ANNUAL EDITIONS

Health 13/14

Thirty-Fourth Edition

EDITOR

Eileen L. Daniel
SUNY at Brockport

Eileen Daniel, a registered dietitian and licensed nutritionist, is a Professor in the Department of Health Science and Associate Vice Provost for Academic Affairs at the State University of New York at Brockport. She received a BS in Nutrition and Dietetics from the Rochester Institute of Technology in 1977, an MS in Community Health Education from SUNY at Brockport in 1987, and a PhD in Health Education from the University of Oregon in 1986. A member of the American Dietetics Association and other professional and community organizations, Dr. Daniel has published more than 40 journal articles on issues of health, nutrition, and health education. She is also the editor of *Taking Sides: Clashing Views on Controversial Issues in Health and Society,* tenth edition (McGraw-Hill/ Contemporary Learning Series, 2012).

ANNUAL EDITIONS: HEALTH, THIRTY-FOURTH EDITION

Published by McGraw-Hill, a business unit of The McGraw-Hill Companies, Inc., 1221 Avenue
of the Americas, New York, NY 10020. Copyright © 2013 by The McGraw-Hill Companies, Inc.
All rights reserved. Previous editions © 2012, 2011, and 2010. Printed in the United States of
America. No part of this publication may be reproduced or distributed in any form or by any means,
or stored in a database or retrieval system, without the prior written consent of The McGraw-Hill
Companies, Inc., including, but not limited to, in any network or other electronic
storage or transmission, or broadcast for distance learning.

Some ancillaries, including electronic and print components, may not be available to customers
outside the United States.

This book is printed on acid-free paper.

Annual Editions® is a registered trademark of The McGraw-Hill Companies, Inc.
Annual Editions is published by the **Contemporary Learning Series** group within the
McGraw-Hill Higher Education division.

1 2 3 4 5 6 7 8 9 0 QDB/QDB 1 0 9 8 7 6 5 4 3 2

ISBN: 978–0–07–813592–7
MHID: 0–07–813592–3
ISSN: 0278-4653 (print)

Managing Editor: *Larry Loeppke*
Marketing Director: *Adam Kloza*
Marketing Manager: *Nathan Edwards*
Developmental Editor: *David Welsh*
Senior Project Manager: *Joyce Watters*
Buyer: *Nichole Birkenholz*
Cover Designer: *Studio Montage, St. Louis, MO*
Senior Content Licensing Specialist: *Shirley Lanners*
Media Project Manager: *Sridevi Palani*

Compositor: Laserwords Private Limited
Cover Image Credits: MichaelSvoboda/Getty Images (inset), Image Source/Corbis (background)

Editors/Academic Advisory Board

Members of the Academic Advisory Board are instrumental in the final selection of articles for each edition of ANNUAL EDITIONS. Their review of articles for content, level, and appropriateness provides critical direction to the editors and staff. We think that you will find their careful consideration well reflected in this volume.

ANNUAL EDITIONS: Health 13/14
34th Edition

EDITOR

Eileen L. Daniel
SUNY at Brockport

ACADEMIC ADVISORY BOARD MEMBERS

Preface

America is in the midst of a revolution that is changing the way millions of Americans view their health. Traditionally, most people delegated responsibility for their health to their physicians and hoped that medical science would be able to cure whatever ailed them. This approach to health care emphasized the role of medical technology and funneled billions of dollars into medical research. The net result of all this spending is the most technically advanced and expensive health care system in the world. In an attempt to rein in health care costs, the health care delivery system moved from privatized health care coverage to what is termed "managed care." While managed care has turned the tide regarding the rising cost of health care, it has done so by limiting reimbursement for many cutting edge technologies. Unfortunately, many people also feel that it has lowered the overall quality of care that is being given. Perhaps the saving grace is that we live at a time in which chronic illnesses rather than acute illnesses are our number one health threat, and many of these illnesses can be prevented or controlled by our lifestyle choices. The net result of these changes has prompted millions of individuals to assume more personal responsibility for safeguarding their own health. Evidence of this change in attitude can be seen in the growing interest in nutrition, physical fitness, dietary supplements, and stress management. If we as a nation are to capitalize on this new health consciousness, we must devote more time and energy to educate Americans in the health sciences, so that they will be better able to make informed choices about their health. Health is a complex and dynamic subject, and it is practically impossible for anyone to stay abreast of all the current research findings. In the past, most of us have relied on books, newspapers, magazines, and television as our primary sources for medical/health information, but today, with the widespread use of personal computers connected to the World Wide Web, it is possible to access vast amount of health information, any time of the day, without even leaving one's home. Unfortunately, quantity and availability does not necessarily translate into quality, and this is particularly true in the area of medical/health information. Just as the Internet is a great source for reliable timely information, it is also a vehicle for the dissemination of misleading and fraudulent information.

Currently there are no standards or regulations regarding the posting of health content on the Internet, and this has led to a plethora of misinformation and quackery in the medical/health arena. Given this vast amount of health information, our task as health educators is two-fold: (1) To provide our students with the most up-to-date and accurate information available on major health issues of our time and (2) to teach our students the skills that will enable them to sort out facts from fiction, in order to become informed consumers. *Annual Editions: Health 13/14* was designed to aid this task. It offers a sampling of quality articles that represents the latest thinking on a variety of health issues, and it also serves as a tool for developing critical thinking skills.

The articles in this volume were carefully chosen on the basis of their quality and timeliness. Because this book is revised and updated annually, it contains information that is not generally available in any standard textbook. As such, it serves as a valuable resource for both teachers and students. This edition of *Annual Editions: Health* has been updated to reflect the latest thinking on a variety of contemporary health issues. We hope that you find this edition to be a helpful learning tool filled with information and the presentation user friendly. The 10 topical areas presented in this edition mirror those that are normally covered in introductory health courses: Promoting Healthy Behavior Change, Stress and Mental Health, Nutritional Health, Exercise and Weight Management, Drugs and Health, Sexuality and Relationships, Preventing and Fighting Disease, Health Care and the Health Care System, Consumer Health, and Contemporary Health Hazards. Because of the interdependence of the various elements that constitute health, the articles selected were written by authors with diverse educational backgrounds and expertise including naturalists, environmentalists, psychologists, economists, sociologists, nutritionists, consumer advocates, and traditional health practitioners.

Annual Editions: Health 13/14 was designed to be one of the most useful and up-to-date publications currently available in the area of health. Any anthology can be improved. This one will be—annually.

Eileen L. Daniel
Editor

The Annual Editions Series

VOLUMES AVAILABLE

Adolescent Psychology

Aging

American Foreign Policy

American Government

Anthropology

Archaeology

Assessment and Evaluation

Business Ethics

Child Growth and Development

Comparative Politics

Criminal Justice

Developing World

Drugs, Society, and Behavior

Dying, Death, and Bereavement

Early Childhood Education

Economics

Educating Children with Exceptionalities

Education

Educational Psychology

Entrepreneurship

Environment

The Family

Gender

Geography

Global Issues

Health

Homeland Security

Human Development

Human Resources

Human Sexualities

International Business

Management

Marketing

Mass Media

Microbiology

Multicultural Education

Nursing

Nutrition

Physical Anthropology

Psychology

Race and Ethnic Relations

Social Problems

Sociology

State and Local Government

Sustainability

Technologies, Social Media, and Society

United States History, Volume 1

United States History, Volume 2

Urban Society

Violence and Terrorism

Western Civilization, Volume 1

Western Civilization, Volume 2

World History, Volume 1

World History, Volume 2

World Politics

Contents

UNIT 1
Promoting Healthy Behavior Change

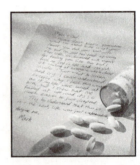

UNIT 2
Stress and Mental Health

The concepts in bold italics are developed in the article. For further expansion, please refer to the Topic Guide.

UNIT 3
Nutritional Health

UNIT 4
Exercise and Weight Management

The concepts in bold italics are developed in the article. For further expansion, please refer to the Topic Guide.

UNIT 5
Drugs and Health

The concepts in bold italics are developed in the article. For further expansion, please refer to the Topic Guide.

UNIT 6
Sexuality and Relationships

UNIT 7
Preventing and Fighting Disease

The concepts in bold italics are developed in the article. For further expansion, please refer to the Topic Guide.

UNIT 8
Health Care and the Health Care System

UNIT 9
Consumer Health

The concepts in bold italics are developed in the article. For further expansion, please refer to the Topic Guide.

UNIT 10
Contemporary Health Hazards

The concepts in bold italics are developed in the article. For further expansion, please refer to the Topic Guide.

The concepts in bold italics are developed in the article. For further expansion, please refer to the Topic Guide.

Correlation Guide

The *Annual Editions* series provides students with convenient, inexpensive access to current, carefully selected articles from the public press. **Annual Editions: Health 13/14** is an easy-to-use reader that presents articles on important topics such as *consumer health, exercise, nutrition,* and many more. For more information on *Annual Editions* and other *McGraw-Hill Contemporary Learning Series* titles, visit www.mhhe.com/cls.

This convenient guide matches the units in **Annual Editions: Health 13/14** with the corresponding chapters in three of our best-selling McGraw-Hill Health textbooks by Hahn et al., Payne et al., and Insel/Roth.

Annual Editions: Health 13/14	Focus on Health, 11/e by Hahn et al.	Understanding Your Health, 12/e by Payne et al.	Core Concepts in Health, Brief, 12/e by Insel/Roth
Unit 1: Promoting Healthy Behavior Change	**Chapter 1:** Shaping Your Health	**Chapter 1:** Shaping Your Health	**Chapter 1:** Taking Charge of Your Health
Unit 2: Stress and Mental Health	**Chapter 2:** Achieving Psychological Health **Chapter 3:** Managing Stress	**Chapter 2:** Achieving Psychological Health **Chapter 3:** Managing Stress	**Chapter 2:** Stress: The Constant Challenge **Chapter 3:** Psychological Health
Unit 3: Nutritional Health	**Chapter 5:** Understanding Nutrition and Your Diet	**Chapter 5:** Understanding Nutrition and Your Diet	**Chapter 9:** Nutrition Basics
Unit 4: Exercise and Weight Management	**Chapter 4:** Becoming Physically Fit **Chapter 6:** Maintaining a Healthy Weight	**Chapter 4:** Becoming Physically Fit **Chapter 6:** Maintaining a Healthy Weight	**Chapter 10:** Exercise for Health and Fitness **Chapter 11:** Weight Management
Unit 5: Drugs and Health	**Chapter 7:** Making Decisions About Drug and Alcohol Use **Chapter 8:** Rejecting Tobacco Use	**Chapter 7:** Making Decisions About Drug Use **Chapter 8:** Taking Control of Alcohol Use **Chapter 9:** Rejecting Tobacco Use	**Chapter 7:** The Use and Abuse of Psychoactive Drugs **Chapter 8:** Alcohol and Tobacco
Unit 6: Sexuality and Relationships	**Chapter 12:** Understanding Sexuality **Chapter 13:** Managing Your Fertility	**Chapter 14:** Exploring the Origins of Sexuality **Chapter 15:** Understanding Sexual Behavior and Relationships **Chapter 16:** Managing Your Fertility **Chapter 17:** Becoming a Parent	**Chapter 4:** Intimate Relationships and Communication **Chapter 5:** Sexuality, Pregnancy, and Childbirth **Chapter 6:** Contraception and Abortion
Unit 7: Preventing and Fighting Disease	**Chapter 9:** Reducing Your Risk of Cardiovascular Disease **Chapter 10:** Living with Cancer and Chronic Conditions **Chapter 11:** Preventing Infectious Diseases	**Chapter 10:** Enhancing Your Cardiovascular Health **Chapter 11:** Living with Cancer **Chapter 12:** Managing Chronic Conditions **Chapter 13:** Preventing Infectious Diseases	**Chapter 12:** Cardiovascular Health and Cancer **Chapter 13:** Immunity and Infection
Unit 8: Health Care and the Health Care System	**Chapter 14:** Becoming an Informed Health Care Consumer	**Chapter 18:** Becoming an Informed Health Care Consumer	**Chapter 15:** Conventional and Complementary Medicine **Chapter 17:** The Challenge of Aging
Unit 9: Consumer Health	**Chapter 15:** Protecting Your Safety	**Chapter 19:** Protecting Your Safety	**Chapter 16:** Personal Safety
Unit 10: Contemporary Health Hazards	**Chapter 16:** The Environment and Your Health	**Chapter 20:** The Environment and Your Health	**Chapter 14:** Environmental Health

Topic Guide

This topic guide suggests how the selections in this book relate to the subjects covered in your course. You may want to use the topics listed on these pages to search the Web more easily.

On the following pages a number of websites have been gathered specifically for this book. They are arranged to reflect the units of this Annual Editions reader. You can link to these sites by going to www.mhhe.com/cls

All the articles that relate to each topic are listed below the bold-faced term.

Internet References

The following Internet sites have been selected to support the articles found in this reader. These sites were available at the time of publication. However, because websites often change their structure and content, the information listed may no longer be available. We invite you to visit www.mhhe.com/cls for easy access to these sites.

Annual Editions: Health 13/14

General Sources

National Institute on Aging (NIA)
www.nia.nih.gov

The NIA, one of the institutes of the U.S. National Institutes of Health, presents this home page to lead you to a variety of resources on health and lifestyle issues on aging.

U.S. Department of Agriculture (USDA)/Food and Nutrition Information Center (FNIC)
www.nal.usda.gov/fnic

Use this site to find nutrition information provided by various USDA agencies, to find links to food and nutrition resources on the Internet, and to access FNIC publications and databases.

U.S. Department of Health and Human Services
www.os.dhhs.gov

This site has extensive links to information on such topics as the health benefits of exercise, weight control, and prudent lifestyle choices.

U.S. National Institutes of Health (NIH)
www.nih.gov

Consult this site for links to extensive health information and scientific resources. Comprising 24 separate institutes, centers, and divisions, the NIH is one of eight health agencies of the Public Health Service, which, in turn, is part of the U.S. Department of Health and Human Services.

U.S. National Library of Medicine
www.nlm.nih.gov

This huge site permits a search of a number of databases and electronic information sources such as MEDLINE. You can learn about research projects and programs and peruse the national network of medical libraries here.

World Health Organization
www.who.int/en

This home page of the World Health Organization will provide links to a wealth of statistical and analytical information about health around the world.

UNIT 1: Promoting Healthy Behavior Change

Columbia University's Go Ask Alice!
www.goaskalice.columbia.edu/index.html

This interactive site provides discussion and insight into a number of personal issues of interest to college-age people and often those younger and older. Many questions about physical and emotional health and well-being are answered.

The Society of Behavioral Medicine
www.sbm.org

This site provides listings of major, general health institutes and organizations as well as discipline-specific links and resources in medicine, psychology, and public health.

UNIT 2: Stress and Mental Health

The American Institute of Stress
www.stress.org

This site provides comprehensive information on stress, its dangers, the beliefs that build helpful techniques for overcoming stress, and so on. This easy-to-navigate site has good links to information on anxiety and related topics.

National Mental Health Association (NMHA)
www.nmha.org/index.html

The NMHA is a citizen volunteer advocacy organization that works to improve the mental health of all individuals. The site provides access to guidelines that individuals can use to reduce stress and improve their lives in small, yet tangible, ways.

Self-Help Magazine
www.selfhelpmagazine.com/index.html

Reach lots of links to self-help resources on the Net at this site, including resources on stress, anxiety, fears, and more.

UNIT 3: Nutritional Health

The American Dietetic Association
www.eatright.org

This organization, along with its National Center of Nutrition and Dietetics, promotes optimal nutrition, health, and well-being. This easy-to-navigate site presents FAQs about nutrition and dieting, nutrition resources, and career and member information.

Center for Science in the Public Interest (CSPI)
www.cspinet.org

CSPI is a nonprofit education and advocacy organization that focuses on improving the safety and nutritional quality of our food supply and on reducing the health problems caused by alcohol. This agency also evaluates the nutritional composition of fast foods, movie popcorn, and chain restaurants. There are also good links to related sites.

Food and Nutrition Information Center
www.nalusda.gov/fnic/index.html

This is an official Agriculture Network Information Center website. The FNIC is one of several information centers at the National Agriculture Library, the Agricultural Research Service, and the U.S. Department of Agriculture. The website has information on nutrition-related publications, an index of food and nutrition related Internet resources, and an online catalog of materials.

UNIT 4: Exercise and Weight Management

American Society of Exercise Physiologists (ASEP)
www.asep.org

The ASEP is devoted to promoting people's health and physical fitness. This extensive site provides links to publications related to exercise and career opportunities in exercise physiology.

Internet References

Cyberdiet
www.cyberdiet.com

This site, maintained by a registered dietician, offers Cyberdiet's interactive nutritional profile, food facts, menus and meal plans, and exercise and food-related sites.

Shape Up America!
www.shapeup.org

At the Shape Up America! website you will find the latest information about safe weight management, healthy eating, and physical fitness.

UNIT 5: Drugs and Health

Food and Drug Administration (FDA)
www.fda.gov

This site includes FDA news, information on drugs, and drug toxicology facts.

National Institute on Drug Abuse (NIDA)
www.nida.nih.gov

Use this site index for access to NIDA publications and communications, information on drugs of abuse, and links to other related websites.

UNIT 6: Sexuality and Relationships

Planned Parenthood
www.plannedparenthood.org

This home page provides links to information on contraceptives (including outercourse and abstinence) and to discussions of other topics related to sexual health.

Sexuality Information and Education Council of the United States (SIECUS)
www.siecus.org

SIECUS is a nonprofit, private advocacy group that affirms that sexuality is a natural and healthy part of living. This home page offers publications, what's new, descriptions of programs, and a listing of international sexuality education initiatives.

UNIT 7: Preventing and Fighting Disease

American Cancer Society
www.cancer.org

Open this site and its various links to learn the concerns and lifestyle advice of the American Cancer Society. It provides information on tobacco and alternative cancer therapies.

American Diabetes Association Home Page
www.diabetes.org

This site offers information on diabetes including treatment, diet, and insulin therapy.

American Heart Association
www.amhrt.org

This award-winning, comprehensive site of the American Heart Association offers information on heart disease, prevention, patient facts, eating plans, what's new, nutrition, smoking cessation, and FAQs.

National Institute of Allergy and Infectious Diseases (NIAID)
www.niaid.nih.gov

Open this site and its various links to learn the concerns and lifestyle advice of the National Institute of Allergy and Infectious Diseases.

UNIT 8: Health Care and the Health Care System

American Medical Association (AMA)
www.ama-assn.org

The AMA offers this site to find up-to-date medical information, peer-review resources, discussions of such topics as HIV/AIDS and women's health, examination of issues related to managed care, and important publications.

MedScape: The Online Resource for Better Patient Care
www.medscape.com

For health professionals and interested consumers, this site offers peer-reviewed articles, self-assessment features, medical news, and annotated links to Internet resources. It also contains the Morbidity & Mortality Weekly Report, which is a publication of the Centers for Disease Control and Prevention.

UNIT 9: Consumer Health

FDA Consumer Magazine
www.fda.gov/fdac

This site offers articles and information that appears in the *FDA Consumer Magazine.*

Global Vaccine Awareness League
www.gval.com

This site addresses side effects related to vaccination. Its many links are geared to provide copious information.

UNIT 10: Contemporary Health Hazards

Centers for Disease Control and Behaviors
www.cdc.gov

This site is a wealth of information on diseases, epidemics, and disease prevention.

Environmental Protection Agency
www.epa.gov

Use this site to find environmental health information provided by various EPA agencies.

Food and Drug Administration
www.fda.gov

This site includes FDA news, information on drugs, and drug toxicology facts.

World Health Organization
www.who.org

This site offers information on health issues throughout the world. For data specific to Haiti, click www.who.int/countries/hti/en

UNIT 1

Promoting Healthy Behavior Change

Unit Selections

1. **Crimes of the Heart,** Walter C. Willett and Anne Underwood
2. **The Perils of Higher Education,** Steven Kotler
3. **Carrots, Sticks, and Health Care Reform—Problems with Wellness Incentives,** Harald Schmidt, MA, Kristin Voigt, DPhil/, PhD and Daniel Wikler, DPhil/, PhD

Learning Outcomes

After reading this Unit, you will be able to:

- Describe why people continue to engage in behaviors that negatively affect their health even when they know about the ill effects these behaviors have on their well-being.

- Describe some programs/policies that could be pursued to help prevent heart disease.

- Explain how the negative behaviors practiced by college students contribute to academic difficulties.

- Discuss the role of incentives in promoting healthy behaviors.

- Describe the factors that contribute to a successful lifestyle change.

- Describe the relationship between health care reform and positive health behaviors.

Student Website

www.mhhe.com/cls

Internet References

Columbia University's Go Ask Alice!
    www.goaskalice.columbia.edu/index.html
The Society of Behavioral Medicine
    www.sbm.org

"Those of us who protect our health daily and those of us who put our health in constant jeopardy have exactly the same mortality: one hundred percent. The difference, of course, is the timing." This quotation from Elizabeth M. Whelan, Sc.D., M.P.H., reminds us that we must all face the fact that we are going to die sometime. The question that is decided by our behavior is when and, to a certain extent, how. This book, and especially this unit, is designed to assist students to develop the cognitive skills and knowledge that, when put to use, help make the moment of our death come as late as possible in our lives and to maintain our health and vitality as long as possible. While we cannot control many of the things that happen to us, we must all strive to accept personal responsibility for, and make informed decisions about, things that we can control. This is no minor task, but it is one in which the potential reward is life itself. Perhaps the best way to start this process is by educating ourselves on the relative risks associated with the various behaviors and lifestyle choices we make. To minimize all the risks to life and health would significantly limit the quality of our lives, and while this might be a choice that some would make, it certainly is not the goal of health education. A more logical approach to risk reduction would be to educate the public on the relative risks associated with various behaviors and lifestyle choices, so that they are capable of making informed decisions. While it may seem obvious that certain behaviors, such as smoking and excessive drinking, entail a high level of risk, the significance of others such as toxic waste sites and food additives are frequently blown out of proportion to the actual risks involved. The net result of this type of distortion is that many Americans tend to minimize the dangers of known hazards such as tobacco, obesity, and alcohol and focus attention, instead, on potentially minor health hazards over which they have little or no control.

Educating the public on the relative risk of various health behaviors is only part of the job that health educators must tackle in order to assist individuals in making informed choices regarding their health and well-being. They must also teach the skills that will enable people to evaluate the validity and significance of new information as it becomes available. Just how important informed decision making is in our daily lives is evidenced by the numerous health-related media announcements and articles that fill our newspapers, computer screens, magazines, and television broadcasts. Rather than informing and enlightening the public on significant new medical discoveries, many of these announcements do little more than add to the level of confusion or exaggerate or sensationalize health issues. Let's assume for a minute that the scientific community is in general agreement that certain behaviors clearly promote our health while others damage our health. Given this information, are you likely to make adjustments to your lifestyle to comply with the findings? Logic would suggest that of course you would,

© Design Pics / PunchStock

but experience has taught us that information alone isn't enough to bring about behavioral change in many people. Why is it that so many people continue to make bad choices regarding their health behaviors when they are fully aware of the risks involved? We can take vows to try and undo or minimize the negative health behaviors of our past. While strategies such as these may work for those who feel they are at risk, how do we help those who do not feel that they are at risk, or those who feel that it is too late in their lives for the changes to matter?

Three articles which address health behaviors and wellness decisions were chosen for this unit. They include "Crimes of the Heart" by Walter Willett and Anne Underwood which discusses major health behavior improvements among residents of a small town in Minnesota. The changes were based on the city's decision to become involved in a project to help support healthy behavior change for its citizens. The town helped to support healthy behavior change by changing the town's environment to include ways that encouraged a healthier lifestyle. In "The Perils of Higher Education," Steven Kotler maintains that while college is a place to learn and grow, for many students it becomes four years of bad diet, too little sleep, and too much alcohol. These negative health behaviors affect not only the students' health, but their grades too. While the negative health behavior of college students are detrimental to their overall current and future health, there is evidence that engaging in these poor health habits can be devastating to learning and memory. In "Carrots, Sticks, and Health Care Reform—Problems with Wellness Incentives," the authors address the issue of using incentives to influence positive health behaviors.

Crimes of the Heart

It's time society stopped reinforcing the bad behavior that leads to heart disease—and pursued policies to prevent it.

WALTER C. WILLETT AND ANNE UNDERWOOD

Until last year, the residents of Albert Lea, Minn., were no healthier than any other Americans. Then the city became the first American town to sign on to the AARP/Blue Zones Vitality Project—the brainchild of writer Dan Buettner, whose 2008 book, *The Blue Zones,* detailed the health habits of the world's longest-lived people. His goal was to bring the same benefits to middle America—not by forcing people to diet and exercise, but by changing their everyday environments in ways that encourage a healthier lifestyle.

What followed was a sort of townwide makeover. The city laid new sidewalks linking residential areas with schools and shopping centers. It built a recreational path around a lake and dug new plots for community gardens. Restaurants made healthy changes to their menus. Schools banned eating in hallways (reducing the opportunities for kids to munch on snack food) and stopped selling candy for fundraisers. (They sold wreaths instead.) More than 2,600 of the city's 18,000 residents volunteered, too, selecting from more than a dozen heart-healthy measures—for example, ridding their kitchens of supersize dinner plates (which encourage larger portions) and forming "walking schoolbuses" to escort kids to school on foot.

The results were stunning. In six months, participants lost an average of 2.6 pounds and boosted their estimated life expectancy by 3.1 years. Even more impressive, health-care claims for city and school employees fell for the first time in a decade—by 32 percent over 10 months. And benefits didn't accrue solely to volunteers. Thanks to the influence of social networks, says Buettner, "even the curmudgeons who didn't want to be involved ended up modifying their behaviors."

Isn't it time we all followed Albert Lea's example? Diet and exercise programs routinely fail not for lack of willpower, but because the society in which we live favors unhealthy behaviors. In 2006, cardiovascular disease cost $403 billion in medical bills and lost productivity. By 2025 an aging population is expected to drive up the total by as much as 54 percent. But creative government programs could help forestall the increases—and help our hearts, too. A few suggestions:

Require graphic warnings on cigarette packages. It's easy to disregard a black-box warning that smoking is "hazardous to your health." It's not so easy to dismiss a picture of gangrenous limbs, diseased hearts, or chests sawed open for autopsy. These are exactly the types of images that the law now requires on cigarette packages in Brazil. In Canada, such warning images must cover at least half the wrapping. In 2001, the year after the Canadian law took effect, 38 percent of smokers who tried to quit cited the images. Think of it as truth in advertising.

Sponsor "commitment contracts" to quit smoking. Yale economist Dean Karlan spearheaded a test program in the Philippines in which smokers who wanted to quit deposited the money they would have spent on cigarettes into a special bank account. After six months those who had succeeded got their money back, while those who had failed lost it. Such a program could be run here by public-health clinics and offer greater incentives, such as letting winners divvy up the money forfeited by losers. Even without such an enhancement, says Karlan, "Filipino participants were 39 percent more likely to quit than those who were not offered the option."

Subsidize whole grains, fruits, and vegetables in the food-stamp program. The underprivileged tend to have disastrously unhealthy diets, and no wonder: $1 will buy 100 calories of carrots—or 1,250 calories of cookies and chips. The government should offer incentives for buying produce. The Wholesome Wave Foundation has shown the way in 12 states, providing vouchers redeemable at farmers' markets to people in the SNAP program (the official name for food stamps). "We've seen purchases of fruits and vegetables double and triple among recipients," says president and CEO Michel Nischan.

Set targets for salt reduction. The average American consumes twice the recommended daily maximum of sodium, most of it from processed foods. The result: high blood pressure, heart attacks, and strokes. But New York City is leading a campaign to encourage food manufacturers to reduce added sodium over the next five years. Consumers will barely notice the changes because they will occur so gradually. The FDA should follow New York's lead.

> **One urban-planning expert advocates a "road diet" in which towns eliminate a lane or two of traffic and substitute sidewalks. "When roads slim down, so do people," he says.**

Incorporate physical education into No Child Left Behind. American children may be prepping like crazy for standardized tests, but they're seriously lagging in physical fitness. Regular exercise improves mood, concentration, and academic achievement. It can also help reverse the growing trend toward type 2 diabetes and early heart disease in children and teenagers.

Require that sidewalks and bike lanes be part of every federally funded road project. The government already spends 1 percent of transportation dollars on such projects. It should increase the level to 2 to 3 percent. When sidewalks are built in neighborhoods and downtowns, people start walking. "The big win for city government is that anything built to a walkable scale leases out for three to five times more money, with more tax revenue on less infrastructure," says Dan Burden, executive director of the Walkable and Livable Communities Institute. He recommends a "road diet" in which towns eliminate a lane or two of downtown traffic and substitute sidewalks. "When roads slim down, so do people," he says.

It's all reasonable. But Dan Buettner isn't waiting for any of these measures to surmount the inevitable industry hurdles. This year he's looking to scale up the Blue Zones Vitality Project to a city of 100,000 or more. "If this works, it could provide a template for the government that's replicable across the country," says his colleague Ben Leedle, CEO of Healthways, which is developing the next phase of the project. The challenges will be much steeper in large cities. But with measures like these, we could one day find ourselves growing fitter without specifically dieting or exercising. Finally, a New Year's resolution we can all keep.

Critical Thinking

1. What motivates people to engage in healthy behaviors?
2. How did changing the environment contribute to healthy behaviors?
3. What role did the behavioral changes make to heart health?

WALTER C. WILLETT is a physician, chair of the department of nutrition at the Harvard School of Public Health, and coauthor of *The Fertility Diet*. **ANNE UNDERWOOD** is a Newsweek contributor.

Willett, Walter and Underwood, Anne. From *Newsweek*, February 15, 2010, pp. 42–43. Copyright © 2010 by Anne Underwood and Walter Willett. Reprinted by permission of Anne Underwood.

The Perils of Higher Education

Can't remember the difference between declensions and derivatives? Blame college. The undergrad life is a blast, but it may lead you to forget everything you learn.

STEVEN KOTLER

We go to college to learn, to soak up a dazzling array of information intended to prepare us for adult life. But college is not simply a data dump; it is also the end of parental supervision. For many students, that translates into four years of late nights, pizza banquets and boozy weekends that start on Wednesday. And while we know that bad habits are detrimental to cognition in general—think drunk driving—new studies show that the undergrad urges to eat, drink and be merry have devastating effects on learning and memory. It turns out that the exact place we go to get an education may in fact be one of the worst possible environments in which to retain anything we've learned.

Dude, I Haven't Slept in Three Days!

Normal human beings spend one-third of their lives asleep, but today's college students aren't normal. A recent survey of undergraduates and medical students at Stanford University found 80 percent of them qualified as sleep-deprived, and a poll taken by the National Sleep Foundation found that most young adults get only 6.8 hours a night.

All-night cramfests may seem to be the only option when the end of the semester looms, but in fact getting sleep—and a full dose of it—might be a better way to ace exams. Sleep is crucial to declarative memory, the hard, factual kind that helps us remember which year World War I began, or what room the French Lit class is in. It's also essential for procedural memory, the "know-how" memory we use when learning to drive a car or write a five-paragraph essay. "Practice makes perfect," says Harvard Medical School psychologist Matt Walker, "but having a night's rest after practicing might make you even better."

Walker taught 100 people to bang out a series of nonsense sequences on a keyboard—a standard procedural memory task. When asked to replay the sequence 12 hours later, they hadn't improved. But when one group of subjects was allowed to sleep overnight before being retested, their speed and accuracy improved by 20 to 30 percent. "It was bizarre," says Walker. "We were seeing people's skills improve just by sleeping."

For procedural memory, the deep slow-wave stages of sleep were the most important for improvement—particularly during the last two hours of the night. Declarative memory, by contrast, gets processed during the slow-wave stages that come in the first two hours of sleep. "This means that memory requires a full eight hours of sleep," says Walker. He also found that if someone goes without sleep for 24 hours after acquiring a new skill, a week later they will have lost it completely. So college students who pull all-nighters during exam week might do fine on their tests but may not remember any of the material by next semester.

Walker believes that the common practice of back-loading semesters with a blizzard of papers and exams needs a rethink. "Educators are just encouraging sleeplessness," says Walker. "This is just not an effective way to force information into the brain."

Who's up for Pizza?

Walk into any college cafeteria and you'll find a smorgasbord of French fries, greasy pizza, burgers, potato chips and the like. On top of that, McDonald's, Burger King, Wendy's and other fast-food chains have been gobbling up campus real estate in recent years. With hectic schedules and skinny budgets, students find fast food an easy alternative. A recent Tufts University survey found that 50 percent of students eat too much fat, and 70 to 80 percent eat too much saturated fat.

But students who fuel their studies with fast food have something more serious than the "freshman 15" to worry about: They may literally be eating themselves stupid. Researchers have known since the late 1980s that bad eating habits contribute to the kind of cognitive decline found in diseases like Alzheimer's. Since then, they've been trying to find out exactly how a bad diet might be hard on the brain. Ann-Charlotte Granholm, director of the Center for Aging at the Medical University of South Carolina, has recently focused on trans fat, widely used in fast-food cooking because it extends the shelf life of foods. Trans fat is made by bubbling hydrogen through unsaturated fat, with copper or zinc added to speed the chemical reaction along. These metals are frequently found in the brains of people with Alzheimer's, which sparked Granholm's concern.

To investigate, she fed one group of rats a diet high in trans fat and compared them with another group fed a diet that was just as greasy but low in trans fat. Six weeks later, she tested the animals in a water maze, the rodent equivalent of a final exam in organic chemistry. "The trans-fat group made many more errors," says Granholm, especially when she used more difficult mazes.

When she examined the rats' brains, she found that trans-fat eaters had fewer proteins critical to healthy neurological function. She also saw inflammation in and around the hippocampus, the part of the brain responsible for learning and memory. "It was alarming," says Granholm. "These are the exact types of changes we normally see at the onset of Alzheimer's, but we saw them after six weeks," even though the rats were still young.

Students who fuel their studies with fast food have something serious to worry about: They may literally be eating themselves stupid.

Her work corresponds to a broader inquiry conducted by Veerendra Kumar Madala Halagaapa and Mark Mattson of the National Institute on Aging. The researchers fed four groups of mice different diets—normal, high-fat, high-sugar and high-fat/high-sugar. Each diet had the same caloric value, so that one group of mice wouldn't end up heavier. Four months later, the mice on the high-fat diets performed significantly worse than the other groups on a water maze test.

The researchers then exposed the animals to a neurotoxin that targets the hippocampus, to assess whether a high-fat diet made the mice less able to cope with brain damage. Back in the maze, all the animals performed worse than before, but the mice who had eaten the high-fat diets were the most seriously compromised. "Based on our work," says Mattson, "we'd predict that people who eat high-fat diets and high-fat/high-sugar diets are not only damaging their ability to learn and remember new information, but also putting themselves at much greater risk for all sorts of neurodegenerative disorders like Alzheimer's."

Welcome to Margaritaville State University

It's widely recognized that heavy drinking doesn't exactly boost your intellect. But most people figure that their booze-induced foolishness wears off once the hangover is gone. Instead, it turns out that even limited stints of overindulgence may have long-term effects.

Less than 20 years ago, researchers began to realize that the adult brain wasn't just a static lump of cells. They found that stem cells in the brain are constantly churning out new neurons, particularly in the hippocampus. Alcoholism researchers, in turn, began to wonder if chronic alcoholics' memory problems had something to do with nerve cell birth and growth.

In 2000, Kimberly Nixon and Fulton Crews at the University of North Carolina's Bowles Center for Alcohol Studies subjected lab rats to four days of heavy alcohol intoxication. They gave the rats a week to shake off their hangovers, then tested them on and off during the next month in a water maze. "We didn't find anything at first," says Nixon. But on the 19th day, the rats who had been on the binge performed much worse. In 19 days, the cells born during the binge had grown to maturity—and clearly, the neurons born during the boozy period didn't work properly once they reached maturity. "[The timing] was almost too perfect," says Nixon.

While normal rats generated about 2,500 new brain cells in three weeks, the drinking rats produced only 1,400. A month later, the sober rats had lost about half of those new cells through normal die-off. But all of the new cells died in the brains of the binge drinkers. "This was startling," says Nixon. "It was the first time anyone had found that alcohol not only inhibits the birth of new cells but also inhibits the ones that survive." In further study, they found that a week's abstinence produced a twofold burst of neurogenesis, and a month off the sauce brought cognitive function back to normal.

What does this have to do with a weekend keg party? A number of recent studies show that college students consume far more alcohol than anyone previously suspected. Forty-four percent of today's collegiates drink enough to be classified as binge drinkers, according to a nationwide survey of 10,000 students done at Harvard University. The amount of alcohol consumed by Nixon's binging rats far exceeded intake at a typical keg party—but other research shows that the effects of alcohol work on a sliding scale. Students who follow a weekend of heavy drinking with a week of heavy studying might not forget everything they learn. They just may struggle come test time.

Can I Bum a Smoke?

If this ledger of campus menaces worries you, here's something you really won't like: Smoking cigarettes may actually have some cognitive benefits, thanks to the power of nicotine. The chemical improves mental focus, as scientists have known since the 1950s. Nicotine also aids concentration in people who have ADHD and may protect against Alzheimer's disease. Back in 2000, a nicotine-like drug under development by the pharmaceutical company Astra Arcus USA was shown to restore the ability to learn and remember in rats with brain lesions similar to those found in Alzheimer's patients. More recently Granholm, the scientist investigating trans fats and memory, found that nicotine enhances spatial memory in healthy rats. Other researchers have found that nicotine also boosts both emotional memory (the kind that helps us *not* put our hands back in the fire after we've been burned) and auditory memory.

5

There's a catch: Other studies show that nicotine encourages state-dependent learning. The idea is that if, for example, you study in blue sweats, it helps to take the exam in blue sweats. In other words, what you learn while smoking is best recalled while smoking. Since lighting up in an exam room might cause problems, cigarettes probably aren't the key to getting on the dean's list.

Nonetheless, while the number of cigarette smokers continues to drop nationwide, college students are still lighting up: As many as 30 percent smoke during their years of higher education. The smoking rate for young adults between the ages of 18 and 24 has actually risen in the past decade.

All this news makes you wonder how anyone's ever managed to get an education. Or what would happen to GPAs at a vegetarian university with a 10 P.M. curfew. But you might not need to go to such extremes. While Granholm agrees that the excesses of college can be "a perfect example of what you shouldn't do to yourself if you are trying to learn," she doesn't recommend abstinence. "Moderation," she counsels, "just like in everything else. Moderation is the key to collegiate success."

Critical Thinking

1. Why do so many college students engage in negative health behaviors? What negative behaviors impact grades?

2. Discuss the relationship between fast food and the brain.

3. Address the relationship among college student health behaviors, learning, and memory.

STEVEN KOTLER, based in Los Angeles, has written for *The New York Times Magazine, National Geographic, Details, Wired* and *Outside.*

Carrots, Sticks, and Health Care Reform—Problems with Wellness Incentives

Harald Schmidt, MA, Kristin Voigt, DPhil, and Daniel Wikler, PhD

C hronic conditions, especially those associated with overweight, are on the rise in the United States (as elsewhere). Employers have used both carrots and sticks to encourage healthier behavior.

The current health care reform bills seek to expand the role of incentives, which promise a win–win bargain: employees enjoy better health, while employers reduce health care costs and profit from a healthier workforce.

However, these provisions cannot be given an ethical free pass. In some cases, the incentives are really sticks dressed up as carrots. There is a risk of inequity that would further disadvantage the people most in need of health improvements, and doctors might be assigned watchdog roles that might harm the therapeutic relationship. We believe that some changes must be made to reconcile incentive use with ethical norms.

Under the 1996 Health Insurance Portability and Accountability Act (HIPAA), a group health plan may not discriminate among individuals on the basis of health factors by varying their premiums. But HIPAA does not prevent insurers from offering reimbursements through "wellness programs." These include what could be called participation incentives, which offer a premium discount or other reimbursement simply for participating in a health-promotion program, and attainment incentives, which provide reimbursements only for meeting targets—for example, a particular body-mass index or cholesterol level. Subsequent regulations specified that attainment incentives must not exceed 20% of the total cost of an employee's coverage (i.e., the combination of the employer's and employee's contributions).[1]

The health care reform measures currently before Congress would substantially expand these provisions (see box). However, ethical analysis and empirical research suggest that the current protections are inadequate to ensure fairness.

Attainment incentives provide welcome rewards for employees who manage to comply but may be unfair for those who struggle, particularly if they fail. The law demands the provision of alternative standards for those who cannot or should not participate because of medical conditions, but those categories are narrowly defined. For all others, the implicit assumption is that they can achieve targets if they try. This assumption is hard to reconcile with what we know about lifestyle change. Most diets, for example, do not result in long-lasting weight reduction, even though participants want and try to lose weight. Attainment-incentive programs make no distinction between those who try but fail and those who do not try.

Proponents of attainment incentives typically do not view this situation as inequitable. Steven Burd, the chief executive officer of Safeway, whose "Healthy Measures" program offers reimbursements for meeting weight, blood-pressure, cholesterol, and tobacco-use targets, compared his company's program to automobile insurance, in which for decades "driving behavior has been correlated with accident risk and has therefore translated into premium differences among drivers." In other words, says Burd, "the auto-insurance industry has long recognized the role of personal responsibility. As a result, bad behaviors (like speeding, tickets for failure to follow the rules of the road, and frequency of accidents) are considered when establishing insurance premiums. Bad driver premiums are not subsidized by the good driver premiums."[2]

If people could lose weight, stop smoking, or reduce cholesterol simply by deciding to do so, the analogy might be appropriate. But in that case, few would have had weight, smoking, or cholesterol problems in the first place. Moreover, there is a social gradient. A law school graduate from a wealthy family who has a gym on the top floor of his condominium block is more likely to succeed in losing weight if he

Summary of Wellness Incentives in the Current Legislation

The "Affordable Health Care for America Act" (House of Representatives), section 112, requires that qualifying programs:

- Be evidence-based and certified by the Department of Health and Human Services.
- Provide support for populations at risk for poor health outcomes.
- Include designs that are "culturally competent [and] physically and programmatically accessible (including for individuals with disabilities)."
- Be available to all employees without charge.
- Not link financial incentives to premiums.
- Entail no cost shifting.

The "Patient Protection and Affordable Care Act" (Senate), section 2705, proposes to increase reimbursement levels to 30% of the cost of employee-only coverage, or up to 50% with government approval. In part restating provisions for current wellness programs, it also requires that qualifying programs:

- Be "available to all similarly situated individuals."
- Have "a reasonable chance of improving the health of, or preventing disease in, participating individuals."
- Not be "overly burdensome, [be] a subterfuge for discriminating based on a health status factor, [or be] highly suspect in the method chosen to promote health or prevent disease."
- Provide an alternative standard for employees whose medical condition—as certified by a physician—precludes participation in attainment-incentive programs.
- Not pose an "undue burden for individuals insured in the individual insurance market."
- Entail no cost shifting.
- Be evaluated in pilot studies and a 10-state demonstration project.

tries than is a teenage mother who grew up and continues to live and work odd jobs in a poor neighborhood with limited access to healthy food and exercise opportunities. And he is more likely to try. In Germany, where both participation and attainment incentives have been offered since 2004, participation rates among people in the top socioeconomic quintile are nearly double the rates among those in the poorest quintile.[3]

Incentive schemes are defended on the grounds of personal responsibility, but as Kant observed, "ought" implies "can." Although alternative standards must be offered to employees for whom specific targets are medically inappropriate, disadvantaged people with multiple coexisting conditions may refrain from making such petitions, seeing them as degrading or humiliating. These potential problems are important in view of the proposed increases in reimbursement levels.

The reform proposals prohibit cost shifting, but provisions in the Senate bill could result in a substantial increase in financial burden on employees who do not meet targets (or alternative standards). On the basis of the average cost of $4700 for employee-only coverage, a 20% incentive amounts to $940; 30% would equal $1410 and 50%, $2350. In practice, insurers may stay below the maximum levels. Some may elect to absorb the full cost of reimbursements, in part because some or all of these costs may be offset by future savings from a healthier workforce. Alternatively, however, insurers might recoup some or all of the costs by increasing insurance contributions from insurance holders. In the extreme case, the incentive might then simply consist of being able to return to the previous level of contributions. Similar effects can be achieved by varying applicable copayments or deductibles.[4] Direct and indirect increases would disproportionately hurt lower-paid workers, who are generally less healthy than their higher-paid counterparts and thus in greater need of health care, less likely to meet the targets, and least likely to be able to afford higher costs. Some employees might decide to opt out of employer-based health insurance—and indeed, one wellness consulting firm, Benicomp, implies in its prospectus that such a result might be desirable, pointing out that employees who do not comply might be "motivated to consider other coverage options" and highlighting the savings that would result for employers.[4]

Proponents emphasize that wellness incentives are voluntary. But the scenarios above show that voluntariness can become dubious for lower-income employees, if the only way to obtain affordable insurance is to meet the targets. To them, programs that are offered as carrots may feel more like sticks. It is worth noting that countries such as Germany generally use far lower reimbursements ($45 to $130 per year, or a maximum of 6% of an employee's contribution) and often use in-kind incentives (such as exercise equipment, heart-rate monitors, or vouchers contributing to the cost of a "wellness holiday") rather than cash.[3]

There are also questions about the effect on the therapeutic relationship. When the German Parliament passed a law making lower copayments conditional on patients' undergoing certain cancer screenings and complying with therapy, medical professionals rejected it, partly out of concern about being put in a policing position.[3] American physicians expressed concern when West Virginia's Medicaid program charged participating doctors with monitoring patients' adherence to the requirements set out in the member agreement.[5] Requiring physicians to certify an employee's medical unsuitability for an incentive scheme or to attest to their achievement of a target might similarly introduce an adversarial element into the doctor–patient relationship.

Incentives for healthy behavior may be part of an effective national response to risk factors for chronic disease. Wrongly implemented, however, they can introduce substantial inequity into the health insurance system. It is a problem if the people who are less likely to benefit from the programs are those who may need them more. The proposed increases in reimbursement levels threaten to further exacerbate inequities. Reform legislation should therefore not raise the incentive cap. Attainment incentives that primarily benefit the well-off and healthy should be phased out, and the focus should shift to participation-incentive schemes tailored to the abilities and needs of lower-paid employees. Moreover, it is crucial that the evaluation of pilots include an assessment of the socioeconomic and ethnic backgrounds of both users and nonusers to ascertain the equitability of programs.

Notes

1. Mello MM, Rosenthal MB. Wellness programs and lifestyle discrimination—the legal limits. *N Engl J Med* 2008;359:192–9.

2. Burd SA. How Safeway is cutting health-care costs. *Wall Street Journal.* June 12, 2009.

3. Schmidt H, Stock S, Gerber A. What can we learn from German health incentive schemes? *BMJ* 2009;339:b3504.

4. Detailed overview, 2009. Ft. Wayne, IN: BeniComp Advantage. (Accessed December 22, 2009, at www.benicompadvantage.com/products/overview.htm.)

5. Bishop G, Brodkey A. Personal responsibility and physician responsibility—West Virginia's Medicaid plan. *N Engl J Med* 2006;355:756–8.

Critical Thinking

1. Distinguish between the carrot and stick approach to health practices.

2. Discuss the advantages and disadvantages of wellness incentives.

3. Identify what particular health behaviors respond well to incentives and why.

Financial and other disclosures provided by the authors are available with the full text of this article at NEJM.org.

From the Harvard School of Public Health and the Harvard University Program in Ethics and Health, Boston.

UNIT 2

Stress and Mental Health

Unit Selections

Learning Outcomes

After reading this Unit, you will be able to:

- Explain why antidepressants may not be the best choice for all patients.

- Understand the cause and effect of major depression.

- Understand why direct attempts to build self esteem tend to fail.

- Contrast positive and negative stressors in shaping one's life.

- Explain the risks and causes of Internet addiction.

Student Website

www.mhhe.com/cls

Internet References

The American Institute of Stress
   www.stress.org
National Mental Health Association (NMHA)
   www.nmha.org/index.html
Self-Help Magazine
   www.selfhelpmagazine.com/index.html

The brain is one organ that still mystifies and baffles the scientific community. While more has been learned about this organ in the last decade than in all the rest of recorded history, our understanding of the brain is still in its infancy. What has been learned, however, has spawned exciting new research and has contributed to the establishment of new disciplines, such as psychophysiology and psychoneuroimmunology (PNI).

Traditionally, the medical community has viewed health problems as either physical or mental and has treated each type separately. This dichotomy between the psyche (mind) and soma (body) is fading in the light of scientific data that reveal profound physiological changes associated with mood shifts. What are the physiological changes associated with stress? Hans Selye, the father of stress research, described stress as a nonspecific physiological response to anything that challenges the body. He demonstrated that this response could be elicited by both mental and physical stimuli. Stress researchers have come to regard this response pattern as the "flight-or-fight" response, perhaps an adaptive throwback to our primitive ancestors. Researchers now believe that repeated and prolonged activation of this response can trigger destructive changes in our bodies and contribute to the development of several chronic diseases. So profound is the impact of emotional stress on the body that current estimates suggest that approximately 90 percent of all doctor visits are for stress-related disorders. If emotional stress elicits a generalized physiological response, why are there so many different diseases associated with it? Many experts believe that the answer may best be explained by what has been termed "the weak-organ theory." According to this theory, every individual has one organ system that is most susceptible to the damaging effects of prolonged stress.

Mental illness, which is generally regarded as a dysfunction of normal thought processes, has no single identifiable etiology. One may speculate that this is due to the complex nature of the organ system involved. There is also mounting evidence to suggest that there is an organic component to the traditional forms of mental illness such as schizophrenia, chronic depression, and manic depression. The fact that certain mental illnesses tend to occur within families has divided the mental health community into two camps: those who believe that there is a genetic factor operating and those who see the family tendency as more of a learned behavior. In either case, the evidence supports mental illness as another example of the weak-organ theory. The reason one person is more susceptible to the damaging effects of stress than another may not be altogether clear, but evidence is mounting that one's perception or attitude plays a key role in the stress equation. A prime example demonstrating this relationship comes from the research that relates cardiovascular disease to stress. The realization that our attitude has such a significant impact on our health has led to a burgeoning new movement in psychology termed "positive psychology." Dr. Martin Seligman, professor of psychology at the University of Pennsylvania and father of the positive psychology movement, believes that optimism is a key factor in maintaining not only our mental health, but our physical health as well. Dr. Seligman notes that while some people are naturally more optimistic than others, optimism can be learned.

One area in particular that appears to be influenced by the positive psychology movement is the area of stress management. Traditionally, stress management programs have focused on the elimination of stress, but that is starting to change as new strategies approach stress as an essential component of life and a potential source of health. It is worth noting that this concept, of stress serving as a positive force in a person's life, was presented by Dr. Hans Selye in 1974 in his book *Stress Without Distress*. Dr. Selye felt that there were three types of stress: negative stress (distress), normal stress, and positive stress (eustress). He maintained that positive stress not only increases a person's self-esteem but also serves to inoculate the person against the damaging

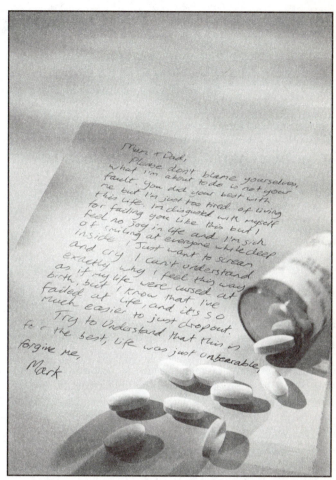

© Stockbyte/Getty Images

effects of distress. Only time will tell if this change of focus in the area of stress management makes any real difference in patient outcome.

The causes of stress are many, but for some individuals, the coming of winter is a very difficult time. Many of these folks experience periods of depression during the shorter days of winter. Workplace stress is another form of distress that causes the economy billions of dollars per year due to sick leave and thereby loss of productivity. Researchers have made significant strides in their understanding of the mechanisms that link emotional stress to physical ailments, but they are less clear on the mechanisms by which positive emotions bolster one's health. Although significant gains have been made in our understanding of the relationship between body and mind, much remains to be learned. What is known indicates that perception and one's attitude are the key elements in shaping our responses to stressors.

Three articles in this section address mental health issues. "The Depressing News about Antidepressants" address the side effects and withdrawal symptoms associated with these medications. The article also describes research that shows the drugs are not more beneficial than a placebo among depressed patients. In "The Boom and Bust Ego," the author describes how to build a healthy self esteem. While many of us use the Internet as a source of information and entertainment, some individuals become addicted. Author Greg Beato discusses how this addiction affects the balance of people's lives in "Internet Addiction."

The Depressing News about Antidepressants

Studies suggest that the popular drugs are no more effective than a placebo. In fact, they may be worse.

SHARON BEGLEY

Although the year is young, it has already brought my first moral dilemma. In early January a friend mentioned that his New Year's resolution was to beat his chronic depression once and for all. Over the years he had tried a medicine chest's worth of antidepressants, but none had really helped in any enduring way, and when the side effects became so unpleasant that he stopped taking them, the withdrawal symptoms (cramps, dizziness, headaches) were torture. Did I know of any research that might help him decide whether a new antidepressant his doctor recommended might finally lift his chronic darkness at noon?

The moral dilemma was this: oh, yes, I knew of 20-plus years of research on antidepressants, from the old tricyclics to the newer selective serotonin reuptake inhibitors (SSRIs) that target serotonin (Zoloft, Paxil, and the granddaddy of them all, Prozac, as well as their generic descendants) to even newer ones that also target norepinephrine (Effexor, Wellbutrin). The research had shown that antidepressants help about three quarters of people with depression who take them, a consistent finding that serves as the basis for the oft-repeated mantra "There is no question that the safety and efficacy of antidepressants rest on solid scientific evidence," as psychiatry professor Richard Friedman of Weill Cornell Medical College recently wrote in *The New York Times*. But ever since a seminal study in 1998, whose findings were reinforced by landmark research in *The Journal of the American Medical Association* last month, that evidence has come with a big asterisk. Yes, the drugs are effective, in that they lift depression in most patients. But that benefit is hardly more than what patients get when they, unknowingly and as part of a study, take a dummy pill—a placebo. As more and more scientists who study depression and the drugs that treat it are concluding, that suggests that antidepressants are basically expensive Tic Tacs.

Hence the moral dilemma. The placebo effect—that is, a medical benefit you get from an inert pill or other sham treatment—rests on the holy trinity of belief, expectation,

and hope. But telling someone with depression who is being helped by antidepressants, or who (like my friend) hopes to be helped, threatens to topple the whole house of cards. Explain that it's all in their heads, that the reason they're benefiting is the same reason why Disney's Dumbo could initially fly only with a feather clutched in his trunk—believing makes it so—and the magic dissipates like fairy dust in a windstorm. So rather than tell my friend all this, I chickened out. Sure, I said, there's lots of research showing that a new kind of antidepressant might help you. Come, let me show you the studies on PubMed.

It seems I am not alone in having moral qualms about blowing the whistle on antidepressants. That first analysis, in 1998, examined 38 manufacturer-sponsored studies involving just over 3,000 depressed patients. The authors, psychology researchers Irving Kirsch and Guy Sapirstein of the University of Connecticut, saw—as everyone else had—that patients did improve, often substantially, on SSRIs, tricyclics, and even MAO inhibitors, a class of antidepressants that dates from the 1950s. This improvement, demonstrated in scores of clinical trials, is the basis for the ubiquitous claim that antidepressants work. But when Kirsch compared the improvement in patients taking the drugs with the improvement in those taking dummy pills—clinical trials typically compare an experimental drug with a placebo—he saw that the difference was minuscule. Patients on a placebo improved about 75 percent as much as those on drugs. Put another way, three quarters of the benefit from antidepressants seems to be a placebo effect. "We wondered, what's going on?" recalls Kirsch, who is now at the University of Hull in England. "These are supposed to be wonder drugs and have huge effects."

The study's impact? The number of Americans taking antidepressants doubled in a decade, from 13.3 million in 1996 to 27 million in 2005.

To be sure, the drugs have helped tens of millions of people, and Kirsch certainly does not advocate that patients suffering from depression stop taking the drugs. On the contrary. But they are not necessarily the best first choice. Psychotherapy, for instance, works for moderate, severe, and even very severe depression. And although for some patients, psychotherapy in combination with an initial course of prescription antidepressants works even better, the question is, *how* do the drugs work? Kirsch's study and, now, others conclude that the lion's share of the drugs' effect comes from the fact that patients expect to be helped by them, and not from any direct chemical action on the brain, especially for anything short of very severe depression.

As the inexorable rise in the use of antidepressants suggests, that conclusion can't hold a candle to the simplistic "antidepressants work!" (unstated corollary: "but don't ask how") message. Part of the resistance to Kirsch's findings has been due to his less-than-retiring nature. He didn't win many friends with the cheeky title of the paper, "Listening to Prozac but Hearing Placebo." Nor did it inspire confidence that the editors of the journal *Prevention & Treatment* ran a warning with his paper, saying it used meta-analysis "controversially." Although some of the six invited commentaries agreed with Kirsch, others were scathing, accusing him of bias and saying the studies he analyzed were flawed (an odd charge for defenders of antidepressants, since the studies were the basis for the Food and Drug Administration's approval of the drugs). One criticism, however, could not be refuted: Kirsch had analyzed only some studies of antidepressants. Maybe if he included them all, the drugs would emerge head and shoulders superior to placebos.

Kirsch agreed. Out of the blue, he received a letter from Thomas Moore, who was then a health-policy analyst at George Washington University. You could expand your data set, Moore wrote, by including everything drug companies sent to the FDA—published studies, like those analyzed in "Hearing Placebo," but also unpublished studies. In 1998 Moore used the Freedom of Information Act to pry such data from the FDA. The total came to 47 company-sponsored studies—on Prozac, Paxil, Zoloft, Effexor, Serzone, and Celexa—that Kirsch and colleagues then pored over. (As an aside, it turned out that about 40 percent of the clinical trials had never been published. That is significantly higher than for other classes of drugs, says Lisa Bero of the University of California, San Francisco; overall, 22 percent of clinical trials of drugs are not published. "By and large," says Kirsch, "the unpublished studies were those that had failed to show a significant benefit from taking the actual drug.") In just over half of the published and unpublished studies, he and colleagues reported in 2002, the drug alleviated depression no better than a placebo. "And the extra benefit of antidepressants was even less than we saw when we analyzed only published studies," Kirsch recalls. About 82 percent of the response to antidepressants—not the 75 percent he had calculated from examining only published studies—had also been achieved by a dummy pill.

Only in patients with very severe symptoms was there a clinically meaningful drug benefit, the *JAMA* study found.

The extra effect of real drugs wasn't much to celebrate, either. It amounted to 1.8 points on the 54-point scale doctors use to gauge the severity of depression, through questions about mood, sleep habits, and the like. Sleeping better counts as six points. Being less fidgety during the assessment is worth two points. In other words, the clinical significance of the 1.8 extra points from real drugs was underwhelming. Now Kirsch was certain. "The belief that antidepressants can cure depression chemically is simply wrong," he told me in January on the eve of the publication of his book *The Emperor's New Drugs: Exploding the Antidepressant Myth.*

The 2002 study ignited a furious debate, but more and more scientists were becoming convinced that Kirsch—who had won respect for research on the placebo response and who had published scores of scientific papers—was on to something. One team of researchers wondered if antidepressants were "a triumph of marketing over science." Even defenders of antidepressants agreed that the drugs have "relatively small" effects. "Many have long been unimpressed by the magnitude of the differences observed between treatments and controls," psychology researcher Steven Hollon of Vanderbilt University and colleagues wrote—"what some of our colleagues refer to as 'the dirty little secret.'" In Britain, the agency that assesses which treatments are effective enough for the government to pay for stopped recommending antidepressants as a first-line treatment, especially for mild or moderate depression.

But if experts know that antidepressants are hardly better than placebos, few patients or doctors do. Some doctors have changed their prescribing habits, says Kirsch, but more "reacted with anger and incredulity." Understandably. For one thing, depression is a devastating, underdiagnosed, and undertreated disease. Of course doctors recoiled at the idea that such drugs might be mirages. If that were true, how were physicians supposed to help their patients?

Two other factors are at work in the widespread rejection of Kirsch's (and, now, other scientists') findings about antidepressants. First, defenders of the drugs scoff at the idea that the FDA would have approved ineffective drugs. (Simple explanation: the FDA requires two well-designed clinical trials showing a drug is more effective than a placebo. That's two, period—even if many more studies show no such effectiveness. And the size of the "more effective" doesn't much matter, as long as it is statistically significant.) Second, doctors see with their own eyes, and feel with their hearts, that the drugs lift the black cloud from many of their depressed patients. But since doctors are not exactly in the habit of prescribing dummy pills, they have no experience comparing how their patients do on them, and therefore never see that a placebo would be almost as effective as a $4 pill. "When they prescribe a treatment and it works," says Kirsch, "their natural tendency is to attribute the cure to the treatment." Hence the widespread "antidepressants work" refrain that persists to this day.

Drug companies do not dispute Kirsch's aggregate statistics. But they point out that the average is made up of some patients in whom there is a true drug effect of antidepressants and some in whom there is not. As a spokesperson for Lilly (maker of Prozac) said, "Depression is a highly individualized illness," and "not all patients respond the same way to a particular treatment." In addition, notes a spokesperson for GlaxoSmithKline (maker of Paxil), the studies analyzed in the *JAMA* paper differ from studies GSK submitted to the FDA when it won approval for Paxil, "so it is difficult to make direct comparisons between the results. This study contributes to the extensive research that has helped to characterize the role of antidepressants," which "are an important option, in addition to counseling and life-style changes, for treatment of depression." A spokesperson for Pfizer, which makes Zoloft, also cited the "wealth of scientific evidence documenting [antidepressants'] effects," adding that the fact that antidepressants "commonly fail to separate from placebo" is "a fact well known by the FDA, academia, and industry." Other manufacturers pointed out that Kirsch and the *JAMA* authors had not studied their particular brands.

Even Kirsch's analysis, however, found that antidepressants are a little more effective than dummy pills—those 1.8 points on the depression scale. Maybe Prozac, Zoloft, Paxil, Celexa, and their cousins do have some non-placebo, chemical benefit. But the small edge of real drugs compared with placebos might not mean what it seems, Kirsch explained to me one evening from his home in Hull. Consider how research on drugs works. Patient volunteers are told they will receive either the drug or a placebo, and that neither they nor the scientists will know who is getting what. Most volunteers hope they get the drug, not the dummy pill. After taking the unknown meds for a while, some volunteers experience side effects. Bingo: a clue they're on the real drug. About 80 percent guess right, and studies show that the worse side effects a patient experiences, the more effective the drug. Patients apparently think, this drug is so strong it's making me vomit and hate sex, so it must be strong enough to lift my depression. In clinical-trial patients who figure out they're receiving the drug and not the inert pill, expectations soar.

That matters because belief in the power of a medical treatment can be self-fulfilling (that's the basis of the placebo effect). The patients who correctly guess that they're getting the real drug therefore experience a stronger placebo effect than those who get the dummy pill, experience no side effects, and are therefore disappointed. That might account for antidepressants' slight edge in effectiveness compared with a placebo, an edge that derives not from the drugs' molecules but from the hopes and expectations that patients in studies feel when they figure out they're receiving the real drug.

The boy who said the emperor had no clothes didn't endear himself to his fellow subjects, and Kirsch has fared little better. A nascent collaboration with a scientist at a medical school ended in 2002 when the scientist was warned not to submit a grant proposal with Kirsch if he ever wanted to be funded again. Four years later, another scientist wrote a paper questioning the effectiveness of antidepressants, citing Kirsch's work. It was published in a prestigious journal. That ordinarily brings accolades. Instead, his department chair dressed him down and warned him not to become too involved with Kirsch.

But the question of whether antidepressants—which in 2008 had sales of $9.6 billion in the U.S., reported the consulting firm IMS Health—have any effect other than through patients'

belief in them was too important to scare researchers off. Proponents of the drugs have found themselves making weaker and weaker claims. Their last stand is that antidepressants are more effective than a placebo in patients suffering the most severe depression.

So concluded the *JAMA* study in January. In an analysis of six large experiments in which, as usual, depressed patients received either a placebo or an active drug, the true drug effect—that is, in addition to the placebo effect—was "nonexistent to negligible" in patients with mild, moderate, and even severe depression. Only in patients with very severe symptoms (scoring 23 or above on the standard scale) was there a statistically significant drug benefit. Such patients account for about 13 percent of people with depression. "Most people don't need an active drug," says Vanderbilt's Hollon, a coauthor of the study. "For a lot of folks, you're going to do as well on a sugar pill or on conversations with your physicians as you will on medication. It doesn't matter what you do; it's just the fact that you're doing something." But people with very severe depression are different, he believes. "My personal view is the placebo effect gets you pretty far, but for those with very severe, more chronic conditions, it's harder to knock down and placebos are less adequate," says Hollon. Why that should be remains a mystery, admits coauthor Robert DeRubeis of the University of Pennsylvania.

Like every scientist who has stepped into the treacherous waters of antidepressant research, Hollon, DeRubeis, and their colleagues are keenly aware of the disconnect between evidence and public impression. "Prescribers, policy makers, and consumers may not be aware that the efficacy of [antidepressants] largely has been established on the basis of studies that have included only those individuals with more severe forms of depression," something drug ads don't mention, they write. People with anything less than very severe depression "derive little specific pharmacological benefit from taking medications. Pending findings contrary to those reported here . . . efforts should be made to clarify to clinicians and prospective patients that . . . there is little evidence to suggest that [antidepressants] produce specific pharmacological benefit for the majority of patients."

Right about here, people scowl and ask how antidepressants—especially those that raise the brain's levels of serotonin—can possibly have no direct chemical effect on the brain. Surely raising serotonin levels should right the synapses' "chemical imbalance" and lift depression. Unfortunately, the serotonin-deficit theory of depression is built on a foundation of tissue paper. How that came to be is a story in itself, but the basics are that in the 1950s scientists discovered, serendipitously, that a drug called iproniazid seemed to help some people with depression. Iproniazid increases brain levels of serotonin and norepinephrine. Ergo, low levels of those neurotransmitters must cause depression. More than 50 years on, the presumed effectiveness of antidepressants that act this way remains the chief support for the chemical-imbalance theory of depression. Absent that effectiveness, the theory hasn't a leg to stand on. Direct evidence doesn't exist. Lowering people's serotonin levels does not change their mood. And a new drug, tianeptine,

14

The Placebo Effect

In addition to depression, many illnesses show a strong response to placebo treatments. These tend to be conditions for which the body's own biochemicals, such as opiates and dopamine, act as natural medications. Because placebos trigger the production of these compounds, dummy pills can be almost as effective as real ones. Among the conditions that have been successfully treated with placebos:

Hypertension pain parkinson's disease psoriasis rheumatoid arthritis ulcers

Illnesses that do not respond to the body's natural opiates and other compounds show little to no placebo response either. These include:

Atherosclerosis cancer growth-hormone deficiency high cholesterol infertility obsessive-compulsive disorder

which is sold in France and some other countries (but not the U.S.), turns out to be as effective as Prozac-like antidepressants that keep the synapses well supplied with serotonin. The mechanism of the new drug? It *lowers* brain levels of serotonin. "If depression can be equally affected by drugs that increase serotonin and by drugs that decrease it," says Kirsch, "it's hard to imagine how the benefits can be due to their chemical activity."

Perhaps antidepressants would be more effective at higher doses? Unfortunately, in 2002 Kirsch and colleagues found that high doses are hardly more effective than low ones, improving patients' depression-scale rating an average of 9.97 points vs. 9.57 points—a difference that is not statistically significant. Yet many doctors increase doses for patients who do not respond to a lower one, and many patients report improving as a result. There's a study of that, too. When researchers gave such nonresponders a higher dose, 72 percent got much better, their symptoms dropping by 50 percent or more. The catch? Only half the patients really got a higher dose. The rest, unknowingly, got the original, "ineffective" dose. It is hard to see the 72 percent who got much better on ersatz higher doses as the result of anything but the power of expectation: the doctor upped my dose, so I believe I'll get better.

Something similar may explain why some patients who aren't helped by one antidepressant do better on a second, or a third. This is often explained as "matching" patient to drug, and seemed to be confirmed by a 2006 federal study called STAR*D. Patients still suffering from depression after taking one drug were switched to a second; those who were still not better were switched to a third drug, and even a fourth. No placebos were used. At first blush, the results offered a ray of hope: 37 percent of the patients got better on the first drug, 19 percent more on their second, 6 percent more improved on their third try, and 5 percent more on their fourth. (Half of those who recovered relapsed within a year, however.)

So does STAR*D validate the idea that the key to effective treatment of depression is matching the patient to the drug?

Maybe. Or maybe people improved in rounds two, three, and four because depression sometimes lifts due to changes in people's lives, or because levels of depression tend to rise and fall over time. With no one in STAR*D receiving a placebo, it is not possible to conclude with certainty that the improvements in rounds two, three, and four were because patients switched to a drug that was more effective for them. Comparable numbers might have improved if they had switched to a placebo. But STAR*D did not test for that, and so cannot rule it out.

It's tempting to look at the power of the placebo effect to alleviate depression and stick an "only" in front of it—as in, the drugs work *only* through the placebo effect. But there is nothing "only" about the placebo response. It can be surprisingly enduring, as a 2008 study found: "The widely held belief that the placebo response in depression is short-lived appears to be based largely on intuition and perhaps wishful thinking," scientists wrote in the *Journal of Psychiatric Research.* The strength of the placebo response drives drug companies nuts, since it makes showing the superiority of a new drug much harder. There is a strong placebo component in the response to drugs for pain, asthma, irritable-bowel syndrome, skin conditions such as contact dermatitis, and even Parkinson's disease. But compared with the placebo component of antidepressants, the placebo response accounts for a smaller fraction of the benefit from drugs for those disorders—on the order of 50 percent for analgesics, for instance.

Which returns us to the moral dilemma. In any year, an estimated 13.1 million to 14.2 million American adults suffer from clinical depression. At least 32 million will have the disease at some point in their life. Many of the 57 percent who receive treatment (the rest do not) are helped by medication. For that benefit to continue, they need to believe in their pills. Even Kirsch warns—in boldface type in his book, which is in stores this week—that patients on antidepressants not suddenly stop taking them. That can cause serious withdrawal symptoms, including twitches, tremors, blurred vision, and nausea—as well as depression and anxiety. Yet Kirsch is well aware that his book may have the same effect on patients as the crows did on Dumbo when they told him the "magic feather" wasn't really giving him the power of flight: the little elephant began crashing to earth. Friends and colleagues who believe Kirsch is right ask why he doesn't just shut up, since publicizing the finding that the effectiveness of antidepressants is almost entirely due to people's hopes and expectations will undermine that effectiveness.

If placebos can make people better, then depression can be treated without drugs that come with serious side effects, not to mention costs.

It's all well and good to point out that psychotherapy is more effective than either pills or placebos, with dramatically lower relapse rates. But there's the little matter of reality. In the U.S., most patients with depression are treated by primary-care doctors, not psychiatrists. The latter are in short supply, especially outside cities and especially for children and adolescents. Some insurance plans discourage such care, and some psychiatrists do not accept insurance. Maybe keeping patients in the dark about the ineffectiveness of antidepressants, which for many are their only hope, is a kindness.

Or maybe not. As shown by the explicit criticism of drug companies by the authors of the recent *JAMA* paper, more and more scientists believe it is time to abandon the "don't ask, don't tell" policy of not digging too deeply into the reasons for the effectiveness of antidepressants. Maybe it is time to pull back the curtain and see the wizard for what he is. As for Kirsch, he insists that it is important to know that much of the benefit of antidepressants is a placebo effect. If placebos can make people better, then depression can be treated without drugs that come with serious side effects, not to mention costs. Wider recognition that antidepressants are a pharmaceutical version of the emperor's new clothes, he says, might spur patients to try other treatments. "Isn't it more important to know the truth?" he asks. Based on the impact of his work so far, it's hard to avoid answering, "Not to many people."

Critical Thinking

1. Distinguish between depression and sadness.
2. Discuss the risks versus benefits of taking antidepressants.
3. Identify what alternatives there are to antidepressant medication.

The Boom and Bust Ego

Self-esteem, as a concept, has had wild ups and downs since the '70s. The newest take is that the less you think about your own self-esteem, the healthier you'll be.

HARRIET BROWN

Back in her college dorm room, in the 1980s, Anneli Rufus had a revelation: "I saw that my roommate looked in the mirror without automatically saying bad things about her body or clothes or face. She just did her best to get ready for the day and went out the door. Watching her once, it dawned on me that other people don't automatically assume the worst about themselves."

Around that same time, Rufus met her future husband (the two were married in '89.) "He'd say things like, 'You're wonderful, you're beautiful.' I thought, 'Well, he's saying that because that's what guys say, or because he feels sorry for me, or because he knows that I'm psychologically fragile, and he doesn't want to upset me.' I never believed a compliment. Information comes to me and I process it in a completely different way than a 'normal' person would," she says. "This is life with low self-esteem."

Rufus can look back on her college years and say that she was an intelligent, kind, interesting, humorous, nice-looking young woman, and that it was not at all unreasonable for someone to fall in love with her. But she would never have been able to see that then. Although she was an aspiring writer, after graduating from UC Berkeley she didn't try to get internships or introduce herself to editors. "I walked around like a shlump," she says. "I didn't know how to present myself or look good or dress right. I didn't think I deserved it, and no one taught me how, and I didn't seek to find out how."

Despite years of such self-undermining behaviors, Rufus's talent and hard work shone through. She's published well-received books and writes regularly for top magazines and websites. She and her husband have kept their relationship strong and happy. "I've had accomplishments," she says, "and I've spent my entire life not really appreciating them. Let's say I win a writing prize. Do I go out to dinner to celebrate and feel great? No. The person with low self-esteem just wants any acknowledgment to be over in this weird subconscious way."

For decades, psychologists pushed people like Rufus to work at raising their self-esteem. Countless books and articles urged those with low self-esteem to build it up by thinking positively, listing achievements and good qualities, and airing shameful feelings, among other methods. Legitimate researchers and self-help gurus alike told them that learning to love themselves—or at least like themselves—would lead to more success at work and at home.

So they tried. They wrote post-it notes listing their best qualities and stuck them to bathroom mirrors. They muttered mantras under their breath. They told their kids they were extra-super-special.

"At one point I was in a women's group with a few friends," Rufus says. "We'd get together and have these talks about how women are fantastic and can rule the world. One night we took turns chanting our own names, loudly. It made me feel worse."

Psychologists have proved what Rufus felt to be true: Direct attempts to build self-esteem generally do not work. A few years ago, Joanne Wood, a professor of psychology at the University of Waterloo in Ontario, set out to test the notion that affirmations and other such self-talk make people feel better about themselves. The subjects in her study who started out with high self-esteem did report feeling a little better after engaging in positive self-talk. But those with low self-esteem—the very people you'd expect to use such techniques—felt worse. "The blithe recommendations to engage in positive self-statements are based on an intuition that they'll work," Wood says. "And they don't, often." Because these positive statements are so starkly different from the negative thoughts of the person with low self-esteem, they likely underscore the discouragingly long distance between where the person is and where she would like to be. The low-self-esteem sufferer is left feeling like a double failure.

Jennifer Crocker, a psychologist at the University of Michigan, studies "contingent self-esteem," or feelings of self-worth that depend on outside validation or praise in a realm that matters to a person. Scoring a victory in that particular area does raise self-esteem, but the boost doesn't last. "How does it feel after you pass your dissertation orals?" asks Crocker, "You feel good for a day, but then your worries come back."

The more a person's self-esteem is contingent on particular outcomes, the harder she will crash if she fails. Success is not extra sweet for these people—but failure is extra bitter.

Success is not extra sweet for these people—but failure is extra bitter.

Contingent self-esteem is by definition a chimera. Even the most accomplished, beautiful, and celebrated human beings don't get a steady stream of compliments and positive feedback. And chasing the chimera can, paradoxically, lead to self-sabotage. "When people want to boost self-esteem or avoid a drop, they may do things that undermine them as a whole," says Crocker. Her research shows that those with contingent self-esteem often shy away from situations that might produce even a temporary dip in how they view themselves—which can make them more prone to failure: Imagine a surgeon reluctant to practice new techniques in the operating room because he might not do them perfectly at first—hardly an attitude that would help his career over time.

Now that the evidence is clear that chasing self-esteem either doesn't work or leads people to self-defeating behaviors, it's particularly tragic to acknowledge that we, as a culture, are more driven to chase ego-affirming highs than ever. Crocker and colleagues found that college students value boosts to their self-esteem (such as receiving a good grade or a compliment) more than any other pleasant activity they were asked about—including sex, favorite foods, drinking alcohol, seeing a best friend, or receiving a paycheck! The researchers interpret the findings as showing that students want boosts to their self-esteem even more than they actually "like" those things that inflate their egos. So much for young hedonism; they'd rather (joylessly) make the honor roll.

Too Much Self-Love is Loathsome, Too

Perhaps the collective failure to raise low self-esteem, whether from racking up achievements in one's field or howling out one's own name, was a blessing in disguise. A few years ago, researchers like Jean Twenge, author of *Generation Me*, started sounding the alarm on the dangers of *too much* self-esteem. Twenge and others believe that today's twentysomethings—raised by parents who rewarded every burp and blink with "Good job!"—may in fact be a generation of entitled narcissists. There is such a thing as feeling too good about yourself, and it may be just as unhealthy as feeling inferior. It can lead to attention-seeking, a focus on appearance and status, and an inability to form real relationships.

Although a direct cause-and-effect relationship has not been established, Nicholas Emler of the University of Surrey in England found that those with low self-esteem are at an increased risk of developing eating disorders, depression, and committing suicide, while those with high self-esteem are a threat to society as well as to themselves: They are more likely to be racist, violent, and criminal.

"When I was a child, people spanked their kids and said terrible things like 'You're a bad boy.' Now, it's just the opposite: All kids are fabulous. That's not realistic, either," Rufus says. "If, in childhood, some wonderful angel would come down and give us a reality check by saying, 'Look, you're good at singing, you're kind of messy but you can work on it, brush your teeth, but, hey, you're very nice to animals,' I think we'd all have an optimal level of self-esteem. We wouldn't be unrealistic about ourselves at one end of the spectrum or the other."

Self-Esteem Doesn't Affect How You Turn Out

It was a bombshell for those who put so much faith in self-esteem and its powers to improve our society: Roy Baumeister of Florida State University, a pioneering researcher and believer in the value of self-esteem starting in the '70s, was forced to do an about-face on his own research in the '80s. Eventually, he conducted a meta-analysis on the relationship between self-esteem and external markers of success in school, at work, and in relationships. In 2003, Baumeister and his colleagues reported that they found no evidence that high self-esteem made people better students, more successful at work, or healthier.

"After all these years," Baumeister says on his university's website, "my recommendation is this: Forget about self-esteem and concentrate more on self-control and self-discipline. Recent work suggests this would be good for the individual and good for society and might even be able to fill some of those promises that self-esteem once made but could not keep."

A Clear-Eyed View on Low Self-Esteem

So If low self-esteem can't be removed through sheer will, and doesn't affect objective outcomes in life anyway, is there a more accurate way to think about it? Jonathon D. Brown, a social psychologist at the University

of Washington, has been pondering the question for years (he's one of social psychology's most frequently cited authors). He believes that we all have a baseline level of self-esteem that is set during childhood interactions with parents. Rather than respect or admiration, he defines self-esteem as a more fundamental affection for oneself. Those with healthy self-esteem maintain deep-down self-acceptance even when they feel bad in the face of rejection or failure. Those with low self-esteem lack an internal "safety net," and thus plunge lower than others when they experience life's slings and arrows. They even perceive rejection and failure where it doesn't exist.

Even the most beautiful and celebrated human beings don't get a steady stream of compliments.

The safety net of solid self-esteem grows out of a secure attachment to a parent; it can fail to form if a parent is inconsistently supportive or lacks empathy and concern for his or her child. "If you love somebody and they screw up, it doesn't change the way you feel about them," Brown points out. "You don't love somebody because of his accomplishments or characteristics. You love somebody in a way that's organic or emotional." The same holds true for how one loves oneself, if all goes well.

Rufus's childhood was a textbook case for the development of low self-esteem. "I got this feeling very early on that it was really up to others, and not up to me, to decide whether I was good or bad," she says.

Her parents were enchanted by her writing and drawing abilities; they saw those efforts as miraculous since they themselves weren't artistic. But they were also convinced that their daughter was a horrible slob, though she remembers her room as being typically messy, not a disaster area. "It was just disorganized because I don't have that natural knack. They didn't teach me how to do it. Instead, their solution was to scream at me. They would storm into my room and say, 'You're a f***ing slob! Look at this pigsty! Why do you do this? Do you do this because you hate us?' Other kids do bad things on purpose, they break things or paint on walls. I never did anything mischievous, because I lived in fear. But I still got punished."

"Low self-esteem comes when you question everything you do," Rufus observes. "You're always tiptoeing around because you're sure you're going to piss someone off without even knowing that you're doing it because you are a terrible person at your core."

While peers can sometimes provide a refuge from an upsetting home life, Rufus was also mocked in school, for wearing orthopedic shoes and for her general nerdiness in an environment where scholastic achievement wasn't prized. The teasing only served to confirm her suspicions about her worthiness.

Jonathon Brown believes that those with low self-esteem are often doomed for life, as the set point can't be inched up too much. Depressing as his message sounds on the surface, it is compellingly honest. And it goes on to convey a means of damage control: If you have low self-esteem, you may not be able to change the way you feel about yourself, but you can learn strategies for better weathering the effects negative thoughts have on your mood and on the decisions you make. "It's like the difference between a dog and a duck," Brown explains. "A duck goes in the water and doesn't get wet. That's a gift ducks get early in life. A dog goes in the water and it has to shake itself dry. Maybe you're never going to be a duck, but you can learn to be a better dog. You can learn to handle life better."

Less Hoping, More Coping

Low self-esteem may not predict anything, but it still doesn't feel very good. So it's valuable for those with low self-esteem to know they can definitely learn to cope with it better and, as a result, spend less time feeling unnecessarily worried, rejected, or inferior. As Joanne Wood has found, people with high self-esteem are automatically more likely than those with less to relish happy moments and force themselves out of funks. Those with low self-esteem confirm their negative beliefs about themselves, downplay their own moments of joy, and wallow in their low periods.

"When I don't get a return call or email, I automatically assume the person is mad at me," Rufus says. "And then there are my conversation hangovers. When I meet with someone, especially when it's important or when it's the first time, I go over it afterward, thinking 'You idiot! Why didn't you act more interested in them, why didn't you say this, why did you forget that?' I can't just let the conversation be in the past and trust that I did the best I could."

In short, those with low self-esteem might be subtly choosing to gather proof of their unworthiness rather than enjoying their bright moments. That's useful information—it can help counter a downward spiral of thoughts. Disciplining oneself to question critical thoughts that discount good wishes or events—a cognitive-behavioral technique—can break patterns of self-doubt and rumination.

Researchers like Jennifer Crocker have found ways for people to nudge their self-esteem upward—by taking their ego out of the equation and refraining tasks that push self-esteem buttons, Crocker's most recent study, yet to be published, looks at college freshmen who met for the first time when they were assigned to room together. Over a period of 10 weeks, Crocker found that when one roommate consciously set out to be supportive of the other, the other student noticed and became more supportive in return. The upshot: Both students' self-esteem rose. "It's the giving that's responsible, not the receiving," says Crocker. "And if you do it in order to boost your self-esteem, other people may feel there's something phony about it."

Crocker attributes the effect to the fact that people's lives become more meaningful when they have constructive goals, especially those goals that make a difference for others. "Focus on what you really care about and what you want to do," she suggests. "You have low self-esteem. So what? You can still make a contribution at work and be supportive of people you care about. And when you do that, you take the attention off yourself. The pain of low self-esteem comes from being preoccupied with the idea that you don't measure up. When you shift attention to something outside yourself, you might find relief."

You have low self-esteem. So what? You can still make a contribution.

Kristin Neff, a professor of educational psychology at the University of Texas at Austin, used to believe self-criticism motivated people to do and be their best. People who weren't satisfied with themselves would work harder to improve. Then while taking a meditation class, Neff stumbled onto the concept of self-compassion. The more she learned about it, the more she came to believe that the key to self-esteem issues was not to focus more energy and attention on them but less.

Neff explains that in American culture, people tend to acquire a sense of self-worth from feeling special. "And that's where all the problems start," she says. A musician who compares herself to a less-talented musician will feel superior, even special, and will probably feel a rise in contingent self-esteem. But if she compares herself to someone more talented, she'll likely feel worse—even though her own talent and skills haven't changed. Social comparison is inevitable, looking for our place in the social universe we inhabit. And we all do it. But it's not exactly a recipe for self-confidence, because there are always people who do what you do both better and worse than you. Especially if you live in populous places, as most of us do now.

Neff sees self-compassion as being different from those old "affirmations" in that rather than glossing over one's mistakes or imperfections as affirmations do, self-compassion acknowledges them—but also acknowledges that flaws are part of being human and that failure therefore connects us to others. Rather than comparing ourselves to other people and watching our self-esteem bounce around as a result, we can remind ourselves that everyone suffers and feels painful emotions. Studies have shown that those who are self-compassionate are less depressed and have stabler feelings of self-worth than others. They are less likely to ride the roller coaster of contingent self-esteem.

Techniques for building self-compassion include cultivating mindfulness—an awareness of the present with a nonjudgmental attitude toward one's own fleeting thoughts and feelings—and simply talking to oneself about problems and concerns as with a friend—with honesty, love, and support, rather than harsh criticisms.

For Rufus, being aware of her low self-esteem and then learning to cope with it better have been a long haul. But she has made progress. A light bulb went on one night when she was 24. "I realized that I'd never thought bad things about my Mom or Dad. I just believed everything they said. I thought, 'Wait, all that yelling was inappropriate.' I wasn't perfect, but I wasn't terrible, either. They were very black-and-white in their thinking, and I never knew if I was the slob who hated them or the prize-winning little writer."

The constructive goal that most takes Rufus's mind off low self-esteem is her work. "Writing, for me, is the ladder to the stars," she says. "I realize at this point in life that I'm pretty good at it. When I'm doing it, I feel better; I feel somewhat normal." The fact that a few of her books, such as *Stuck: Why We Can't Move On,* have an unconventional yet "self-help" bent—and have resulted in hundreds of "thank you" emails from readers—gives her the sense that she is contributing to the world and easing others' concerns.

By her own report, having a rock-solid and temperamentally sanguine life partner has kept Rufus afloat during her darker moments. A few months after she met her husband, they were sitting on a curb while she sobbed and blurted out "Every one hates me," and "I'm a terrible person." In response, he said "Why can't you just let me love you?" It's a mantra she thinks back on and tries to adhere to.

"I think people with low self-esteem need real lessons on the tiny little steps you have to take to stop wasting your time with worries, to stop loathing yourself," she says. "In my mind, I often go back to my college dorm, where I saw my roommate getting ready—just being a normal person. I don't need to overcome my low self-esteem in this massive way. Just getting those lessons from watching others has been great for me."

Critical Thinking

1. Discuss why the more a person's self esteem is contingent on a particular outcome, the more one will crash if one fails.

2. Distinguish between ego and self esteem.

3. Can someone really change their level of self esteem? Explain.

Internet Addiction

What once was parody may soon be diagnosis.

GREG BEATO

In 1995, in an effort to parody the way the American Psychiatric Association's hugely influential *Diagnostic and Statistical Manual of Mental Disorders* medicalizes every excessive behavior, psychiatrist Ivan Goldberg introduced on his website the concept of "Internet Addiction Disorder." Last summer Ben Alexander, a 19-year-old college student obsessed with the online multiplayer game *World of Warcraft,* was profiled by CBS News, NPR, the Associated Press, and countless other media outlets because of his status as client No. 1 at reSTART, the first residential treatment center in America for individuals trying to get themselves clean from Azeroth, iPhones, and all the other digital narcotics of our age.

At reSTART's five-acre haven in the woods near Seattle, clients pay big bucks to detox from pathological computer use by building chicken coops, cooking hamburgers, and engaging in daily therapy sessions with the program's two founders, psychologist Hilarie Cash and clinical social worker and life coach Cosette Rae. With room for just six addicts at a time and a $14,500 program fee, reSTART isn't designed for the masses, and so far it seems to have attracted more reporters than paying clients. When I spoke with Rae in May, she said "10 to 15" people had participated in the 45-day program to date.

Still, the fact that reSTART exists at all shows how far we've progressed in taking Dr. Goldberg's spoof seriously. You may have been too busy monitoring Kim Kardashian's every passing thought-like thing on Twitter to notice, but Digital Detox Week took place in April, and Video Game Addiction Awareness Week followed on its heels in June. Internet addiction disorder has yet to claim a Tiger Woods of its own, but the sad, silly evidence of our worldwide cyber-bingeing mounts on a daily basis. A councilman in the Bulgarian city of Plovdiv is ousted from his position for playing *Farmville* during budget meetings. There are now at least three apps that use the iPhone's camera to show the world right in front of you so you can keep texting while walking down the street, confident in your ability to avoid sinkholes, telephone poles, and traffic. Earlier this year, 200 students taking a class in media literacy at the University of Maryland went on a 24-hour media fast for a group study, then described how "jittery," "anxious," "miserable," and "crazy" they felt without Twitter, Facebook, iPods, and laptops.

"I clearly am addicted," one student concluded, "and the dependency is sickening."

In the early days of the Web, dirty talk was exchanged at the excruciatingly slow rate of 14.4 bits per second, connectivity charges accrued by the hour instead of the month, and the only stuff for sale online was some overpriced hot sauce from a tiny store in Pasadena. It took the patience of a Buddhist monk, thousands of dollars, and really bad TV reception to overuse the Web in a self-destructive manner. Yet even then, many people felt Ivan Goldberg's notes on Internet addiction worked better as psychiatry than comedy. A year before Goldberg posted his spoof, Kimberly Young, a psychologist at the University of Pittsburgh, had already begun conducting formal research into online addiction. By 1996 the Harvard-affiliated McLean Hospital had established a computer addiction clinic, a professor at the University of Maryland had created an Internet addiction support group, and *The New York Times* was running op-eds about the divorce epidemic that Internet addiction was about to unleash.

Fifteen years down the line, you'd think we'd all be introverted philanderers by now, isolating ourselves in the virtual Snuggie of *World of Warcraft* by day and stepping out at night to destroy our marriages with our latest hook-ups from AshleyMadison.com. But the introduction of flat monthly fees, online gaming, widespread pornography, MySpace, YouTube, Facebook, WiFi, iPhones, netbooks, and free return shipping on designer shoes with substantial markdowns does not seem to have made the Internet any more addictive than it was a decade ago.

In 1998 Young told the Riverside *Press-Enterprise* that "5 to 10 percent of the 52 million Internet users [were] addicted or 'potentially addicted.'" Doctors today use similar numbers when estimating the number of online junkies. In 2009 David Greenfield, a psychiatrist at the University of Connecticut, told the *San Francisco Chronicle* that studies have shown 3 percent to 6 percent of Internet users "have a problem." Is it possible that the ability to keep extremely close tabs on Ashton Kutcher actually has reduced the Internet's addictive power?

Granted, 3 percent is an awful lot of people. Argue all you like that a real addiction should require needles, or spending time in seedy bars with people who drink vodka through their eyeballs, or at least the overwhelming and nihilistic urge to invest thousands of dollars in a broken public school system through the purchase of lottery tickets. Those working on the front lines of technology overuse have plenty of casualties to point to. In our brief conversation, Cosette Rae tells me about a Harvard student who lost a scholarship because he spent too much time playing games, a guy who spent so many sedentary hours at his computer that he developed blood clots in his leg and had to have it amputated, and an 18-year-old who chose homelessness over gamelessness when his parents told him he either had to quit playing computer games or move out.

A few minutes on Google yields even more lurid anecdotes. In 2007 an Ohio teenager shot his parents, killing his mother and wounding his father, after they took away his Xbox. This year a South Korean couple let their real baby starve to death because they were spending so much time caring for their virtual baby in a role-playing game called *Prius Online.*

On a pound-for-pound basis, the average *World of Warcraft* junkie undoubtedly represents a much less destructive social force than the average meth head. But it's not extreme anecdotes that make the specter of Internet addiction so threatening; it's the fact that Internet overuse has the potential to scale in a way that few other addictions do. Even if Steve Jobs designed a really cool-looking syringe and started distributing free heroin on street corners, not everyone would try it. But who among us doesn't already check his email more often than necessary? As the Internet weaves itself more and more tightly into our lives, only the Amish are completely safe.

As early as 1996, Kimberly Young was promoting the idea that the American Psychiatric Association (APA) should add Internet addiction disorder to the *Diagnostic and Statistical Manual of Mental Disorders* (*DSM*). In February, the APA announced that its coming edition of the *DSM,* the first major

revision since 1994, will for the first time classify a behavior-related condition—pathological gambling—as an "addiction" rather than an "impulse control disorder." Internet addiction disorder is not being included in this new category of "behavioral addictions," but the APA said it will consider it as a "potential addition . . . as research data accumulate."

If the APA does add excessive Internet use to the *DSM,* the consequences will be wide-ranging. Health insurance companies will start offering at least partial coverage for treatment programs such as reSTART. People who suffer from Internet addiction disorder will receive protection under the Americans With Disabilities Act if their impairment "substantially limits one or more major life activities." Criminal lawyers will use their clients' online habits to fashion diminished capacity defenses.

Which means that what started as a parody in 1995 could eventually turn more darkly comic than ever imagined. Picture a world where the health care system goes bankrupt because insurers have to pay for millions of people determined to kick their Twitter addictions once and for all. Where employees who view porn at work are legally protected from termination. Where killing elves in cyberspace could help absolve you for killing people in real life. Is it too late to revert to our older, healthier, more balanced ways of living and just spend all our leisure hours watching *Love Boat* reruns?

Critical Thinking

1. How can electronic devices become addicting? Is it a true addiction?
2. What can be done to treat Internet addiction?
3. Do you believe that group homes for Internet addiction are effective? Discuss.

UNIT 3
Nutritional Health

Unit Selections

Learning Outcomes

After reading this Unit, you will be able to:

- List the four nutrients that function as antioxidants. Identify the best food sources of these nutrients in foods that you commonly eat.

- Identify the four groups that should pay particular attention to sodium content of foods and consume no more than 1,500 mg of sodium per day, as recommended in the Dietary Guidelines for Americans.

- Discuss the merits of taking supplemental vitamin D.

- Explain the possible link between food coloring and behavior change in children.

Student Website
www.mhhe.com/cls

Internet References

Center for Science in the Public Interest (CSPI)
   www.cspinet.org
Food and Nutrition Information Center
   www.nalusda.gov/fnic/index.html

The American Dietetic Association
   www.eatright.org

For years, the majority of Americans paid little attention to nutrition, other than to eat three meals a day and, perhaps, take a vitamin supplement. While this dietary style was generally adequate for the prevention of major nutritional deficiencies such as scurvy, medical evidence began to accumulate linking the American diet to a variety of chronic illnesses including cancer and heart disease. In an effort to guide Americans in their dietary choices, the United States Department of Agriculture and the United States Public Health Service review and publish Dietary Guidelines every five years. The most recent Dietary Guidelines' recommendations are no longer limited to food choices; they include advice on the importance of maintaining a healthy weight and engaging in daily exercise. In addition to the Dietary Guidelines, the Department of Agriculture developed the Food Guide Pyramid to show the relative importance of food groups. Meat and dairy products are no longer recommended to be the focus of the diet. Rather fruits, vegetables, and whole grains should make up most of what we eat.

Despite an apparent ever-changing array of dietary recommendations from the scientific community, five recommendations remain constant: (1) eat a diet low in saturated fat (beef, pork, butter, and whole milk dairy products), (2) eat whole grain foods (whole wheat bread, brown rice), (3) drink plenty of fresh water daily, (4) limit your daily intake of sugar and salt, and (5) eat a diet rich in fruits and vegetables. These recommendations, while general in nature, are seldom heeded and in fact many Americans don't eat enough fruits and vegetables and eat too much sugar, salt, and saturated fat.

Of all the nutritional findings, the link between dietary saturated fat and coronary heart disease remains the most consistent throughout the literature. Current recommendations suggest that the types of fats consumed may play a much greater role in disease processes than the total amount of fat consumed. As it currently stands, most experts agree that it is prudent to limit our intake of trans fat found in margarine, fried foods, and baked goods made with solid shortening. These fats appear to raise LDLs, the bad cholesterol, and lower HDLs, the good cholesterol, thus increasing the risk of heart disease. There's also evidence that trans fats increase the risk of diabetes.

Although the basic advice on eating healthy remains fairly constant, many Americans are still confused about exactly what to eat. Should their diet be low carbohydrate, high protein, or low fat? When people turn to standards such as the Food Guide Pyramid, even here there is some confusion. The pyramid, designed by the Department of Agriculture over 20 years ago, recommends a diet based on grains, fruits, and vegetables with several servings of meats and dairy products. It also restricts the consumption of fats, oils, and sweets. While the pyramid offers guidelines as to food groups, individual nutrients are not emphasized. And many people have difficulty translating food pyramid recommendations into breakfast, lunch, and dinner.

© James Gathany/CDC

To add to the confusion, the media, particularly the Internet, continues to bombard us with articles and television segments on nutrition-related issues, adding to the lack of clarity about which foods are healthy. Of all the topic areas in health, food and nutrition is certainly one of the most interesting, if for no other reason than the rate at which dietary recommendations change. One constant piece of advice is to eat plenty of fruits and vegetables. Though this information is widely disseminated, a surprisingly number of children and adults don't eat the recommended number of servings. Despite all the controversy and conflict, the one message that seems to remain constant is the importance of balance and moderation in everything we eat.

Four articles were selected for this unit. "Antioxidants: Fruitful Research and Recommendations" by Pamela S. Brummit discusses antioxidants and the best food sources for these naturally occurring promoters of health. As described in "Vitamin D: Dandy? Dastardly? Or Debatable? Allen C. Bowling reviews studies on vitamin D in relation to health and disease risks including multiple sclerosis. Unfortunately, it's not totally clear whether or not vitamin D will increase or decrease the risk of other health issues including osteoporosis. One mineral, sodium, is vital to life, but too much sodium has been linked to high blood pressure among sensitive individuals. In "Keeping a Lid on Salt: Not So Easy" Nanci Hellmich addresses the challenges of restricting sodium in the current U.S. food environment. Food coloring is another additive that may need to be restricted. Gardiner Harris explores the possible link between behavioral problems and food coloring in "F.D.A. Panel to Consider Warnings for Artificial Food Colorings."

Antioxidants: Fruitful Research and Recommendations

PAMELA S. BRUMMIT, MA, RD/LD

Free radicals, which are produced during food metabolism and by external factors such as radiation and smog, can damage cells and may contribute to some diseases—notably heart disease and cancer—and many experts believe antioxidants can help prevent this damage.

The body's immune system helps defend against oxidative stress. As we age, this defense becomes less effective, which contributes to poor health. Clinical studies hypothesize that when we consume antioxidants, we provide our bodies with protection and health benefits.

Antioxidants Defined

The USDA identifies beta-carotene (vitamin A), selenium, vitamin C, vitamin E, lutein, and lycopene as antioxidant substances.

Lycopene is a pigment that gives vegetables and fruits such as tomatoes, pink grapefruit, and watermelon their red hue. Several studies suggest that consuming foods rich in lycopene is associated with a lower risk of prostate cancer and cardiovascular disease. Lycopene is better absorbed when consumed in processed tomato products rather than in fresh tomatoes.

Selenium is a trace mineral that is essential to good health but required only in small amounts. Its antioxidant properties help prevent cellular damage from free radicals. Plant foods are the major dietary sources of selenium, but the content in a particular food depends on the selenium content of the soil where it's grown. Soils in the high plains of northern Nebraska and the Dakotas have very high levels of selenium.

Lutein is found in large amounts in the lens and retina of our eyes and is recognized for its eye health benefits. It may also protect against damage caused by UVB light and is a critical component to overall skin health. Lutein is found naturally in foods such as dark green, leafy vegetables and egg yolks.

The antioxidant function of beta-carotene (precursor to vitamin A) is its ability to reduce free radicals and protect the cell membrane lipids from the harmful effects of oxidation. In addition, beta-carotene may provide some synergism to vitamin E.

As a water-soluble antioxidant, vitamin C reduces free radicals before they can damage the lipids. These antioxidant properties fight free radicals that can promote wrinkles, age spots, cataracts, and arthritis. Also, the antioxidants in vitamin C have been found to fight free radicals that prey on organs and blood vessels.

As an antioxidant, vitamin E may help prevent or delay cardiovascular disease and cancer and has been shown to play a role in immune function. DNA repair, and other metabolic processes.

Fruits and vegetables, nuts, grains, poultry, and fish are major sources of antioxidants.

Research

Researchers have studied antioxidants and disease processes for years. Some studies have found that an increased intake of beta-carotene is associated with decreased cardiovascular mortality in older adult populations. Studies on the effects of vitamin E on aging have shown potential relationships between the vitamin and the prevention of atherosclerosis, cancer, cataracts, arthritis, central nervous system disorders such as Parkinson's disease, Alzheimer's disease, and impaired glucose tolerance. Studies on vitamin C suggest that it may help protect against vascular dementia, and studies on selenium point to its potential role in cancer prevention. Beta-carotene, vitamin C, and vitamin E showed a positive improvement in muscle strength and may improve physical performance in older adults.

One lycopene study found that eating 10 or more servings per week of tomato products was associated with up to a 35% reduced risk of prostate cancer. Another study suggested that men who had the highest amount of lycopene in their body fat were one half as likely to suffer a heart attack as those with the least amount. Numerous studies correlate a high intake of lycopene-containing foods or high lycopene serum levels with reduced incidence of cancer, cardiovascular disease, and macular degeneration. However, estimates of lycopene consumption have been based on reported tomato intake, not on the use of lycopene supplements. Since tomatoes are sources of other nutrients, including vitamin C, folate, and potassium, it is unclear whether lycopene itself is beneficial.

Some researchers suggest that eliminating free radicals may actually interfere with a natural defense mechanism within the body. Large doses of antioxidants may keep immune systems from fighting off invading pathogens.

Three out of four intervention trials using high-dose beta-carotene supplements did not show protective effects against cancer or cardiovascular disease. Rather, the high-risk population (smokers and asbestos workers) showed an increase in cancer and angina cases. It appears that beta-carotene can promote health when taken at dietary levels but may have adverse effects when taken in high doses by subjects who smoke or who have been exposed to asbestos.

Results from one study indicate that antioxidant supplementation may not be beneficial for disease prevention. This study showed no consistent, clear evidence for health effects. However, the preliminary studies suggest antioxidants may block the heart-damaging effects of oxygen on arteries and the cell damage that might encourage some kinds of cancer.

There remains a lack of knowledge regarding the safety of long-term mega-doses of vitamins. Research continues to be inconclusive and the data incomplete. Research has not been able to validate a link between oxidative stress and chronic disease. As with all research, the studies have been too diverse to provide conclusions.

Recommendations

The American Dietetic Association and the American Heart Association (AHA) recommend that people eat a variety of nutrient-rich foods from all of the food groups on a daily basis because this provides necessary nutrients, including antioxidants. Some researchers believe antioxidants are effective only when they are consumed in foods that contain them.

The recognized beneficial roles that fruits and vegetables play in the reduced risk of disease has led health organizations to develop programs encouraging consumers to eat more antioxidant-rich fruits and vegetables. The AHA and the American Cancer Society recommend that healthy adults eat five or more servings per day. The World Cancer Research Fund and the American Institute for Cancer Research report that "evidence of dietary protection against cancer is strongest and most consistent for diets high in vegetables and fruits."

Given the high degree of scientific consensus regarding the benefits of a diet high in fruits and vegetables—particularly those that contain dietary fiber and vitamins A and C—the FDA released a health claim for fruits and vegetables in relation to cancer. Food packages that meet FDA criteria may now carry the claim, "Diets low in fat and high in fruits and vegetables may reduce the risk of some cancers." The FDA also released a dietary guidance message for consumers: "Diets rich in fruits and vegetables may reduce the risk of some types of cancer and other chronic diseases." The 2005 Dietary Guidelines for Americans states, "Increased intakes of fruits, vegetables, whole grains, and fat-free or low-fat milk and milk products are likely to have important health benefits for most Americans."

Antioxidant research continues to grow and emerge as researchers discover new, beneficial components of food. Reinforced by current research, the message remains that antioxidants obtained from food sources, including fruits, vegetables, and whole grains, may reduce disease risk and can benefit human health.

Using the latest research technologies, USDA nutrition scientists measured the antioxidant levels in more than 100 different foods, including fruits, vegetables, nuts, dried fruits, spices, and cereals. The top 20 ranked foods that interfere with or prevent damage from free radicals are artichokes (cooked), black beans, black plums, blackberries, cranberries, cultivated blueberries, Gala apples, Granny Smith apples, pecans, pinto beans, plums, prunes, raspberries, Red Delicious apples, red kidney beans, Russet potatoes (cooked), small red beans, strawberries, sweet cherries, and wild blueberries.

How can we encourage older adults to eat more fruits and vegetables, especially those high in antioxidants? Share this helpful list with your older adult clients and patients.

1. Try one new fruit or vegetable per week. Variety is key!
2. Keep washed, ready-to-eat fruits and vegetables on hand and easily accessible. On the run? Take a bag of fruits or vegetables with you to munch on.
3. Serve fruits and vegetables with other favorite foods.
4. Add vegetables to casseroles, stews, and soups and puréed fruits and vegetables to sauces. Include vegetables in sandwiches and pastas.
5. Sprinkle vegetables with Parmesan cheese or top with melted low-fat cheese or white sauce made with low-fat milk.
6. Experiment with different methods of cooking fruits and vegetables.
7. Enjoy vegetables with low-fat dip for a snack.
8. Try commercial prepackaged salads and stir-fry mixes to save time.
9. Drink 100% fruit juice instead of fruit-flavored drinks or soda.
10. Serve fruit for dessert.
11. Keep a bowl of apples, bananas, and/or oranges on the dining room table.
12. Choose a side salad made with a variety of leafy greens.
13. Bake with raisin, date, or prune purée to reduce fat intake and increase fiber consumption.
14. Order vegetable toppings on your pizza.
15. Sip fruit smoothies for breakfast or snacks. Blend papaya with pineapple for a cool afternoon treat, or sip on a glass of fresh tomato juice at dinner.
16. Make a fruit salad to try many different types of fruit at once.
17. Learn to recognize a serving of fruits and vegetables: a medium-sized piece of fruit or ½ cup of most fresh, canned, or cooked fruits and vegetables.
18. Start your day with fruit. For example, add fruit to cereal or yogurt or pile on waffles. Or add vegetables—tomatoes, onions, potatoes—to an omelet or scrambled eggs.
19. Top meat and fish with salsa made from tomatoes, onions, corn, mangos, or other fruits and vegetables.
20. Try vegetarian choices: Vegetable stir fry, bean burrito, etc.

Critical Thinking

1. What are the benefits of consuming foods rich in antioxidants?
2. What foods provide high levels of antioxidants?
3. What vitamins/minerals are considered antioxidants?

Pamela S. Brummit, MA, RD/LD, is the founder and president of Brummit & Associates, Inc, a dietary consulting firm. She has held more than 20 board positions in local, state, and national dietetic associations and is past chair of Consultant Dietitians in Health Care Facilities dietetic practice group.

Keeping a Lid on Salt: Not So Easy

Known as a silent killer, it's part of how we live.

Nanci Hellmich

For years, Americans have been advised to consume less sodium, and they've taken that advice with a grain of salt.

Even many health-conscious consumers figured it was the least of their worries, especially compared with limiting their intake of calories, saturated fat, trans fat, cholesterol and sugar.

All that changed last week when a report from the Institute of Medicine urged the government to gradually reduce the maximum amount of sodium that manufacturers and restaurants can add to foods, beverages and meals. The report put a spotlight on what doctors and nutritionists have argued is a major contributor to heart disease and stroke.

More than half of Americans have either high blood pressure or pre-hypertension, says cardiologist Clyde Yancy, president of the American Heart Association and medical director at the Baylor Heart and Vascular Institute in Dallas.

"That puts a lot of us in the bucket of people who need to be on a lower sodium diet. Sodium contributes to most people's high blood pressure, and for some it may be the primary driver."

Cutting back on sodium could save thousands of people from early deaths caused by heart attacks and strokes each year, and it could save billions of dollars in health care costs, he says.

Others second that. "Salt is the single most harmful element in our food supply, silently killing about 100,000 people each year," says Michael Jacobson, executive director of the Washington, D.C.-based Center for Science in the Public Interest. "That's like a crowded jetliner crashing every single day. But the food industry has fended off government action for more than three decades."

Now salt has our attention.

But reducing it in the American diet is easier said than done. "We have, in essence, ignored the advice because we are driven by convenience, and sodium makes a fast-food lifestyle very easy," Yancy says. "To change, we would need to live and eat differently."

Very differently.

Americans now consume an average of about 3,400 milligrams of sodium a day, or about 1½ teaspoons, government data show. Men consume more than women.

But most adults—including those with high blood pressure, African Americans, the middle-aged and the elderly—should consume no more than 1,500 milligrams a day, according to the dietary guidelines from the U.S. Department of Agriculture. Others should consume less than 2,300 milligrams, or less than a teaspoon, the guidelines say.

And yet it's virtually impossible to limit yourself to such amounts if you often eat processed foods, prepared foods or restaurant fare, including fast food. Most Americans' sodium intake comes from those sources, not the salt shaker on the table.

Some restaurant entrees have 2,000 milligrams or more in one dish. Fast-food burgers can have more than 1,000 milligrams. Many soups

are chock-full of sodium. So are many spaghetti sauces, broths, lunch meats, salad dressings, cheeses, crackers and frozen foods.

Can't see it, can't taste it.

Salt serves many functions in products. Besides adding to a food's taste, it is a preservative. "You can't see it," Yancy says. "You can't even taste it because you are so accustomed to it. If you want the freedom to make healthy choices, you are limited by today's foods. That's a problem."

To change that, food companies and restaurants will have to come up with new ways to formulate products and recipes to help consumers gradually lower their salt levels, which would wean them off the taste.

That's a huge challenge, but nutritionists and public health specialists say it can be done and will be worth it. "There is no health benefit to a high-sodium diet, and there is considerable risk," says Linda Van Horn, a professor of preventive medicine at Northwestern University Feinberg School of Medicine.

Even those whose blood pressure is in the normal range should watch their intake, Yancy says. "Here's a wake-up call: Every American who is age 50 or older has a 90% chance of developing hypertension. That increases the risk of heart disease and stroke. This is a preventable process, and it's preventable with sodium reduction, weight control and physical activity."

Why It Can Be Harmful

There are several theories for why sodium increases blood pressure, Yancy says, "but the most obvious one is that it makes us retain fluids, and that retention elevates blood pressure," which injures blood vessels and leads to heart disease and stroke. "It's a connect-the-dots phenomenon."

Some people, especially some African Americans, are more salt-sensitive than others, Yancy says.

"When they are exposed to sodium, they retain more fluid, and because of the way their kidneys handle sodium, they may have a greater proportional rise in blood pressure," he says.

The cost of this damage? An analysis by the Rand Corp. found that if the average sodium intake of Americans was reduced to 2,300 milligrams a day, it might decrease the cases of high blood pressure by 11 million, improve quality of life for millions of people and save about $18 billion in annual health care costs.

The estimated value of improved quality of life and living healthier longer: $32 billion a year. Greater reductions in sodium consumption in the population would save more lives and money, says Roland Sturm, a senior economist with Rand.

Yancy says the country doesn't just need health care reform, "we need health reform. If we don't adjust the demand part of the equation, no system will work. Remarkably, people might be overall healthier by simply reducing sodium."

But Yancy says people need to keep in mind that sodium is just one of the factors that increase the risk of heart disease and stroke. Others include obesity, consuming too much sugar and too few fruits and vegetables, lack of physical activity and smoking.

Salt Industry Disagrees

Leaders in the salt industry say their product is being unfairly maligned. The Institute of Medicine report and the government "are focusing on one small aspect of health, which is a small increase in blood pressure in a small segment of population," says Lori Roman, president of the Salt Institute, an industry group.

Some of the research that ties salt to health risks is based on faulty assumptions and extrapolations, Roman says. She says a recent worldwide study indicated there is no country where people eat an average of less than 1,500 milligrams a day. "That's way below the normal range," Roman says. The Italians eat more sodium than Americans, but their cardiovascular health is better than Americans', and the reason is they eat a lot of fruits and vegetables, she says.

"This is the real story that the government is missing," Roman says. "It is the secret to good health."

She says people may end up following a less healthy diet if they cut back on sodium. "Have you ever bought a can of low-sodium string beans and then tried to season it to taste good? It's impossible," Roman says. "Here's one of the unintended consequences of this recommendation: People will eat fewer vegetables, and by eating fewer vegetables, they will be less healthy."

Yancy says the first step for many people is making the decision to cut back on salt intake. He knows from experience that it can be done.

An African American, Yancy, 52, has high blood pressure and a family history of heart disease and stroke. He's lean and exercises for an hour a day, but still he has to take medication for hypertension. Before he started watching his sodium intake a few years ago, Yancy says, he was consuming more than 4,000 milligrams a day, partly because he grew up in southern Louisiana and was used to a salty, high-fat diet.

But he has weaned himself off the taste. He doesn't have a salt shaker in his house, and he reads the labels on grocery store items and doesn't buy any that have more than 100 milligrams of sodium in a serving.

"I taste the salt in items and put them aside. I find it difficult to enjoy prepared soups. I can taste the salt in prepared meals. I've learned to make my own soups."

When he eats out, he orders salads and asks for his fish and meat to be grilled. "Typically, I eat fish with lemon juice and pepper."

Even so, he believes his sodium intake is probably higher than it should be because he often eats in restaurants and cafeterias, and many foods have hidden sodium.

Changes in food products need to be made over time as the Institute of Medicine report suggests, says Van Horn, a research nutritionist at Northwestern. "If we drop the sodium overnight, people will be desperately seeking salt shakers."

So how hard is it going to be to reduce the salt in processed and prepared foods?

"We've been trying to reduce the sodium in foods for more than 30 years. If this were easy, it would have been accomplished," says Roger Clemens, a professor of pharmacology at the University of Southern California and a spokesman for the Institute of Food Technologists.

The primary dietary source of sodium is sodium chloride, also known as table salt, he says. There are other sodium salts, such as sodium bicarbonate (baking soda) in baking and sodium benzoate (preservative) in bread and beverages. And there are potassium salts that are used in foods—as emulsifiers in cheese and buffers in beverages, he says.

"Salt is a natural preservative. It has been used in the food supply to ensure food safety for centuries," Clemens says. "It's critical for preserving bacon, olives, lunch meats, fish and poultry."

"Some foods, such as cheese, can only be produced with salt. No other compound allows the proteins to knit together to become cheese."

If It Doesn't Taste Good...

To make cheese that is lower in sodium, foodmakers must put the cheese through a special procedure that basically extracts some of the sodium. "It's a very long, tedious process," he says.

Salt also is crucial for making most breads. To get dough to rise, manufacturers use sodium chloride and sodium bicarbonate, Clemens says. "If you were to eat a sodium-free product, the texture and flavor would be markedly different. It would be more compressed. I don't think you'd like it at first."

He says some manufacturers have experimented with low-sodium items, and in some cases consumers have turned up their noses. "If it doesn't taste good, consumers won't buy it."

Melissa Musiker, a nutrition spokeswoman for the Grocery Manufacturers Association, agrees. "You can't get ahead of consumers," she says. "You work on the recipes, test them, see how consumers respond and go back and tweak."

There is no one single alternative for replacing it in various foods, she says. "It has to be replaced on an ingredient-by-ingredient basis."

Clemens says food companies will continue to try to develop new technologies to lower the sodium.

"It has taken us 30 years to get this far, and it will probably take us another decade to get a significant difference in the intake. If we can lower sodium in our diet, we'll have a huge health impact on generations to come."

Critical Thinking

1. What are the health risks of excessive sodium?
2. What foods are high in sodium?
3. Should everyone be on a sodium-restricted diet?
4. Is there a downside to reducing sodium?

Vitamin D: Dandy? Dastardly? Or Debatable?

The vitamin D story is all over the map in more ways than one. Dr. Bowling reviews the scene and offers some basic information.

ALLEN C. BOWLING, MD, PhD

It was once assumed that Americans had adequate vitamin D intake and that vitamin D was only involved in bone health. However, recent scientific and clinical studies indicate that vitamin D may have effects on many tissues—not just bone—and that vitamin D deficiency might worsen or even cause many medical conditions, including multiple sclerosis. In addition, many studies over the past several years have raised the possibility that vitamin D deficiency is widespread in the United States.

As a result of the high level of public and professional interest, many people have had blood tests for vitamin D levels, and vitamin D supplements—sometimes in very high doses—have been recommended for MS, for general health, and for a wide array of other conditions.

In the midst of all the excitement about potential benefits, other recent reports raise concerns about the safety of high-dose vitamin D supplements. We are seeing reports with differing—and sometimes conflicting—messages about how to translate current understandings of vitamin D into practical guidelines.

A Search for Standards

The United States and Canadian governments commissioned the Food and Nutrition Board of the Institute of Medicine (IOM), the organization that establishes appropriate dietary intake values for vitamins and minerals, to formally review studies on vitamin D and calcium and develop new recommendations. The IOM report was released in November, 2010—but it has not settled matters. It is considered by some to be too conservative and has been the source of significant controversy and debate.

Vitamin D Basics

There are several sources for vitamin D. A unique source is sun exposure, which allows the body to make its own vitamin D. This is why vitamin D is often referred to as the "sunshine vitamin." Vitamin D may also be consumed in foods and dietary supplements. However, only a few foods, most notably oily fish (such as salmon), naturally contain significant amounts of vitamin D. In the United States, a limited number of other foods, including dairy products, cereals and orange juice, are fortified with vitamin D.

Vitamin D levels in the body are measured with a blood test, which reports on blood levels as "nanograms per milliliter" or "ng/ml." Many clinical laboratories and publications define "sufficient" levels as 30–100 ng/ml, "insufficient" levels as 20–30 ng/ml and levels below 20 ng/ml as "deficient." Some have argued that the lower range of

"sufficient" should be 40, not 30 ng/ml. But the recent IOM report proposes that the lower range of "sufficient" should be 20 ng/ml.

The IOM report also recommends an increase in intake, also known as the Recommended Daily Amount, or RDA, for vitamin D. The RDA is the daily intake that is thought to meet or exceed the requirements for 97.5% of the population. The newly developed RDA for vitamin D for adults is 600–800 international units (IU). The adult RDA for calcium is now 1,000–1,300 milligrams (mg).

Some professional organizations, physicians and scientists don't agree. They propose that the RDA for vitamin D should be significantly higher than 600–800 mg, based on the results of studies in a variety of conditions.

Vitamin D Deficiency

The prevalence of vitamin D deficiency may be difficult to determine precisely. Since vitamin D is synthesized in the body by sunlight exposure, vitamin D levels naturally vary with geographic location and time of year. And, as noted, there is controversy about what levels of vitamin D are considered deficient. The IOM report, using lower levels for deficiency, analyzing intake, and averaging results from many studies, concluded that vitamin D deficiency is **not common** in the United States or Canada. However, other studies in the United States and Europe have concluded that 40–100% of elderly people are vitamin D deficient. One study of American adults who had a reasonable intake of vitamin D found that about one-third of them were vitamin D deficient as measured by their blood levels.

Biological Effects of Vitamin D

For years it has been known that vitamin D regulates calcium absorption and thus maintains bone health. Recent studies have found that many other cells and tissues of the body have the biochemical machinery to synthesize and respond to vitamin D. Thus, vitamin D may have important effects on general health and on many disease processes. For example, vitamin D has effects on nerve, muscle, and immune cells that could potentially affect the disease process of MS.

Medical Conditions Associated with Vitamin D Deficiency

Presumably through immune system effects, vitamin D deficiency has been associated with increased risk and increased disease severity of MS and other immune diseases, including diabetes and rheumatoid arthritis. Vitamin D deficiency may also increase the risk or severity of a long list of other diseases, including heart disease and multiple forms of cancer. Inadequate vitamin D has also been associated with muscle weakness and an increased risk of falls.

Study Quality

When evaluating studies of vitamin D and specific diseases, it is critical to understand the quality of the studies. At this point, the most rigorous research on vitamin D has been done in relation to bone health. There is general consensus, due to well-conducted epidemiologic and clinical trial studies, that low vitamin D intake leads to decreased bone density and that vitamin D supplements may improve bone density. In its mild form, low bone density is known as **osteopenia** and in its severe form as **osteoporosis**.

But beyond bone health, the effects of vitamin D are less certain because the studies done to date are not as rigorous. The studies for non-skeletal conditions are generally "observational studies" in which a group of people with a particular disease or condition are found to have low vitamin D levels. This may establish an association between low vitamin D and that condition but it does not prove that vitamin D deficiency **causes** the condition or that vitamin D supplements could **prevent or provide therapeutic effects** for that condition.

Risks of Vitamin D Supplements

It has been known for decades that very high doses of vitamin D [50,000 IU or more daily] may trigger high blood calcium levels, impaired kidney function and other serious side effects. More recent studies have raised the possibility—**but have certainly not proven**—that long-term intake of moderately high doses of vitamin D, could increase the risk of death and the risk of pancreatic, breast, or prostate cancers, heart disease, bone fractures, and falls.

The recent IOM report—which was based on a review of a wide range of studies of vitamin D and calcium—stated that the Tolerable Upper Intake Level (UL) for adults, which is the safe upper limit for regular daily use, should be 4,000 IU for vitamin D and 2,000–3,000 mg for calcium. The report expressed concern that adverse effects of vitamin D could possibly be seen when blood levels are higher than 50 ng/ml.

Are You Confused Yet?

Some sources of information, such as the IOM report, caution against the use of high doses of vitamin D and downplay the prevalence of vitamin D deficiency, while other sources state that widespread vitamin D deficiency is causing many diseases and strongly encourage use of high supplement doses. Between these two extremes are middle-of-the road approaches that offer "best guess" strategies for using the current evidence. For example, "The Vitamin D Summit Meeting" in Paris in November 2009, an international conference of 25 vitamin D experts from 12 different countries, concluded that the appropriate blood level range is 30–100 ng/ml and that in people with MS and many other vitamin D-associated conditions it is reasonable to test vitamin D blood levels and to take supplements if the levels are low.

My Thoughts on the Matter

Through its widespread effects on the body, vitamin D may indeed have important implications for MS. However, at this time, the most definitive effect of vitamin D is on bone health. People with MS are known to be prone to osteoporosis, and clearly vitamin D deficiency could increase the risk for, or worsen, this condition. In addition, MS-associated weakness and with it the risk of falling could be caused by, or worsened by, vitamin D deficiency.

Information about vitamin D is evolving and much additional research needs to be done. In the meantime, one certainly cannot be dogmatic. There are several reasonable options for people with MS.

1. **Get a measurement and supplement if needed:** Determine your personal vitamin D level with a standard blood test known as "25-hydroxy-vitamin D." If the level is normal (between 20–30 ng/ml up to 100 ng/ml), there is no known benefit to taking vitamin D supplements. If the vitamin D level is below 20–30 ng/ml, vitamin D-rich foods and vitamin D supplements may be taken. But due to concerns about possible side effects, it may be best to avoid doses higher than 4,000 IU daily and blood levels higher than 50 ng/ml. If vitamin D deficiency or insufficiency is found, increasing vitamin D intake may improve bone health and could possibly slow the disease course of MS, increase strength, and even improve general health.

   The disadvantages of this approach include lack of definitive risk-benefit information, inconvenience and expense. The blood test alone may cost $50 to $250.

2. **Use supplements "blindly":** You may consider skipping the blood test and simply taking vitamin D supplements. This blind approach avoids the inconvenience and cost of the test, but it adds uncertainty about appropriate dosage. Specifically, it may lead to unnecessary or inadequate supplement use.

3. **Wait and see:** For some, it may seem reasonable to do nothing and wait until there is more definitive safety and effectiveness information. The disadvantage of this approach is that vitamin D-deficient people will not be diagnosed and, therefore, will not receive the potential benefits of supplements.

A Bottom Line

People with MS should discuss an appropriate vitamin D strategy with their health-care providers. And due to the possible preventive effect of vitamin D on inherited risk of MS, people with MS may also want to discuss vitamin D issues with their siblings, their children and with their children's health-care providers. Finally, since understanding of vitamin D is rapidly changing, people with MS should stay informed about it.

Please visit our Web site at www.nationalMSsociety.org/sund for a complete list of references for this article.

Critical Thinking

1. Name three functions of vitamin D.
2. What health benefits have been linked to vitamin D?
3. Why has vitamin D been called the "nutrient of the decade"?

Dr. **ALLEN BOWLING** is the medical director of the Multiple Sclerosis Service at the Colorado Neurological Institute (CNI) and clinical associate professor of Neurology at the University of Colorado-Denver and Health Sciences Center. Additional information about dietary supplements may be found in his book, *Complementary and Alternative Medicine and Multiple Sclerosis* (2nd edition, Demos Medical Publishing), and on his Web site, www.NeurologyCare.net.

F.D.A. Panel to Consider Warnings for Artificial Food Colorings

GARDINER HARRIS

Washington—After staunchly defending the safety of artificial food colorings, the federal government is for the first time publicly reassessing whether foods like Jell-O, Lucky Charms cereal and Minute Maid Lemonade should carry warnings that the bright artificial colorings in them worsen behavior problems like hyperactivity in some children.

The Food and Drug Administration concluded long ago that there was no definitive link between the colorings and behavior or health problems, and the agency is unlikely to change its mind any time soon. But on Wednesday and Thursday, the F.D.A. will ask a panel of experts to review the evidence and advise on possible policy changes, which could include warning labels on food.

The hearings signal that the growing list of studies suggesting a link between artificial colorings and behavioral changes in children has at least gotten regulators' attention—and, for consumer advocates, that in itself is a victory.

In a concluding report, staff scientists from the F.D.A. wrote that while typical children might be unaffected by the dyes, those with behavioral disorders might have their conditions "exacerbated by exposure to a number of substances in food, including, but not limited to, synthetic color additives."

Renee Shutters, a mother of two from Jamestown, N.Y., said in a telephone interview on Tuesday that two years ago, her son Trenton, then 5, was having serious behavioral problems at school until she eliminated artificial food colorings from his diet. "I know for sure I found the root cause of this one because you can turn it on and off like a switch," Ms. Shutters said.

But Dr. Lawrence Diller, a behavioral pediatrician in Walnut Creek, Calif., said evidence that diet plays a significant role in most childhood behavioral disorders was minimal to nonexistent. "These are urban legends that won't die," Dr. Diller said.

There is no debate about the safety of natural food colorings, and manufacturers have long defended the safety of artificial ones as well. In a statement, the Grocery Manufacturers Association said, "All of the major safety bodies globally have reviewed the available science and have determined that there is no demonstrable link between artificial food colors and hyperactivity among children."

In a 2008 *petition* filed with federal food regulators, the Center for Science in the Public Interest, a consumer advocacy group, argued that some parents of susceptible children do not know that their children are at risk and so "the appropriate public health approach is to remove those dangerous and unnecessary substances from the food supply."

The federal government has been cracking down on artificial food dyes for more than a century in part because some early ones were not only toxic but were also sometimes used to mask filth or rot. In 1950, many children became ill after eating Halloween candy containing Orange No. 1 dye, and the F.D.A. banned it after more rigorous testing suggested that it was toxic. In 1976, the agency banned Red No. 2 because it was suspected to be carcinogenic. It was then replaced by Red No. 40.

Many of the artificial colorings used today were approved by the F.D.A. in 1931, including Blue No. 1, Yellow No. 5 and Red No. 3. Artificial dyes were developed—just as aspirin was—from coal tar, but are now made from petroleum products.

In the 1970s, Dr. Benjamin Feingold, a pediatric allergist from California, had success treating the symptoms of hyperactivity in some children by prescribing a diet that, among other things, eliminated artificial colorings. And some studies, including one published in The Lancet medical journal in 2007, have found that artificial colorings might lead to behavioral changes even in typical children.

The consumer science group asked the government to ban the dyes, or at least require manufacturers to include prominent warnings that "artificial colorings in this food cause hyperactivity and behavioral problems in some children."

Citizen petitions are routinely dismissed by the F.D.A. without much comment. Not this time. Still, the agency is not asking the experts to consider a ban during their two-day meeting, and agency scientists in lengthy analyses expressed skepticism about the scientific merits of the Lancet study and others suggesting any definitive link between dyes and behavioral issues. Importantly, the research offers almost no clue about the relative risks of individual dyes, making specific regulatory actions against, say, Green No. 3 or Yellow No. 6 almost impossible.

The F.D.A. scientists suggested that problems associated with artificial coloring might be akin to a peanut allergy, or "a unique intolerance to these substances and not to any inherent neurotoxic properties" of the dyes themselves. As it does for peanuts and other foods that can cause reactions, the F.D.A. already requires manufacturers to disclose on food labels the presence of artificial colorings.

A spokeswoman for General Mills refused to comment. Valerie Moens, a spokeswoman for Kraft Foods Inc., wrote in an e-mail that all of the food colors the company used were approved and clearly labeled, but that the company was expanding its "portfolio to include products without added colors," like Kool-Aid Invisible, Capri Sun juices and Kraft Macaroni and Cheese Organic White Cheddar.

The panel will almost certainly ask that more research on the subject be conducted, but such calls are routinely ignored. Research on pediatric behaviors can be difficult and expensive to conduct since it often involves regular and subjective assessments of children by parents and teachers who should be kept in the dark about the specifics of the test. And since the patents on the dyes expired long ago, manufacturers have little incentive to finance such research themselves.

Popular foods that have artificial dyes include Cheetos snacks, Froot Loops cereal, Pop-Tarts and Hostess Twinkies, according to an extensive listing in the consumer advocacy group's petition. Some grocery chains, including Whole Foods Market and Trader Joe's, refuse to sell foods with artificial coloring.

Critical Thinking

1. Identify risks associated with artificial food colorings.
2. What foods contain artificial food colorings?
3. Should the FDA warn people about food coloring? Why or why not?

UNIT 4

Exercise and Weight Management

Unit Selections

Learning Outcomes

After reading this Unit, you will be able to:

- Address ways to combat childhood obesity.

- Identify seven steps to incorporating the Mediterranean lifestyle.

- Explain how one can lose weight on a limited budget.

- Explain why it is important to exercise to achieve optimal health.

- Differentiate between the new and old physical education classes.

- Discuss why disrupted sleep patterns are linked to obesity.

Student Website
www.mhhe.com/cls

Internet References

American Society of Exercise Physiologists (ASEP)
www.asep.org
Cyberdiet
www.cyberdiet.com
Shape Up America!
www.shapeup.org

Recently, a new set of guidelines, dubbed "Exercise Lite," has been issued by the U.S. Centers for Disease Control and Prevention in conjunction with the American College of Sports Medicine. These guidelines call for 30 minutes of exercise, five days a week, which can be spread over the course of a day. The primary focus of this approach to exercise is improving health, not athletic performance. Examples of activities that qualify under the new guidelines are walking your dog, playing tag with your kids, scrubbing floors, washing your car, mowing the lawn, weeding your garden, and having sex. From a practical standpoint, this approach to fitness will likely motivate many more people to become active and stay active. Remember, since the benefits of exercise can take weeks or even months before they become apparent, it is very important to choose an exercise program that you enjoy so that you will stick with it. Ron Schachter discusses why it's important for students in physical education classes to develop life-long fitness goals. While a good diet cannot compensate for the lack of exercise, exercise can compensate for a less than optimal diet. Exercise not only makes people physically healthier, it also keeps their brains healthy. While the connection hasn't been proven, there is evidence that regular workouts may cause the brain to better process and store information, which results in a smarter brain.

While exercise and a nutritious diet can keep people fit and healthy, many Americans are not heeding this advice. For the first time in our history, the average American is now overweight when judged according to the standard height/weight tables. In addition, more than 25 percent of Americans are clinically obese, and the number appears to be growing.

Why is this happening, given the prevailing attitude that Americans have toward fat? One theory that is currently gaining support suggests that while Americans have cut back on their consumption of fatty snacks and desserts, they have actually increased their total caloric intake by failing to limit their consumption of carbohydrates. The underlying philosophy goes something like this: Fat calories make you fat, but you can eat as many carbohydrates as you want and not gain weight. The truth is that all calories count when it comes to weight gain, and if cutting back on fat calories prevents you from feeling satiated, you will naturally eat more to achieve that feeling. While this position seems reasonable enough, some groups, most notably supporters of the Atkins diet, have suggested that eating a high-fat diet will actually help people lose weight because of fat's high satiety value in conjunction with the formation of ketones (which suppress appetite). Whether people limit fat or carbohydrates, they will not lose weight unless their total caloric intake is less than their energy expenditure.

America's preoccupation with body weight has given rise to a billion dollar industry. When asked why people go on diets, the predominant answer is for social reasons such as appearance and group acceptance, rather than concerns regarding health. Why do diets and diet aids fail? One of the major reasons lies in the mindset of the dieter. Many dieters do not fully understand the biological and behavioral aspects of weight loss, and consequently they have unrealistic expectations regarding the process.

Being overweight not only causes health problems; it also carries with it a social stigma. Overweight people are often thought of as weak-willed individuals with little or no self-respect. The notion that weight control problems are the result of personality defects is being challenged by new research findings. Evidence is mounting

© Ingram Publishing

that suggests that physiological and hereditary factors may play as great a role in obesity as do behavioral and environmental factors. Researchers now believe that genetics dictate the base number of fat cells an individual will have, as well as the location and distribution of these cells within the body. The study of fat metabolism has provided additional clues as to why weight control is so difficult. These metabolic studies have found that the body seems to have a "setpoint," or desired weight, and it will defend this weight through alterations in basal metabolic rate and fat-cell activities. While this process is thought to be an adaptive throwback to primitive times when food supplies were uncertain, today, with our abundant food supply, this mechanism only contributes to the problem of weight control.

It should be apparent by now that weight control is both an attitudinal and a lifestyle issue. Fortunately, a new, more rational approach to the problem of weight control is emerging. This approach is based on the premise that you can be perfectly healthy and good looking without being pencil-thin. The primary focus of this approach to weight management is the attainment of your body's "natural ideal weight" and not some idealized, fanciful notion of what you would like to weigh. The concept of achieving your natural ideal body weight suggests that we need to take a more realistic approach to both fitness and weight control and also serves to remind us that a healthy lifestyle is based on the concepts of balance and moderation.

The articles chosen for this unit address both exercise and weight management. Strategies to maintain a healthy weight are addressed in "The Hungry Brain" which also discusses neurological bases for people's desire to overeat. How to eat a healthy, low-calorie diet without spending a fortune is discussed in "Dieting on a Budget." The Mediterranean diet is widely accepted as a healthy way of eating. This acceptance by the medical community and popular press are encouraging Americans to adopt principles and foods of the Mediterranean lifestyle. "Eat Like a Greek" from *Consumer Reports on Health* leads the reader through practical steps of how to incorporate the Mediterranean lifestyle into daily life. Even more alarming, a large percentage of the children in America are overweight or obese. Tina Schwager suggests ways to combat this problem in "Defeating Childhood Obesity."

Defeating Childhood Obesity

Are you ready to step up to the challenge?

TINA SCHWAGER

There was a time when we, as kids, could ask our moms, "Can we go outside and play?" And they would respond, "OK, just be back by dinner time." Then we'd hop on our bikes and off we'd go. And we would play outside . . . all day long. In those days, we didn't have computers, or video games, or cell phones. Every kid knew how to throw and kick a ball, play a game of tag that could last for hours, and find things to keep busy until it was time to head home.

Things are different now. Today, kids can "play" with friends in a virtual world, and going outside simply to goof around is a rarity. An overabundance of conveniences makes most everything we do easier, faster and more connected with the mere push of a button. But those conveniences are a part of what is helping to destroy our kids.

To be blunt, a large percentage of kids in America are fat and unhealthy. In the past 20 years, "the prevalence of obesity among children ages 6 to 11 years has more than doubled," and more than tripled in adolescents ages 12 to 19.[2] Organizations such as the Centers for Disease Control and Prevention (CDC) and the American Obesity Association (AOA) have amassed the numbers on this disturbing epidemic: 30.3% of kids ages 6 to 11 are overweight, 15.3% are classified as obese, and for adolescents, 30.4% are estimated to be overweight and 15.5% obese.[5] The tendency toward overweight is slightly greater in boys than girls (32.7% to 27.8%[5]) and is an even bigger problem among lower-income and ethnic minority families where African-American, Hispanic and Native-American kids ". . . have a particularly high obesity prevalence."[5]

The American Obesity Association (AOA) defines overweight as being at or above 85% of one's Body Mass Index (BMI), and obesity as 95% of BMI.[5]

So, who or what is to blame? Unfortunately, multiple factors come into play, making ultimate victory over this problem something that demands a multifaceted attack.

Heredity

Several generations ago, a "chunky" kid was often attributed to some hefty relative, and the family gene pool took the hit. The unspoken assumption was that there is nothing one can do about heredity. But heredity alone is not responsible, since ". . . genetic characteristics of the human population have not changed in the last three decades, but the prevalence of obesity has tripled . . . ."[8] Combining poor dietary habits and lack of physical activity with a family history is what truly increases the risk for overweight and obesity.

Media

Call it entertainment, or a learning tool . . . it doesn't matter what you call it. Media tools such as computers, cell phones, video games, high-tech TVs and hand-held media devices (like music and movie players) are helping make young people fat. In 2007, the national Youth Risk Behavior Survey done by the Department of Health and Human Services, Centers for Disease Control and Prevention, found that 25% of high school kids played ". . . video or computer games or used a computer for something that was not school work for 3 or more hours per day on an average school day." And as for TV, 35% watched 3 or more hours a day.[6]

Sitting in front of a screen and watching others do things that grown-ups used to get out and actually do; playing with virtual friends or against foes instead of running around outside; texting instead of riding bikes together—all these tools of convenience lead to a reduction in physical activity and lots of mindless snacking. Studies like those done at Stanford Prevention Research Center indicate that kids snack more on unhealthy foods while involved in media activities, and ". . . may not stop eating when they are full because of the distraction."[4] Watching TV has been found to contribute to poor food choices in several ways—the ads often tout unhealthy or high-fat foods; passively watching robs kids of physical play time; and TV watching was actually found to lower kids' metabolic rates.[8]

What Is BMI?

There are many methods that try and determine fitness and health levels. The simplest and most practical way to screen for overweight and obesity is Body Mass Index, or BMI. It addresses the issue based solely on someone's weight in relation to their height. According to the CDC, BMI is the most widely accepted method to screen for overweight and obesity in kids and teens because:

- It is easy to obtain height and weight measurements
- It is noninvasive
- It correlates with body fatness.[7]

Less Physical Activity

For many kids, getting outside and playing has been replaced by technological interaction. While being at school used to guarantee at least a little bit of physical activity via recess and PE classes, funds to support physical education programs are, in many cases, simply not there. So unless a kid plays in a sports league or can afford to work with a pro of some type, their sports experience tends to be limited, and so does their overall level of physical exertion.

In addition, it simply isn't as safe as it used to be for kids to go outside and play. "Today's youth are considered the most inactive generation in history, caused in part by reduction in school physical education programs and unavailable or unsafe community recreation facilities."[5] Statistically, as of a 2007 study, 65% of high school students didn't meet recommended levels of physical activity and 70% didn't attend PE classes daily.[6] The CDC reports that daily PE participation among adolescents dropped from 42% in 1991 to 28% in 2003.[8]

Poor Nutrition

Everything is big these days—big TVs, big cars and big food portions. The airwaves show commercial after commercial advertising unhealthy foods and giant portions. And you can bet the mindless snacking that comes with too much media exposure doesn't include carrot sticks and hummus. Media driven snacking undoubtedly consists of empty calories that do nothing to contribute to growth and development while preventing kids from putting something nutritious into their bodies. High-fat, high-sodium, high-calorie snacks are everywhere. Media overload puts those items right in front of their hungry little faces.

According to the CDC, ". . . large portion sizes for food and beverages, eating meals away from home, [and] frequent snacking on energy-dense foods . . ."[8] are all factors in our kids' high-calorie world. And unlike a calorie conscious adult, kids don't know to change their intake at meals to balance the extra snack calories.

Another ticket to poor nutrition is the on-the-go lifestyle most families lead. The family schedule is often so jam-packed that meals are frequently eaten on the run. And, "when schedules get hectic, busy families turn to fast food."[4]

The Future Outlook

While multiple factors are responsible for the obesity epidemic among children, it's the fallout for the future that is undeniably frightening. Excess fat and body weight are directly linked to what are termed "diseases of excess," chronic conditions that used to be the burden of adults who overdid it by eating too much fatty, fried, salty and generally unhealthy food—coronary heart disease, high blood pressure, diabetes and certain forms of cancer. But now those conditions are showing up in our kids. Check out these statistics from the CDC and the AOA:

- Type 2 diabetes, formerly known as adult onset diabetes, accounted for 2 to 4% of childhood diabetics prior to 1992, but by 1994 that number jumped to 16%.[5]
- Type 2 diabetes has become so prevalent that it is estimated one in three American children born in 2000 will develop it in their lifetime.[1]
- Children who become obese by age 8 are found to be more severely obese as adults.[2]
- Eighty percent of kids who were overweight at age 10 to 15 were obese adults at age 25.[3]
- Early indicators of atherosclerosis are being seen in childhood and adolescence.[2]
- Elevated blood pressure levels occurred nine times more often in obese kids and adolescents.[5]
- Since developing bones and cartilage can't bear excess weight, orthopedic problems frequently develop in overweight kids, or lead to degenerative conditions in adulthood.[5]

So Now What?

The picture looks pretty grim. But government efforts through committees such as the CDC's Division of Adolescent and School Health are attempting to educate families and school personnel and create policies that help monitor and improve nutrition and activity habits at school. For example, the Coordinated School Health Program consists of eight components addressing the problem: health education, physical education, health services, nutrition services, counseling and social services, health promotion for staff, and community involvement.[1]

Outside of school, hope may lie in the hands of fitness professionals trained to reach out and educate young people. Some suggestions include:

- Create a basic level or specialty program just for kids and teens
- Offer seminars or other community outreach activities to teach kids strategies for taking control of their own well-being (nutrition classes, boot camp for teens, yoga for kids and dance-infused aerobics)
- Create a newsletter for your clients that is also available at local businesses or nearby schools to market your programs that help local youth.

Knowing the magnitude of this problem may inspire your facility to create something that could change not only the present, but the future of young lives. One at a time, a difference can be made.

References

1. "Addressing childhood obesity through nutrition and physical activity." U.S. Department of health and human services, centers for disease control and prevention. www.cdc.gov (Accessed Jun 29, 2010).

2. www.allergan.com/assets/pdf/obesity_fact_sheet.pdf (Accessed Jul 19, 2010).

3. "Childhood obesity: A growing problem." Stanford prevention research center. prevention.standford.Edu (Accessed Jun 29, 2010).

4. "Childhood overweight and obesity," 3/31/10. Centers for disease control and prevention. www.cdc.gov (Accessed Jun 29, 2010).

5. Overweight and obesity. www.cdc.gov/obesity/childhood/causes.html (Accessed Jul 19, 2010).

6. "Defining childhood overweight and obesity," 10/20/09. Centers for disease control and prevention. www.cdc.gov/obesity/childhood/defining.html (Accessed Jul 19, 2010).

7. "Nutrition and the health of young people," Nov 2008. U.S. Department of Health and Human Services, Centers for Disease Control and Prevention. www.cdc.gov/healthyouth/nutrition/facts.htm (Accessed Jul 20, 2010).

8. "The obesity epidemic and united states students." Department of health and human services, centers for disease control and prevention. www.cdc.gov/healthyyouth/yrbs/pdf/us_obesity-combo.pdk (Accessed Jul 19, 2010).

Critical Thinking

1. What type of fitness program would most benefit obese children?

2. Describe some of the problems associated with childhood obesity.

3. Why has childhood obesity increased during the past 30 years?

TINA SCHWAGER, ATC, PTA, *is a certified Athletic Trainer and Physical Therapy Assistant with over 20 years' experience in outpatient orthopedic rehabilitation and sports conditioning. She is also the author of three self-help books for teenage girls, published by Free Spirit Publishing:* The Right Moves: A Girl's Guide to Getting Fit and Feeling Good, Gutsy Girls: Young Women Who Dare, *and* Cool Women, Hot Jobs. *Schwager has written extensively on topics related to fitness, sports medicine and motivation; created an informative online newsletter covering issues related to health, sports medicine and nutrition; and continues to publish articles nationally, both online and in print.*

Eat Like a Greek

Want flavor plus good health? The Mediterranean style of dining has it all.

Diets are often doomed to fail because they focus more on what you can't eat than what you can. Don't eat bread. Don't eat sugar. Don't eat fat. On some diets, even certain fruits and vegetables are forbidden. After a few weeks of being told "no," our inner toddler throws a tantrum and runs screaming to Krispy Kreme.

That's what is so appealing about the Mediterranean diet, which isn't really a diet at all but a style of eating that focuses on an abundance of delicious, hearty, and nutritious food. Just looking at the pyramid at right, developed by Oldways Preservation Trust, a nonprofit organization that encourages healthy food choices, may be enough to make you look forward to the next meal.

"What I like about this approach to food is that it's very easy," says Sara Baer-Sinnott, executive vice president of Oldways. "It's not a fancy way of eating, but you'll never feel deprived because the foods have so much flavor."

The best part is that eating like a Greek not only satisfies your need to say yes to food, but has been scientifically proven to be good for your health. Decades of research has shown that traditional Mediterranean eating patterns are associated with a lower risk of several chronic diseases, including the big three—cancer, heart disease, and type 2 diabetes. Most recently, a systematic review of 146 observational studies and 43 randomized clinical trials published in the April 13, 2009, issue of the *Archives of Internal Medicine* found strong evidence that a Mediterranean diet protects against cardiovascular disease. Other recent research has linked the eating style to a lower risk of cognitive decline and dementia.

So, where do you start? Your next meal is as good a place as any. Just walk through our guide for menu planning.

Stepping into a Mediterranean Lifestyle

Although a trip to southern Italy or Greece would be nice, you needn't go farther than your local supermarket. If your menu planning usually begins with a meat entrée, then adds a starch and a vegetable side dish as an afterthought, you'll want to reprioritize your food choices. "Think about designing a plate where a good half of it is taken up with vegetables, another one-quarter is healthy grains—whole-grain pasta, rice, couscous, quinoa—and the remaining quarter is

lean protein," says Katherine McManus, R.D., director of nutrition at Brigham and Women's Hospital in Boston and a consultant on the most recent version of the Mediterranean pyramid. "Of course, you needn't physically separate your foods in that fashion, but it gives you a good idea of the proportions to aim for."

STEP 1: Start with plant foods. Build your menus around an abundance of fruits and vegetables (yes, even potatoes); breads and grains (at least half of the servings should be whole grains); and beans, nuts, and seeds. To maximize the health benefits, emphasize a variety of minimally processed and locally grown foods.

STEP 2: Add some lean protein. The Mediterranean diet draws much of its protein from the sea, reflecting its coastal origins. Fish is not only low in saturated fat but can also be high in heart-healthy omega-3 fatty acids. Aim for two servings of fish a week, especially those, such as salmon and sardines, that are high in omega-3s but lower in mercury. You

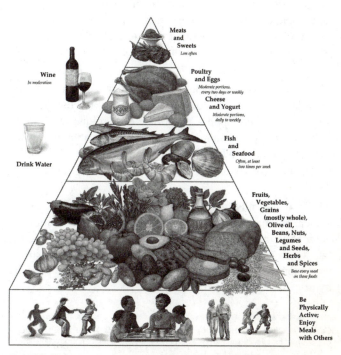

© 2009 Oldways Preservation Trust, www.oldwayspt.org

A Day in the Mediterranean Life

Breakfast

It's hard to go wrong with whole-grain cereal, fruit, and low-fat milk. Variations on the theme include low-fat yogurt with fresh berries and granola, or meaty steel-cut oats topped with fresh fruit, applesauce, whipped yogurt, or a sprinkle of nuts. Enjoy eggs? Try sautéing vegetables or greens in a bit of olive oil until soft and then scramble in a beaten egg. Go Greek with chopped olives and feta, or top with salsa and avocado for a Tex-Mex flair.

Lunch

Whether you're at home or brown-bagging, a Mediterranean lunch is tastier and healthier than drive-through fare and often faster and cheaper, too. Bagged salad greens provide a base for whatever you have on hand—fruit, vegetables, nuts, cheese, or a bit of leftover grilled chicken or fish. Consider topping it with a low-fat ranch dressing, an olive-oil vinaigrette, or just a drizzle of flavorful oil and a squeeze of fresh lemon. Or fill a whole-wheat pita pocket with hummus and as much fresh lettuce, peppers, cucumbers, and tomatoes as you can stuff in. If you're really pressed for time, heat up a can of low-sodium lentil, minestrone, or vegetable soup.

Snack Time

Keep a ready supply of fruit and veggies on hand so you'll grab them at snack time. Hummus, low-fat yogurt, and salad dressings pair nicely with them. If you don't want to invest the prep time, buy pre-cut. It's also a good idea to keep some nonperishable snacks at your desk or in your car—raisins or other dried fruit, nuts, and whole-grain crackers or pretzels.

Dinner

This is when many of us lose sight of nutrition goals because it's so easy after a long day to fall into old, comfortable habits. Fortunately, Mediterranean-style dining emphasizes simple foods and cooking methods.

While your pasta boils, for example, you can sauté a variety of vegetables in olive oil and garlic, then toss in a few shrimp and cook until they turn pink. Mix it all with a sprinkle of cheese, pour yourself a glass of wine, and you're sitting down to a relaxing dinner in less than 20 minutes.

In much the same manner, you can put together a quick stir-fry with slices of chicken breast, vegetables, and rice. Fresh fish is the simplest of entrées because it cooks quickly and doesn't take much dressing up. Spritz it with olive oil and your favorite seasonings and broil it, or coat it in bread crumbs and pan fry in a bit of olive oil. Squeeze on fresh lemon juice and adorn with parsley just before serving.

Two things you should have on hand for your evening meal: frozen vegetables, which are usually just as nutritious as fresh, and a plastic container of salad, preferably filled with a variety of greens. It's also a good idea to stock your crisper with seasonal fruit. A bowl of ripe berries, a chunk of melon, or a soft, farm-fresh peach is a delicious and satisfying end to any meal.

Oldways Preservation Trust, a nonprofit organization that promotes healthful eating, has more recipes and menu ideas on the two websites it sponsors: www.oldwayspt.org and www.mediterraneanmark.org.

can also include moderate amounts of poultry and even eggs. Or substitute with vegetarian sources of protein, such as beans, nuts, or soy products. Limit red meat to a couple of servings a month, and minimize consumption of processed meats.

STEP 3: Say cheese. Include some milk, yogurt, or cheese in your daily meal. While low-fat versions are preferable, others are fine in small amounts. A sprinkle of high-quality Romano or Parmesan, for example, adds a spark to vegetables and pasta. Soy-based dairy products are fine, too, if you prefer them or are lactose intolerant.

STEP 4: Use oils high in "good" fats. Canola oil is a good choice, but many Mediterranean recipes call for olive oil. Both are high in unsaturated fat. Minimize artery-clogging saturated fat, which comes mainly from animal sources, and avoid the even more heart-harming trans fat, which comes from partially hydrogenated vegetable oil.

STEP 5: End meals with the sweetness of fruit. Make sugary and fatty desserts just an occasional indulgence.

STEP 6: Drink to your health. A moderate amount of alcohol—especially red wine—may help protect your heart. But balance that against the increased risks from drinking alcohol, including breast cancer in women. A moderate amount is one drink a day for women, two for men.

STEP 7: Step out. "The Mediterranean lifestyle is built around daily activity," McManus says. Go for a walk after dinner. And choose leisure activities that keep you moving.

Critical Thinking

1. Discuss why a Greek diet may reduce the risks of cancer and heart disease.
2. What types of foods make up a Greek menu plan?
3. How feasible would it be to adopt a Greek diet?

Dieting on a Budget

Plus the secrets of thin people, based on our survey of 21,000 readers.

With jobs being cut and retirement accounts seemingly shrinking by the day, it's too bad our waistlines aren't dwindling, too. We can't rectify that cosmic injustice, but in this issue we aim to help you figure out the most effective, least expensive ways to stay trim and fit.

Though most Americans find themselves overweight by middle age, an enviable minority stay slim throughout their lives. Are those people just genetically gifted? Or do they, too, have to work at keeping down their weight?

To find out, the Consumer Reports National Research Center asked subscribers to *Consumer Reports* about their lifetime weight history and their eating, dieting, and exercising habits. And now we have our answer:

People who have never become overweight aren't sitting in recliners with a bowl of corn chips in their laps. In our group of always-slim respondents, a mere 3 percent reported that they never exercised and that they ate whatever they pleased. The eating and exercise habits of the vast majority of the always-slim group look surprisingly like those of people who have successfully lost weight and kept it off.

Both groups eat healthful foods such as fruits, vegetables, and whole grains and eschew excessive dietary fat; practice portion control; and exercise vigorously and regularly. The only advantage the always-slim have over the successful dieters is that those habits seem to come a bit more naturally to them.

"When we've compared people maintaining a weight loss with controls who've always had a normal weight, we've found that both groups are working hard at it; the maintainers are just working a little harder," says Suzanne Phelan, Ph.D., an assistant professor of kinesiology at California Polytechnic State University and co-investigator of the National Weight Control Registry, which tracks people who have successfully maintained a weight loss over time. For our respondents, that meant exercising a little more and eating with a bit more restraint than an always-thin person—plus using more monitoring strategies such as weighing themselves or keeping a food diary.

A total of 21,632 readers completed the 2007 survey. The always thin, who had never been overweight, comprised 16 percent of our sample. Successful losers made up an additional 15 percent. We defined that group as people who, at the time of the survey, weighed at least 10 percent less than they did at their heaviest, and had been at that lower weight for at least three years. Failed dieters, who said they would like to slim down yet still weighed at or near their lifetime high, were, sad to say, the largest group: 42 percent. (The remaining 27 percent of respondents, such as people who had lost weight more recently, didn't fit into any of the categories.)

An encouraging note: More than half of our successful losers reported shedding the weight themselves, without aid of a commercial diet program, a medical treatment, a book, or diet pills. That confirms

---

Price vs. Nutrition: Making Smart Choices

Although healthful foods often cost more than high-calorie junk such as cookies and soda, we unearthed some encouraging exceptions. As illustrated below, two rich sources of nutrients, black beans and eggs, cost mere pennies per serving—and less than plain noodles, which supply fewer nutrients. And for the same price as a doughnut, packed with empty calories, you can buy a serving of broccoli.

- **Cooked black beans**
  - Serving size 1/2 cup
  - Calories per serving 114
  - Cost per serving 74¢

- **Hard-boiled egg**
  - Serving size one medium
  - Calories per serving 78
  - Cost per serving 94¢

- **Cooked noodles**
  - Serving size 3/4 cup
  - Calories per serving 166
  - Cost per serving 134¢

- **Glazed doughnut**
  - Serving size 1 medium
  - Calories per serving 239
  - Cost per serving 324¢

- **Cooked broccoli**
  - Serving size 1/2 cup chopped
  - Calories per serving 27
  - Cost per serving 334¢

- **Chicken breast**
  - Serving size 4 oz.
  - Calories per serving 142
  - Cost per serving 364¢

Sources: Adam Drewnowski, Ph.D., director of the Center for Public Health Nutrition, University of Washington: USDA Nutrient Database for Standard Reference.

---

what we found in our last large diet survey, in 2002, in which 83 percent of "superlosers"—people who'd lost at least 10 percent of their starting weight and kept it off for five years or more—had done it entirely on their own.

Stay-Thin Strategies

Successful losers and the always thin do a lot of the same things—and they do them more frequently than failed dieters do. For the dietary strategies below, numbers reflect those who said they are that way at least five days a week, a key tipping point, our analysis found. (Differences of less than 4 percentage points are not statistically meaningful.)

Lifetime Weight History

Failed dieters: overweight and have tried to lose, but still close to highest weight. **Always thin:** never overweight. **Successful losers:** once overweight but now at least 10 percent lighter and have kept pounds off for at least three years.

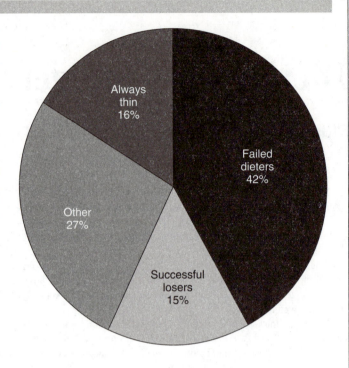

Strength Train at Least Once a Week

Always thin	31%
Successful loser	32%
Failed dieter	23%

Do Vigorous Exercise at Least Four Days a Week

Always thin	35%
Successful loser	41%
Failed dieter	27%

Eat Fruit and Vegetables at Least Five Times a Day

Always thin	49%
Successful loser	49%
Failed dieter	38%

Eat Whole Grains, Not Refined

Always thin	56%
Successful loser	61%
Failed dieter	49%

Eat Less Than 1/3 Calories from Fat

Always thin	47%
Successful loser	53%
Failed dieter	35%

Observe Portion Control at Every Meal

Always thin	57%
Successful loser	62%
Failed dieter	42%

Count Calories

Always thin	9%
Successful loser	47%
Failed dieter	9%

6 Secrets of the Slim

Through statistical analyses, we were able to identify six key behaviors that correlated the most strongly with having a healthy body mass index (BMI), a measure of weight that takes height into account. Always thin people were only slightly less likely than successful losers to embrace each of the behaviors—and significantly more likely to do so than failed dieters. By following the behaviors, you can, quite literally, live like a thin person.

Watch portions. Of all the eating behaviors we asked about, carefully controlling portion size at each meal correlated most strongly with having a lower BMI. Successful losers—even those who were still overweight—were especially likely (62 percent) to report practicing portion control at least five days per week. So did 57 percent of the always thin, but only 42 percent of failed dieters.

Portion control is strongly linked to a lower BMI.

Limit fat. Specifically, that means restricting fat to less than one-third of daily calorie intake. Fifty-three percent of successful losers and 47 percent of the always thin said they did that five or more days a week, compared with just 35 percent of failed dieters.

Eat fruits and vegetables. The more days that respondents ate five or more servings of fruits or vegetables, the lower their average BMI score. Forty-nine percent of successful losers and the always thin said they ate that way at least five days a week, while 38 percent of failed dieters did so.

Choose whole grains over refined. People with lower body weights consistently opted for whole-wheat breads, cereals, and other grains over refined (white) grains.

Eat at home. As the number of days per week respondents are restaurant or takeout meals for dinner increased, so did their weight. Eating at home can save a lot of money, too.

Exercise, exercise, exercise. Regular vigorous exercise—the type that increases breathing and heart rate for 30 minutes or longer—was strongly linked to a lower BMI. Although only about one quarter of respondents said they did strength training at least once a week, that practice was significantly more prevalent among successful losers (32 percent) and always thin respondents (31 percent) than it was among failed dieters (23 percent).

What Didn't Matter

One weight-loss strategy is conspicuously absent from the list: going low-carb. Of course we asked about it, and it turned out that limiting carbohydrates was linked to higher BMIs in our survey. That doesn't necessarily mean low-carb plans such as the Atkins or South Beach diets don't work. "If you go to the hospital and everyone there is sick, that doesn't mean the hospital made them sick," says Eric C. Westman, M.D., associate professor of medicine and director of the Lifestyle Medicine Clinic at Duke University Medical School. "Just as people go to hospitals because they're ill, people may go to carb restriction because they have a higher BMI, not the other way around." At the same time, the findings do suggest that cutting carbs alone, without other healthful behaviors such as exercise and portion control, might not lead to great results.

Eating many small meals, or never eating between meals, didn't seem to make much difference one way or another. Including lean protein with most meals also didn't by itself predict a healthier weight.

Realistic Expectations

Sixty-six percent of our respondents, all subscribers to *Consumer Reports,* were overweight as assessed by their body mass index; that's the same percentage as the population as a whole. One third of the overweight group, or 22 percent of the overall sample, qualified as obese.

Although that might seem discouraging, the survey actually contains good news for would-be dieters. Our respondents did much better at losing weight than published clinical studies would predict. Though such studies are deemed successful if participants are 5 percent lighter after a year, our successful losers had managed to shed an average of 16 percent of their peak weight, an average of almost 34 pounds. They had an impressive average BMI of 25.7, meaning they were just barely overweight.

One key to weight loss success is having realistic goals and our subscribers responses proved encouraging. A staggering 70 percent of them said they currently wanted to lose weight. But when we asked how many pounds they hoped to take off, we found that their goals were modest: The vast majority reported wanting to lose 15 percent or less of their overall body weight; 65 percent sought to lose between 1 and 10 percent. Keeping expectations in check might help dieters from becoming discouraged when they don't achieve, say, a 70-pound

---

Are You Overweight?

A body mass index under 25 is considered normal weight: from 25 to 29, overweight; and 30 or above, obese. To calculate your BMI, multiply your weight in pounds by 703, then divide by your height squared in inches.

---

weight loss or drop from a size 20 to a size 6—a common problem in behavioral weight loss studies.

Realistic goals are one key to weight loss.

What You Can Do

Weight loss is a highly individual process, and what matters most is finding the combination of habits that work for you. But our findings suggest that there are key behaviors common to people who have successfully lost weight and to those who have never gained it in the first place. By embracing some or all of those behaviors, you can probably increase your chances of weight-loss success, and live a healthier life in the process. In addition to following the steps above, consider these tips:

Don't get discouraged. Studies show that prospective dieters often have unrealistic ideas about how much weight they can lose. A 10 percent loss might not sound like much, but it significantly improves overall health and reduces risk of disease.

Ask for support. Though only a small minority of respondents overall reported that a spouse or family member interfered with their healthful eating efforts, that problem was much more likely among failed dieters, 31 percent of whom reported some form of spousal sabotage in the month prior to the survey. Ask housemates to help you stay on track by, for example, not pestering you to eat foods you're trying to avoid, or not eating those foods in front of you.

Get up and move. While regular vigorous exercise correlated most strongly with healthy body weight, our findings suggest that any physical activity is helpful, including activities you might not even consider exercise. Everyday activities such as housework, yard work, and playing with kids were modestly tied to lower weight. By contrast, hours spent sitting each day, whether at an office desk or at home watching television, correlated with higher weight.

Critical Thinking

1. Is it possible to diet on a limited food budget? Explain.
2. Why should exercise be included in any weight control program?
3. What foods are both low cost and low fat/calorie?

The New Phys Ed.

Dodgeball is passé; schools are teaching lifelong fitness.

RON SCHACHTER

I t's not unusual for kids to bike or skateboard before school and then count down the minutes until they get to play video games after school. But what would you think of including skateboarding or Wii in the school day?

That's just what a growing number of physical education teachers are doing, in an attempt to make exercise more engaging—and lifelong—for elementary and middle school students. A new generation of P.E. classes is introducing youngsters to everything from step aerobics and yoga to inline skating and mountain biking.

Experts agree that these approaches to exercise provide an attractive alternative to team sports and stay with students long after they leave school. "The newer physical education, which you will see more and more of in schools, focuses on personal challenges rather than team competition," explains Stephen Cone, a professor of health and exercise science at Rowan University in Glassboro, New Jersey. "And it provides skills that students can take with them to have a healthy life."

The change from the traditional P.E. diet of dodgeball, volleyball, and jumping jacks is taking place as the fitness of today's youngsters, along with a looming obesity crisis, has become a central concern for educators and parents.

Solo Sports

Craig Coleman, who teaches physical education at Hayes Elementary School in Fridley, Minnesota, is one educator who appreciates the changing landscape. "When I was in school, we played dodgeball, basketball, and soccer," he recalls. "I picked up skateboarding and ice skating outside of school."

While team activities are not about to become extinct at Hayes, Coleman is steering his classes in a different direction. "I'm trying to get away from team sports," he says. "When these kids get older, they're not likely to play team sports. I'm assuming they'll quit."

That won't be the case, Coleman figures, with the individual sports—inline skating, ice skating, and skateboarding, among them—that he's added to the curriculum. "Ninety-five percent of our kids have never touched a skateboard before," Coleman says. "But they've picked it up really well."

For the past three years, the school's third and fourth graders have donned protective helmets, as well as knee, wrist, and elbow pads, and hopped onto skateboards that have stickier wheels to grip the gym floor without causing any damage.

Coleman launched the program with a $5,000 grant, purchasing equipment and materials from Colorado-based Skate Pass, which offers a curriculum covering everything from learning how to fall to turning correctly and even hosts a certification program for teachers.

P.E. on Wheels

Coleman's not the only teacher putting kids on a roll. At Benjamin Franklin Middle School in Teaneck, New Jersey, physical education teacher Carol Ann Chiesa introduced inline skating to her students 14 years ago. With a $10,000 grant from the National Association for Sport and Physical Education, Chiesa acquired 40 pairs of skates in different sizes and the requisite pads and helmets.

The school's 300 fifth and sixth graders skate during three-week P.E. units in the fall and between the more conventional units Chiesa teaches. "I ask them, 'On a scale of one to ten, of all the things you do in gym, which do you like best?' and the skating always gets a nine or ten," she says. "They're doing something to increase their aerobic capacity, and they don't even realize it. They're getting a great workout."

Even though inline skating is not as popular as it was when she started the program, Chiesa remains convinced that it has staying power. "It's a lifetime sport," she says. "They have the basics now, and as they get older, they won't be afraid to come back to it."

Just outside of Pittsburgh, Pennsylvania, meanwhile, physical education teacher Mark Gartner is fixed as much on the future as the present at Hampton Middle School. Three years ago, the school acquired 60 Trek 820 21-speed mountain bikes, as well as three years' worth of replacement parts, with $14,000 provided through grants and fundraisers.

"We were trying to make our program most beneficial to students as adults," says Gartner. "The statistics show that only two percent of adults past the age of thirty-five participate in competitive sports. If you're teaching something that's irrelevant, what's the point?"

Gartner teaches the basics of gear shifting, as well as bicycle safety and respect for the outdoor environments through which his students will be riding. Those students, some of whom have never ridden before, progress from the blacktop outside of the school to the more challenging trails surrounding it.

Hampton's bike classes belong to a larger program built on the same philosophy that students should be able to take with them what they have learned in P.E. "We have a fitness center that—in my opinion—rivals what you would find in a local gym," Gartner says, adding that students can choose from weight machines, treadmills, exercise bikes, and stair climbers. They can also take aerobic dance classes.

Gartner offers a telling measure of the program's success. "In the past, if you didn't want to do P.E., you forgot your clothes," he observes. "We have almost a zero rate of that."

Exercise on TV

While advanced gym equipment can be costly, some schools are finding less expensive ways to deliver life-long physical education. At Alamo Elementary School in Otsego, Michigan, Kyle Uramkin's classes have taken the electronic route by making use of Wii Sports and Wii Fitness activities.

These interactive video games allow users to participate in sports by moving their arms, legs, and bodies in simulated tennis and bowling matches, aerobics sessions, and fitness courses. Uramkin usually sets up four or five stations featuring different sports, through which the 25 students in his physical education classes rotate. He projects the interactive programs for some activities—such as step aerobics—on a large screen in the gym for the entire class to follow.

The students get a workout, Uramkin notes, and something more. "Kids who might have been hesitating

to participate or weren't giving a hundred percent really take to it," he says, adding that the "exergaming" program has even reached students' homes. "I've had parents come in and say, 'We're thinking about getting one.' That's not just extending the physical activity of the kid, but who knows, may be the parent will get more active."

Stretch Breaks

There's also the growing conviction in some schools that physical activity belongs in the classroom. At French Road Elementary School in Brighton, New York, most of the teachers lead their classes in yoga breaks throughout the day. Those teachers have received a three-hour, after-school training from a certified yoga instructor.

French Road assistant principal Carolyn Rabidoux, who introduced the yoga-in-the-classroom initiative three years ago, also provides materials from Indiana-based YogaKids International, including cards that show different yoga positions. "A teacher can pull out a pose to help children focus, get energy, or just relax," explains Rabidoux, who has also created a series of online videos in which French Road teachers and their yoga instructor demonstrate those poses.

Some classrooms even have a yoga station, where individual students can go over, consult a card, and assume a pose. "It gives them a positive way of focusing instead of yelling out or acting out," Rabidoux says.

Fifth-grade French Road teacher Lara Liu says she uses yoga with her students regularly. "It energizes them after lunch and helps them focus before tests," she says. "I also use it as a transition piece, to get them on the same page and looking at me before we move on."

That transition can be as simple as Liu calling out, "Give me a five." In response, students raise their arms releasing one finger at a time as they take a long breath, and do the reverse as they breathe out. One of their favorites, Liu continues, is called the Volcano, in which they place their palms together at their chest, breathe in deeply, and then "explode" as they exhale, raising their hands over their heads then returning them to their sides.

Good Results

Educators who've taken advantage of the new P.E. are more than happy with the results. "Kids are really incorporating yoga into who they are," says Rabidoux, who tells the story of one student recently stuck in an elevator during a visit to New York City. While the adults surrounding her were starting to panic, the youngster took some yoga breaths to calm herself down.

"More teachers are recognizing that students cannot sit for very long and are putting in short movement breaks," adds Theresa Cone, an assistant professor of health and exercise science at Rowan University, who together with her husband, Stephen, has coauthored several books on new approaches to physical education. "I had one student teacher who convinced the entire school to stop every afternoon and do two minutes of exercise," she recalls, explaining that the student teacher delivered instructions for simple movements over the school's intercom. "The teachers and students loved it."

Cone also insists that the same movements—such as twisting side to side, circling arms, reaching up and down, marching forward and backward—can be practiced in any classroom by students standing next to their desks. She also suggests having small groups of students take turns devising and leading a one-minute activity break every day. The results will be pleasantly surprising, she promises, "and they'll be using the 21st-century skills of collaboration, problem solving, and creativity."

Critical Thinking

1. How does the new PE differ from the traditional PE curriculum?

2. What are the benefits of the new PE?

The Hungry Brain

The urge to eat too much is wired into our heads. **Tackling obesity may require bypassing the stomach** and short-circuiting our brains.

Dan Hurley

At 10:19 P.M. on a Monday evening in October, I sat in a booth at Chevys Fresh Mex in Clifton, New Jersey, reviewing the latest research into the neurobiology of hunger and obesity. While I read I ate a shrimp and crab enchilada, consuming two-thirds of it, maybe less. With all this information in front of me, I thought, I had an edge over my brain's wily efforts to thwart my months-long campaign to get under 190 pounds. But even as I was taking in a study about the powerful lure of guacamole and other salty, fatty foods, I experienced something extraordinary. That bowl of chips and salsa at the edge of the table? It was whispering to me: *Just one more. You know you want us. Aren't we delicious?* In 10 minutes, all that was left of the chips, and my willpower, were crumbs.

I am not alone. An overabundance of chips, Baconator Double burgers, and Venti White Chocolate Mochas have aided a widespread epidemic of obesity in this country. Our waists are laying waste to our health and to our health-care economy: According to a study published by the Centers for Disease Control and Prevention in 2010, nine states had an obesity rate of at least 30 percent—compared with zero states some 10 years earlier—and the cost of treatment for obesity-related conditions had reached nearly 10 percent of total U.S. medical expenditure. So-called normal weight is no longer normal, with two-thirds of adults and one third of children and adolescents now classified as overweight or obese. Dubbed the "Age of Obesity and Inactivity" by the *Journal of the American Medical Association,* this runaway weight gain threatens to decrease average U.S. life span, reversing gains made over the past century by lowering risk factors from smoking, hypertension, and cholesterol. We all know what we should do—eat less, exercise more—but to no avail. An estimated 25 percent of American men and 43 percent of women attempt to lose weight each year; of those who succeed in their diets, between 5 and 20 percent (and it is closer to 5 percent) manage to keep it off for the long haul.

The urgent question is, why do our bodies seem to be fighting against our own good health? According to a growing number of neurobiologists, the fault lies not in our stomachs but in our heads. No matter how convincing our conscious plans

and resolutions, they pale beside the brain's power to goad us into noshing and hanging on to as much fat as we can. With that in mind, some scientists were hopeful that careful studies of the brain might uncover an all-powerful hormone that regulates food consumption or a single spot where the cortical equivalent of a neon sign blinks "Eat Heavy," all the better to shut it off.

After extensive research, the idea of a single, simple cure has been replaced by a much more nuanced view. The latest studies show that a multitude of systems in the brain act in concert to encourage eating. Targeting a single neuronal system is probably doomed to the same ill fate as the failed diets themselves. Because the brain has so many backup systems all geared toward the same thing—maximizing the body's intake of calories—no single silver bullet will ever work.

The brain's prime directive to eat and defend against the loss of fat emerged early in evolution.

"I call it the 'hungry brain syndrome'," says Hans-Rudolf Berthoud, an expert in the neurobiology of nutrition at the Pennington Biomedical Research Center in Baton Rouge, Louisiana. The brain's prime directive to eat and defend against the loss of fat emerged early in evolution, because just about every creature that ever trotted, crawled, swam, or floated was beset by the uncertainty of that next meal. "The system has evolved to defend against the slightest threat of weight loss, so you have to attack it from different directions at once."

With the obesity epidemic raging, the race for countermeasures has kicked into high gear. Neuroscientists are still seeking hormones that inhibit hunger, but they have other tactics as well. One fruitful new avenue comes from the revelation that hunger, blood sugar, and weight gained per calorie consumed all ratchet up when our sleep is disrupted and our circadian rhythms—the 24-hour cycle responding to light and dark—[are] thrown into disarray. All this is compounded by stress, which decreases metabolism while increasing the yen for high-calorie food. We might feel in sync with our high-tech world, but the obesity epidemic is a somber sign that our biology and lifestyles have diverged.

Seeking Silver Bullets, Shooting Blanks

The path forward seemed so simple back in 1995, when three papers in *Science* suggested a panacea for the overweight: A hormone that made animals shed pounds, rapidly losing body fat until they were slim. Based on the research, it seemed that doctors might soon be able to treat obesity the way they treat diabetes, with a simple metabolic drug.

Fat cells release that "diet" hormone—today named leptin, from the Greek *leptos,* meaning thin—to begin a journey across the blood-brain barrier to the hypothalamus, the pea-size structure above the pituitary gland. The hypothalamus serves as a kind of thermostat, setting not only body temperature but playing a key role in hunger, thirst, fatigue, and sleep cycles. Leptin signals the hypothalamus to reduce the sense of hunger so that we stop eating.

In early lab experiments, obese mice given extra leptin by injection seemed sated. They ate less, their body temperature increased, and their weight plummeted. Even normal-weight mice became skinnier when given injections of the hormone.

Once the pharmaceutical industry created a synthetic version of human leptin, clinical trials were begun. But when injected into hundreds of obese human volunteers, leptin's effect was clinically insignificant. It soon became clear why. In humans, as in mice, fat cells of the obese already produced plenty of leptin—more in fact than those of their thin counterparts, since the level of leptin was directly proportional to the amount of fat. The early studies had worked largely because the test mice were, by experimental design, leptin-deficient. Subsequent experiments showed that in normal mice—as in humans—increases in leptin made little difference to the brain, which looked to *low* leptin levels as a signal to eat more, essentially disregarding the kind of high levels that had caused deficient mice to eat less. This made leptin a good drug for maintaining weight loss but not a great candidate for getting the pounds off up front.

Despite that disappointment, the discovery of leptin unleashed a scientific gold rush to find other molecules that could talk the brain into turning hunger off. By 1999 researchers from Japan's National Cardiovascular Center Research Institute in Osaka had announced the discovery of ghrelin, a kind of antileptin that is released primarily by the gut rather than by fat cells. Ghrelin signals hunger rather than satiety to the hypothalamus. Then, in 2002, a team from the University of Washington found that ghrelin levels rise before a meal and fall immediately after. Ghrelin (from the Indo-European root for the word "grow") increased hunger while jamming on the metabolic brakes to promote the body's storage of fat.

So began another line of attack on obesity. Rather than turning leptin on, researchers began exploring ways to turn ghrelin off. Some of them began looking at animal models, but progress has been slow; the concept of a ghrelin "vaccine" has been floated, but clinical trials are still years off.

Seeking a better understanding of the hormone, University of Washington endocrinologist David Cummings compared ghrelin levels in people who had lost considerable amounts of weight through diet with those who shed pounds by means of gastric bypass surgery—a technique that reduces the capacity of the stomach and seems to damage its ghrelin-producing capacity as well. The results were remarkable. For dieters, the more weight lost, the greater the rise in ghrelin, as if the body were telling the brain to get hungry and regain that weight. By contrast, the big losers in the surgical group saw ghrelin levels fall to the floor. Surgical patients never felt increases in appetite and had an easier time maintaining their weight loss as a result. (A newer weight-loss surgery removes most of the ghrelin-producing cells outright.)

Based on such findings, a ghrelin-blocking drug called rimonabant was approved and sold in 32 countries, though not in the United States. It remained available as recently as 2008, even though it also increased the risk of depression and suicidal thinking; it has since been withdrawn everywhere. The verdict is still out on a newer generation of combination pharmaceuticals, including one that contains synthetic versions of leptin and the neurohormone amylin, known to help regulate appetite. In a six-month clinical trial, the combination therapy resulted in an average weight loss of 25 pounds, or 12.7 percent of body weight, with greater weight loss when continued for a full 52 weeks; those who stopped taking the drug midway regained most of their weight.

The Circadian Connection

The limited results from tackling the hypothalamus sent many scientists looking at the other gyres and gears driving obesity in the brain, especially in regions associated with sleep. The first big breakthrough came in 2005, when *Science* published a landmark paper on mice with a mutated version of the Clock gene, which plays a key role in the regulation of the body's circadian rhythms. The mutant mice not only failed to follow the strict eat-by-night, sleep-by-day schedule of normally nocturnal mice, they also became overweight and developed diabetes. "There was a difference in weight gain based on when the food was eaten, whether during day or night," says the study's senior author, endocrinologist Joe Bass of Northwestern University. "That means the metabolic rate must differ under those two conditions."

Could *my* late-night hours be the undoing of my weight-loss plans? Four days after my humiliating defeat by a bowl of tortilla chips, I met with Alex Keene, a postdoctoral researcher at New York University with a Matisse nude tattooed on his right forearm and a penchant for studying flies. His latest study asked whether a starved fly would take normal naps or sacrifice sleep to keep searching for food. He found that like humans (and most other creatures), flies have a neurological toggle between two fundamental yet incompatible drives: to eat or to sleep. "Flies only live a day or two when they're starved,"

Keene told me as we walked past graduate students peering at flies under microscopes. "If they decide to sleep through the night when they're starved, it's a bad decision on their part. So their brains are finely tuned to suppress their sleep when they don't have food and to sleep well after a meal."

For a major study published last year, Keene bred flies with dysfunctional mutations of the Clock gene and also of Cycle, another gene involved in circadian rhythms. He found that the genes together regulate the interaction between the two mutually exclusive behaviors, sleep and feeding, kicking in to suppress sleep when a fly is hungry.

Even when fed, flies without working versions of the Clock and Cycle genes tended to sleep poorly—about 30 percent as much as normal flies. "It was as if they were starving right away," Keene explains. Keene went even further, pinpointing where, amid the 100,000 or so neurons in the fly brain, the Clock gene acts to regulate the sleeping-feeding interaction: a region of just four to eight cells at the top of the fly brain.

"My father is an anthropologist," Keene told me as we stood in the fly room, its air pungent with the corn meal and molasses the flies feed on. "It's ironic, right? He looks at how culture determines behavior, while I look at how genes determine behavior. I used to get him so mad he'd storm out of the house."

Perhaps it takes an anthropologist's son to see that the excess availability of cheap, high-calorie chow cannot fully explain the magnitude and persistence of the problem in our culture. The rebellion against our inborn circadian rhythms wrought by a 24-hour lifestyle, lit by neon and fueled by caffeine, also bears part of the blame. The powerful effect of disordered sleep on metabolism has been seen not just in flies but also in humans. A 2009 study by Harvard University researchers showed that in just 10 days, three of eight healthy volunteers developed prediabetic blood-sugar levels when their sleep-wake schedule was gradually shifted out of alignment.

"It's clear from these types of studies that the way we're keeping the lights on until late at night, the way in which society demands that we stay active for so much longer, could well be contributing to aspects of the metabolic disease we're seeing now," says Steve Kay, a molecular geneticist at the University of California, San Diego.

These insights have fostered collaboration between once-diverse groups. "Physicians who specialized in obesity and diabetes for years are now discovering the importance of circadian effects," Kay says. At the same time, "basic research scientists like me, who have been studying the circadian system for so many years, are now looking at its metabolic effects. When so many people's research from so many areas starts to converge, you know we're in the midst of a paradigm shift. This is the slow rumbling before the volcano blows."

This past April, the National Institute of Diabetes and Digestive and Kidney Diseases (NIDDK) of the National Institutes of Health organized a first-ever national conference focused solely on how circadian rhythms affect metabolism. "What has become obvious over the past few years is that metabolism, all those pathways regulating how fats and carbohydrates are used, is affected by the circadian clock," says biochemist Corinne Silva, a program director at the NIDDK. Her goal is to find drugs that treat diabetes and obesity by targeting circadian pathways. "The mechanisms by which circadian rhythms are maintained and the cross talk with metabolic signaling are just beginning to be elucidated," she says, but they should lead to novel therapeutic approaches in the years ahead.

In Keene's view, the newfound link between sleep and obesity could be put to use right now. "People who are susceptible to diabetes or have weight issues might just get more sleep. I get only about six hours of sleep myself. I usually run in the middle of the night. I'm not a morning person," the enviably thin, 29-year-old Keene states.

My visit to his fly room convinced me to try a new angle in my quest to get under 190 pounds: Rather than focus on *how much* food I put in my mouth, I would focus on *when* I eat. I decided I would no longer eat after 10 P.M.

The Pleasure Factor

Timing may be everything for some folks, but it wasn't for me. No wonder: The brain has no shortage of techniques to goad us into eating. Another line of evidence suggests that the brains of overweight people are wired to feel more pleasure in response to food. Sleep deprived or not, they just enjoy eating more. To study such differences, clinical psychologist Eric Stice of the Oregon Research Institute mastered the delicate task of conducting fMRI brain scans while people were eating. The food he chose to give the volunteers inside the tunnel-like scanners was a milk shake. And let the record show, it was a *chocolate* milk shake.

Brains of the overweight are wired to feel more pleasure in response to food.

Obese adolescent girls, Stice found, showed greater activation compared with their lean peers in regions of the brain that encode the sensory experience of eating food—the so-called gustatory cortex and the somatosensory regions, archipelagoes of neurons that reach across different structures in the brain. At the same time, the obese girls sipping milk shakes showed decreased activation in the striatum, a region near the center of the brain that is studded with dopamine receptors and known to respond to stimuli associated with rewards. Stice wondered whether, even among normal-weight girls, such a pattern might predict an increased risk of overeating and weight gain.

To test his hypothesis, he followed a group of subjects over time, finding that those with reduced activation in the dorsal (rear) region of the striatum while sipping a milk shake were ultimately more likely to gain weight than those with normal activation. The most vulnerable of these girls were also more likely to have a DNA polymorphism—not a mutation, per se, but a rather routine genetic variation—in a dopamine receptor gene, causing reduced dopamine signaling in the striatum and placing them at higher risk. "Individuals may overeat," Stice and his colleagues concluded, "to compensate for a hypofunctioning dorsal striatum, particularly those with genetic polymorphisms thought to attenuate dopamine signaling in this region."

Stice was initially surprised by the results. "It's totally weird," he admits. "Those who experienced less pleasure were at increased risk for weight gain." But his more recent studies have convinced him that the reduced pleasure is a result of years of overeating among the obese girls—the same phenomenon seen in drug addicts who require ever-greater amounts of their drug to feel the same reward. "Imagine a classroom of third graders, and everyone is skinny," he says. "The people who initially find that milk shake most orgasmic will want more of it, but in so doing they cause neuroplastic changes that downregulate the reward circuitry, driving them to eat more and more to regain that same feeling they crave."

Even among people of normal weight, individual differences in brain functioning can directly affect eating behaviors, according to a 2009 study by Michael Lowe, a research psychologist at Drexel University. He took fMRI brain scans of 19 people, all of them of normal weight. Nine of the volunteers reported following strict diets; the other 10 typically ate whenever and whatever they wanted. Lowe had all of them sip a milk shake immediately before getting scanned. The brains of the nondieters, he found, lit up just as one would expect, showing activations in areas associated with satiation and memory, as if saying, "Mmmm, that was good." The chronic dieters showed activations in areas of the brain associated with desire and expectation of reward, however. If anything, the milk shake had made them hungrier.

"What we have shown is that these chronic dieters may actually have a reason to restrain themselves, because they are more susceptible than average to overeating," Lowe says.

Yet inborn differences in hunger and desire, too, turn out to be only part of the weighting game. Eating behaviors are also linked to areas of the brain associated with self-control (such as the left superior frontal region) and visual attention (such as the right middle temporal region). A recent fMRI study led by Jeanne McCaffery, a psychologist at Brown Medical School, showed that successful weight losers had greater activation in those regions, compared with normal-weight people and obese people, when viewing images of food.

The effects of stress on eating behaviors also has a neurobiological basis, according to University of Pennsylvania neurobiologist Tracy Bale. She showed that neural pathways associated with stress link directly to areas of the brain associated with seeking rewards. "Few things are more rewarding evolutionarily than calorie-dense food," Bale told me a few days after presenting a seminar on the subject at last fall's Society for Neuroscience meeting in San Diego. "Under stress people don't crave a salad; they crave something high-calorie. It's because those stress pathways in the limbic system feed into the reward centers, and they drive reward-seeking behaviors. What that tells us is that in addition to drug companies' trying to target appetite, they need to look at the reward centers. We're not necessarily fat because we're hungry but because we're looking for something to deal with stress."

Aha! Perhaps it was stress that was messing with my latest, clock-based diet. Back in March 2010, a tree had fallen on my family's home during a major storm, crushing the roof, destroying half the house, and forcing us to flee to a nearby apartment. By November, as I researched this story, we had finally moved back into our rebuilt house. With nerves fully frayed, I found myself drawn as never before to the Tick Tock Diner, where the motto literally is "Eat Heavy," and where the french fries never tasted better. Instead of losing a few pounds to get under 190, by Thanksgiving I had hit 196.

How to Fix a Hungry Brain

Neuroscience has yet to deliver a weight-loss elixir for paunchy 53-year-old journalists like me, much less for those suffering from serious obesity. But that day will come, Steve Kay asserts, once researchers figure out the correct combination of drugs that work simultaneously on multiple triggers of eating and metabolism, just as hypertension is now routinely treated with two- or three-drug combinations.

Some scientists think a more radical approach is called for. Since the triggers of obesity lie in the brain, neurosurgeons at West Virginia University Health Sciences Center are attempting to rewire those triggers directly using deep brain stimulation (DBS). Since 2009 they have performed surgery on three obese patients to implant electrodes that emit rhythmic electric shocks into the hypothalamus. Having failed other medical therapies for obesity, the three agreed to volunteer for DBS, a treatment already approved for treating the tremors and dystonia of Parkinson's disease. "These patients weren't eating all that much; it was mainly a problem of having very slow metabolisms," says Donald M. Whiting, one of the neurosurgeons leading the study. "Our goal was to speed it up." On the basis of successful animal studies, he adds, "we thought we'd switch on the energy and collect our Nobel Prize."

All three patients experienced significantly less hunger when the electrodes were switched on, and all regained their normal hunger when the electrodes were switched off. Unfortunately, none lost a significant amount of weight in the study's first year. The problem, Whiting concludes, is that there are many ways to adjust DBS. With four contact points on the electrodes, each placed half a millimeter apart and each adjustable for voltage, frequency, and pulse width, the research team has been seeking the combination of settings that most effectively rev up metabolism. So far they have found settings that work only temporarily.

"The brain is really pretty smart," Whiting says. "It tends to want to reboot to factory settings whenever it can. We find that we can reset things for a week or two, but then the brain gets back to where it wants." Despite the challenges, Whiting remains convinced that finding a safe and effective medical treatment for weight control will be essential to turn the obesity epidemic around—and that no amount of preaching from Oprah, no behavior program from Weight Watchers nor food from Jenny Craig, will ever suffice.

"This mystification that obesity is caused by a lack of willpower or just eating the wrong foods is simply a misconception," Joe Bass of Northwestern told me. "There is so much social stigma attached to weight that we make a lot of value judgments. The effort in science is to peel back those layers of belief and try to understand things in an experimental, rational mode. Just as we have made progress against heart disease with statins and blood pressure drugs, we will find medications that can safely and substantially lower weight."

Months after my investigation of the brain-gut connection began, I faced the acid test. In early March I stepped back onto my bathroom scale for a final weigh-in. Rather than slip below 190, for the first time in my life I had tipped, by a single pound, over 200. You might blame it on insufficient exercise or on the cheese and crackers I failed to remove from my late-night work ritual. I'm blaming it on my brain.

Critical Thinking

1. What foods seems to trigger overeating?

2. How do stress and lack of sleep contribute to the desire to overeat?

3. Why have leptin and ghrelin failed to affect weight?

4. Do some people derive more pleasure from food than others? Why?

From *Discover*, June 2011, pp. 53–59. Copyright © 2011 by Discover Syndication. Reprinted by permission via PARS International.

UNIT 5
Drugs and Health

Unit Selections

Learning Outcomes

After reading this Unit, you will be able to:

- Understand the risks of Ketamine use and abuse.

- Be aware of the dangers of synthetic marijuana.

- Address the health risks associated with the use of caffeinated alcoholic beverages marketed to young people.

Student Website
www.mhhe.com/cls

Internet References

Food and Drug Administration (FDA)
  www.fda.gov
National Institute on Drug Abuse (NIDA)
  www.nida.nih.gov

As a culture, Americans have come to rely on drugs not only as a treatment for disease but also as an aid for living normal, productive lives. This view of drugs has fostered a casual attitude regarding their use and resulted in a tremendous drug abuse problem. Drug use and abuse has become so widespread that there is no way to describe the typical drug abuser.

There is no simple explanation for why America has become a drug-taking culture, but there certainly is evidence to suggest some of the factors that have contributed to this development. From the time that we are children, we are constantly bombarded by advertisements about how certain drugs can make us feel and look better. While most of these ads deal with proprietary drugs, the belief created is that drugs are a legitimate and effective way to help us cope with everyday problems. Certainly drugs can have a profound effect on how we feel and act, but research has also demonstrated that our mind plays a major role in the healing process.

Growing up, most of us probably had a medicine cabinet full of prescription and over-the-counter (OTC) drugs, freely dispensed to family members to treat a variety of ailments. This familiarity with drugs, coupled with rising health care costs, has prompted many people to diagnose and medicate themselves with over-the-counter, non-prescription medications without sufficient knowledge of the possible side effects. Though most of these preparations have a limited potential for abuse, it does not mean that they are innocuous. Generally speaking, over-the-counter drugs are relatively safe if taken at the recommended dosage by healthy people, but the risk of dangerous side effects rises sharply when people exceed the recommended dosage. Another potential danger associated with the use of over-the-counter drugs is the drug interactions that can occur when they are taken in conjunction with prescription medications. The gravest danger associated with the use of over-the-counter drugs is that an individual may use them to control symptoms of an underlying disease and thus prevent its early diagnosis and proper treatment.

While over-the-counter drugs can be abused, an increasing number of drug-related deaths over the past five years have been linked to prescription drugs. These drugs such as opiate-based painkillers include OxyContin, Darvon, and Vicodin and are often used as an alternative to an illicit high.

As a culture, we have grown up believing that there is, or should be, a drug to treat any malady or discomfort that befalls us. Would we have a drug problem if there was no demand for drugs? One drug that is used widely in the United States is alcohol, especially on college campuses. Every year over 1,000 students die from alcohol-related causes, mostly drinking and driving. About one in ten adults has a serious alcohol problem which negatively affects work and home.

For this unit, three drugs that are used on high school and college campuses are addressed and include caffeinated alcoholic beverages, synthetic marijuana, and ketamine. Caffeinated alcoholic beverages including the brand Four Loko, were originally marketed as energy drinks and contained alcohol, caffeine, taurine, and guarana. These products have had multiple concerns including ethical, health, and legal related to the companies marketing them to minors and the risks of combining caffeine and alcohol. Many states banned these beverages which forced companies to reconfigure the product. Today, Four Loko contains alcohol and is marketed as a malt beverage.

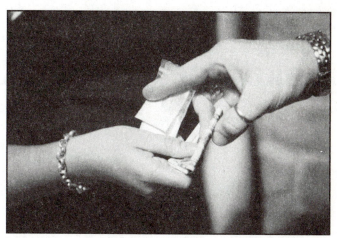

© Stockbyte/Getty Images

Illicitly sold Ketamine comes either from diverted legal supplies and semi-legitimate suppliers, or from theft of legitimate suppliers. Ketamine is very short-acting, its hallucinatory effects typically last sixty minutes when injected and up to two hours when ingested, The total experience lasts no more than a couple of hours. The drug produces a dissociative state, characterized by a sense of detachment from one's physical body and the external world. At sufficiently high doses, users may experience what is called the "K-hole, a state somewhat like schizophrenia."

New York State recently placed a statewide ban on the sales of synthetic marijuana and issued a warning of the dangers of the drug, which can be significantly more severe than natural marijuana. Study after study has found that synthetic pot is linked to serious side effects, which often require emergency room visits and medical intervention. Synthetic marijuana has been shown to bring about severe reactions including death and acute renal failure, and commonly cause: tachycardia (increased heart rate); paranoid behavior, agitation, and irritability; nausea and vomiting; confusion; drowsiness; headache; hypertension; electrolyte abnormalities; seizures; and syncope (loss of consciousness). In "Caffeinated Alcohol in a Can, Four Loko Does the Job, Students Agree," author Don Troop discusses risks associated with students drinking caffeinated alcoholic beverages, including missed classes, falling behind in school work, damage to property, traffic accidents, and injuries that occur while under the influence of alcohol. Other drugs of abuse among young people include ketamine and synthetic marijuana. The use of both these drugs is increasing as addressed in "Ketamine Use: A Review" and "This Drug Shouldn't Be Out There." Ketamine use as a recreational drug has recently spread in many parts of the world. There are increasing concerns about the harmful physical and psychological consequences of repeated misuse of this drug which remains an important medicine in both anesthesia and pain management. Synthetic cannabis (marijuana) is sold under the brands K2 and Spice and is dangerous to users. The drug's qualities are similar to LSD, cocaine, and organic marijuana. Synthetic marijuana is made up of a mixture of herbs and spices and sprayed with a chemical similar to THC, the active ingredient in non-synthetic marijuana. Many states are trying to make the drug illegal to limit its use.

Caffeinated Alcohol in a Can, Four Loko Does the Job, Students Agree

DON TROOP

It's friday night in this steep-hilled college town, and if anyone needs an excuse to party, here are two: In 30-minutes the Mountaineers football team will kick off against the UConn Huskies in East Hartford, Conn., and tonight begins the three-day Halloween weekend.

A few blocks from the West Virginia University campus, young people crowd the aisles of Ashebrooke Liquor Outlet, an airy shop that is popular among students. One rack in the chilled-beverage cooler is nearly empty—the one that is usually filled with 23.5-ounce cans of Four Loko, a fruity malt beverage that combines the caffeine of two cups of coffee with the buzz factor of four to six beers.

"That's what everyone's buying these days," says an employee. "Loko and Burnett's vodka," a line of distilled spirits that are commonly mixed with nonalcoholic energy drinks like Red Bull and Monster to create fruity cocktails with a stimulating kick.

Four Loko's name comes from its four primary ingredients—alcohol (12 percent by volume), caffeine, taurine, and guarana. Although it is among dozens of caffeinated alcoholic drinks on the market, Four Loko has come to symbolize the dangers of such beverages because of its role in binge-drinking incidents this fall involving students at New Jersey's Ramapo College and at Central Washington University. Ramapo and Central Washington have banned Four Loko from their campuses, and several other colleges have sent urgent e-mail messages advising students not to drink it. But whether Four Loko is really "blackout in a can" or just the highest-profile social lubricant of the moment is unclear.

Just uphill from Asherbrooke Liquor Outlet, four young men stand on a porch sipping cans of Four Loko—fruit punch and cranberry-lemonade. All are upperclassmen except for one, Philip Donnachie, who graduated in May. He says most Four Loko drinkers he knows like to guzzle a can at home before meeting up with friends, a custom that researchers in the field call "predrinking."

"Everyone that's going to go out for the night, they're going to start with a Four Loko first," Mr. Donnachie says, adding that he generally switches to beer.

A student named Tony says he paid $5.28 at Ashebrooke for two Lokos—a bargain whether the goal is to get tipsy or flat-out drunk.

Before the drink became infamous, he says, he would see students bring cans of it into classrooms. "The teachers didn't know what it was," Tony says, and if they asked, the student would casually reply, "It's an energy drink."

Farther uphill, on the sidewalk along Grant Avenue, the Tin Man from *The Wizard of Oz* carries a Loko—watermelon flavor, judging by its color. Down the block a keg party spills out onto the front porch, where guests sprawl on a sofa and flick cigarette ashes over the railing. No one here is drinking Four Loko, but most are eager to talk about the product because they've heard that it could be banned by the federal government as a result of the student illnesses.

It's among dozens of caffeinated alcoholic drinks on the market, but Four Loko has come to symbolize the dangers of them all because of its role in binge-drinking incidents on colleges campuses this fall.

Research Gap

That's not likely to happen anytime soon, according to the Food and Drug Administration.

"The FDA's decision regarding the regulatory status of caffeine added to various alcoholic beverages will be a high priority for the agency," Michael L. Herndon, an FDA spokesman, wrote in an e-mail message. "However, a decision regarding the use of caffeine in alcoholic beverages could take some time." The FDA does not consider such drinks to be "generally recognized as safe." A year ago the agency gave 27 manufacturers 30 days to provide evidence to the contrary, if it existed. Only 19 of the companies have responded.

Dennis L. Thombs is chairman of the department of social and behavioral sciences at the University of North Texas Health Science Center, in Fort Worth. He knows a great deal about the drinking habits of young people.

Last year he was the lead author of a paper submitted to the journal *Addictive Behaviors* that described his team's study of bar patrons' consumption of energy drinks and alcohol in the college town of Gainesville, Fla.

After interviewing 802 patrons and testing their blood-alcohol content, Mr. Thombs and his fellow researchers concluded that energy drinks' labels should clearly describe the ingredients, their amounts, and the potential risks involved in using the products.

But Mr. Thombs says the government should have more data before it decides what to do about alcoholic energy drinks.

"There's still a big gap in this research," he says. "We need to get better pharmacological measures in natural drinking environments," like bars.

He says he has submitted a grant application to the National Institutes of Health in hopes of doing just that.

"Liquid Crack"

Back at the keg party in Morgantown, a student wearing Freddy Krueger's brown fedora and razorblade glove calls Four Loko "liquid crack" and says he prefers not to buy it for his underage friends. "I'll buy them something else," he says, "but not Four Loko."

Dipsy from the *Teletubbies* says the people abusing Four Loko are younger students, mostly 17- and 18-year-olds. He calls the students who became ill at Ramapo and Central Washington "a bunch of kids that don't know how to drink."

Two freshmen at the party, Gabrielle and Meredith, appear to confirm that assertion.

"I like Four Loko because it's cheap and it gets me drunk," says Gabrielle, 19, who seems well on her way to getting drunk tonight, Four Loko or not. "Especially for concerts. I drink two Four Lokos before going, and then I don't have to spend $14 on a couple drinks at the stadium."

Meredith, 18 and equally intoxicated, says that although she drinks Four Loko, she favors a ban. "They're 600 calories, and they're gross."

An interview with Alex, a 19-year-old student at a religiously affiliated college in the Pacific Northwest, suggests one reason that the drink might be popular among a younger crowd. In his state and many others, the laws that govern the sale of Four Loko and beer are less stringent than those for hard liquor.

That eases the hassle for older friends who buy for Alex. These days that's not a concern, though. He stopped drinking Four Loko because of how it made him feel the next day.

"Every time I drank it I got, like, a blackout," says Alex. "Now I usually just drink beer."

Critical Thinking

1. What role does Four Loko play in binge drinking?
2. Why is the drink so appealing to college students?
3. Why is Four Loko marketed to college students?

Ketamine Use: A Review

Celia J. A. Morgan & H. Valerie Curran
on behalf of the Independent Scientific Committee on Drugs (ISCD)

Introduction

Since it was first introduced as an anaesthetic in 1964, ketamine has had a fascinating history. Its safety profile made it the key anaesthetic for American soldiers injured during the Vietnam War. Today it remains the most widely used anaesthetic in veterinary medicine. Ketamine's psychosis-like effects have led to it being used as a pharmacological 'model' of schizophrenia. These same effects have also contributed to it becoming used as a recreational drug. Famously, the physician John Lilly took ketamine repeatedly in the late 1970s, describing his experience as like being 'a peeping Tom at the keyhole of eternity'. Recreational use of ketamine ('K', 'ket', 'Special K') has increased over recent years in many parts of the world and new problems have emerged—especially for those using heavily—including physical harms and addiction. At the same time, ketamine now plays a medical role in pain management and is being explored for its possible anti-depressant effects.

Pharmacologically, ketamine's main action is on glutamate, the major excitatory neurotransmitter in the brain. It is a non-competitive antagonist at one of the three glutamate receptors: the N-methyl d-aspartate (NMDA) receptor. Because of its role in synaptic plasticity, the NMDA-receptor is central to learning and memory. Ketamine also has less prominent actions at other receptor sites. It blocks muscarinic acetylcholine receptors and may potentiate the effects of gamma-aminobutyric acid (GABA) synaptic inhibition. Ketamine also induces activation of dopamine release [1] and acts as a weak agonist at mμ opioid receptors [2]. Ketamine exists as two optimal isomers—(S)-(+) and (R)-(-)-2-(2-chlorophenyl)-2-(methylamino) cyclohexanone with differing affinities at the NMDA-receptor. Both the more potent S-(+) and the less potent R(-) enantiomers have similar pharmacokinetic profiles.

Medical Uses of Ketamine

Ketamine's important medical uses should be clearly distinguished from its non-medical use. Ketamine was first synthesized as a replacement for phencyclidine (PCP, 'angel dust'), which had a range of adverse effects. Like phencyclidine, ketamine was shown to be a potent 'dissociative anaesthetic' that produced profound analgesia and amnesia without any slowing of heart rate or breathing. However, patients often reported a variety of unusual symptoms when recovering from ketamine anaesthesia. These 'emergence phenomena' included delusions, hallucinations, delirium and confusion, and sometimes 'out-of-body' and 'near-death' experiences. In turn, these phenomena led to ketamine being withdrawn from mainstream anaesthetic use with humans.

Ketamine is still used today in specialist anaesthesia, particularly paediatrics, veterinary anaesthesia and field medicine. Its good safety profile (relative preservation of airway reflexes and haemodynamic stability; spontaneous ventilation) has also led to it being the anaesthetic drug of choice in parts of the world that have limited availability of resuscitation equipment. In veterinary medicine, ketamine is the most widely used anaesthetic agent in all animal species. Its popularity in equine medicine is reflected in a common street name: 'the horse tranquillizer'.

Ketamine also has a role in pain management in both human and veterinary medicine. It is a potent analgesic which prevents 'wind-up', where neurones in the spinal cord become sensitized to painful stimuli [3]. In this way, low doses of ketamine given before, during and after surgery improves post-operative pain relief. In humans, low doses (0.1–0.5 mg/kg/hour) of ketamine can be used as local anaesthetics and co-analgesics, and are particularly effective for neuropathic pain [4] which is notoriously difficult to treat. Low-dose ketamine is also effective in treating complex regional pain syndrome [5]. It can also be used to relieve acute pain, although its psychosis-like side effects may make co-administration of a benzodiazepine necessary. Ketamine has also been used in intensive care management of cases of prolonged epileptic seizures [6].

Other potential medical uses of ketamine are currently being researched (see [7]), particularly in treatment-resistant depression (e.g. [8]) and in heroin and alcohol addiction [9]. There are also experimental studies using single doses to explore the 'ketamine model' of psychosis (e.g. [10,11]).

Non-medical Use of Ketamine

Precisely those effects that limited the clinical use of ketamine made the drug appealing to recreational drug users. The first reports of non-medical ketamine use appeared in the 1960s [12], but use remained rare in Europe until the 1990s, when it appeared on the 'rave' scene as an adulterant to ecstasy tablets [13]. At low doses ketamine induces distortion of time and space, hallucinations and mild dissociative effects. According to users, the most appealing aspects of ketamine use are 'melting into the surroundings', 'visual hallucinations', 'out-of-body experiences' and 'giggliness' [30]. At large doses, ketamine induces a more severe dissociation commonly referred to as a 'K-hole', wherein the user experiences intense detachment to the point that their perceptions appear completely divorced from their previous reality. Some users—astronauts of the psyche or 'psychonauts'—value these profoundly altered states of consciousness, whereas others see the resulting decreased sociability as a less appealing aspect of ketamine use.

Ketamine is primarily obtained in a powder form and administered through snorting or inhaling. Other forms of ingestion include liquid injected intramuscularly or occasionally intravenously. Ketamine is rarely taken orally, as by this route ketamine is metabolized to norketamine quickly and produces a more sedative and less psychedelic experience.

Although a controlled drug in many countries, ketamine is not currently under international control and figures on its use world-wide are unavailable. The United Nations *World Drug Report* [14] describes the spread of the drug across East Asia, Australia, North America and Europe and stressed: 'the dramatically increasing use and availability of ketamine in parts of South-East Asia linked to the absence of international restrictions on the drug' (p. 114). In Hong Kong, ketamine was deemed to be the single most abused drug. Diversion from the legitimate trade remains the primary source of ketamine but industrial-scale manufacture of illicit ketamine is now emerging. For example, in 2009, China reported the seizure from two illicit laboratories of 8.5 million tons of the immediate precursor chemical for ketamine [14].

In the United Kingdom, ketamine was classified as a Class C substance in 2006. According to the annual DrugScope [15] survey, the average price of a gram of ketamine in the United Kingdom fell from £30 to £20 between 2005 and 2008 and has since become cheaper still. Ketamine has been included in the British Crime Survey (BCS) since 2006 and estimates suggest an increase in numbers of ketamine users from around 85 000 in 2006/07 to 113 000 in 2008/09 [16]. Use in the previous year among young people aged 16–24 doubled between 2007/08 and 2008/09 (from 0.9% to 1.9%) but was steady in 2009/10 (1.7%) [17]. This compares with 2009/10 use of cannabis (16.1%), cocaine (5.5%), ecstasy (4.3%), amyl nitrate (3.2%), amphetamines (2.4%) and magic mushrooms (1.2%). Numbers in this age group having ever used ketamine have unsurprisingly increased (2.2% 2007/8; 3.6% 2008/9; 4% 2009/10). In the United States, ketamine is a schedule III drug which has been 'ever used' by an estimated 1–2% of 10th- and 12th-graders [18].

While the use of ketamine was initially confined to certain subcultures [13], it has recently become more mainstream. For example, a survey of clubbers in 2001 found that 25% of respondents had taken ketamine [19], while a similar survey in 2009 showed that this had increased to 68% [20]. These latest data show a third of respondents reported using ketamine in the previous month, suggesting that ketamine is now the fourth most popular drug among UK clubbers after cannabis, ecstasy and cocaine.

Since ketamine was classified in the United Kingdom and its use has become more widespread, further data have emerged suggesting a range of risks associated with ketamine use that were not known at the time of the original review by the Advisory Council on the Misuse of Drugs (ACMD) [21]. Therefore the Independent Scientific Committee on Drugs (ISCD) decided to review ketamine again in the light of this new information.

Methodology

The 'rational scale' developed by Nutt and colleagues [22] was used as a framework for assessing the harms associated with ketamine use. This divides the harms associated with psychoactive substances into a matrix of nine under three broad categories, each with three subcategories: 'physical harms' (acute physical risks, chronic risks, propensity for intravenous use); 'dependence-related harms' (acute pleasure, risk of physical dependence, propensity for psychological dependence) and 'social harms' (acute social harms of intoxication, harms to the individual within society, costs to the health service).

A comprehensive search syntax was developed using indexed keywords (e.g. MeSH). The following databases were searched: MEDLINE, PsycINFO, Web of Knowledge and Google Scholar. The outputs of searches were considered against pre-specified inclusion and exclusion criteria. Initially all evidence was reviewed to September 2010. Conclusions were drawn from studies on the basis of a pre-defined hierarchy of research design:

- Level 1: Pre-existing systematic research syntheses of clinical data (systematic reviews, meta-analyses, syntheses of qualitative data)
- Level 2: Controlled observational studies (cohort studies, case–control studies, etc.)
- Level 3: Uncontrolled observational evidence (case reports and case series)
- Level 4: Pre-clinical data

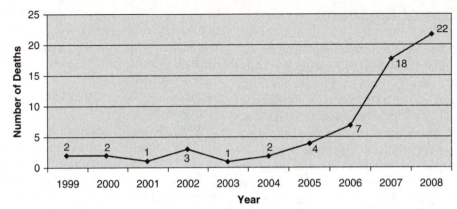

Figure 1 UK post-mortem toxicology mentions of ketamine in the United Kingdom 1999–2008 [105]; additional data courtesy of Dr J. Corkery]

Preferred evidence was levels 1 and 2, but due to the limited research on ketamine, levels 3 and 4 data were also included. Authors were also contacted where necessary for clarification and any new data. Additionally, sweeps of drug user forum sites, using the same search criteria, were made to monitor any mentions of ketamine harms not noted in the scientific literature.

A Note on Terminology: Frequency of Ketamine Use

There is a very marked variation in how often individuals use ketamine. Much published research has used the term 'ketamine addict', 'heavy user' or 'frequent user' without fully defining what is meant in terms of frequency, dose or duration of use. In this review, the terms given within the particular published articles have been used. The terms 'recreational ketamine user' and 'infrequent user' generally refer to non-dependent ketamine users whose use is confined predominantly to weekends.

Physical and Psychological Harms
Acute Physical Risks
Safety Ratio

One of the ways in which the acute physical risk associated with a drug is assessed is the 'safety ratio'. For drugs of abuse, this is the ratio of a usual recreational dose to a fatal or lethal dose (LD). Gable [23] gave ketamine a safety ratio of 25 based on reports that the rodent oral ketamine median lethal dose (LD_{50}: the dose of a drug that produces death in 50% of experimental animals tested) averaged around 600 mg/kg [24] or approximately 4.2 g for a 70 kg human (although other papers with mice suggest it may be much lower at 42.9mg/kg [25]. Rodent data were reduced by a factor of 10 to take into account interspecies differences. This also assumed a greater human oral LD_{50} of 4.2 g, with

an oral recreational dose of 175 mg [26]. It is important to emphasize that all these estimates are extrapolated from rodent data and based on oral doses.

Risk of Death from an Acute Dose

In humans, ketamine has a wide margin of safety, with no adverse outcomes reported even in medical settings of marked overdose [27]. Green et al. [28] reported no adverse outcomes in nine cases in which children in emergency departments were injected inadvertently with five to 100 times the intended dose. This may reflect special properties of ketamine anaesthesia whereby patients are able to maintain their own airway, and so it can be used safely in special populations and circumstances such as in the 'field'. These respiratory properties reduce the potential risks for the recreational user. Coughing and swallowing reflexes are also maintained, again protecting recreational users from harm because there is no suppression of the gag reflex even when extremely intoxicated.

Other data, shown in Fig. 1, reported the number of unexplained deaths in the United Kingdom between 1999 and 2008 in which ketamine was mentioned. Although the levels are low, they increased 10-fold over this period. In the majority of cases, ketamine was mentioned alongside a range of other psychotropics. Further, these data should also be evaluated cautiously, because toxicology screens are only performed in two-thirds of cases and among these, ketamine is not tested routinely.

Acute Physical Risk of Death from Accidents

Both Jansen [29] and Stewart [30] concluded that accidental death when intoxicated was the highest mortality risk. Two frequent ketamine users from a sample of 30 in a longitudinal study by Morgan et al. [31] died between baseline testing and 12-month follow-up as a result of their acute ketamine use—one through drowning in a bath and one of hypothermia.

Despite anecdotal reports of a high risk of accidental injury while acutely intoxicated with ketamine, due largely to the dissociation and analgesia (e.g. [32,33]), there are sparse scientific data on this risk. Because ketamine is a powerful analgesic, the intoxicated user is more vulnerable to being damaged. One case study reported a hospital worker who had injected ketamine collapsing with their face on an electric fire and suffering third-degree burns (cf. [34]). Muetzelfeldt et al. [35] found that of 90 ketamine users, 13% reported personally being involved in an accident as a direct result of taking ketamine, whereas 83% knew someone who had. An important harm reduction message is therefore that those acutely intoxicated with ketamine should not be left alone in case of accidents as well as being accompanied by someone who has not taken the drug.

Acute Ketamine Poisoning and ER Admissions

The UK National Poisons Unit provides information for doctors on poisons in their TOXBASE website. Of 570 000 TOXBASE hits in 2008/2009, 0.3% were ketamine-related (1710 cases), a sixfold increase from 2000 (0.05%; 285 cases).

There are currently few data on the number of emergency room (ER) presentations of patients with ketamine toxicity. In a London teaching hospital, Wood et al. [36] recorded 116 ER presentations involving recreational ketamine use, only 11% of which involved ketamine alone [co-ingested drugs included ethanol (39%), gamma hydroxy-butyrate/gamma-butyrolactone (GHB/GBL) (47%), cocaine (19%) and 3,4-methylenedioxymethamphetamine (MDMA) (53%)]. Most cases (72%) were discharged directly from the ED, and no case where ketamine alone had been ingested required admission to critical care.

Ng et al. [37] reviewed 233 cases of ER presentations of ketamine users in Hong Kong. Users had an average age of 22 years, two-thirds were male and the most common presenting symptoms were: impaired consciousness (45%); abdominal pain (21%); lower urinary tract symptoms (12%); and dizziness (12%), suggesting a lack of severe acute physical health consequences. The most common physical 'symptoms' reported as helping to identify acute ketamine intoxication were high blood pressure (40%), tachycardia (39%), abdominal tenderness (18%) and white powder in the nostrils (17%).

Acute Cardiac Risks from Ketamine Use

Ketamine stimulates the cardiovascular system leading to increased heart rate, cardiac output and blood pressure. Therefore, taking ketamine may present an acute risk for people with hypertension and severe cardiac disease, those at risk of a stroke or with raised intracranial pressure. Acute cardiac risk is increased when ketamine is taken in conjunction with stimulant drugs.

Chronic Physical and Psychological Effects of Ketamine
Ketamine-induced Ulcerative Cystitis

Ketamine-induced ulcerative cystitis is a recently identified condition which can have a severe and potentially long-lasting impact on the individual. Shahani et al. [38] first documented cases in nine dependent ketamine users, describing symptoms such as frequency and urgency of urination, dysuria, urge incontinence and occasionally painful haematuria (blood in urine). Computerized tomography (CT) scans of these individuals revealed a marked thickening of the bladder wall, a small bladder capacity and perivesicular stranding consistent with severe inflammation. At cystoscopy all patients had severe ulcerative cystitis. Biopsies in four of these cases found denuded urothelial mucosa with thin layers of reactive and regenerating epithelial cells and ulcerations with vascular granulation tissue and scattered inflammatory cells. Cessation of ketamine use provided some relief of symptoms.

Since then a number of case reports of ketamine-induced ulcerative cystitis have been published (e.g. [39,40]), all describing 'ketamine addicts' or 'near-daily' users. Oxley et al. [41] conducted a histopathology study of 17 'addicts' and suggested that ketamine mimics carcinoma in-situ and could increase the risk of bladder cancer. It is clearly important that young people presenting with urinary tract symptoms are asked about their drug use when no other causes are found.

A larger study of 59 'ketamine bladder' patients [42] found 42 (71%) had a cystoscopy that showed various degrees of epithelial inflammation similar to that seen in chronic interstitial cystitis. Urodynamically, either detrusor overactivity or decreased bladder compliance with or without vesico-ureteric reflux was detected to some degree in 47 patients and eight also had raised serum creatinine. Prevalence data are difficult to obtain. Of 90 UK ketamine users, 30% reported urinary tract symptoms while they used ketamine [35]. Among frequent users, nearly half had sought medical attention for ketamine-induced cystitis. Cottrell & Gillatt [43] suggest that the course of disease varies, with approximately one-third of cases resolving after stopping ketamine use, one-third remaining static and one-third worsening.

The aetiology of ketamine-induced ulcerative cystitis is unclear. It appears to be most common in those misusing the drug frequently, mainly daily, over an extended period. Ketamine is commonly administered as a few repeated doses in veterinary and medical anaesthesia and analgesia. We found only one case study reporting ketamine-induced ulcerative cystitis during its medical use—a 16-year-old treated for chronic pain [40]. Her urinary tract symptoms remitted completely following reduction of her of ketamine dose.

Kidney Dysfunction

Another emergent physical health problem associated with frequent, high-dose ketamine use appears to be hydronephrosis (water on the kidney) secondary to urinary tract problems. In their study of ketamine-induced ulcerative cystitis, Chu *et al.* [42] reported that 30 (51%) patients presented with either unilateral (7%) or bilateral (44%) hydronephrosis (water on the kidney). On the initial assessment four patients also showed papillary necrosis (destruction of kidney cells), and this led to renal failure in one, who had complete obstruction of the urethra.

'K-cramps'

A third of 90 ketamine users in one study spontaneously reported 'K-cramps'—intense abdominal pain—as a result of prolonged, heavy ketamine use [35]. Frequent ketamine users often report taking more ketamine to alleviate this pain and this can make attempts to quit using fail. The aetiology of K-cramps remains unclear, but three small case studies (one, three and two patients, respectively) have reported the existence of 'colicky' upper gastric pain in young ketamine users [44–46], all of whom also presented with abnormal liver function. CT scans of these patients found dilation of the common bile duct with a smooth tapered end, mimicking choledochal cysts (congenital conditions associated with benign cystic dilatation of bile ducts). These symptoms abated when the patients stopped using ketamine.

A larger study of ER presentations [46] also reported that 21% of ketamine patients presented with abdominal pains and 15% with abnormal liver function, which concur with these reports of biliary problems.

Among ketamine users there is a belief that 'K-cramps' or 'K-belly' arises from swallowing the drips when ketamine is snorted intranasally. Some harm reduction advice given on user forums (partvibe.org; drugforum.net; squatjuice.org) is not to swallow the drips. However, this advice would seem to be incorrect based on evidence reviewed above.

Depression

Increased depression (assessed with the Beck Depression Inventory) in both daily users and ex-ketamine users was found over the course of 1 year in our longitudinal study [31] but not in current infrequent (>1 per month, >3 times per week) users. However, this elevated depression was not at clinical levels and the increase was not correlated with changes in ketamine use.

In contrast, a preliminary study of seven patients suggested that one dose of ketamine can have rapid and relatively prolonged antidepressant effects in depressed patients who did not respond to usual treatments [47]. Enthusiasm for this approach was rekindled by a larger study of 18 treatment-resistant patients administered 0.5 mg/kg ketamine over 40 minutes [48]. Twelve of the patients showed an immediate 50% reduction in measures of depression compared with none of 14 patients given placebo. The anti-depressant effects of one dose lasted 1–2 weeks in eight patients, but they all relapsed thereafter, leading to calls for repeated ketamine treatment of depression (e.g. [8]). In the first clinical trial, Aan het Rot *et al.* [49] gave depressed patients six infusions of ketamine (on days 0, 3, 5, 8, 10 and 12). Of the nine patients who received repeated infusions (dependent upon their response to the first infusion), eight relapsed within an estimated mean 30 days after the first infusion or 19 days after the sixth infusion. The rapid response to ketamine contrasts with the 3–4-week lag in response to mainstream anti-depressants. However, the chronic effects of the drug should be monitored if repeated dosing is to be a strategy in the treatment of depression.

Psychosis

In healthy volunteers, one dose of ketamine induces transient positive and negative symptoms of schizophrenia (e.g. [50]). In schizophrenic patients who have been stabilized on antipsychotic medication, ketamine causes a resurgence of psychotic symptoms [51] which are remarkably similar to those each individual exhibited in the acute phase of their illness [52].

Pre-clinical studies giving small numbers (~ 5) of repeated doses of ketamine to rats have also found 'schizophrenia-like' changes such as abnormal hippocampal neurogenesis, particularly reductions in hippocampal parvalbumin containing GABAergic interneurons [53], as well as increased dopamine binding in the hippocampus and decreased glutamate binding in the prefrontal cortex [54]. Studies with infrequent (>1 per month <3 times per week) and daily ketamine users assessing subclinical psychotic symptomatology have found that scores on measures of delusions, dissociation and schizotypy are higher in daily ketamine users compared to infrequent users and in infrequent users compared to polydrug controls who do not use ketamine [31,55]. Morgan *et al.* [31] found that daily ketamine users showed a similar pattern of 'basic symptoms' to individuals prodromal for schizophrenia. However, there is no evidence of clinical psychotic symptoms in infrequent ketamine users [56]. Despite anecdotes (e.g. [32,34]), there is little evidence of any link between chronic, heavy use of ketamine and diagnosis of a psychotic disorder.

Cognitive Impairment

The NMDA receptor is thought to underpin the form of synaptic plasticity known as long-term potentiation, which is central for learning and memory. Given that the principle action of ketamine is at this NMDA receptor, the consequences of ketamine use on cognition have been fairly widely investigated. In humans, a single dose of ketamine induces marked, dose-dependent impairments in working and episodic memory which would impact profoundly on users' ability to function [57]. In mice, impaired fear memory (decreasing fear in a fear conditioning paradigm) has been found after 4 but not 2 weeks of daily injection of 5 mg/kg [58].

Several studies have examined cognitive function in infrequent and frequent ketamine users (e.g. [11,55,56,59–61]). Overall, infrequent or recreational ketamine use does not appear to be associated with long-term cognitive impairment (e.g. [56]). The most robust findings are that frequent ketamine users exhibit profound impairments in both short- and long-term memory (for review see [57]). Many studies have been cross-sectional and cannot address causation. However, in a longitudinal study, frequent ketamine use caused impairments in visual recognition and spatial working memory that correlated with changes in level of ketamine use over 12 months [30]. Other impairments in planning and frontal functions have been observed, but appear so far to be unrelated to measures of ketamine use [11]. Memory impairments may be reversible when individuals stop using the drug, as they were not found in a group of 30 ex-ketamine users who had been abstinent for at least a year. The cognitive consequences of repeated ketamine use in paediatric anaesthesia would also merit further investigation [62].

Neurological Changes

Increased D1 receptor binding in the right dorsolateral prefrontal cortex of ketamine users has been reported, indicating upregulation of dopaminergic receptors [56]. White matter abnormalities have been observed in ketamine addicts compared to controls [63]. Reduced fractional anisotropy correlated with the degree of ketamine use in the bilateral frontal and left temporoparietal regions. However, similar changes have been observed in other drug-dependent populations [64], so these may not be specific effects of ketamine. There were also small changes in the temporal region that may relate to the drug's impairment of episodic memory.

Dependence-Related Harms
Acute Pleasure Associated with Taking the Drug
Neurochemical Actions

Dopaminergic modulation may underpin the reinforcing properties of many recreational drugs (e.g. [65]). Acutely, ketamine increases extracellular dopamine (DA) concentrations in the rat striatum and prefrontal cortex [66] and some positron emission tomography (PET) studies in humans have shown that it elicits striatal DA release [67–69].

Ketamine also interacts with μ-opioid receptors and non-opioid σ receptor sites, which may also relate to its rewarding properties, although affinity of the drug for these receptors is relatively low. There has been a suggestion that different isoforms of ketamine may have different neurochemical and

possibly reinforcing properties [33]. S + ketamine has a much greater affinity for the NMDA-receptor, and R- ketamine has a greater opioid action.

Pharmacokinetic Parameters and Route of Administration

The most common way in which ketamine is taken recreationally is 'snorted' intranasally, like cocaine. In the United States intravenous use of ketamine is rare even among injecting users of other drugs [70]. Insufflation of ketamine leads to a relatively rapid (~ 5 minutes) onset of effects on the brain. A rapid 'high' is thought to increase the abuse potential of a substance. In addition, the short half-life of ketamine (1–2 hours) may both promote bingeing and increase its appeal over longer-lasting hallucinogens such as lysergic acid diethylamide (LSD) or 'magic' mushrooms [71].

Acute Reinforcing Effects in Animals and Humans

Pre-clinical findings suggest clear similarities between ketamine and other addictive drugs in a wide range of behavioural paradigms. Rats will self-administer ketamine [72,73], show conditioned place preference [74] and locomotor sensitization following repeated doses has been observed [75–77]. Furthermore, ketamine substitutes for ethanol in drug discrimination paradigms in rats [78,79]. Humans dependent on alcohol show enhanced NMDA receptor function [80], and in recently detoxified alcoholics ketamine produces ethanol-like subjective effects, including a 'high'[81].

Studies with healthy volunteers have found that ketamine increases subjective ratings of 'high'[82] and this relates to its abuse potential. In one study, subanaesthetic doses (0.4 mg/kg and 0.8 mg/kg) or placebo were infused intravenously to healthy, ketamine-naive volunteers [83]. They rated how much they 'liked' the drug and 'wanted more' of it. An inverted U-shaped dose–response curve was found. Shortly after the infusion started, they both liked and wanted more of both doses. Towards the end of the 80-minute infusion, these ratings had markedly reduced in the high-dose group, whereas the low-dose group still liked and wanted more of the drug.

Psychological and Physical Dependence
Incidence of Ketamine Dependence

There are some case reports of ketamine dependence in the literature (e.g. [84–87]) but no large-scale studies, and so the incidence of ketamine dependence is unknown. An interview study of 90 ketamine users found that 57% of frequent users, 43% of infrequent users and 60% of ex-users expressed concerns about ketamine addiction [35]. The majority of frequent users in that study reported using the drug without stopping until supplies ran out, so compulsive patterns of behaviour are also a concern.

Withdrawal Symptoms Following Abstinence

There is conflicting evidence of the existence of a 'withdrawal syndrome' following cessation of ketamine use. Cravings seem to be a key problem in frequent users: 28 of the 30 daily users in a study by Morgan et al. [88] reported having tried to stop taking the drug but failed; all reported ketamine cravings as the reason for failure. The same study found 12 of the 30 daily users reported withdrawal symptoms characterized by anxiety, shaking, sweating and palpitations when they stopped using. A few published case studies also show craving and somatic and psychological aspects of anxiety as withdrawal symptoms [89–91]. However, a specific ketamine withdrawal syndrome has not yet been described.

Tolerance

The need for increasing doses is one index of a substance's addictive potential. Studies with rats [92] and monkeys [93] as well as children undergoing anaesthesia (e.g. [94]) have convincingly demonstrated a rapid development of tolerance—'tachyphylaxis'—with repeated ketamine dosing. This may be due to induction of liver enzymes [95]. It is also possible that it reflects neuronal adaptations in receptor numbers or receptor sensitivity.

Frequent ketamine users report escalating doses over time, with one study finding a 600% increase from first use to current use [88]. Objective data from hair analyses showed a doubling of ketamine concentrations in hair over a year in infrequent ketamine users [31]. Frequent users' hair ketamine did not change, but they were probably already using maximal amounts.

Social Harms of Ketamine
Social Harms of Intoxication
Risk of Accidental Injury

As a dissociative anaesthetic, ketamine can render an individual oblivious to their environment. This puts the user not only at risk of accidental injury to themselves, as already discussed, but also more vulnerable to assault by others. Ketamine also impairs psychomotor performance dose-dependently, such as hand–eye movement coordination and balance [96]. This increases the risks of causing accidents in complex motor tasks such as driving. Over a 4-year period, 21% of fatal vehicle crashes in Hong Kong involved alcohol or drugs and 9% of those involved ketamine [97]. Recreational users often seek out safe 'chill-out' areas to consume the drug and reduce risks [71], whereas more dependent users report using the drug in most situations, including while driving [35].

Risk-taking Behaviour

Ketamine use has been found to be associated with an increased incidence of unsafe sex among gay men in the United States (e.g. [98]). Ketamine is not associated with violent behaviour, so the risk of social violence is not increased [21].

Harms to the Ketamine User within Society

There is little information about the degree to which ketamine use affects users' place within society. For frequent users, most social risks are similar to those of any addictive illegal drug such as disruptions to education and employment.

Educational and Professional Achievement

Dependent ketamine users in the United Kingdom are often part of subcultures, such as the 'traveller' and 'free party' scenes, that may have limited interest in participating in mainstream society [99,100]. Irrespective of their ketamine use, many of their educational and professional achievements may have differed from the norm. At present there are no data on how ketamine dependence impacts on achievement. An interview study of 100 recreational users found that 20% perceived employment related problems to result from their ketamine use [101]. Morgan et al. [31] found that frequent/daily users had spent significantly fewer years in education than infrequent or non-users.

Engagement in Criminal Activities

The degree to which ketamine may lead users towards criminal activities to fund their use is unknown, partly as there are no drug treatment orders for ketamine use. Since its classification, ketamine smuggling has become an organized crime and the drug's street price has decreased [15]. There were 1266 ketamine seizures in 2008/09 in the UK and arrests for ketamine appear to be increasing [102].

Ketamine Use in Pregnancy

No data on human use of ketamine in pregnancy were available. Research with rats has shown that cocaine and a combination of cocaine and ketamine reduced fetal birth weight but not ketamine alone [103].

Cost to the Health Service

The majority of costs will stem from chronic physical health problems. In particular, ketamine-induced ulcerative cystitis is associated with a variety of costly procedures, as symptoms may be difficult to manage. A number of cystoscopies may be required, as well as catheterization of the bladder for symptomatic relief, and in severe cases, bladder reconstruction or ultimately cystectomy (bladder removal; [43]). In such cases the patient will need to be followed-up for life, at a very high cost to the health service. Treatment of ketamine dependence may be another emerging cost.

Discussion

After nearly 50 years of medical use, ketamine still occupies a unique place in the pharmacological tool boxes of anaesthetists, pain clinicians and veterinarians [104]. More recent research suggests that it may potentially have other clinical applications, including treatment of resistant depression [7]. It is also an important experimental compound used in medical research.

At the same time, this review has highlighted a number of harms stemming from the chronic, recreational use of ketamine. Of most concern is ketamine-induced ulcerative cystitis which appears more common in, but is not restricted to, those using the drug on a frequent, often daily basis. It is important that young people presenting with urinary tract symptoms are asked about drug use when no other causes are found. Key questions which research needs to address are what mechanisms lead to this condition and why do some users develop it while others do not?

There is also concern that some individuals develop dependence, although the incidence of this is currently hard to gauge. Although a specific withdrawal syndrome has not yet been identified, tolerance to the drug develops rapidly. Many daily users report having tried but failed to stop using ketamine. Anecdotally, we have encountered many frequent users who have difficulties stopping the drug and yet cannot gain access to drug treatment services in the United Kingdom.

There is a need for joined-up treatment of those who have developed ketamine-induced ulcerative cystitis. Urological interventions should be coordinated with psychosocial interventions that promote future abstinence from the drug.

Young people should be made aware of the long-term physical risks of using ketamine. Ulcerative cystitis and loss of bladder control do not mesh well with desirable images of being young and attractive, and so a strong harm-reduction message could be constructed. Similarly, users should minimize the risk of accidental injury or death by ensuring that intoxicated friends are always accompanied by others who are not intoxicated. In a similar vein, the potential of neurological and cognitive changes following frequent use of the drug should be communicated and implications stressed for poor performance at school, college or work. The long-term neurological, neurocognitive and psychiatric effects must be investigated further in longitudinal designs which also follow-up on those who subsequently stop using ketamine. Such studies could ideally be interdisciplinary and allow further investigation of ketamine's physical effects, including K-cramps and effects on kidney function.

There is variation across the world in the legal status of ketamine. The current classification of ketamine in the United Kingdom under the Misuse of Drugs Act (Class C) suggests that its harms are less severe than some other drugs such as cannabis (class B) or ecstasy (class A). Our review of the scientific evidence suggests that this classification of ketamine does not reflect accurately its known and potentially severe harms. At the same time, there is currently little evidence that changing a drug's legal classification impacts on drug users' behaviours; in fact, since classification the prevalence of ketamine has increased and cost decreased, and a more stringent classification would present many practical hurdles for the legitimate, medical use of ketamine.

Declaration of Interest
None.

Critical Thinking

1. What are the dangers of using the drug Ketamine?
2. Why has its popularity increased in recent years?
3. Discuss the legitimate uses of the drug.

References

1. Rabiner E. A. Imaging of striatal dopamine release elicited with NMDA antagonists: is there anything there to be seen? *J Psychopharmacol* 2007; **21:** 253–8.
2. Oye I., Paulsen O., Maurset A. Effects of ketamine on sensory perception: evidence for a role of N-methyl-D-aspartate receptors. *J Pharmacol Exp Ther* 1992; **260:** 1209–13.
3. Sunder R. A., Toshniwal G., Dureja G. P. Ketamine as an adjuvant in sympathetic blocks for management of central sensitization following peripheral nerve injury. *J Brachial Plex Peripher Nerve Inj* 2008; **3:** 22–8.
4. Lynch M. E., Clark A. J., Sawynok J., Sullivan M. J. Topical amitriptyline and ketamine in neuropathic pain syndromes: an open-label study. *J Pain* 2005; **6:** 644–9.
5. Correll G. E., Maleki J., Gracely E. J., Muir J. J., Harbut R. E. Subanesthetic ketamine infusion therapy: a retrospective analysis of a novel therapeutic approach to complex regional pain syndrome. *Pain Med* 2004; **5:** 263–75.
6. Fujikawa D. G. Neuroprotective effect of ketamine administered after status epilepticus onset. *Epilepsia* 1995; **36:** 186–95.
7. Aroni F., Iacovidou N., Dontas I., Pourzitaki C., Xanthos T. Pharmacological aspects and potential new clinical applications of ketamine: reevaluation of an old drug. *J Clin Pharmacol* 2009; **49:** 957–64.
8. Krystal J. H. Ketamine and the potential role for rapid-acting antidepressant medications. *Swiss Med Wkly* 2007; **137:** 215–6.
9. Krupitsky E. M., Grinenko A. Y. Ketamine psychedelic therapy (KPT): a review of the results of ten years of research. *J Psychoact Drugs* 1997; **29;** 165–83.
10. Fletcher P. C., Honey G. D. Schizophrenia, ketamine and cannabis: evidence of overlapping memory deficits. *Trends Cogn Sci* 2006; 10: 167–74.
11. Morgan C. J., Muetzelfeldt L., Curran H. V. Ketamine use, cognition and psychological wellbeing: a comparison of frequent, infrequent and ex-users with polydrug and non-using controls. *Addiction* 2009; **104:** 77–87.

12. Siegel R. K. Phencyclidine and ketamine intoxication: a study of four populations of recreational users. *NIDA Res Monogr* 1978; **21:** 119–47.

13. Dalgarno P. J., Shewan D. Illicit use of ketamine in Scotland. *J Psychoact Drugs* 1996; **28:** 191–9.

14. United Nations Office on Drug Control (UNODC). *World Drug Report 2010.* New York: United Nations Publications; 2010. United Nations Publication Sales no. E.10.XI.132010. Available from http://www.unodc.org /unodc/en/data-and-analysis/WDR-2010.html (accessed 19 July 2011; archived by Webcite at http://www .webcitation.org/60IJkzhGx).

15. DrugScope. K mart. *Druglink* 2009; **24:** 4–7.

16. Hoare J. Drug misuse declared: findings from the 2008/09 British Crime Survey England and Wales. Home Office Statistical Board. London: Home Office; 2009.

17. Hoare J., Moon D. Drug misuse declared: findings from the 2009/10. British Crime Survey England and Wales. Home Office Statistical Board. London: Home Office; 2010.

18. Johnston L. D., O'Malley P. M., Bachman J. G., Schulenberg J. E. *Monitoring the Future National Results on Adolescent Drug Use: Overview of Key Findings, 2009.* Bethesda, MD: National Institute on Drug Abuse; 2010.

19. McCambridge J., Winstock A., Hunt N., Mitcheson L. 5-Year trends in use of hallucinogens and other adjunct drugs among UK dance drug users. *Eur Addict Res* 2007; **13:** 57–64.

20. Dick D., Torrance C. MixMag drugs survey. *Mix Mag* 2010; **2010:**44–53.

21. L; Nutt D, King L. A. ACMD Technical Committee: Report on Ketamine. London: Home Office; 2004. Home Office. Available from http://www.homeoffice.gov, uk /publications/alcohol-drugs/drugs/acmdl/ketamine-report .pdf?view=Binary. (accessed 19 July 2011; archived by WebCite al htlp://www.webcitation.org/60HvqMVlK).

22. Nutt D., King L. A., Saulsbury W., Blakemore C. Development of a rational scale to assess the harm of drugs of potential misuse. *Lancet* 2007; **369:** 1047–53.

23. Gable R. S. Acute toxic effects of club drugs. *J Psychoact Drugs* 2004; **36:** 303–13.

24. Derelanko M. J., Hollinger M. A. *CRC Handbook of Toxicology.* Boca Raton, FL: CRC Press; 1995.

25. Ben-Shlomo I, Rosenbaum A., Hadash O., Katz Y. Intravenous midazolam significantly enhances the lethal effect of thiopental but not that of ketamine in mice. *Pharmacol Res* 2001; **44:** 509–12.

26. Hansen G., Jensen S. B., Chandresh L., Hilden T. The psychotropic effect of ketamine. *J Psychoact Drugs* 1988; **20:** 419–25.

27. Long H. N. L. S., Hofmann R. S. Ketamine medication error resulting in death. *J Toxicol Clin Toxicol* 2002; **40:** 1.

28. Green S. M., Clark R., Hostetler M. A., Cohen M., Carlson D., Rothrock S. G. Inadvertent ketamine overdose in children: clinical manifestations and outcome. *Ann Emerg Med* 1999; **34:** 492–7.

29. Jansen K. L. A review of the nonmedical use of ketamine: use, users and consequences. *J Psychoact Drugs* 2000; **32:** 419–33.

30. Stewart C. E. Ketamine as a street drug. *Emerg Med Serv* 2001: **30:** 30. 2, 4 passim.

31. Morgan C. J., Muetzelfeldt L., Curran H. V. Consequences of chronic ketamine self-administration upon neurocognitive function and psychological wellbeing: a 1-year longitudinal study. *Addiction* 2010; **105:** 121–33.

32. Lilly J. *The Scientist: A Novel Autobiography.* New York: J.B. Lippincott; 1978.

33. Moore M., Altounian H. *Journeys into the Bright World.* Rockport, MA: Para Research Inc.; 1978.

34. Jansen K. *Ketamine: Dreams and Realities.* Sarasota, FL: Multidisciplinary Association for Psychedelic Studies; 2001.

35. Muetzelfeldt L., Kamboj S. K., Rees H., Taylor J., Morgan C. J., Curran H. V. Journey through the K-hole: phenomenological aspects of ketamine use. *Drug Alcohol Depend* 2008; **95:** 219–29.

36. Wood D. M., Nicolaou M., Dargan P. I. Epidemiology of recreational drug toxicity in a nightclub environment. *Subst Use Misuse* 2009; **44:** 1495–502.

37. Ng S. H., Tse M. L., Ng H. W., Lau F. L. Emergency department presentation of ketamine abusers in Hong Kong: a review of 233 cases. *Hong Kong Med J* 2010; **16:** 6–11.

38. Shahani R., Streutker C, Dickson B., Stewart R. J. Ketamine-associated ulcerative cystitis: a new clinical entity. *Urology* 2007: **69:** 810–2.

39. Cottrell A., Warren K., Ayres R., Weinstock P., Kumar V., Gillatt D. The destruction of the lower urinary tract by ketamine abuse: a new syndrome? *BJU Int* 2008; **102:** 1178–9; author reply 9.

40. Gregoire M. C., MacLellan D. L., Finley G. A. A pediatric case of ketamine-associated cystitis [Letter to the Editor re: Shahani R, Streutker C, Dickson B *et al.* Ketamine-associated ulcerative cystitis: a new clinical entity. *Urology* 2007; 69: 810–812]. *Urology* 2008; **71:** 1232–3.

41. Oxley J. D., Cottrell A. M., Adams S., Gillatt D. Ketamine cystitis as a mimic of carcinoma in situ. *Histopathology* 2009; **55:** 705–8.

42. Chu P. S., Ma W. K., Wong S. C., Chu R. W., Cheng C. H., Wong S. *et al.* The destruction of the lower urinary tract by ketamine abuse: a new syndrome? *BJU Int* 2008; **102:** 1616–22.

43. Cottrell A. M., Gillatt D. Consider ketamine misuse in patients with urinary symptoms. *Practitioner* 2008; **252:** 5.

44. Wong S. W., Lee K. F., Wong J., Ng W. W., Cheung Y. S., Lai P. B. Dilated common bile ducts mimicking choledochal cysts in ketamine abusers. *Hong Kong Med J* 2009; **15:** 53–6.

45. Selby N. M., Anderson J., Bungay P., Chesterton L., Kohle N. V. Obstructive nephropathy and kidney injury associated with ketamine abuse. *NDT Plus* 2008; **1:** 2.

46. Ng S. H., Lee H. K., Chan Y. C., Lau F. L. Dilated common bile ducts in ketamine abusers. *Hong Kong Med J* 2009; **15:** 157. author reply.

47. Berman R. M., Cappiello A., Anand A., Oren D. A., Heninger G. R., Charney D. S. *et al.* Antidepressant effects of ketamine in depressed patients. *Biol Psychiatry* 2000; **47:** 351–4.

48. Zarate C. A. Jr, Singh J. B., Carlson P. J., Brutsche N. E., Ameli R., Luckenbaugh D. A. *et al.* A randomized trial of an N-methyl-D-aspartate antagonist in treatment-resistant major depression. *Arch Gen Psychiatry* 2006; **63:** 856–64.

49. Aan het Rot M., Collins K. A., Murrough J. W., Perez A. M., Reich D. L., Charney D. S. *et al.* Safety and efficacy of repeated-dose intravenous ketamine for treatment-resistant depression. *Biol Psychiatry* 2010; **67:** 139–45,

50. Krystal J. H., Karper L. P., Seibyl J. P., Freeman G. K., Delaney R., Bremner J. D. *et al.* Subanesthetic effects of the noncompetitive NMDA antagonist, ketamine, in humans. Psychotomimetic, perceptual, cognitive, and neuroendocrine responses. *Arch Gen Psychiatry* 1994; **51:** 199–214.

51. Lahti A. C., Koffel B., LaPorte D., Tamminga C. A. Subanesthetic doses of ketamine stimulate psychosis in schizophrenia. *Neuropsychopharmacology* 1995; **13:** 9–19.

52. Malhotra A. K., Pinals D. A., Adler C. M., Elman I., Clifton A., Pickar D. et al. Ketamine-induced exacerbation of psychotic symptoms and cognitive impairment in neuroleptic-free schizophrenics. *Neuropsychopharmacology* 1997; **17:** 141–50.

53. Keilhoff G., Bernstein H. G., Becker A., Grecksch G., Wolf G. Increased neurogenesis in a rat ketamine model of schizophrenia. *Biol Psychiatry* 2004; **56:** 317–22.

54. Becker A., Peters B., Schroeder H., Mann T., Huether G., Grecksch G. Ketamine-induced changes in rat behaviour: a possible animal model of schizophrenia. *Prog Neuropsy-chopharmacol Biol Psychiatry* 2003; **27:** 687–700.

55. Curran H. V., Morgan C. Cognitive, dissociative and psychotogenic effects of ketamine in recreational users on the night of drug use and 3 days later. *Addiction* 2000; **95:** 575–90.

56. Narendran R., Frankle W. G., Keefe R., Gil R., Martinez D., Slifstein M. *et al.* Altered prefrontal dopaminergic function in chronic recreational ketamine users. *Am J Psychiatry* 2005; **162:** 2352–9.

57. Morgan C. J., Curran H. V. Acute and chronic effects of ketamine upon human memory: a review. *Psychopharmacology (Berl)* 2006; **188:** 408–24.

58. Amann L. C., Halene T. B., Ehrlichman R. S., Luminais S. N., Ma N., Abel T. *et al.* Chronic ketamine impairs fear conditioning and produces long-lasting reductions in auditory evoked potentials. *Neurobiol Dis* 2009; **35:** 311–7.

59. Curran H. V., Monaghan L. In and out of the K-hole: a comparison of the acute and residual effects of ketamine in frequent and infrequent ketamine users. *Addiction* 2001; **96:** 749–60.

60. Morgan C. J., Perry E. B., Cho H. S., Krystal J. H., D'Souza D. C. Greater vulnerability to the amnestic effects of ketamine in males. *Psychopharmacology (Berl)* 2006; **187:** 405–14.

61. Morgan C. J., Rossell S. L., Pepper F., Smart J., Blackburn J., Brandner B. *et al.* Semantic priming after ketamine acutely in healthy volunteers and following chronic self-administration in substance users. *Biol Psychiatry* 2006; **59:** 265–72.

62. Istaphanous G. K., Loepke A. W. General anesthetics and the developing brain. *Curr Opin Anaesthesiol* 2009; **22:** 368–73.

63. Liao Y., Tang J., Ma M., Wu Z., Yang M., Wang X. *et al.* Frontal white matter abnormalities following chronic ketamine use: a diffusion tensor imaging study. *Brain* 2010; **133:** 2115–22.

64. Nestler E. J. Is there a common molecular pathway for addiction? *Nat Neurosci* 2005; **8:** 1445–9.

65. Robinson T. E., Berridge K. C. The neural basis of drug craving: an incentive-sensitization theory of addiction. *Brain Res Brain Res Rev* 1993; **18:** 247–91.

66. Moghaddam B., Adams B., Verma A., Daly D. Activation of glutamatergic neurotransmission by ketamine: a novel step in the pathway from NMDA receptor blockade to dopaminergic and cognitive disruptions associated with the prefrontal cortex. *J Neurosci* 1997; **17:** 2921–7.

67. Breier A., Malhotra A. K., Pinals D. A., Weisenfeld N. I., Pickar D. Association of ketamine-induced psychosis with focal activation of the prefrontal cortex in healthy volunteers. *Am J Psychiatry* 1997; **154:** 805–11.

68. Smith G. S., Schloesser R., Brodie J. D., Dewey S. L., Logan J., Vitkun S. A. *et al.* Glutamate modulation of dopamine measured *in vivo* with positron emission tomography (PET) and 11C-raclopride in normal human subjects. *Neuropsy-chopharmacology* 1998; **18:** 18–25.

69. Vollenweider F. X., Leenders K. L., Scharfetter C., Antonini A., Maguire P., Missimer J. *et al.* Metabolic hyperfrontality and psychopathology in the ketamine model of psychosis using positron emission tomography (PET) and [18F]fluorodeoxyglucose (FDG). *Eur Neuropsychopharmacol* 1997; **7:** 9–24.

70. Lankenau S. E., Bloom J. J., Shin C. Longitudinal trajectories of ketamine use among young injection drug users. *Int J Drug Policy* 2010; **21**: 306–14.

71. Moore K., Measham F. 'It's the most fun you can have for twenty quid': meanings, motivations, and consequences of British ketamine use. *Addict Res Theory* 2008; **16**: 13.

72. Winger G., Hursh S. R., Casey K. L., Woods J. H. Relative reinforcing strength of three N-methyl-D-aspartate antagonists with different onsets of action, *J Pharmacol Exp Ther* 2002; **301**: 690–7.

73. Marquis K. L., Webb M. G., Moreton J. E. Effects of fixed ratio size and dose on phencyclidine self-administration by rats. *Psychopharmacology (Berl)* 1989; **97**: 179–82.

74. Suzuki T, Kato H., Aoki T., Tsuda M., Narita M., Misawa M. Effects of the non-competitive NMDA receptor antagonist ketamine on morphine-induced place preference in mice. *Life Sci* 2000; **67**: 383–9.

75. Meyer P. J., Phillips T. J. Behavioral sensitization to ethanol does not result in cross-sensitization to NMDA receptor antagonists. *Psychopharmacology (Berl)* 2007; **195**: 103–15.

76. Trujillo K. A., Zamora J. J., Warmoth K. P. Increased response to ketamine following treatment at long intervals: implications for intermittent use. *Biol Psychiatry* 2008; **63**: 178–83.

77. Wiley J. L., Evans R. L., Grainger D. B., Nicholson K. L. Age-dependent differences in sensitivity and sensitization to cannabinoids and 'club drugs' in male adolescent and adult rats. *Addict Biol* 2008; **13**: 277–86,

78. Shelton K. L. Substitution profiles of N-methyl-D-aspartate antagonists in ethanol-discriminating inbred mice. *Alcohol* 2004; **34**: 165–75.

79. Harrison Y. E., Jenkins J. A., Rocha B. A., Lytle D. A., Jung M. E., Oglesby M. W. Discriminative stimulus effects of diazepam, ketamine and their mixture: ethanol substitution patterns. *Behav Pharmacol* 1998; **9**: 31–40.

80. Krystal J. H., Petrakis I. L., Limoncelli D., Nappi S. K., Trevisan L., Pittman B. *et al.* Characterization of the interactive effects of glycine and d-cycloserine in men: further evidence for enhanced NMDA receptor function associated with human alcohol dependence. *Neuropsychopharmacology* 2011; **36**: 701–10.

81. Krystal J. H., Petrakis I. L., Webb E., Cooney N. L., Karper L. P., Namanworth S. *et al.* Dose-related ethanol-like effects of the NMDA antagonist, ketamine, in recently detoxified alcoholics. *Arch Gen Psychiatry* 1998; **55**: 354–60.

82. Krystal J. H., D'Souza D. C., Karper L. P., Bennett A., Abi-Dargham A., Abi-Saab D. *et al.* Interactive effects of subanesthetic ketamine and haloperidol in healthy humans. *Psychopharmacology (Berl)* 1999; **145**: 193–204.

83. Morgan C. J., Mofeez A., Brandner B., Bromley L., Curran H. V. Ketamine impairs response inhibition and is positively reinforcing in healthy volunteers: a dose-response study. *Psychopharmacology (Berl)* 2004; **172**: 298–308.

84. Pal H. R., Berry N., Kumar R., Ray R. Ketamine dependence. *Anaesth Intensive Care* 2002; **30**: 382–4.

85. Hurt P. H., Ritchie E. C. A case of ketamine dependence. *Am J Psychiatry* 1994; **151**: 779.

86. Jansen K. L. Ketamine—can chronic use impair memory? *Int J Addict* 1990; **25**: 133–9.

87. Moore N. N., Bostwick J. M. Ketamine dependence in anesthesia providers. *Psychosomatics* 1999; **40**: 356–9.

88. Morgan C. J., Rees H., Curran H. V. Attentional bias to incentive stimuli in frequent ketamine users. *Psychol Med* 2008; **38**: 1331–40.

89. Blachut M., Solowiow K., Janus A., Ruman J., Cekus A., Matysiakiewicz J. *et al.* A case of ketamine dependence. *Psychiatr Pol* 2009; **43**: 593–9.

90. Critchlow D. G. A case of ketamine dependence with discontinuation symptoms. *Addiction* 2006: **101**: 1212–3.

91. Lim D. K. Ketamine associated psychedelic effects and dependence. *Singapore Med J* 2003; **44**: 31–4.

92. Cumming J. F. The development of an acute tolerance to ketamine. *Anesth Analg* 1976; **55**: 788–91.

93. Bree M. M., Feller I., Corssen G. Safety and tolerance of repeated anesthesia with CI 581 (ketamine) in monkeys. *Anesth Analg* 1967; **46**: 596–600.

94. Byer D. E., Gould A. B. Jr. Development of tolerance to ketamine in an infant undergoing repeated anesthesia. *Anesthesiology* 1981; **54**: 255–6.

95. Livingston A., Waterman A. E. The development of tolerance to ketamine in rats and the significance of hepatic metabolism. *Br J Pharmacol [In Vitrof]* 1978; **64**: 6.3–9.

96. Lofwall M. R., Griffiths R. R., Mintzer M. Z. Cognitive and subjective acute dose effects of intramuscular ketamine in healthy adults. *Exp Clin Psychopharmacol* 2006; **14**: 439–49.

97. Cheng W. C, Ng K. M., Chan K. K., Mok V. K., Cheung B. K. Roadside detection of impairment under the influence of ketamine—evaluation of ketamine impairment symptoms with reference to its concentration in oral fluid and urine. *Forensic Sci Int* 2007; **170**: 51–8.

98. Darrow W. W., Biersteker S., Geiss T., Chevalier K., Clark J., Marrero Y. *et al.* Risky sexual behaviors associated with recreational drug use among men who have sex with men in an international resort area: challenges and opportunities. *J Urban Health* 2005; **82**: 601–9.

99. Newcombe R. Ketamine case study: the phenomenology of a ketamine experience. *Addict Res Theory* 2008; **16**: 6.

100. Riley S. Ketamine: the divisive dissociative. A discourse analysis of the constructions of ketamine by participants of a free party (rave) scene. *Addict Res Theory* 2008; **16**: 13.

101. Dillon P., Copeland J., Jansen K. Patterns of use and harms associated with non-medical ketamine use. *Drug Alcohol Depend* 2003; **69**: 23–8.

102. Bulletin H. O. S. *Crime in England and Wales 2008/09 Volume 1. Findings from the British Crime Survey and Police Recorded Crime.* London, UK: Home Office; 2009.

103. Abdel-Rahman M. S., Ismail E. E. Teratogenic effect of ketamine and cocaine in CF-1 mice. *Teratology* 2000; **61:** 291–6.

104. Persson J. Wherefore ketamine? *Curr Opin Anaesthesiol* 2010; **23:** 455–60.

105. Schifano F., Corkery J., Oyefeso A., Tonia T., Ghodse A. H. Trapped in the "K-hole": overview of deaths associated with ketamine misuse in the UK (1993–2006). *J Clin Psychopharmacol* 2008; **28:** 114–6.

Critical Thinking

1. What are the dangers of using the drug Ketamine?
2. Why has its popularity increased in recent years?
3. Discuss the legitimate uses of the drug.

Acknowledgements—For helpful comments on sections of an early draft of this review, the authors gratefully thank Dr Polly Taylor, Dr John Oxley, Dr Ange Cottrell, Dr Daniel Wood, Pete Weinstock, Rachael Ayres, Dr Fiona Measham, Dr John Corkery, Dr Robert Gable and Professor David Nutt. We also thank Sharinjeet Dhiman and Gráinne Schafer for compiling the references. The ISCD provided a small allowance to fund the literature search.

"This Drug Shouldn't Be Out There"

Synthetic cannabis, sold under the brands K2 and Spice, is a dangerous drug that teenagers are abusing.

JOHN DICONSIGLIO

Tracy heard rumors about the new drug in town. Some of her friends called it "fake weed." It was supposed to be like marijuana. Some of her friends said the high was more intense, even if it didn't last as long. At the time, the drug was legal. Her boyfriend bought it at a gas station.

Some friends called the drug K2. Others referred to it as Spice. Both are brand names used to market what is really one drug—synthetic cannabis. Tracy didn't like the look of K2. It was a crumple of sticky, brownish herbs. And it smelled nasty—like burned leaves.

K2 has characteristics of various drugs. It is chemically similar to marijuana. Like LSD, it can cause a person to hallucinate. And it can cause a person's heart rate to soar, which happens to people who use cocaine and other drugs. Besides being called K2 and Spice, the drug is also sold under the names Genie, Zohai, Yucatan Fire, and Silver Surfer.

No Longer Legal

Recently, the U.S. Drug Enforcement Administration made it illegal to possess or sell the five chemicals used to make synthetic cannabis. This makes sense to John Huffman, a Clemson University chemist, who created many of the chemicals used to manufacture synthetic cannabis.

"Anyone who tries this drug is an idiot," Huffman says. "Smoking this is like playing Russian roulette. It's insane."

Huffman says he created the chemicals by mistake. In 1995, he created the chemical compound as an appetite stimulant for people with glaucoma, a disease that can cause blindness.

Huffman published his results in a scientific journal—only later to find out that someone was spraying the drug on leaves and selling the product. "This drug shouldn't be out there," Huffman says.

Tracy's Tale

Unfortunately, Tracy did end up smoking synthetic cannabis. The 19-year-old from Michigan was an addict who had been arrested three times for drug use. Because of her legal troubles, Tracy had to undergo regular drug tests. Tracy knew that one failed urine test would land her in jail.

Her boyfriend told her that smoking synthetic cannabis would get her high—and wouldn't show up in a drug test. So she gave it a try and was hit with an intense rush. "I thought it wouldn't do anything, but I took one hit, and I was really tripping," Tracy says.

Her heart began racing and she could barely catch her breath. "I thought I was having a heart attack," Tracy says. "I tried to calm down, but I was panting. I screamed, 'What is this stuff?'"

Synthetic cannabis is a mix of dried herbs and spices that have been sprayed with a "synthetic cannabinoid"—a chemical that is similar to THC, the active ingredient in marijuana. The drug is marketed as incense or herbal tobacco. The back of the packets even display a warning: "Not for human consumption."

"It's like the Surgeon General's warning on cigarettes," Tracy says. "No one takes it seriously. We all know they have to put it on the package to keep it legal."

Although it's possible to detect the drug in urine, most drug tests do not yet test for synthetic cannabis, so it's become popular among kids on probation. Tracy takes a drug test three times a week, and although she smokes synthetic cannabis daily, she has never failed a drug test.

Each sample of the drug is unique—and that's not a good thing. "From bag to bag, you just don't know what a person is taking and how his or her body is going to react to it," says Dr. Anthony Scalzo, director of toxicology at St. Louis University.

Different Reaction

The receptors in each person's brain react differently to certain chemicals, according to Scalzo. As a result, the drug may have relatively minor effects on one person, while another will experience physical distress in the form of a rapid heart rate, raised blood pressure, and hallucinations.

Scalzo says the most dangerous side effect of the drug is the radical mood swings it causes. "You have a happy-go-lucky kid, who is not depressed. Then he smokes this stuff and all of a sudden he kills himself," he says.

In 2009, poison centers received only 14 calls regarding synthetic cannabis, according to the American Association of Poison Control Centers. By September 2010, more than 1,500 people reported experiencing synthetic cannabis symptoms such as racing heartbeats, elevated blood pressure, and nausea.

Fatal Use

So far, the drug has been linked to at least one death. In June 2010, an 18-year-old man in Iowa became agitated and violent after trying synthetic cannabis for the first time. Later that day, he shot himself with his father's hunting rifle. Scalzo says he has treated a 14-year-old user who tried to jump out a fifth-story window and a 21-year-old college student who claimed to have hallucinations after smoking synthetic cannabis.

Experts at Branches Counseling, a drug-counseling service in the Midwest, say they have seen a steady increase in teen patients who have abused synthetic cannabis. Many of these users don't even like the drug, says therapist Beth Bunn. "They say it hurts or burns when they smoke it," she says. Other users have experienced withdrawal symptoms similar to those experienced with heroin, symptoms such as severe aches and pains, heart palpitations, and seizures.

Unfortunately, Tracy is still using synthetic cannabis. Smoking the drug makes her feel like there are burning ashes on the back of her throat. But she doesn't plan to quit using it. "I know it's not good for me, but I just can't give it up," Tracy admits.

Discussion Questions

1. Had you ever heard of synthetic cannabis before reading this article? How dangerous a drug do you think it is?
2. Do you think Tracy will ever be able to stop using synthetic cannabis? Explain.

Critical Thinking

1. What are the risks of synthetic marijuana?
2. Why is the drug so appealing?
3. Should it legal or illegal? Discuss.

DiConsiglio, John. From *Scholastic Choices*, February/March 2011, pp. 10–12. Copyright © 2011 by Scholastic Inc. Reprinted by permission.

UNIT 6

Sexuality and Relationships

Unit Selections

Learning Outcomes

After reading this Unit, you will be able to:

- Understand how to end a relationship with dignity.

- Explain why the right partner is one who is interested and capable of supporting the needs of the partner.

- Understand the link between online pornography and sexual addiction.

- Identify the detrimental effects of sexual addiction.

Student Website

www.mhhe.com/cls

Internet References

Planned Parenthood
www.plannedparenthood.org
Sexuality Information and Education Council of the United States (SIECUS)
www.siecus.org

Sexuality is an important part of both self-awareness and intimate relationships. But how important is physical attraction in establishing and maintaining intimate relationships? Researchers in the area of evolutionary psychology have proposed numerous theories that attempt to explain the mutual attraction that occurs between the sexes. The most controversial of these theories postulates that our perception of beauty or physical attractiveness is not subjective but rather a biological component hardwired into our brains. It is generally assumed that perceptions of beauty vary from era to era and culture to culture, but evidence is mounting that suggests that people all over share a common sense of beauty that is based on physical symmetry. In addition to a sense of physical beauty, researchers believe that scent is an important component of who we end up with. Physical attraction may be based on smell, which may be a significant component of what we think of as "chemistry" between partners.

While physical attraction is clearly an important issue when it comes to dating, how important is it in long-term loving relationships? For many Americans the answer may be very important, because we tend to be a "Love Culture," a culture that places a premium on passion in the selection of our mates. Is passion an essential ingredient in love, and can passion serve to sustain a long-term meaningful relationship? Since most people can't imagine marrying someone that they don't love, we must assume that most marriages are based on this feeling we call love. That being the case, why is it that so few marriages survive the rigors of day-to-day living? Perhaps the answer has more to do with our limited definition of love rather than love itself.

Another important topic of interest and controversy in the area of human sexuality is sex education. While most states mandate some type of school-based sex education, many parents believe that they should be the source of their children's sex education and not the schools. Although the concept of "safe sex" is nothing new, the degree of open and public discussion regarding sexual behaviors is. With the emergence of AIDS as a disease of epidemic proportions and the rapid spreading of other sexually transmitted diseases (STDs), the surgeon general of the United States initiated an aggressive educational campaign, based on the assumption that knowledge would change behavior. If STD rates among teens are any indication of the effectiveness of this approach, then we must conclude that our educational efforts are failing. Conservatives believe that while education may play a role in curbing the spread of STDs, the root of the problem is promiscuity, and that promiscuity rises when a society is undergoing a moral decline. The solution, according to conservatives, is a joint effort between parents and educators to teach students the importance of values such as respect, responsibility, and integrity. Liberals, on the other hand, think that preventing promiscuity is unrealistic. They believe that the focus should be on establishing open and frank discussions between the sexes. Their premise is that we are all sexual beings, and the best way to combat STDs is to establish open discussions between sexual partners, so that condoms will be used correctly when couples engage in intercourse.

While education undoubtedly has had a positive impact on slowing the spread of STDs, perhaps it was unrealistic to think that education alone was the solution, given the magnitude and

© Design Pics / Darren Greenwood

the nature of the problem. Most experts agree that for education to succeed in changing personal behaviors, the following conditions must be met: (1) The recipients of the information must first perceive themselves as vulnerable and, thus, be motivated to explore replacement behaviors and (2) the replacement behaviors must satisfy the needs that were the basis of the problem behaviors. To date most education programs have failed to meet these criteria. Given all the information that we now have on the dangers associated with AIDS and STDs, why is it that people do not perceive themselves at risk? It is not so much the denial of risks as it is the notion of most people that they use good judgment when it comes to choosing sex partners. Unfortunately, most decisions regarding sexual behavior are based on subjective criteria that bear little or no relationship to one's actual risk. Even when individuals do view themselves as vulnerable to AIDS and STDs, there are currently only two viable options for reducing the risk of contracting these diseases. The first is the use of a condom and the second is sexual abstinence, neither of which is an ideal solution to the problem.

Articles for this unit address three topics: the breakup of a relationship, choosing the right mate, and sexual addiction. The breakup of a relationship can be painful. Elizabeth Svoboda delves into how to end a relationship with dignity and without devaluing oneself or the other person in "The Thoroughly Modern Guide to Breakups." She also maintains that relationships can be ended with minimal distress and offers advice on how this can be accomplished. "Are You with the Right Mate?" focuses on marriage and choosing the right mate. The article quotes a family therapist who states that real marriage begins when initial physical attraction diminishes, marking the need to start growing as an individual. The idea that pornography is related to sexual addiction has been a topic of discussion in recent years. Chris Lee discusses this problem in "This Man Is Addicted to Sex." With the increase in online options to view pornography, there appears to be a connection to the destructive addiction which has a detrimental effect on a person's career, relationships, and self esteem leading to depression, job loss, and high-risk sexual behavior.

The Thoroughly Modern Guide to Breakups

Yes, breaking up is hard to do, and we're primed to avoid delivering or digesting such deeply threatening news. Still, It's possible to end affairs with dignity and minimal distress.

ELIZABETH SVOBODA

Julie Spira isn't just any writer. She bills herself as an expert on Internet dating, and wrote a book called *The Perils of Cyber-Dating.* When, in 2005, she met The Doctor on an online dating site, Spira was positive she'd finally found The One. "He seemed very solid and close to his family," Spira recalls. He made it clear on their first date that, after the end of a lengthy marriage and a year of serial dating, he was looking for an enduring relationship. "That was very appealing to me."

She took it as a sign of his integrity. It didn't hurt that he was handsome, too. Eight months of exclusive dating later, The Doctor asked her to marry him.

They planned a simple wedding. But first, they put their individual homes up for sale so they could buy a place together. They went house-hunting together nearly every weekend. When her father got sick, The Doctor saved his life.

Fourteen months into their engagement, Spira received an email from her fiancé titled, simply, "Please Read This." She put the message aside to savor after work and other commitments. When she finally clicked on it, she wished she hadn't. "The email had an attached document. It said I was not the woman for him, that the relationship was over, and to please send back the ring. It said my belongings would be delivered tomorrow," Spira says. "I sat there and my whole body started to shake."

Spira had to plaster on a happy face for a few days—her parents were renewing their marriage vows at a family party on the other side of the country and she wasn't yet ready to tell anyone about the broken engagement. "I wore my ring. I pretended my fiancé had an emergency and couldn't make it. Then I went to my room and sobbed in secret." Once home, she cried every day for a month. Then another electronic communiqué arrived from The Doctor. It said, in its entirety, "Are you OK?"

That was all she ever heard from him.

The breakup left her socially paralyzed. She didn't, couldn't, date, even after many months. She remains single today, three years later. Disappointment ignites anger when she thinks about what happened. "It was cowardly and cruel. Where's the human side of it? Where's the respect from someone who was devoted to you for two years?" It's scant comfort when people tell her that Berger dumped Carrie by Post-it note on *Sex and the City.* "With email, you don't even have a guarantee that the person got your message."

Saying good-bye is heartbreaking, and most of us are total jerks about it. Bad dumping behavior is booming, especially among the young. In one recent survey, 24 percent of respondents aged 13 to 17 said it was completely OK to break up with someone by texting, and 26 percent of them admitted to doing so. "It's always been hard to break up with someone face to face," says Stanford University sociologist Clifford Nass, author of *The Man Who Lied to His Laptop,* "but lack of social skills makes it harder. And we're learning fewer and fewer social skills."

As a result, remote shortcuts like electronic endings look deceptively appealing—although, at the very least, they chip away at the self-respect of the dumpers and deprive dumpees of a needed shot at closure. Little wonder that hypersensitivity to rejection is on the rise, and it's contributing to large increases in stalking behavior, especially on college campuses. More than 3 million people report being stalking victims each year, the ultimate measure of collective cluelessness about ending love affairs well.

Hypersensitivity to rejection is on the rise, and it's contributing to large increases in stalking behavior.

As drive-by breakups like Spira's become more common, mastering the art of the ending is more necessary than ever. The average age of first marriage now hovers around 27, five years later than in 1970. Most people are having more and more serious relationships before they find the one that works. The emerging social reality demands some preparation for romantic rejection, given its potential to shatter one's sense of self.

The Clean Dozen: 12 Rules of Better Breakups

No question, breaking up is incredibly difficult because it involves giving, or receiving, bad news that engages our deepest vulnerability—the fear that we are unlovable. Most of us are designed not only to minimize discomfort but to dislike rupturing attachments, priming us for sleights of avoidance in delivering or digesting such deeply threatening information. It takes courage to recognize we have a moral obligation to put aside personal discomfort in approaching someone we cared for and who loved us—especially when means of ducking that responsibility are so readily available. But courage pays dividends in self-respect and accelerated recovery.

Not only do our biology, psychology, and morality influence how we weather breakups, but so do the circumstances of the act. There may be little anyone can do to alter biological responsiveness, but everyone can control the way breaking up is conducted. Here, say the experts, is how to do it so that both parties remain emotionally intact, capable of weathering the inevitable pain and sadness.

1. **Take full responsibility for initiating the breakup.** If your feelings or needs have changed, your dreams diverged, or your lives are going in opposite directions, don't provoke your partner into doing the breakup. Shifting responsibility is not only a weasel tactic that diminishes the doer, says Paul Falzone, CEO of the online dating service eLove, it's confusing. Adds Russell Friedman, executive director of the California-based Grief Recovery Institute and author of *Moving On,* "Trying to manipulate your partner into breaking up, like suddenly giving one-word answers in an attempt to make them say, 'The heck with it,' creates a sense of real distortion." The partner may not initially get the message that you want to break up, but "will start to question themselves: 'Am I not a valuable human being? Am I unattractive?'" The target may also question their own instincts and intuition. "You're setting up the sense that the other person is to blame. You have bypassed their intuition—they can't trust what they felt, saw, heard in the relationship." That kind of uncertainty can cripple them in future relationships; they may not be willing to trust a new partner's devotion or suitability.

2. **Do it only face to face.** Humans evolved to communicate face to face, which provides some built-in consolations. We may experience many nonverbal cues that reassure us of our essential lovability—the quick touch on the arm that says you're still valued even as the relationship ends. Anything less than face-to-face sends a distressing message: "You don't matter."

   Some dumpers might think that delivering the news by email, text, or even a Facebook statement is less cruel than directly speaking the truth. But remote modes of delivery actually inflict psychic scars on the dumpee that can impede future partnerships. "When you don't get any explanation, you spend a huge amount of time trying to figure out what's wrong with you," says eLove's Paul Falzone. "And you'll be hesitant about entering another relationship."

Being on the receiving end of remote dumping can leave us stuck in emotional limbo, says University of Chicago neuroscientist John Cacioppo. "The pain of losing a meaningful relationship can be especially searing in the absence of direct social contact." With no definitive closure, we're left wondering what the heck happened, which can lead to the kind of endless rumination that often leads to depression.

"Situations where you have an incomplete picture of what's going on are perfect ground for the development of rumination," says Yale University psychologist Susan Nolen-Hoeksema. "It can send people into a tailspin." Many dumpees emerge from the tailspin distrustful of others, making it difficult for them to establish closeness with future partners. "When you begin to distrust others, you make less of an investment in them," adds Bernardo Carducci, professor of psychology at Indiana University Southeast. "So the person you meet next is going to suffer for the sins of a stranger."

Dumpers themselves may come to regret surrogate sayonaras once they realize how badly their vanishing act hurt their former partners—and how little concern they showed. "Five years on, you don't want to be ashamed of how you handled this," says John Portmann, a moral philosopher at the University of Virginia. Guilt and shame encumber future interactions.

3. **Act with dignity.** Since a breakup is a potentially explosive scenario, resolve in advance to bite back any insults that are poised to fly out of your mouth. Preserving your partner's self-respect has the compound effect of salvaging your own.

4. **Be honest.** "I'm not in love with you anymore" is actually OK. But honesty need not be a bludgeon, nor does it demand total disclosure. If you secretly think your partner is a complete snooze in bed, you're probably better off keeping that opinion to yourself. "You have an obligation to watch out for the other person's self-esteem," Virginia's Portmann says. "Do not cut them down in such a way that it's impossible for them to have another successful relationship. Why rub salt in their wounds? That's torture."

   "The message to get across is, 'You're not what I'm looking for,'" adds Florida State University psychologist Roy Baumeister. "That doesn't imply that there's something wrong or deficient about your partner." It's simply straightforward.

5. **Avoid big, bad clichés like "It's not you, it's me."** Such generic explanations ring false and communicate a lack of respect. You owe your partner a genuine explanation, however brief, of why things aren't working. One big caveat: If you suspect that your partner might react violently to your decision to end the relationship, don't stick around to justify your reasoning; safety comes first.

6. **Avoid a point-by-point dissection of where things fell apart.** "It's not a good idea because there's never going to be agreement," says Russell Friedman. "I'll say, 'This is what happened,' and you'll say, 'No, no.'"

Prolonged back-and-forth often degenerates into a fight—or worse: If your partner gains the upper hand, he or she may succeed in luring you back into a dysfunctional relationship you've decided you want to end.

7. **Make it a clean break.** Do not try to cushion the blow by suggesting future friendly meetups. "Saying 'Let's be friends' might be a way for the rejecter to try to handle their own guilt, but it's not always good for the person being rejected," Baumeister observes. Such a misguided attempt to spare a partner pain can leave him or her hopeful there might be a chance at future reconciliation, which can hinder the efforts of both parties to move on.

8. **Communicate ongoing appreciation of the good times you shared.** In exchanging good-byes, it's even desirable, says Friedman. It's equally fine to confide disappointment that the hopes you shared for a future together won't be realized. Such statements convey a continued belief in your partner's inherent value.

9. **Don't protest a partner's decision.** And don't beg him or her to reconsider later on. The best thing a dumpee can do to speed emotional healing is to accept that the relationship has come to an unequivocal end. In her neuroimaging studies, Helen Fisher found that the withdrawal-like reaction afflicting romantic rejectees diminished with time, indicating that they were well on their way to healing. But the recovery process is fragile, says Fisher, and last-ditch attempts to make contact or win back an ex can scuttle it. "If you suddenly get an email from the person, you can get right into the craving for them again." To expedite moving on, she recommends abstaining from any kind of contact with the rejecter: "Throw out the cards and letters. Don't call. And don't try to be friends."

10. **Don't demonize your ex-partner.** It's a waste of your energy. And avoid plotting revenge; it will backfire by making him or her loom ever larger in your thoughts and postpone your recovery.

11. **Don't try to blot out the pain you're feeling, either.** Short of the death of a loved one, the end of a long-term relationship is one of the most severe emotional blows you'll ever experience. It's perfectly normal—in fact, necessary—to spend time grieving the loss. "Love makes you terribly vulnerable," Portmann says. "If you allow yourself to fall in love, you can get hurt really badly." The sooner you face the pain, the sooner it passes.

12. **Resist thinking you've lost your one true soul mate.** Don't tell yourself you've lost the one person you were destined to be with forever, says Baumeister. "There's something about love that makes you think there's only one person for you, and there's a mythology surrounding that. But there's nothing magical about one person." In reality, there are plenty of people with whom each of us is potentially compatible. It might be difficult to fathom in the aftermath of a breakup, but chances are you'll find someone else.

For both parties, the experience influences how—or even whether—one moves on with life and love.

The best breakups, if there is such a thing, enable acceptance and minimize psychic wreckage, so that the pain of the ending doesn't overwhelm the positive trace of the relationship. For the partnership will take up permanent residence in memory, likely to be revisited many times over the years. The challenge of breaking up is to close the relationship definitively and honorably, without devaluing oneself or the person who previously met one's deepest needs. Yes, Virginia, people can fall out of love with grace and dignity—if only they learn how to give breakups a chance.

Initially, everyone reacts to rejection like a drug user going through withdrawal.

Battered by Biology

Because our brains are wired from the beginning for bonding, breakups batter us biologically. Initially, says Rutgers University anthropologist Helen Fisher, everyone reacts to rejection like a drug user going through withdrawal. In the early days and weeks after a breakup, she has found, just thinking about the lover who dumped us activates several key areas of the brain—the ventral tegmental area of the midbrain, which controls motivation and reward and is known to be involved in romantic love; the nucleus accumbens and the orbitofrontal/ prefrontal cortex, part of the dopamine reward system and associated with craving and addiction; and the insular cortex and anterior cingulate, associated with physical pain and distress.

As reported in a recent issue of the *Journal of Neurophysiology,* Fisher rounded up 15 people who had just experienced romantic rejection, put them in an fMRI machine, and had them look at two large photographs: an image of the person who had just dumped them and an image of a neutral person to whom they had no attachment. When the participants looked at the images of their rejecters, their brains shimmered like those of addicts deprived of their substance of choice. "We found activity in regions of the brain associated with cocaine and nicotine addiction," Fisher says. "We also found activity in a region associated with feelings of deep attachment, and activity in a region that's associated with pain."

Fisher's work corroborates the findings of UCLA psychologist Naomi Eisenberger, who discovered that social rejection activates the same brain area—the anterior cingulate—that generates an adverse reaction to physical pain. Breakups likely stimulate pain to notify us how important social ties are to human survival and to warn us not to sever them lightly.

Although Eisenberger didn't study romantic rejection, she expects that it actually feels much worse than the social rejection she did document. "If you're getting pain-related activity from someone you don't care about, it would presumably be a lot more painful from someone you share memories with," she points out.

The intensity of the pain may be what compels some spurned lovers to stalk their ex-partners; they're willing to do just about anything to make the hurt go away. Fisher believes that activation of addictive centers in response to breakups also fuels stalking behavior, explaining "why the beloved is so difficult to give up."

A Time of Broken Dreams

Biology is nowhere near the whole story. Attachment styles that emerge early in life also influence how people handle break-ups later on—and how they react to them. Those with a secure attachment style—whose caregivers, by being generally responsive, instilled a sense of trust that they would always be around when needed—are most likely to approach breakups with psychological integrity. Typically, they clue their partners in about any changes in their feelings while taking care not to be hurtful.

On the receiving end of a breakup, "the secure person acknowledges that the loss hurts, but is sensible about it," says Phillip Shaver, a University of California, Davis psychologist who has long studied attachment behavior. "They're going to have an undeniable period of broken dreams, but they express that to a reasonable degree and then heal and move on."

By contrast, people who develop an anxious or insecure attachment style—typically due to inconsistent parental attention during the first years of life—are apt to try to keep a defunct relationship going rather than suffer the pain of dissolving it. "The anxious person is less often the one who takes the initiative in breaking up," Shaver says. "More commonly, they hang on and get more angry and intrusive."

On the receiving end of a breakup, the insecurely attached react poorly. "They don't let go," says Shaver. "They're more likely to be stalkers, and they're more likely to end up sleeping with the old partner." Their defense against pain—refusing to acknowledge that the relationship is over—precludes healing. They pine on for the lost love with little hope of relief.

Whether we bounce back from a breakup or wallow in unhappiness also depends on our general self-regard. In a University of California, Santa Barbara study where participants experienced rejection in an online dating exchange, people with low self-esteem took rejection the worst: They were most likely to blame themselves for what had happened and to rail against the rejecter. Their levels of the stress hormone cortisol ran particularly high. Such reactivity to romantic rejection often creates unhealthy coping strategies—staying home alone night after night, for example, or remaining emotionally closed off from new partners.

People with high self-esteem were not immune to distress in the face of romantic rejection, whether they were rejecter or rejectee, but they were less inclined to assume a lion's share of the blame for the split. Best of all, they continued to see themselves in a positive light despite a brush-off.

Critical Thinking

1. What recommendations does the author give to end a relationship with dignity?
2. How can affairs end with minimal distress?
3. Why do many breakups end badly?

ELIZABETH SVOBODA is a freelance writer in San Jose, California.

Are You with the Right Mate?

REBECCA WEBBER

Elliott Katz was stunned to find himself in the middle of a divorce after two kids and 10 years of marriage. The Torontonian, a policy analyst for the Ottawa government, blamed his wife. "She just didn't appreciate all I was doing to make her happy." He fed the babies, and he changed their diapers. He gave them their baths, he read them stories, and put them to bed. Before he left for work in the morning, he made them breakfast. He bought a bigger house and took on the financial burden, working evenings to bring in enough money so his wife could stay home full-time.

He thought the solution to the discontent was for her to change. But once on his own, missing the daily interaction with his daughters, he couldn't avoid some reflection. "I didn't want to go through this again. I asked whether there was something I could have done differently. After all, you can wait years for someone else to change."

What he decided was, indeed, there were some things he could have done differently—like not tried as hard to be so noncontrolling that his wife felt he had abandoned decision-making entirely. His wife, he came to understand, felt frustrated, as if she were "a married single parent," making too many of the plans and putting out many of the fires of family life, no matter how many chores he assumed.

Ultimately, he stopped blaming his wife for their problems. "You can't change another person. You can only change yourself," he says. "Like lots of men today" he has since found, "I was very confused about my role as partner." After a few post-divorce years in the mating wilderness, Katz came to realize that framing a relationship in terms of the right or wrong mate is by itself a blind alley.

"We're given a binary model," says New York psychotherapist Ken Page. "Right or wrong. Settle or leave. We are not given the right tools to think about relationships. People need a better set of options."

Sooner or later, there comes a moment in *all* relationships when you lie in bed, roll over, look at the person next to you and think it's all a dreadful mistake, says Boston family therapist Terrence Real. It happens a few months to a few years in. "It's an open secret of American culture that disillusionment exists. I go around the country speaking about 'normal marital hatred.' Not one person has ever asked what I mean by that. It's extremely raw."

What to do when the initial attraction sours? "I call it the first day of your real marriage," Real says. It's not a sign that you've chosen the wrong partner. It is the signal to grow as an individual—to take responsibility for your own frustrations. Invariably, we yearn for perfection but are stuck with an imperfect human being. We all fall in love with people we think will deliver us from life's wounds but who wind up knowing how to rub against us.

A new view of relationships and their discontents is emerging. We alone are responsible for having the relationship we want. And to get it, we have to dig deep into ourselves while maintaining our connections. It typically takes a dose of bravery—what Page calls "enlightened audacity." Its brightest possibility exists, ironically, just when the passion seems most totally dead. If we fail to plumb ourselves and speak up for our deepest needs, which admittedly can be a scary prospect, life will never feel authentic, we will never see ourselves with any clarity, and everyone will always be the wrong partner.

The Way Things Are

Romance itself seeds the eventual belief that we have chosen the wrong partner. The early stage of a relationship, most marked by intense attraction and infatuation, is in many ways akin to cocaine intoxication, observes Christine Meinecke, a clinical psychologist in Des Moines, Iowa. It's orchestrated, in part, by the neurochemicals associated with intense pleasure. Like a cocaine high, it's not sustainable.

But for the duration—and experts give it nine months to four years—infatuation has one overwhelming effect: Research shows that it makes partners overestimate their similarities and idealize each other. We're thrilled that he loves Thai food, travel, and classic movies, just like us. And we overlook his avid interest in old cars and online poker.

Eventually, reality rears its head. "Infatuation fades for everyone," says Meinecke, author of *Everybody Marries the Wrong Person*. That's when you discover your psychological incompatibility, and disenchantment sets in. Suddenly, a switch is flipped, and now all you can see are your differences. "You're focusing on what's wrong with *them*. They need to get the message about what *they* need to change."

You conclude you've married the wrong person—but that's because you're accustomed to thinking, Cinderella-like, that there *is* only one right person. The consequences of such a pervasive belief are harsh. We engage in destructive behaviors, like blaming our partner for our unhappiness or searching for some one outside the relationship.

Along with many other researchers and clinicians, Meinecke espouses a new marital paradigm—what she calls "the self responsible spouse." When you start focusing on what isn't so great, it's time to shift focus. "Rather than look at the other person, you need to look at yourself and ask, 'Why am I suddenly so unhappy and what do I need to do?'" It's not likely a defect in your partner.

In mature love, says Meinecke, "we do not look to our partner to provide our happiness, and we don't blame them for our unhappiness. We take responsibility for the expectations that we carry, for our own negative emotional reactions, for our own insecurities, and for our own dark moods."

But instead of looking at ourselves, or understanding the fantasies that bring us to such a pass, we engage in a thought process that makes our differences tragic and intolerable, says William Doherty, professor of psychology and head of the marriage and family therapy program at the University of Minnesota. It's one thing to say, "I wish my spouse were more into the arts, like I am." Or, "I wish my partner was not just watching TV every night but interested in getting out more with me." That's something you can fix.

It's quite another to say, "This is intolerable. I need and deserve somebody who shares my core interests." The two thought processes are likely to trigger differing actions. It's possible to ask someone to go out more. It's not going to be well received to ask someone for a personality overhaul, notes Doherty, author of *Take Back Your Marriage*.

No one is going to get all their needs met in a relationship, he insists. He urges fundamental acceptance of the person we choose and the one who chooses us. "We're all flawed. With parenting, we know that comes with the territory. With spouses, we say 'This is terrible.'"

The culture, however, pushes us in the direction of discontent. "Some disillusionment and feelings of discouragement are normal in the love-based matches in our culture," explains Doherty. "But consumer culture tells us we should not settle for anything that is not ideal for us."

As UCLA psychologist Thomas Bradbury puts it, "You don't have a line-item veto when it comes to your partner. It's a package deal; the bad comes with the good."

Further, he says, it's too simplistic an interpretation that your partner is the one who's wrong. "We tend to point our finger at the person in front of us. We're fairly crude at processing some information. We tend not to think, 'Maybe I'm not giving her what she needs.' 'Maybe he's disgruntled because I'm not opening up to him.' Or, 'Maybe he's struggling in his relationships with other people.' The more sophisticated question is, 'In what ways are we failing to make one another happy?'"

Now in a long-term relationship, Toronto's Katz has come to believe that "Marriage is not about *finding* the right person. It's about *becoming* the right person. Many people feel they married the wrong person, but I've learned that it's truly about growing to become a better husband."

Eclipsed by Expectations

What's Most Noticeable about Sarah and Mark Holdt of Estes Park, Colorado, is their many differences. "He's a Republican, I'm a Democrat. He's a traditional Christian, I'm an agnostic. He likes meat and potatoes, I like more adventurous food," says Sarah. So Mark heads off to church and Bible study every week, while Sarah takes a "Journeys" class that considers topics like the history of God in America. "When he comes home, I'll ask, 'What did you learn in Bible Study?'" she says. And she'll share her insights from her own class with him.

But when Sarah wants to go to a music festival and Mark wants to stay home, "I just go," says Sarah. "I don't need to have him by my side for everything." He's there when it matters most—at home, at the dinner table, in bed. "We both thrive on touch," says Sarah, "so we set our alarm a half hour early every morning and take that time to cuddle." They've been married for 14 years.

It takes a comfortable sense of self and deliberate effort to make relationships commodious enough to tolerate such differences. What's striking about the Holdts is the time they take to share what goes on in their lives—and in their heads—when they are apart. Research shows that such "turning toward" each other and efforts at information exchange, even in routine matters, are crucial to maintaining the emotional connection between partners.

Say one partner likes to travel and the other doesn't. "If you view this with a feeling of resentment, that's going to hurt, over and over again," says Doherty. If you can accept it, that's fine—provided you don't start living in two separate worlds.

"What you don't want to do," he says, "is develop a group of single travel friends who, when they are on the road, go out and flirt with others. You start doing things you're not comfortable sharing with your mate." Most often, such large differences are accompanied by so much disappointment that partners react in ways that do not support the relationship.

The available evidence suggests that women more than men bring some element of fantasy into a relationship. Women generally initiate more breakups and two-thirds of divorces, becoming more disillusioned than men. They compare their mates with their friends much more than men do, says Doherty.

He notes, "They tend to have a model or framework for what the relationship should be. They are more prone to the comparison between what they have and what they think they should have. Men tend to monitor the gap between what they have and what they think they deserve only in the sexual arena. They don't monitor the quality of their marriage on an everyday basis."

To the extent that people have an ideal partner and an ideal relationship in their head, they are setting themselves up for disaster, says family expert Michelle Givertz, assistant professor of communication studies at California State University, Chico. Relationship identities are negotiated between two individuals. Relationships are not static ideals; they are always works in progress.

To enter a relationship with an idea of what it should look like or how it should evolve is too controlling, she contends. It takes two people to make a relationship. One person doesn't get to decide what it should be. And to the extent that he or she does, the other partner is not going to be happy.

"People can spend their lives trying to make a relationship into something it isn't, based on an idealized vision of what should be, not what is," she says. She isn't sure why, but she finds that such misplaced expectations are increasing. Or, as Doherty puts it, "A lot of the thinking about being married to the wrong mate is really self-delusion."

Yes, Virginia, Some Mates Really *Are* Wrong

Sometimes, however, we really do choose the wrong person— someone ultimately not interested in or capable of meeting our needs, for any of a number of possible reasons. At the top of the list of people who are generally wrong for *anyone* are substance abusers—whether the substance is alcohol, prescription drugs, or illicit drugs—who refuse to get help for the problem.

"An addict's primary loyalty is not to the relationship, it's to the addiction," explains Ken Page. "Active addicts become cheaper versions of themselves and lose integrity or the ability to do the righ thing when it's hard. Those are the very qualities in a partner you need to lean on." Gamblers fall into the same compulsive camp, with the added twist that their pursuit of the big win typically lands them, sooner or later, into deep debt that threatens the foundations of relationship life.

People who cheated in one or more previous relationships are not great mate material. They destroy the trust and intimacy basic to building a relationship. It's possible to make a case for a partner who cheats once, against his own values, but not for one who compulsively and repeatedly strays. Doherty considers such behavior among the "hard reasons" for relationship breakup, along with physical abuse and other forms of over controlling. "These are things that nobody should have to put up with in life," he says.

But "drifting apart," "poor communication," and "we're just not compatible anymore" are in a completely different category. Such "soft reasons," he insists, are, by contrast, always two-way streets. "Nobody gets all the soft goodies in life," he finds. "It's often better to work on subtle ways to improve the relationship."

In an ongoing marriage, he adds, "incompatibility is never the real reason for a divorce." It's a reason for breakup of a dating relationship. But when people say "she's a nice person but we're just not compatible," Doherty finds, something happened in which both were participants and allowed the relationship to deteriorate. It's a nice way to say you're not blaming your partner.

The real reason is likely to be that neither attended to the relationship. Perhaps one or both partners threw themselves into parenting. Or a job. They stopped doing the things that they did when dating and that couples need to do to thrive as a partnership—take time for conversation, talk about how their day went or what's on their mind. Or perhaps the real love was undermined by the inability to handle conflict.

"If you get to the point where you're delivering an ultimatum," says Bradbury, you haven't been maintaining your relationship properly. "It's like your car stopping on the side of the road and you say, 'It just isn't working anymore'—but you haven't changed the oil in 10 years." The heart of any relationship, he insists—what makes people the right mates for each other—is the willingness of both partners to be open and vulnerable; to listen and care about each other.

Although there are no guarantees, there are stable personal characteristics that are generally good and generally bad for relationships. On the good side: sense of humor; even temper; willingness to overlook your flaws; sensitivity to you and what you care about; ability to express caring. On the maladaptive side: chronic lying; chronic worrying or neuroticism; emotional over reactivity; proneness to anger; propensity to harbor grudges; low self-esteem; poor impulse control; tendency to aggression; self-orientation rather than an otherorientation. Situations, such as chronic exposure to nonmarital stress in either partner, also have the power to undermine relationships.

In addition, there are people who are specifically wrong for you, because they don't share the values and goals you hold most dear. Differences in core values often plague couples who marry young, before they've had enough life experience to discover who they really are. Most individuals are still developing their belief systems through their late teens and early 20s and still refining their lifestyle choices. Of course, you have to know what you hold most dear, and that can be a challenge for anyone at any age, not just the young.

A Critical Difference

There's a difference between fighting for what you want in your relationship and being in direct control of your partner, demanding that he or she change, says Real.

Firmly stand up for your wants and needs in a relationship. "Most people don't have the skill to speak up for and fight for what they want in a relationship," he observes. "They don't speak up, which preserves the love but builds resentment. Resentment is a choice; living resentfully means living unhappily. Or they speak up—but are not very loving." Or they just complain.

The art to speaking up, he says, is to transform a complaint into a request. Not "I don't like how you're talking to me," but "Can you please lower your voice so I can hear you better?" If you're trying to get what you want in a relationship, notes Real, it's best to keep it positive and future-focused.

One of the most common reasons we choose the wrong partner is that we do not know who we are or what we really want. It's hard to choose someone capable of understanding you and meeting your most guarded emotional needs and with whom your values are compatible when you don't know what your needs or values are or haven't developed the confidence to voice them unabashedly.

Maria Lin is a nonpracticing attorney who married a chef. "I valued character, connection, the heart," she says. "He was charming, funny, treated me amazingly well, and we got along great." But over time, intellectual differences got in the way. "He couldn't keep up with my analysis or logic in arguments or reasoning through something, or he would prove less capable at certain things, or he would misspell or misuse terms. It was never anything major, just little things."

Lin confides that she lost respect for her chef-husband. "I didn't realize how important intellectual respect for my partner would end up being to me. I think this was more about not knowing myself well enough, and not knowing how being intellectually stimulated was important to me, and (even worse) how it would tie to that critical factor of respect."

The Signal to Grow

It is a fact that like the other basic pillars of life, such as work and children, marriage is not always going to be a source of satisfaction. No one is loved perfectly; some part of our authentic self is never going to be met by a partner. Sure, you can always draw a curtain over your heart. But that is not the only or the best response.

"Sometimes marriage is going to be a source of pain and sorrow," says Givertz. "And that's necessary for personal and interpersonal growth." In fact, it's impossible to be deliriously happy in marriage every moment if you are doing anything at all challenging in life, whether raising children, starting a business, or taking care of an aging parent.

Disillusionment becomes an engine for growth because it forces us to discover our needs. Knowing oneself, recognizing one's needs, and speaking up for them in a relationship are often acts of bravery, says Page. Most of us are guarded about our needs, because they are typically our areas of greatest sensitivity and vulnerability.

"You have to discover—and be able to share—what touches you and moves you the most," he observes. "But first, of course, you have to accept that in yourself. Few of us are skilled at this essential process for creating passion and romance. We'd rather complain." Nevertheless, through this process, we clarify ourselves as we move through life.

At the same time, taking the risk to expose your inner life to your partner turns out to be the great opportunity for expanding intimacy and a sense of connection. This is the great power of relationships: Creating intimacy is the crucible for growing into a fully autonomous human being while the process of becoming a fully realized person expands the possibility for intimacy and connection. This is also the work that transforms a partner into the right partner.

Another crucial element of growth in relationships, says Givertz, is a transformation of motivation—away from self-centered preferences toward what is best for the relationship and its future. There is an intrapsychic change that sustains long-term relationships. Underlying it is a broadening process in which response patterns subtly shift. Accommodation (as opposed to retaliation) plays a role. So does sacrifice. So do willingness and ability to suppress an impulse to respond negatively to a negative provocation, no matter how personally satisfying it might feel in the moment. It requires the ability to hold in mind the long-term goals of the relationship. With motivation transformed, partners are more apt to take a moment to consider how to respond, rather than react reflexively in the heat of a moment.

In his most recent study of relationships, UCLA's Bradbury followed 136 couples for 10 years, starting within six months of their marriage. All the couples reported high levels of satisfaction at the start and four years later. What Bradbury and his colleague Justin Lavner found surprising was that some couples who were so satisfied at the four-year pass eventually divorced, despite having none of the risk factors identified in previous studies of relationship dissolution—wavering commitment, maladaptive personality traits, high levels of stress.

The only elements that identified those who eventually divorced were negative and self-protective reactions during discussions of relationship difficulties and nonsupportive reactions in discussing a personal issue. Displays of anger, contempt, or attempts to blame or invalidate a partner augured poorly, even when the partners felt their marriage was functioning well overall, the researchers report in the *Journal of Family Psychology*. So did expressions of discouragement toward a partner talking about a personality feature he or she wanted to change.

In other words, the inability or unwillingness to suppress negative emotions in the heat of the moment eliminates the possibility of a transformation of motivation to a broader perspective than one's own. Eventually, the cumulative impact of negative reactivity brings the relationship down.

"There is no such thing as two people meant for each other," says Michelle Givertz. "It's a matter of adjusting and adapting." But you have to know yourself so that you can get your needs for affection, inclusion, and control met in the ways that matter most for you. Even then, successful couples redefine their relationship many times, says Meinecke. Relationships need to continually evolve to fit ever-changing circumstances. They need to incorporate each partner's changes and find ways to meet their new needs.

"If both parties are willing to tackle the hard and vulnerable work of building love and healing conflict, they have a good chance to survive," says Page. If one party is reluctant, "you might need to say to your partner, 'I need this because I feel like we're losing each other, and I don't want that to happen.'"

In the end, says Minnesota's Doherty, "We're all difficult. Everyone who is married is a difficult spouse. We emphasize that our spouse is difficult and forget how we're difficult for them." If you want to have a mate in your life, he notes, you're going to have to go through the process of idealization and disillusionment—if not with your current partner then with the next. And the next. "You could really mess up your kids as you pursue the ideal mate." What's more, studies show that, on average, people do not make a better choice the second time around. Most often, people just trade one set of problems for another.

Boston's Real reports that he attended an anniversary party for friends who had been together 25 years. When someone commented on the longevity of the relationship, the husband replied: "Every morning I wake up, splash cold water on my face, and say out loud, 'Well, you're no prize either.'" While you're busy being disillusioned with your partner, Real suggests, you'll do better with a substantial dose of humility.

Critical Thinking

1. How can someone determine if they are marrying the right person?
2. Explain the statement: Sometimes marriages bring pain and sorrow and that's necessary for growth.

REBECCA WEBBER is a freelance writer based in New York.

This Man Is Addicted to Sex

It wrecks marriages, destroys careers, and saps self-worth. Yet Americans are being diagnosed as sex addicts in record numbers.

CHRIS LEE

Valerie realized that sex was wrecking her life right around the time her second marriage disintegrated. At 30, and employed as a human-resources administrator in Phoenix, she had serially cheated on both her husbands—often with their subordinates and co-workers—logging anonymous hookups in fast-food-restaurant bathrooms, affairs with married men, and one-night stands too numerous to count. But Valerie couldn't stop. Not even after one man's wife aimed a shotgun at her head while catching them in flagrante delicto. Valerie called phone-sex chat lines and pored over online pornography, masturbating so compulsively that it wasn't uncommon for her to choose her vibrator over going to work. She craved public exhibitionism, too, particularly at strip clubs, and even accepted money in exchange for sex—not out of financial necessity but for the illicit rush such acts gave her.

For Valerie, sex was a form of self-medication: to obliterate the anxiety, despair, and crippling fear of emotional intimacy that had haunted her since being abandoned as a child. "In order to soothe the loneliness and the fear of being unwanted, I was looking for love in all the wrong places," she recalls.

After a decade of carrying on this way, Valerie hit rock bottom. Facing her second divorce as well as the end of an affair, she grew despondent and attempted to take her life by overdosing on prescription medication. Awakening in the ICU, she at last understood what she had become: a sex addict. "Through sexually acting out, I lost two marriages and a job. I ended up homeless and on food stamps," says Valerie, who, like most sex addicts interviewed for this story, declined to provide her real name. "I was totally out of control."

"Sex addiction" remains a controversial designation—often dismissed as a myth or providing talk-show punchlines thanks to high-profile lotharios such as Dominique Strauss-Kahn and Tiger Woods. But compulsive sexual behavior, also called hypersexual disorder, can systematically destroy a person's life much as addictions to alcohol or drugs can. And it's affecting an increasing number of Americans, say psychiatrists and addiction experts. "It's a national epidemic," says Steven Luff, coauthor of *Pure Eyes: A Man's Guide to Sexual Integrity* and leader of the X3LA sexual-addiction recovery groups in Hollywood.

Reliable figures for the number of diagnosed sex addicts are difficult to come by, but the Society for the Advancement of Sexual Health, an education and sex-addiction treatment organization, estimates that between 3 and 5 percent of the U.S. population—or more than 9 million people—could meet the criteria for addiction. Some 1,500 sex therapists treating compulsive behavior are practicing today, up from fewer than 100 a decade ago, say several researchers and clinicians, while dozens of rehabilitation centers now advertise treatment programs, up from just five or six in the same period. The demographics are changing, too. "Where it used to be 40- to 50-year-old men seeking treatment, now there are more females, adolescents, and senior citizens," says Tami VerHelst, vice president of the International Institute for Trauma and Addiction Professionals. "Grandfathers getting caught with porn on their computers by grandkids, and grandkids sexting at 12."

In fact, some of the growth has been fueled by the digital revolution, which has revved up America's carnal metabolism. Where previous generations had to risk public embarrassment at dirty bookstores and X-rated movie theaters, the Web has made pornography accessible, free, and anonymous. An estimated 40 million people a day in the U.S. log on to some 4.2 million pornographic websites, according to the Internet Filter Software Review. And though watching porn isn't the same as seeking out real live sex, experts say the former can be a kind of gateway drug to the latter.

"Not everyone who looks at a nude image is going to become a sex addict. But the constant exposure is going to trigger people who are susceptible," says Dr. David Sack, chief executive of Los Angeles's Promises Treatment Centers.

New high-tech tools are also making it easier to meet strangers for a quick romp. Smartphone apps like Grindr use GPS technology to facilitate instantaneous, no-strings gay hookups in 192 countries. The website AshleyMadison.com promises "affairs guaranteed" by connecting people looking for sex outside their marriages; the site says it has 12.2 million members.

This year the epidemic has spread to movies and TV. In November the Logo television network began airing Bad Sex, a reality series following a group of men and women with severe sexual issues, most notably addiction. And on Dec. 2, the acclaimed psychosexual drama Shame arrives in theaters. The movie follows Brandon (portrayed by Irish actor Michael Fassbender in a career-defining performance), a New Yorker with a libido the size of the Empire State Building. His life devolves into a blur of carnal encounters, imperiling both his job and his self-regard. In perhaps the least sexy sex scene in the history of moviedom, Brandon appears to lose all humanity during a frenzied ménage à trois with two prostitutes. "It's a foursome with the audience," says director and co-writer Steve McQueen. "What we were doing was actually dangerous. Not just in terms of people liking the movie, but psychologically."

However powerful and queasy Shame's odyssey into full-frontal debasement may be, the film only begins to tap into the dark realities connected with sex addiction. Take it from Tony, a 36-year-old from the affluent Westside of Los Angeles, who found his life thrown into turmoil by compulsive sexual behavior. "I was crippled by it," he says. "I would go into trancelike states, lose track of what I was doing socially, professionally, spiritually. I couldn't stop."

He was ashamed of his tireless efforts to find women. "I was meeting girls on the basketball court, in the club, pulling my car over to meet them on the street," Tony recalls. It took joining a Sex and Love Addicts Anonymous 12-step program for him to realize that he wasn't alone.

He also learned that his fixation on **sex** was a way of avoiding his insecurities and tackling the emotional issues that first led to his addictive behavior. "The addiction will take you to a place where you're walking the streets at night, so keyed up, thinking, 'Maybe I'll just see if there's anybody out there,'" he says. "Like looking for prey, kind of. You're totally jacked up, adrenalized. One hundred percent focused on this one purpose. But my self-esteem was shot."

Most treatment programs are modeled on Alcoholics Anonymous, but rather than pushing cold-turkey abstinence, they advocate something called "sexual sobriety." This can take different forms, but typically involves eradicating "unwanted sexual behavior," whether that's obsessive masturbation or sex with hookers. "We treat it very much like sobriety for an eating disorder," says Robert Weiss, founder of the Sexual Recovery Institute in Los Angeles. "They have to define for themselves based on their own goals and belief systems: 'What is healthy eating for me? Can I go to a buffet? Can I eat by myself?' We look at your goals and figure in your sexual behaviors and validate what's going to lead you back to the behavior you don't want to do."

Although sex addicts sometimes describe behavior akin to obsessive-compulsive disorder, research hasn't directly correlated the two. But a growing body of research shows how hypersexual disorder can fit into other forms of addiction. At the Promises treatment centers, clinicians have observed a number of **sex** addicts who have relapsed with drugs or alcohol in order to medicate the shame they felt. Severe depression can also follow after an addict starts to confront the condition. "I realized I was not comfortable in my own skin," says Valerie, who checked herself into four months of treatment for **sex** addiction at Del Amo, a private behavioral-health hospital in Torrance, Calif. "My depression came from the fear I was going to be alone for the rest of my life. Fighting the obsession and rumination, the fear of loneliness and abandonment."

Sex addicts are compelled by the same heightened emotional arousal that can drive alcoholics or drug addicts to act so recklessly, say addiction experts. Research shows that substance abusers and sex addicts alike form a dependency on the brain's pleasure-center neurotransmitter, dopamine. "It's all about chasing that emotional high: losing yourself in image after image, prostitute after prostitute, affair after affair," says the Sexual Recovery Institute's Weiss. "They end up losing relationships, getting diseases, and losing jobs."

Here's what the experts will tell you that sex addiction is most decidedly not: a convenient excuse for sexual indiscretions and marital truancy. Chris Donaghue, a sex therapist who hosts the show Bad Sex, says Tiger Woods, for example, does not qualify as a sex addict, despite his well-documented sexcapades and treatment at a Mississippi rehabilitation center specializing in sex addiction. "Because he didn't honor his integrity and marital boundary does not make him an addict," Donaghue says, adding that people will say, "'Because I get in trouble, because I cheat, I'll just blame it on sex addiction. That's my get-out-of-jail-free card.'"

Contrast Woods's wild-oats sowing against the experiences of Harper, an Atlanta-born television executive who found himself caught in the grips of sex addiction for four years. After joining an online dating service, Harper fell into a pattern of juggling multiple relationships, sexting incessantly and focusing almost singlemindedly on hooking up. He discovered he could usually get his partners into bed on the first date—sometimes within the first hour of meeting. "And these weren't desperate women," he says.

But the fleeting ego gratification Harper derived from his conquests came at a steep price. He describes himself as living in a "stupor." Friendships suffered, and he felt "pathetic" about his sexual urgency. The worst part, he says, was that his sex drive ultimately changed "what I think is normal," as his tolerance grew for increasingly hard-core forms of pornography. "It really is like that monster you can't ever fulfill," says Harper, 30, who has avoided dating for the past eight months and attends a recovery group. "Both with the porn and the sex, something will be good for a while and then you have to move on to other stuff. The worst thing is, toward the end, I was looking at pretend incest porn. And I was like, 'Why is something like that turning me on?!'"

The potential for abuse of online porn is well documented, with research showing that chronic masturbators who engage with online porn for up to 20 hours a day can suffer a "hangover" as a result of the dopamine drop-off. But there are other collateral costs. "What you look at online is going to take you offline," says Craig Gross, a.k.a. the "Porn Pastor," who heads XXXChurch.com, a Christian website that warns against the perils of online pornography. "You're going to do so many things you never thought you'd do."

Exhibit A: "We see a lot of heterosexual men who are addicted to sex and, because culturally and biologically women aren't as readily available to have sex at all times of the day, these men will turn to gay men for gratification," says sex therapist Donaghue. "Imagine what that does to their psychology. 'Now am I gay? What do I tell my wife?'"

That wasn't the issue for Max Dubinsky, an Ohio native and writer who went through a torturous 14-month period of online-pornography dependence. He says a big problem with his addiction was actually what it prevented him from doing. "I couldn't hold down a healthy relationship. I couldn't be aroused without pornography, and I was expecting way too much from the women in my life," recalls Dubinsky, 25, who sought treatment at the X3LA recovery group and is now married.

If discussion of sex addiction can seem like an exclusive domain of men, that's because, according to sex therapists, the overwhelming majority of self-identifying addicts—about 90 percent—are male. Women are more often categorized as "love addicts," with a compulsive tendency to fall into dependent relationships and form unrealistic bonds with partners. That's partly because women are more apt than men to be stigmatized by association with sex addiction, says Anna Valenti-Anderson, a sex-addiction therapist in Phoenix. "We live in a society where there's still a lot more internalized shame for

women and there's a lot more for them to lose," Valenti-Anderson says. "People will say, 'She's a bad mom' for doing these sexual things. As opposed to, 'She's sick and has a disorder.' But very slowly, women are starting to be more willing to come into treatment."

Addicts and therapists alike say they hope a greater awareness of the disease will eventually help addicts of all genders and ages come forward and seek treatment. Many are likely to find that "sex addiction isn't really about sex," as Weiss puts it; it's about "being wanted."

X3LA's Steven Luff says, "Sex is the perfect match for that. 'I matter right now. In this moment, I am loved.' In that sense, an entire culture, an entire nation is looking for meaning."

Critical Thinking

1. Discuss the concept of sex addition and why it can be such a negative factor in someone's life.

2. Address the treatment options for sex addiction.

3. What role does Internet pornography play in sex addiction?

UNIT 7

Preventing and Fighting Disease

Unit Selections

Learning Outcomes

After reading this Unit, you will be able to:

- Understand the symptoms associated with headaches and the common medications used to treat them.

- Understand the hormonal connection to migraine headaches.

- Contrast the treatment and life expectancy of those with HIV/AIDS today versus 30 years ago.

- Identify the ten public health achievements which occurred during the past ten years.

Student Website

www.mhhe.com/cls

Internet References

American Cancer Society
    www.cancer.org
American Diabetes Association Home Page
    www.diabetes.org
American Heart Association
    www.amhrt.org
National Institute of Allergy and Infectious Diseases (NIAID)
    www.niaid.nih.gov

Cardiovascular disease and cancer are the leading killers in this country. This is not altogether surprising given that the American population is growing increasingly older, and one's risk of developing both of these diseases is directly proportional to one's age. Another major risk factor, which has received considerable attention over the past 30 years, is one's genetic predisposition or family history. Historically, the significance of this risk factor has been emphasized as a basis for encouraging at-risk individuals to make prudent lifestyle choices, but this may be about to change as recent advances in genetic research, including mapping the human genome, may significantly improve the efficacy of both diagnostic and therapeutic procedures.

Just as cutting-edge genetic research is transforming the practice of medicine, startling new research findings in the health profession are transforming our views concerning adult health. This new research suggests that the primary determinants of our health as adults are the environmental conditions we experienced during our life in the womb. According to Dr. Peter Nathaniels of Cornell University, conditions during gestation, ranging from hormones that flow from the mother to how well the placenta delivers nutrients to the tiny limbs and organs, program how our liver, heart, kidneys, and especially our brains function as adults. While it is too early to draw any firm conclusions regarding the significance of the "life in the womb factor," it appears that this avenue of research may yield important clues as to how we may best prevent or forestall chronic illness.

Of all the diseases in America, coronary heart disease is this nation's number one killer. Frequently, the first and only symptom of this disease is a sudden heart attack. Epidemiological studies have revealed a number of risk factors that increase one's likelihood of developing this disease. These include hypertension, a high serum cholesterol level, diabetes, cigarette smoking, obesity, a sedentary lifestyle, a family history of heart disease, age, sex, race, and stress. In addition to these well-established risk factors, scientists think they may have discovered several additional risk factors. These include the following: low birth weight, cytomegalovirus, *Chlamydia pneumoniae,* porphyromonas-gingivalis, and c-reactive protein (CRP). CRP is a measure of inflammation somewhere in the body. In theory, a high CRP reading may be a good indicator of an impending heart attack.

One of the most startling and ominous health stories was the recent announcement by the Centers for Disease Control and Prevention (CDC) that the incidence of Type 2 adult onset diabetes increased significantly over the past 15 years. This sudden rise appears to cross all races and age groups, with the sharpest increase occurring among people aged 30 to 39 (about 70 percent). Health experts at the CDC believe that this startling rise in diabetes among 30- to 39-year-olds is linked to the rise in obesity observed among young adults (obesity rates rose from 12 to 20 percent nationally during this same time period). Experts at the CDC believe that there is a time lag of about 10–15 years between the deposition of body fat and the manifestation of Type 2 diabetes. This time lag could explain why individuals in their 30s are experiencing the greatest increase in developing Type 2 diabetes today. Current estimates suggest that 16 million Americans have diabetes; it kills approximately

© McGraw-Hill Companies, Inc./Tim Fuller, photographer

180,000 Americans each year. Many experts now believe that our couch potato culture is fueling the rising rates of both obesity and diabetes. Given what we know about the relationship between obesity and Type 2 diabetes, the only practical solution is for Americans to watch their total calorie intake and exercise regularly.

Cardiovascular disease is America's number one killer, but cancer takes top billing in terms of the "fear factor." This fear of cancer stems from an awareness of the degenerative and disfiguring nature of the disease. Today, cancer specialists are employing a variety of complex agents and technologies, such as monoclonal antibodies, interferon, and immunotherapy, in their attempt to fight the disease. Progress has been slow, however, and the results, while promising, suggest that a cure may be several years away. A very disturbing aspect of this country's battle against cancer is the fact that millions of dollars are spent each year trying to advance the treatment of cancer, while the funding for the technologies used to detect cancer in its early stages is quite limited. A reallocation of funds would seem appropriate, given the medical community posits that early detection and issue related to early detection has arisen.

The four articles in this unit address topics such as fighting and preventing diseases and conditions such as migraines, HIV/AIDS, and infections. In the first, Kent Holtorf discusses the role of hormones in the prevention and treatment of migraine headaches, especially among women in "Fighting Headaches with Hormones." Todd Melby addresses the status of HIV and AIDS, focusing on the 30th anniversary of the recognition of the disease as an epidemic in "The HIV/AIDS Epidemic at 30." Wendy Orent in "The Human Vector" discusses origins of new diseases including the evolution and mutations associated with turning an animal disease into a human one. Finally, the article "Ten Great Public Health Achievements—United States 2001–2010 reports on the achievements that helped the health status of Americans during the past ten years. The introduction of new vaccines, reduced tobacco use, and reduction of infants born with neural tube defects all contributed to the health of the nation during this time period.

Fighting Headaches with Hormones

KENT HOLTORF

With reports dating back to 1500 B.C., headaches have one the longest histories of recognition of all medical disorders—but, beset by myths, unclear causes, and inadequate remedies, they remain one of the most poorly treated conditions in medicine today.

Headaches are one of the most common complaints, with almost everyone having experienced a "splitter" at least once in his or her lifetime. About 75% of individuals have endured a headache in the past year. Headaches can be occasional, chronic, or recurrent, and the pain can be mild or severe enough to disrupt daily activities dramatically, In the U.S., more than 45,000,000 people suffer from chronic headaches.

Headaches involve the network of nerve fibers in the tissue, blood vessels, and muscles in the head and base of the skull. There are various types of headaches, as well as considerable overlap of classifications and effective therapies. For instance, migraines and the muscle tension variety coexist in as many as two-thirds of sufferers. A lot of headaches, however, have a significant hormonal component that usually goes undetected or untreated. With prosper diagnosis, significant improvement be seen in the majority of sufferers.

"There are various types of headaches, as well as considerable overlap of classifications and effective therapies."

Most primary headaches (those not due to underlying disease) fall under three categories: tension, migraine, and cluster.

Tension headaches—also called stress or muscle-contraction headaches—are the type experienced on occasion by most people. They typically are characterized by a dull, steady pain. Tension headaches often are described as tightness or vice-like pain around the forehead or back of the head. They usually occur gradually in the middle of the day and often are associated with stress, anxiety, and depression.

The severity of tension headaches typically grows as frequency increases. Chronic tension headaches usually will become more "migraine-like," being more severe and throbbing in nature. Well-known causes include inadequate sleep, poor posture, emotional or mental stress, depression, hunger, dieting, skipping meals, and over-exertion. Common hormonal causes, which usually go undetected, include low adrenal function and low thyroid. Also, while low estrogen and progesterone are known to be associated with migraine headaches, these hormones also can cause chronic tension headaches.

Migraines are the second most common type of headache. An estimated 30,000 people in the U.S. suffer from them. Women are about four times more likely than men to be afflicted. The word migraine, in Greek, means "half of the skull," as the pain usually is one-sided, but can extend further. Most migraine patients fail to get relief with current therapies. In fact, a large trial found that 64% of migraine patients are dissatisfied with their current remedies.

The exact cause of migraines is unclear but, it is known that they involve abnormal constriction and dilatation of blood vessels and the release of inflammatory chemicals from nerve fibers around these blood vessels. The sympathetic nervous system (which focuses on stress) subsequently is stimulated, causing the typical symptoms of nausea, vomiting, and photophobia (light sensitivity). Some people also experience a variety of mostly visual sensations—an aura before, or with, the onset of the migraine.

Commonly identified triggers of migraines include alcohol, cheese, preservatives, hunger, exertion, fatigue, perfumes, weather changes, and artificial sweeteners. Fluctuations in estrogen and progesterone are well-known triggers of migraines (though typically poorly treated), but low adrenal function and low thyroid are common contributors that often remain undiagnosed.

Standard medications for the acute treatment of migraines include triptans; nonsteroidal anti-inflammatories, or NSAIDS, such as aspirin and ibuprofen; ergots; narcotic pain medications; and Midrin.

Additionally, there are a number of medications that can be used to reduce the frequency and severity of migraines, including anti-seizure and blood-pressure drugs and antidepressants. However, these typically are associated with significant side effects and do not address the underlying abnormal physiology.

The most effective way to treat migraines without side effects is to remedy the hormonal imbalance causing or contributing to the migraines, which include estrogen, progesterone, thyroid, testosterone, cortisol, DHEA, pregnenolone, melatonin, oxytocin, and serotonin. Hormones play a significant part in around 75% of migraines.

Cluster headaches are a much more rare form that strikes in a group or "cluster" with relatively long periods between attacks. The pain typically is one-sided, steady, piercing, behind one eye or temple, and occurs at night or early morning. Men almost are 10 times more likely to suffer from cluster headaches than women. The standard therapy consists of pain medications. As with estrogen and progesterone imbalance causing migraines in women, low and fluctuating testosterone levels can cause cluster headaches in men.

Estrogen is a known culprit in migraines and such association often is called a menstrual migraine, as they usually occur just before or during a women's cycle. In fact, 60% of women who suffer from migraines find a worsening of headaches just before and during their period. Many also will notice an increased frequency of headaches mid cycle (during ovulation). All of these instances are associated with dramatic drops in estrogen and progesterone. Women usually see a reduction in migraines during the last two trimesters of pregnancy when these hormones remain elevated.

To dilate normally, blood vessels require estrogen, progesterone, testosterone, and thyroid hormone. With a deficiency of these hormones or a fluctuation (high to low), the normal constriction and dilatation of blood vessels are compromised and destabilized, potentially precipitating a migraine. Estrogen and progesterone have additional effects that help subdue migraines and tension headaches. Bioidentical estrogen and progesterone decrease vessel inflammation, thus shortcircuiting migraine and tension headaches, and aid in the production of serotonin, which has been shown to prevent the headaches.

Mitigating Migraines

Physicians generally use the medications called triptans or ergotamines for menstrual migraines, but hormone-related migraines are the most resistant to such drugs. The best way to treat them is to prevent the dramatic drop in estrogen and progesterone during the last part of the cycle, although they can occur mid cycle as well. This involves giving bioidentical progesterone during the second part of the cycle (days 16–28), either via a cream or time-released capsule, as the standard progesterone preparation is in a peanut oil base and results in too much fluctuation of levels.

Synthetic progestins should not be used, as they can worsen migraines. A bioidentical low-dose estrogen (usually a combination of estriol and estradiol) is given later in the cycle (typically starling on day 24). The estrogen should be given transdermally (via either cream twice daily or a patch). This delivers a constant level and prevents the peaks and valleys experienced when given orally.

Some physicians will employ birth control pills to "fix" fluctuating hormonal levels. Low doses sometimes are effective, but more often make symptoms worse. Additionally, synthetic estrogens and progestins increase inflammation and are associated with an elevated risk of blood clots and breast cancer.

Undiagnosed low cellular thyroid level is a significant contributor to a large percent of migraines. An adequate thyroid hormone is required for blood vessels to constrict or dilate normally. For instance, low thyroid is a major cause of a condition called Raynaud's phenomenon or syndrome, where the vessels in the hand constrict and endure excessive dilation. After a trigger, such as temperature change or an emotional event, the hands turn white with lack of blood flow and, after a period of lime, they flush as the vessels dilate abnormally. This is very painful, but can be prevented or treated with thyroid supplementation. This is the same phenomenon that occurs in the skull with a migraine.

Thyroid is important for muscle tension headache as well; muscles require significant energy to relax. With low thyroid, the muscle does not have enough energy in the resting phase, so it becomes stiff and painful, which can cause a tension headache and perhaps trigger a migraine.

Hypothyroidism is a common disorder characterized by an inadequate cellular thyroid effect to meet the needs of the tissues. Typical symptoms include fatigue, weight gain, depression, cold extremities, muscle aches, headaches, decreased libido, weakness, cold intolerance, water retention, premenstrual syndrome, dry skin, and headaches.

Low thyroid causes or contributes to the symptoms of many conditions, but the deficiency often is missed by standard testing. This especially is true with depression, obesity, diabetes, chronic fatigue syndrome, fibromyalgia, and migraine headaches. It is not surprising that the two populations with the highest incidence of migraines are depressed patients and those with chronic fatigue syndrome or fibromyalgia, as all of these are shown to have low tissue thyroid levels that are missed by standard blood tests.

Physicians and endocrinologists often use a simple test called TSH (thyroid stimulating hormone) to rule out a thyroid disorder. Relying on it, however, will result in misdiagnosing up to 80% of the cases with low thyroid.

These conditions are associated with poor utilization of thyroid hormone, where they do not convert the inactive version of the a hormone called thyroxine (T4) that is secreted by the thyroid gland into the active version that has metabolic effects called triiodothyronine (T3). Instead, they convert the T4 into a mirror image of the T3—known as reverse T3. This imposter blocks the effects of T3. A low T3 or high reverse T3 level results in cellular thyroid deficiency and can cause or contribute to a number of the conditions previously mentioned. In order to assess a patient's thyroid function adequately, in addition to laboratory analysis, an extensive history should be taken. A laboratory analysis indicating a T3/reverse T3 ratio of less than 1.8 is consistent with low cellular thyroid levels and a trial of thyroid replacement should be considered even if the TSH is normal.

Additionally, a test called sex hormone binding globulin (SHBG) is a marker for cellular thyroid levels. It is stimulated in the liver in response to thyroid hormone and estrogen, so it can be a useful madder for tissue level of thyroid. In a premenopausal woman, the level should be above 70. If not, this is a good indication that there are low tissue levels of thyroid. This especially is true if the woman is on oral thyroid replacement, because, due to first pass metabolism, her liver will have much higher thyroid levels than the rest of the tissues. Thus, if SHBG is low, the rest of the body is characterized by low thyroid. This test is not useful if a woman is on oral estrogen replacement because that will elevate SHBG artificially due to high estrogen levels in the liver. The test is accurate for those using transdermal estrogen preparations, however.

For patients who suffer from migraine headaches and, to some degree, tension headaches, the standard method of thyroid supplementation with T4 preparations often is of little benefit. Effective treatment usually requires that a combination of T4 and T3 be given, or even more effective is all T3 via a time-released preparation.

A major hormone produced in response to stress is cortisol. While some people believe that cortisol causes stress, it actually helps the body deal with it. With acute stress, the body will increase cortisol in relation to the amount of stress. With chronic stress, however, the adrenal output can become compromised, which is termed "adrenal fatigue." This occurs when the body no longer can secrete cortisol and other adrenal hormones such as DHEA adequately. Instead of secreting cortisol and DHEA in response to stress, the body replaces it with adrenaline, resulting in an inability to handle stress that often is associated with anxiety, fatigue, insomnia, muscle pain, sugar cravings, and hypoglycemia.

Low cortisol secretion, caused by stress or missed meals, results in drops in blood sugar that can precipitate a migraine and, because cortisol is anti-inflammatory, adrenal fatigue also can result in an increased amount of inflammatory cytokines (messengers) that can precipitate a migraine.

A migraine triggered by missed meals is a common sign that adrenal fatigue is playing a role. If a person has chronic fatigue syndrome or fibromyalgia, it almost is assured that adrenal dysfunction largely is responsible, as studies show that 90% of such individuals have adrenal dysfunction—and standard blood tests are no better than flipping a coin to differentiate normal and abnormal adrenal function, as a "normal" serum cortisol often is associated with dysfunction.

If migraines occur during missed meals or stress and the fasting serum cortisol level is less than 12, a trial of physiologic replacement of cortisol should be considered. This means that very low doses of natural cortisol are given to bring the cortisol level to a more optimal level. This should not be confused with the use of corticosteroids such as prednisone, which have significant side effects. In contrast, physiologic doses of coltisol from 2.5 to l0 milligrams are shown to have a long-term safety profile that essentially is the same as a placebo.

Testosterone is the primary androgen produced by the testes in men and in the adrenal gland and ovaries in women. It is thought to be mainly a male hormone, but it plays a vital role in maintaining mood, energy, libido, and lean body mass in both sexes.

A common cause of low testosterone in men is stress and exposure to environmental contaminants such as bisphenol-A, which is a component in many plastic containers, including water bottles. In women, a major cause of suppressed testosterone levels is the use of birth control pills. While low testosterone levels can increase the risk of migraines, it particularly is important in men with cluster headaches.

Studies have shown that a suboptimal testosterone level in men that still may be considered "normal" by many doctors is associated with fatigue, depression, poor motivation, obesity, and risk of cluster headaches. The problem is that standard blood tests miss the majority of men who can benefit because they mainly measure inactive levels, which do not decline as rapidly as the active testosterone; thus, the tests do not detect significant testosterone deficiency.

What is Considered "Normal"?

Keep in mind, too, that standard laboratory normal ranges only consider the lowest 2.5% of the population to be abnormal, so many doctors will not treat until that level is reached. Men can suffer with major symptoms due to testosterone deficiency, have a 70-80% reduction in levels, and still be considered "normal" by the laboratory and an unknowing physician.

Any man with migraines or cluster headaches and suboptimal testosterone levels is a good candidate for replacement therapy, especially if associated with fatigue, erectile dysfunction, obesity, or depression. With supplementation, such men can have dramatic improvement in headache frequency, as well as a significantly better quality of life and a reduction in cardiovascular risk.

By the way, the studies clearly demonstrate that the long-held belief that testosterone replacement can increase the risk of prostate cancer is incorrect. It now is demonstrated that low testosterone, not high, increases risk for prostate cancer.

Women with low or suboptimal levels of testosterone may suffer from depression, fatigue, and reduced libido. Supplementation not only help fight such symptoms, but helps reduce the incidence of migraines.

Along with cortisol, DHEA is naturally produced in the body by the adrenal glands. It circulates in the bloodstream and is converted into other hormones like testosterone and estrogen. Low levels are associated with aging, illness, chronic stress, fatigue, low libido, and migraine headaches. Bringing levels back to more optimal readings can reduce the frequency and severity of migraines, especially when given in combination with other hormones. If levels are in the lowest 35 percentile, DHEA supplementation should be considered.

Pregnenolone is the most abundant hormone in the brain—considered to be the "grandmother" hormone, one from with all others are derived. If pregnenolone levels are low, the body cannot produce the other hormones adequately. A proper pregnenolone level is essential for balance, which can reduce migraine frequency and severity. As with DHEA, if levels are in the lowest 35 percentile, supplementation should be considered.

Melatonin is secreted by the pineal gland to regulate the circadian rhythm (sleep cycle) of the body. It also serves as a particularly potent intracellular antioxidant that reduces oxidative stress and inflammation. Migraine patients have a high incidence of insomnia and sleep disorders, and studies show they have diminished secretion of melatonin. While there is no standardized blood test to detect this deficiency, any migraine patient should consider a trial of melatonin supplementation at bedtime, especially those who have insomnia.

While serotonin technically is a neurotransmitter, it works as a hormone when taken orally or by injection. Migraine patients have been shown to have low serotonin levels, which may be at least partially due to the low cellular thyroid levels seen with this condition, as thyroid is needed by the nerves to make serotonin. This especially is true for those who are depressed or have been on long-term antidepressants, as they suppress the body's ability to produce serotonin.

It is interesting that most physicians, neurologists, and psychiatrists are not aware of the effectiveness of bioidentical serotonin supplementation or even its existence as a prescription medication, but the fact is that, if someone has a migraine, a shot of serotonin often will abort the pain immediately without side effects. It also is good as treatment for an acute anxiety attack.

Oxytocin, at very high concentrations, produces uterine contractions during pregnancy. It is known, too, as the "cuddle hormone" for promoting feelings of calmness, security, trust, well-being, social bonding, and romantic attachment. It is produced at time of birth and during sex and meaningful social interactions. It can increase libido and orgasms in women and improve erectile function in men—and, of course, prevent migraines.

Critical Thinking

1. What role do hormones play in the treatment and prevention of headaches?

2. Discuss the physical and mental effects of headaches.

3. Address the three main types of headaches and discuss treatment options for each.

***

KENT HOLTORF is a general internist at UCLA Medical Center who runs private practices on the East and West coasts and is the author of *Ur-Ine Trouble*.

The HIV/AIDS Epidemic at 30

Todd Melby

Fifteen years ago, Craig White noticed an unusual mark on his leg. "I gotta get tested," he told himself.

So White trudged to a free clinic and asked for an HIV test. One week later, a nurse returned with the news: He was HIV-positive. White, a gay man in his early forties, turned to his partner and embraced him.

In 1996, a diagnosis of HIV was often a death sentence. White soon learned that his T lymphocyte count—also known as CD4 count—was just 52, a sign that HIV was attacking his immune system.

"People with your number usually last six months," a physician told him. "I hate to tell you. But that's your prognosis."

Two developments saved White's life, he says. A university oncologist enrolled him in a drug trial that effectively battled his HIV-related cancer. At about the same time, protease inhibitors, a new class of drugs that target infections like HIV, came on the market.

"Things started to go right," White says.

After more than a year of chemotherapy and the new antiretrovirals, the cancer disappeared and his T cell count improved dramatically.

Today, White is a healthy 57-year-old marketing executive living in suburban Chicago. Although he still takes five pills a day to keep his immune system strong, his few health irritations are mostly related to aging, not HIV.

That White—and millions of others like him—are living longer lives is one of the success stories in the fight against HIV/AIDS. New studies suggest novel ways to stop the spread of the disease. But as HIV/AIDS enters its fourth decade on the planet, many challenges remain.

New approaches offer hope, but some communities suffer.

In the United States, blacks and Latinos are contracting HIV at higher rates than other ethnic groups. With government budgets straining under the weight of a long recession, more than 9,000 Americans remain on waiting lists to begin treatment.

Health disparities also abound around the world. HIV-positive patients in poorer countries are still less likely to receive drugs needed to keep them healthy. But there's encouraging news as well. A new study suggests the best way to prevent new cases is to get HIV-positive men and women on antiretrovirals immediately—before signs of immune system weakness.

As activists, researchers and everyday citizens observe World AIDS Day on December 1, we examine some of the important developments and challenges facing decision makers.

Gay and Bisexual Men, Black Americans Hit Hardest

Los Angeles physicians are credited with discovering the disease now known as HIV/AIDS. In a June 1981 issue of the U.S. Centers for Disease Control and Prevention's (CDC) *Morbidity and Mortality Weekly Report,* the doctors noted that five gay men between the ages of 29 and 36 had recently died of pneumonia due to a suppressed immune system.

"The fact that these patients were all homosexual suggests an association between some aspect of a homosexual lifestyle or disease acquired through sexual contact," the report noted.

In the 30 years since that report, 25 million people have died as a result of HIV/AIDS, including more than 617,000 people in the United States. Currently, 34 million people are infected worldwide, including more than 1.1 million Americans.

Among Americans, most of the new diagnoses in 2009 were the result of sexual contact between men (17,005), followed by heterosexual sexual contact (10,393), IV drug users (4,942) and a combination of male sexual contact and IV drug use (1,580).

"We have an epidemic in this country that is primarily among gay men," says Carl Schmid, deputy executive director of the AIDS Institute. "When you think of how small the gay community is . . . the rates are just astronomical."

"We have an epidemic in this country that is primarily among gay men. When you think of how small the gay community is . . . the rates are just astronomical."

— Carl Schmid

The most affected ethnic groups are blacks and Latinos. Although those two groups comprise just 28 percent of the United Status population, they account for 64 percent of all new HIV infections.

Black Americans have been particularly hard hit. They account for 44 percent of all new HIV cases and make up nearly half of all people (46 percent) living with the disease. Blacks are dying at a faster clip than other ethnic groups. Their survival time with the disease is lower than other ethnic groups and in 2007, blacks accounted for 57 percent of all HIV/AIDS deaths.

"The impact on black Americans is striking," says Jen Kates, director of Global Health and HIV policy at the Kaiser Family Foundation (KFF).

Latinos, now the second largest ethnic group in the United States, comprise 16 percent of the country's people and account for 20 percent of new HIV infections. Most HIV-positive Latinos live in New York, California, Puerto Rico, Texas and Florida.

Many Latinos also face barriers to health care, both due to language, immigration status and poverty, says John Hellman, policy advocate at the Latino Commission on AIDS.

An HIV Cost and Services Utilization Study (HCSUS) by the R-and Corporation supports that claim. "Latinos fare more poorly on several important measures of access and quality, differences that diminished over time but were not completely eliminated," according to a KFF summary of several HCSUS studies.

HIV-positive blacks and Latinos are disproportionately poor and many rely on the AIDS Drug Assistance Program (ADAP) for the expensive medical treatment. But that federal and state government effort is falling short.

"There's an ADAP funding crisis," Hellman says. "It's a huge problem."

According to KFF, 9,066 people in need of antiretroviral drugs aren't getting them. There are waiting lists in at least 11 states, including Alabama, Florida, Georgia, Idaho, Louisiana, Montana, North Carolina, Ohio, South Carolina, Utah and Virginia.

About one-third of the people on ADAP waiting lists live in Florida, which prompted Senator Bill Nelson (D-Fla.) and Elton John to pen an opinion editorial for *Politico,* an online political website.

"In these difficult times, we must not lose sight of the fact that prevention and care remain a critical weapon against this epidemic—which is why we must have affordable and accessible treatment for those living with AIDS," Nelson and John wrote.

That will likely happen in 2014, when the Affordable Health Care Act takes effect. The law—referred to as Obamacare by its political opponents—may eliminate ADAP waiting lists.

Another positive step cited by AIDS policy experts is the Obama administration's adoption of a "National HIV/AIDS Strategy for the United States" last year. The policy calls for ways to reduce infections, improve care, reduce inequities and encourage government agencies to coordinate efforts to fight HIV/AIDS.

"It's been very helpful," Schmid says. "It puts the goals out there. It's getting agencies to work together."

The National HIV/AIDS Strategy is changing how HIV prevention funds are being spent. New CDC guidelines are asking cities and states to spend more money on those most affected by the virus, i.e., gay men and black Americans.

"Making the National HIV/AIDS strategy 'real' will require innovation and new focus, including the shift of resources to the communities where HIV is most prevalent," says A. Cornelius Baker, national policy advisor at the National Black Gay Men's Advocacy Coalition. "Black communities in the South and many urban cities are expected to benefit from this shift."

Treating the Disease Immediately Offers Hope

There's still no cure for one of the world's deadliest diseases. But there is new hope.

In June, University of North Carolina at Chapel Hill researcher Myron Cohen announced the findings of a six-year study involving 1,763 couples living in the United States, Brazil, India, Thailand and several other countries. Each of the couples included one HIV-negative person and one HIV-positive person. Once divided into separate groups, half of the HIV-positive people began taking antiretrovirals immediately. The other half didn't begin anti-AIDS drugs until symptoms appeared.

During the $73 million study, 28 partners of people with HIV became infected. In 27 of the cases, treatment had been delayed. That discovery led researchers to stop the study and begin offering treatment to newly infected individuals.

Michel Sibide of UNAIDS, the United Nations program on HIV/ AIDS, calls the results a "game changer." Thomas Coates of the University of California, Los Angeles, told a reporter, "The results are phenomenal."

So while there is no cure, it's conceivable HIV/ AIDS could be wiped out—or at least drastically reduced—through a combination of testing and immediate treatment. After all, HIV-positive patients using antiretrovirals don't appear to pass on the virus to their partners.

While that's theoretically possible, it's not that easy.

"Even if everyone [who is HIV-positive] could get treatment immediately, there's still a need for other interventions," Kates says. "It's not a simple road."

Still, Secretary of State Hillary Clinton has urged policy makers and activists to imagine an "AIDS-free generation" by pushing for earlier treatment and other effective preventative efforts.

"We have a chance to give countless lives and futures to millions of people who are alive today but equally, if not profoundly more importantly, to an entire new generation yet to be born," Clinton added.

"We have a chance to give countless lives and futures to millions of people who are alive today but equally, if not profoundly more importantly, to an entire new generation yet to be born."

Other important approaches include circumcising men, vaginal gels and comprehensive sexuality education about safer sex. Studies in 2005 and 2006 found that circumcised males were much less likely to contract HIV from female partners.

"In these studies, men who had been randomly assigned to the circumcision group had a 60 percent (South Africa), 53 percent (Kenya) and 51 percent (Uganda) lower incidence of HIV infection compared with men assigned to the wait-list group to be circumcised at the end of the study," a CDC report states.

Meanwhile, a 2010 study of 889 women found that those using a vaginal microbicide containing tenofovir, an antiretroviral drug, were 39 percent less likely to contract HIV. Experts say the study needs to be repeated, but early reaction was positive. Sidibe called it "encouraging." And the CDC's Kevin Fenton, director of the National Center for HIV/AIDS, termed it "an exciting step."

Education remains an important worldwide prevention tool. In the most recent "UNAIDS Report on the Global AIDS Epidemic," one of the many charts focused on the "percentage of schools [in each country] that provided life skills-based HIV education in the last academic year."

Costa Rica, Finland, Luxembourg, Japan, Portugal, Sweden, Venezuela and Zimbabwe were among the nations reporting 100 percent. The United States was not listed.

HIV/AIDS prevention, treatment and care doesn't come cheap. A recent KFF and UNAIDS report found that HIV/AIDS donations by rich countries fell 10 percent in the past year. Australia, Germany, the Netherlands, Norway, Spain, Sweden and the United States donated less money to fight HIV/AIDS in 2010.

The U.S. gives more than any other nation—54 percent of all big nation giving to HIV/AIDS comes from America. The Kaiser/UNAIDS report says U.S. giving fell in the most recent year because of the way Congress is allocating funds, not because there is a change in giving patterns.

Still, Kates worries that the global recession and the European debt crisis could cause a decrease in overall available funds.

"This is the first time we saw a drop," she says. "It's a challenging time."

Critical Thinking

1. How has the epidemic changed over the past 30 years?

2. What new treatment options are available for persons with AIDS?

3. Today, which population groups have been most affected by AIDS? Discuss.

The Human Vector

WENDY ORENT

"How do you make preparedness sexy?" Dave Daigle asks. A communications expert in disaster readiness at the Centers for Disease Control and Prevention in Atlanta, Daigle created last year's cheeky Zombie Apocalypse campaign, designed to teach the social media generation how to survive natural disasters and uncontained infectious outbreaks. He never expected the associated Twitter campaign to crash his server and ultimately garner three billion hits. The whole initiative, the most successful in CDC public-relations history, cost taxpayers all of $87—for clip art.

The Zombie Apocalypse campaign instructs you how to prepare for pandemics and catastrophes like hurricanes, tornadoes, and floods. You need a plan. You need flashlights, an all-weather radio, bottled water. You need food you can stock, like peanut butter, canned tuna, and crackers. You need first-aid supplies like bandages, antiseptics, and soap. And you need somewhere safe to stay—a basement room, preferably windowless, where you can hole up for several days until the danger is past.

That style of preparation also resonates with the plots of popular disease-disaster movies, like the recent *Contagion*. The film presents a fictional virus, a construct devised by Columbia University epidemiologist Ian Lipkin, vectoring its way across the planet, killing millions of the fecklessly unprepared and leaving social havoc and innumerable bodies in its wake. The CDC campaign and the film spring from the same conviction: Since nature can always turn on us, we had better be ready for the consequences.

This kind of preparedness for natural catastrophes makes sense, but for pandemics the idea rings false; unlike the scenario in *Contagion*, pandemics don't spring on us like hurricanes. Instead, they are overwhelmingly social phenomena. Mother Nature doesn't create them; human beings do. We create the settings that allow new, deadly diseases to evolve and invade. Understanding those settings, which can be thought of as disease factories, and taking steps to disrupt them are far better preparation than sending families down to huddle in the basement.

The term pandemic almost always refers to waves of acute infectious disease across a wide geographical area. In A.D. 542, during the savage Plague of Justinian, the citizens of Constantinople buried their dead in towers along the city walls and, when there was no more room, in massive pits into which corpses were flung like carrion. That epidemic, almost certainly bubonic plague, rimmed the entire Mediterranean at least as far west as Marseille and killed millions. The Black

Death—caused by a variant of the same germ, Yersinia pestis—swept into Europe from central Asia in 1347 and killed between a quarter and a third of Europe. And plague was not done with Europe yet. Londoners of the 17th century watched additional waves of disease come in by ship from Holland. In a matter of weeks, they too were infected, nailed up in their houses, and left to die. The bodies, stacked like logs on gravediggers' wagons, were carted through the streets and dumped in mass graves, which you can still see in London today.

Blaming pestilence on God's wrath goes back to Homer's Iliad. In the opening pages, a priest asks Apollo to avenge his daughter, who has been taken by the Greek leader, Agamemnon, as a spoil of war. Apollo complies with a rain of arrows, and the Greeks begin to die. The same image of plague as God's punishment crops up during the Plague of Justinian and the Black Death, and something of it remains today, though in the modern narrative it is no longer God but nature that we have offended. Since the publication of Laurie Garrett's influential 1994 book, *The Coming Plague*, people commonly talk about pandemics as nature's retribution: something sprung on us as a penalty for disturbing the world's innate balance, for penetrating too deeply into forests and jungles, for disrupting the order of the Earth's precarious ecosystems. It is our version of God's punishment, and it is just as false.

The idea that new diseases come from human invasions of pristine environments probably stems from HIV, the virus causing AIDS. HIV originated as a simian virus and most likely crossed the species line around 1930. Yet AIDS did not turn into a human pandemic until sexual activity transformed a sluggish disease into an explosive and probably more virulent one, contends evolutionary biologist Paul Ewald of the University of Louisville. It was not just the spark of infection, but what happened to that infection when it entered human society, that converted a simian retrovirus into HIV and then into the deadly pandemic that is AIDS.

This is why pandemics are necessarily social phenomena. Each human pandemic exists because social conditions have allowed it to evolve. Some diseases move across species lines and yet harm us not at all. An example is Ebola-Reston, a virus deadly to monkeys. It infected four people at an animal facility in Reston, Virginia, in November 1989, but no one fell ill; the infections were detectable only through blood tests. At the same time, other, related Ebola viruses ravage the human body. Some particularly notorious strains almost always kill.

What most new diseases, including Ebola, don't do very well is spread from person to person. Without such spread there is no pandemic. There isn't even a new, self-sustaining human disease. If we are looking for the real engine for infection—the driver of the disease factory, if you like—we have to understand what human-to human-transmission is, and how it turns an animal disease into a human one.

To be transmitted, a germ has to be shed from one human host and picked up by another. Some germs, like cholera, make their hosts produce copious diarrhea. If there is poor sanitation or people are crowded together, those germs are likely to infect other hosts. Respiratory infections are shed into the air or onto surfaces. If someone sneezes into her hand and touches a doorknob that you touch afterwards, you may catch her infection. Some germs float through the air and you breathe them in. Measles and tuberculosis spread this way. These germs have to keep their hosts mobile. If you are knocked off your feet right away by an infection and you don't walk around sneezing or coughing, it is harder for the germ to find another person to infect.

But manipulating the host into producing diarrhea or a germ-filled sneeze is not a trivial task. Highly virulent H5N1 avian flu, which many experts thought would trigger a deadly pandemic between 2004 and 2007, has so far been unable to convert from a chicken flu to a human one. On the vast chicken farms of Asia, where millions of birds are crowded under disease-factory conditions, H5N1 gained tremendous virulence, becoming a sophisticated chicken-killing machine. When people are exposed to high doses of this virus, they can succumb as well. But H5N1, well adapted to the higher temperatures and particular cell receptors found in chickens, does not spread from person to person. In its present form, therefore, it has shown no capacity to turn from a well-adapted chicken disease to a human one.

Experts have warned that H5N1 could recombine with a human virus at any moment, mutating so it becomes transmissible. But transmission doesn't just happen; it evolves. It would take a whole series of mutations, and they would have to happen in the bodies of a chain of human beings, not chickens. Nor would a single recombination event be likely to spawn a fully transmissible human disease. Instead, you would have to start with a huge dose of virus, says flu virologist Earl Brown of the University of Ottawa. A huge dose would be more likely to contain many diverse strains. Then you would have to expose those strains to a chain of human hosts. As the virus moved from person to person (assuming it could), the strains that are most easily transmitted would be selected over the others. Eventually you would get a human-adapted virus, though what that virus would look like is anybody's guess. To produce a truly lethal human flu or other virus, you would need the same sort of conditions that produced virulent chicken flu. You would need a disease factory for people.

Yet in 2005 scientists were so terrified of a lethal avian flu pandemic that they devised all sorts of preparations, which surely helped inspire the CDC's Zombie Apocalypse campaign. Tamiflu, an antiviral drug, was stockpiled in enormous quantities, even though the late influenza virologist Edwin Kibourne

noted that it is useless for prophylaxis. The drug also has dangerous side effects—and there are practical limits for how long you could keep people on it, anyway. Governments and drug companies developed candidates for anti-pandemic vaccines, and some experts called for mass prophylactic vaccination, even though no human H5N1 virus existed. Government agencies urged people to stockpile water and peanut butter and tuna fish in preparation for what Michael Osterholm, director of the Center for Infectious Disease Research and Policy at the University of Minnesota, told the press would be "three years of a given hell. . . . I can't think of any other risk, terrorism or Mother Nature included, that could potentially pose any greater risk to society than this."

We never got three years of hell, but we did get a new pandemic influenza. While experts were fixated on birds in Asia, this strain came from pigs in Mexico. Packing pigs into cramped quarters produces another kind of disease factory. In the winter of 2009, people living near a giant industrial pig farm in La Gloria, Mexico, reportedly became ill with a severe respiratory virus. No one except local reporters and a few health officials paid attention.

Then the virus began to spread. By the time the supposed "index case"—a 5-year-old La Gloria child named Edgar Hernandez—was identified, the so-called swine flu had been transmitted widely across Mexico. Within days it landed across the border, and in just weeks it spread across the world. Pigs and people, both mammals, pass flu back and forth quite easily; a pig is more like a person than a chicken when it comes to temperature and cell receptors. Pigs were always more likely to produce a pandemic flu than chickens. But most people weren't looking.

Enormous animal farms remain a source of danger, a far greater danger to people than new viruses emerging straight out of nature. Virologist Brown warns that we have to find new ways to raise animals that don't pack them so closely together in huge industrial farms. Under such crowded conditions, even the most innocuous germs can rapidly evolve virulence. The deadly Escherichia coli outbreak in Germany last year [2011], which sickened more than 4,000 people and killed more than 50, may be traceable to modern factory farming, which uses massive doses of antibiotics to curb animal infections, likely converting a normally benign microbe into an antibiotic-resistant killer.

Hospitals also encourage the emergence of lethal human microbes. Paul Ewald points out that any conditions allowing germs to be transported from a person immobilized by serious illness to new human hosts can produce deadly infections. Ironically, hospitals turn out to be highly efficient disease factories. They allow the proliferation and spread of dangerous germs among patients, and the evolution of those germs to extreme levels of virulence. The last decades have seen the evolution of virulent, antibiotic-resistant staphylococcus germs (MRSA), now spread worldwide, along with potentially lethal strains of Clostridium difficile, a usually benign intestinal infection. And the normally innocuous soil bacterium Acinetobacter baumannii has plagued veterans' hospitals, evolving intense virulence and antibiotic resistance and afflicting wounded soldiers returning from Afghanistan and Iraq.

The CDC's Zombie Apocalypse program is well intentioned, and for natural disasters it gives great advice. But preparing for a pandemic has almost nothing to do with personal supplies of crackers and duct tape. It lies in understanding the real engines of infection: the giant industrial farms and crowded hospitals with insufficient hygiene.

Many European hospitals have reduced their rates of MRSA transmission by screening patients with nasal swabs prior to admission, and some American hospitals are following suit. Shutting down industrial farming should probably come next. These germ incubators need to be replaced with less intensive farms that raise fewer animals on more land. Switching to grass-fed cattle, which live on the open range, would help as well. The price, including the end of cheap chicken, pork,

or beef, might be more than we are willing to pay, even at risk to our health. But as long as there are industrial farms, the possibility of pandemics arising from them persists.

Closing disease factories, wherever they occur, may not make for compelling cinema, but it is the most effective form of pandemic preparation we can devise.

Critical Thinking

1. Explain why pandemics are necessarily social phenomena.
2. Discuss the relationship between animals and human diseases.
3. Why are infectious diseases spreading in hospitals? What can be done to stop this?

Orent, Wendy. From *Discover*, March 2012. Copyright © 2012 by Discover Syndication. Reprinted by permission via PARS International.

Ten Great Public Health Achievements— United States, 2001–2010

Ram Koppaka

During the 20th century, life expectancy at birth among U.S. residents increased by 62%, from 47.3 years in 1900 to 76.8 in 2000, and unprecedented improvements in population health status were observed at every stage of life *(1)*. In 1999, *MMWR* published a series of reports highlighting 10 public health achievements that contributed to those improvements. This report assesses advances in public health during the first 10 years of the 21st century. Public health scientists at CDC were asked to nominate noteworthy public health achievements that occurred in the United States during 2001–2010. From those nominations, 10 achievements, not ranked in any order, have been summarized in this report.

Vaccine-Preventable Diseases

The past decade has seen substantial declines in cases, hospitalizations, deaths, and health-care costs associated with vaccine-preventable diseases. New vaccines (i.e., rotavirus, quadrivalent meningococcal conjugate, herpes zoster, pneumococcal conjugate, and human papillomavirus vaccines, as well as tetanus, diphtheria, and acellular pertussis vaccine for adults and adolescents) were introduced, bringing to 17 the number of diseases targeted by U.S. immunization policy. A recent economic analysis indicated that vaccination of each U.S. birth cohort with the current childhood immunization schedule prevents approximately 42,000 deaths and 20 million cases of disease, with net savings of nearly $14 billion in direct costs and $69 billion in total societal costs *(2)*.

The impact of two vaccines has been particularly striking. Following the introduction of pneumococcal conjugate vaccine, an estimated 211,000 serious pneumococcal infections and 13,000 deaths were prevented during 2000–2008 *(3)*. Routine rotavirus vaccination, implemented in 2006, now prevents an estimated 40,000–60,000 rotavirus hospitalizations each year *(4)*. Advances also were made in the use of older vaccines, with reported cases of hepatitis A, hepatitis B, and varicella at record lows by the end of the decade. Age-specific mortality (i.e., deaths per million population) from varicella for persons age <20 years, declined by 97% from 0.65 in the prevaccine period (1990–1994) to 0.02 during 2005–2007 *(5)*. Average age-adjusted mortality (deaths per million population) from hepatitis A also declined significantly, from 0.38 in the prevaccine period (1990–1995) to 0.26 during 2000–2004 *(6)*.

Prevention and Control of Infectious Diseases

Improvements in state and local public health infrastructure along with innovative and targeted prevention efforts yielded significant progress in controlling infectious diseases. Examples include a 30% reduction from 2001 to 2010 in reported U.S. tuberculosis cases and a 58% decline from 2001 to 2009 in central line–associated blood stream infections *(7,8)*. Major advances in laboratory techniques and technology and investments in disease surveillance have improved the capacity to identify contaminated foods rapidly and accurately and prevent further spread *(9–12)*. Multiple efforts to extend HIV testing, including recommendations for expanded screening of persons aged 13–64 years, increased the number of persons diagnosed with HIV/AIDS and reduced the proportion with late diagnoses, enabling earlier access to life-saving treatment and care and giving infectious persons the information necessary to protect their partners *(13)*. In 2002, information from CDC predictive models and reports of suspected West Nile virus transmission through blood transfusion spurred a national investigation, leading to the rapid development and implementation of new blood donor screening *(14)*. To date, such screening has interdicted 3,000 potentially infected U.S. donations, removing them from the blood supply. Finally, in 2004, after more than 60 years of effort, canine rabies was eliminated in the United States, providing a model for controlling emerging zoonoses *(15,16)*.

Tobacco Control

Since publication of the first Surgeon General's Report on tobacco in 1964, implementation of evidence-based policies and interventions by federal, state, and local public health authorities has reduced tobacco use significantly (17). By 2009, 20.6% of adults and 19.5% of youths were current smokers, compared with 23.5% of adults and 34.8% of youths 10 years earlier. However, progress in reducing smoking rates among youths and adults appears to have stalled in recent years. After a substantial decline from 1997 (36.4%) to 2003 (21.9%), smoking rates among high school students remained relatively unchanged from 2003 (21.9%) to 2009 (19.5%) (18). Similarly, adult smoking prevalence declined steadily from 1965 (42.4%) through the 1980s, but the rate of decline began to slow in the 1990s, and the prevalence remained relatively unchanged from 2004 (20.9%) to 2009 (20.6%) (19). Despite the progress that has been made, smoking still results in an economic burden, including medical costs and lost productivity, of approximately $193 billion per year (20).

Although no state had a comprehensive smoke-free law (i.e., prohibit smoking in worksites, restaurants, and bars) in 2000, that number increased to 25 states and the District of Columbia (DC) by 2010, with 16 states enacting comprehensive smoke-free laws following the release of the 2006 Surgeon General's Report (21). After 99 individual state cigarette excise tax increases, at an average increase of 55.5 cents per pack, the average state excise tax increased from 41.96 cents per pack in 2000 to $1.44 per pack in 2010 (22). In 2009, the largest federal cigarette excise tax increase went into effect, bringing the combined federal and average state excise tax for cigarettes to $2.21 per pack, an increase from $0.76 in 2000. In 2009, the Food and Drug Administration (FDA) gained the authority to regulate tobacco products (23). By 2010, FDA had banned flavored cigarettes, established restrictions on youth access, and proposed larger, more effective graphic warning labels that are expected to lead to a significant increase in quit attempts (24).

Maternal and Infant Health

The past decade has seen significant reductions in the number of infants born with neural tube defects (NTDs) and expansion of screening of newborns for metabolic and other heritable disorders. Mandatory folic acid fortification of cereal grain products labeled as enriched in the United States beginning in 1998 contributed to a 36% reduction in NTDs from 1996 to 2006 and prevented an estimated 10,000 NTD affected pregnancies in the past decade, resulting in a savings of $4.7 billion in direct costs (25–27).

Improvements in technology and endorsement of a uniform newborn-screening panel of diseases have led to earlier lifesaving treatment and intervention for at least 3,400 additional newborns each year with selected genetic and endocrine disorders (28,29). In 2003, all but four states were screening for only six of these disorders. By April 2011, all states reported screening for at least 26 disorders on an expanded and standardized uniform panel (29). Newborn screening for hearing loss increased from 46.5% in 1999 to 96.9% in 2008 (30). The percentage

of infants not passing their hearing screening who were then diagnosed by an audiologist before age 3 months as either normal or having permanent hearing loss increased from 51.8% in 1999 to 68.1 in 2008 (30).

Motor Vehicle Safety

Motor vehicle crashes are among the top 10 causes of death for U.S. residents of all ages and the leading cause of death for persons aged 5–34 years (30). In terms of years of potential life lost before age 65, motor vehicle crashes ranked third in 2007, behind only cancer and heart disease, and account for an estimated $99 billion in medical and lost work costs annually (31,32). Crash-related deaths and injuries largely are preventable. From 2000 to 2009, while the number of vehicle miles traveled on the nation's roads increased by 8.5%, the death rate related to motor vehicle travel declined from 14.9 per 100,000 population to 11.0, and the injury rate declined from 1,130 to 722; among children, the number of pedestrian deaths declined by 49%, from 475 to 244, and the number of bicyclist deaths declined by 58%, from 178 to 74 (33,34).

These successes largely resulted from safer vehicles, safer roadways, and safer road use. Behavior was improved by protective policies, including effective seat belt and child safety seat legislation; 49 states and the DC have enacted seat belt laws for adults, and all 50 states and DC have enacted legislation that protects children riding in vehicles (35). Graduated drivers licensing policies for teen drivers have helped reduce the number of teen crash deaths (36).

Cardiovascular Disease Prevention

Heart disease and stroke have been the first and third leading causes of death in the United States since 1921 and 1938, respectively (37,38). Preliminary data from 2009 indicate that stroke is now the fourth leading cause of death in the United States (39). During the past decade, the age-adjusted coronary heart disease and stroke death rates declined from 195 to 126 per 100,000 population and from 61.6 to 42.2 per 100,000 population, respectively, continuing a trend that started in the 1900s for stroke and in the 1960s for coronary heart disease (40). Factors contributing to these reductions include declines in the prevalence of cardiovascular risk factors such as uncontrolled hypertension, elevated cholesterol, and smoking, and improvements in treatments, medications, and quality of care (41–44).

Occupational Safety

Significant progress was made in improving working conditions and reducing the risk for workplace-associated injuries. For example, patient lifting has been a substantial cause of low back injuries among the 1.8 million U.S. health-care workers in nursing care and residential facilities. In the late 1990s, an evaluation of a best practices patient-handling program that included the use of mechanical patient-lifting equipment demonstrated reductions of 66% in the rates of workers' compensation injury claims and lost workdays and documented that the investment in lifting equipment can be recovered in less than 3 years *(45)*. Following widespread dissemination and adoption of these best practices by the nursing home industry, Bureau of Labor Statistics data showed a 35% decline in low back injuries in residential and nursing care employees between 2003 and 2009.

The annual cost of farm-associated injuries among youth has been estimated at $1 billion annually *(46)*. A comprehensive childhood agricultural injury prevention initiative was established to address this problem. Among its interventions was the development by the National Children's Center for Rural Agricultural Health and Safety of guidelines for parents to match chores with their child's development and physical capabilities. Follow-up data have demonstrated a 56% decline in youth farm injury rates from 1998 to 2009 (National Institute for Occupational Safety and Health, unpublished data, 2011).

In the mid-1990s, crab fishing in the Bering Sea was associated with a rate of 770 deaths per 100,000 full-time fishers *(47)*. Most fatalities occurred when vessels overturned because of heavy loads. In 1999, the U.S. Coast Guard implemented Dockside Stability and Safety Checks to correct stability hazards. Since then, one vessel has been lost and the fatality rate among crab fishermen has declined to 260 deaths per 100,000 full-time fishers *(47)*.

Cancer Prevention

Evidence-based screening recommendations have been established to reduce mortality from colorectal cancer and female breast and cervical cancer *(48)*. Several interventions inspired by these recommendations have improved cancer screening rates. Through the collaborative efforts of federal, state, and local health agencies, professional clinician societies, not-for-profit organizations, and patient advocates, standards were developed that have significantly improved cancer screening test quality and use *(49,50)*. The National Breast and Cervical Cancer Early Detection Program has reduced disparities by providing breast and cervical cancer screening services for uninsured women *(49)*. The program's success has resulted from similar collaborative relationships. From 1998 to 2007, colorectal cancer death rates decreased from 25.6 per 100,000 population to 20.0 (2.8% per year) for men and from 18.0 per 100,000 to 14.2 (2.7% per year) for women *(51)*. During this same period, smaller declines were noted for breast and cervical cancer death rates (2.2% per year and 2.4%, respectively) *(52)*.

Childhood Lead Poisoning Prevention

In 2000, childhood lead poisoning remained a major environmental public health problem in the United States, affecting children from all geographic areas and social and economic levels. Black children and those living in poverty and in old, poorly maintained housing were disproportionately affected. In 1990, five states had comprehensive lead poisoning prevention laws; by 2010, 23 states had such laws. Enforcement of these

statutes as well as federal laws that reduce hazards in the housing with the greatest risks has significantly reduced the prevalence of lead poisoning. Findings of the National Health and Nutrition Examination Surveys from 1976–1980 to 2003–2008 reveal a steep decline, from 88.2% to 0.9%, in the percentage of children aged 1–5 years with blood lead levels ≥ 10 μg/dL. The risks for elevated blood lead levels based on socioeconomic status and race also were reduced significantly. The economic benefit of lowering lead levels among children by preventing lead exposure is estimated at $213 billion per year *(53)*.

Public Health Preparedness and Response

After the international and domestic terrorist actions of 2001 highlighted gaps in the nation's public health preparedness, tremendous improvements have been made. In the first half of the decade, efforts were focused primarily on expanding the capacity of the public health system to respond (e.g., purchasing supplies and equipment). In the second half of the decade, the focus shifted to improving the laboratory, epidemiology, surveillance, and response capabilities of the public health system. For example, from 2006 to 2010, the percentage of Laboratory Response Network labs that passed proficiency testing for bioterrorism threat agents increased from 87% to 95%. The percentage of state public health laboratories correctly subtyping *Escherichia coli* O157:H7 and submitting the results into a national reporting system increased from 46% to 69%, and the percentage of state public health agencies prepared to use Strategic National Stockpile material increased from 70% to 98% *(54)*. During the 2009 H1N1 influenza pandemic, these improvements in the ability to develop and implement a coordinated public health response in an emergency facilitated the rapid detection and characterization of the outbreak, deployment of laboratory tests, distribution of personal protective equipment from the Strategic National Stockpile, development of a candidate vaccine virus, and widespread administration of the resulting vaccine. These public health interventions prevented an estimated 5–10 million cases, 30,000 hospitalizations, and 1,500 deaths (CDC, unpublished data, 2011).

Existing systems also have been adapted to respond to public health threats. During the 2009 H1N1 influenza pandemic, the Vaccines for Children program was adapted to enable provider ordering and distribution of the pandemic vaccine. Similarly, President's Emergency Plan for AIDS Relief clinics were used to rapidly deliver treatment following the 2010 cholera outbreak in Haiti.

Conclusion

From 1999 to 2009, the age-adjusted death rate in the United States declined from 881.9 per 100,000 population to 741.0, a record low and a continuation of a steady downward trend that began during the last century. Advances in public health contributed significantly to this decline; seven of the 10 achievements described in this report targeted one or more of the 15 leading causes of death. Related *Healthy People 2010* data are available at http://www.cdc.gov/mmwr/preview/mmwrhtml/mm6019a5_addinfo.htm. The examples in this report also illustrate the effective application of core public health tools. Some, such as the establishment of surveillance systems, dissemination of guidelines, implementation of research findings, or development of effective public health programs, are classic tools by which public health has addressed the burden of disease for decades.

Although not new, the judicious use of the legal system, by encouraging healthy behavior through taxation or by shaping it altogether through regulatory action, has become an increasingly important tool in modern public health practice and played a major role in many of the achievements described in this report *(55)*. The creative use of the whole spectrum of available options, as demonstrated here, has enabled public health practitioners to respond effectively. Public health practice will continue to evolve to meet the new and complex challenges that lie ahead.

References

1. National Center for Health Statistics. Health, United States, 2010: with special feature on death and dying. Hyattsville, MD: CDC, National Center for Health Statistics, 2011. Available at http://www.cdc.gov/nchs/hus.htm. Accessed May 16, 2011.

2. Zhou F. Updated economic evaluation of the routine childhood immunization schedule in the United States. Presented at the 45th National Immunization Conference. Washington, DC; March 28–31, 2011.

3. Pilishvili T, Lexau C, Farley MM, et al. Sustained reductions in invasive pneumococcal disease in the era of conjugate vaccine. J Infect Dis 2010; 201;32–41.

4. Tate JE, Cortese MM, Payne DC. Uptake, impact, and effectiveness of rotavirus vaccination in the United States: review of the first 3 years of postlicensure data. Pediatr Infect Dis J 2011;30(1 Suppl):S56–60.

5. Marin M, Zhang JX, Seward JF. Near elimination of varicella deaths in the US following implementation of the childhood vaccination program. Pediatrics. In press, 2011.

6. Vogt TM, Wise ME, Bell BP, Finelli L. Declining hepatitis A mortality in the United States during the era of hepatitis A vaccination. J Infect Dis 2008;197:1282–8.

7. CDC. Vital signs: central line–associated blood stream infections—United States, 2001, 2008, and 2009. MMWR 2011;60:243–8.

8. CDC. Trends in tuberculosis—United States, 2010. MMWR 2011;60: 333–7.

9. CDC. Ongoing multistate outbreak of *Escherichia coli* serotype O157:H7 infections associated with consumption of fresh spinach—United States, September 2006. MMWR 2006;55:1045–6.

10. CDC. Multistate outbreak of *Salmonella* serotype Tennessee infections associated with peanut butter—United States, 2006–2007. MMWR 2007;56:521–4.

11. Boxrud D, Monson T, Stiles T, Besser J. The role, challenges, and support of PulseNet laboratories in detecting foodborne disease outbreaks. Public Health Rep 2010;125(Suppl 2):57–62.

12. Gottlieb SL, Newbern EC, Griffin PM, et al. Multistate outbreak of listeriosis linked to turkey deli meat and subsequent changes in US regulatory policy. Clin Infect Dis 2006;42:29–36.

13. CDC. Revised recommendations for HIV testing of adults, adolescents, and pregnant women in health-care settings. MMWR 2006;55(No. RR-14).

14. Pealer LN, Marfin AA, Petersen LR, et al. Transmission of West Nile virus through blood transfusion in the United States in 2002. N Engl J Med 2003;349:1236–45.

15. Blanton JD, Hanlon CA, Rupprecht CE. Rabies surveillance in the United States during 2006. J Am Vet Med Assoc 2007;231:540–56.

16. Rupprecht CE, Barrett J, Briggs D, et al. Can rabies be eradicated? Dev Biol (Basel) 2008;131:95–121.

17. US Department of Health, Education, and Welfare, Public Health Service. Smoking and health: report of the advisory committee to the Surgeon General of the Public Health Service. Washington, DC: US Department of Health Education and Welfare, Public Health Service; 1964.

18. CDC. Trends in the prevalence of tobacco use: national YRBS, 1991–2009. Atlanta, GA: US Department of Health and Human Services, CDC; 2010. Available at http://www.cdc.gov/healthyyouth/yrbs/pdf/us_tobacco_trend_yrbs.pdf. Accessed May 17, 2011.

19. CDC. Vital signs: current cigarette smoking among adults aged ≥18 years—United States, 2009. MMWR 2010;59:1135–40.

20. CDC. Smoking-attributable mortality, years of potential life lost, and productivity losses—United States, 2000–2004. MMWR 2008;57: 1226–8.

21. CDC. State smoke-free laws for worksites, restaurants, and bars—United States, 2000–2010. MMWR 2011;60:472–5.

22. CDC. State Tobacco Activities Tracking and Evaluation (STATE) System. Available at http://www.cdc.gov/tobacco/statesystem. Accessed May 17, 2011.

23. US Government Printing Office. Family Smoking Prevention and Tobacco Control Act. Public Law No. 111-31. Washington DC: US Government Printing Office; 2009. Available at http://www.gpo.gov/fdsys/pkg/PLAW-111publ31/content-detail.html. Accessed May 17, 2011.

24. CDC. CDC grand rounds: current opportunities in tobacco control. MMWR 2010;59:487–92.

25. CDC. Spina bifida and anencephaly before and after folic acid mandate—United States, 1995–1996 and 1999–2000. MMWR 2004;53: 362–5.

26. CDC. CDC grand rounds: additional opportunities to prevent neural tube defects with folic acid fortification. MMWR 2010;59:980–4.

27. Grosse SD, Ouyang L, Collins JS, Green D, Dean JH, Stevenson RE. Economic evaluation of a neural tube defect recurrence-prevention program. Am J Prevent Med 2008;35:572–7.

28. CDC. Using tandem mass spectrometry for metabolic disease screening among newborns. A report of a work group. MMWR 2001;50(No. RR-3).

29. CDC. Impact of expanded newborn screening—United States, 2006. MMWR 2008;57:1012–5.

30. CDC. Summary of infants screened for hearing loss, diagnosed, and enrolled in early intervention, United States, 1999–2008. Atlanta, GA: US Department of Health and Human Services, CDC; 2010. Available at http://www.cdc.gov/ncbddd/hearingloss/2008-data/EHDI_1999_2008.pdf. Accessed May 17, 2011.

31. CDC. Web-based Injury Statistics Query and Reporting System (WISQARS). Available at http://www.cdc.gov/injury/wisqars/index.html. Accessed May 17, 2011.

32. Naumann RB, Dellinger AM, Zaloshnja E, Lawrence BA, Miller TR. Incidence and total lifetime costs of motor vehicle-related fatal and nonfatal injury by road user type, United States, 2005. Traffic Inj Prev 2010;11:353–60.

33. National Highway Traffic Safety Administration. Traffic safety facts, 2009 data: children. Washington, DC: US Department of Transportation; 2010. Report no. DOT HS 811-387.

34. National Highway Traffic Safety Administration. Trafic safety facts 2009 (early edition). Washington, DC: US Department of Transportation; 2010. Report no. DOT HS 811-402.

35. Insurance Institute for Highway Safety. Child passenger safety. Arlington, VA: Insurance Institute for Highway Safety, Highway Loss Data Institute; 2011. Available at http://www.iihs.org/laws/restraintoverview.aspx. Accessed May 17, 2011.

36. Baker SP, Chen L-H, Li G. Nationwide review of graduated driver licensing. Washington, DC: AAA Foundation for Traffic Safety; 2007. Available at http://www.aaafoundation.org/pdf/nationwidereviewofgdl.pdf. Acccessed May 17, 2011.

37. CDC. Leading causes of death 1900–1998. Hyattsville, MD: US Department of Health and Human Services, CDC, National Center for Health Statistics. Available at http://www.cdc.gov/nchs/data/dvs/lead1900_98.pdf. Acccessed May 17, 2011.

38. Xu JQ, Kochanek KD, Murphy SL, Tejada-Vera B. Deaths: final data for 2007. Natl Vital Stat Rep 2010;58(19).

39. Kochanek KD, Xu JQ, Murphy SL, et al. Deaths: preliminary data for 2009. Natl Vital Stat Rep 2010;59(4).

40. CDC. Decline in deaths from heart disease and stroke—United States, 1900–1999. MMWR 1999;48:649–56.

41. Institute of Medicine. A population-based policy and systems change approach to prevent and control hypertension Washington, DC: The National Academies Press; 2010.

42. CDC. Health, United Sates, 2009: with special feature on medical technology. Hyattsville, MD: US Department of Health and Human Services, CDC, National Center for Health Statistics; 2010.

43. CDC. Use of a registry to improve acute stroke care—seven states, 2005–2009. MMWR 2011;60:206–10.

44. Roger VL, Go AS, Lloyd-Jones DM, et al. Heart disease and stroke statistics—2011 update: a report from the American Heart Association. Circulation 2011;123:e18–209.

45. Bureau of Labor Statistics. Table R6: incidence rates for nonfatal occupational injuries and illnesses involving days away from work per 10,000 full-time workers by industry and selected parts of body affected by injury or illness, 2003. Available at http://www.bls.gov/iif/oshwc/osh/case/ostb1384.pdf. Accessed May 17, 2011.

46. Zaloshnja E, Miller TR, Lee BC. Incidence and cost of nonfatal farm youth injury, United States, 2001–2006. J Agromedicine 2011;16:6–18.

47. CDC. Commercial fishing deaths—United States, 2000–2009. MMWR 2010;59:842–5.

48. CDC. The guide to community preventive services. Atlanta, GA: US Department of Health and Human Services, CDC; 2011. Available at http://www.thecommunityguide.org/index.html. Accessed May 17, 2011.

49. CDC. Breast cancer. Atlanta, GA: US Department of Health and Human Services, CDC; 2011. Available at http://www.cdc.gov/cancer/breast. Accessed May 17, 2011.

50. CDC. Colorectal cancer test use among persons aged ≥50 years—United States, 2001. MMWR 2003;52:193–6.

51. Kohler BA, Ward E, McCarthy BJ, et al. Annual report to the nation on the status of cancer, 1975–2007, featuring tumors of the brain and other nervous system. J Natl Cancer Inst 2011;103:714–36.

52. Edwards BK, Ward E, Kohler BA, et al. Annual report to the nation on the status of cancer, 1975–2006, featuring colorectal cancer trends and impact of interventions (risk factors, screening, and treatment) to reduce future rates. Cancer 2010;116:544–73.

53. Grosse SD, Matte TD, Schwartz J, et al. Economic gains resulting from the reduction in children's exposure to lead in the United States. Environ Health Perspect 2002;110:563–9.

54. CDC. Justification of estimates for appropriation committees. Fiscal year 2011. Atlanta, GA: US Department of Health and Human Services, CDC. Available at http://intra-apps.cdc.gov/fmo/appropriations_budget_formulation/appropriations_budget_form_pdf/fy2011_cdc_cj_final.pdf. Accessed May 17, 2011.

55. CDC. Law and public health at CDC. MMWR 2006; 55(Suppl 2): 29–33.

Critical Thinking

1. Why is tobacco control considered a great achievement?

2. Discuss the reasons fewer infants are being born with neural tube defects.

3. Identify new vaccines and discuss their effectiveness as public health measures.

Reported by Domestic Public Health Achievements Team, CDC. Corresponding contributor: **Ram Koppaka**, MD, PhD, Epidemiology and Analysis Program Office, Office of Surveillance, Epidemiology, and Laboratory Services, CDC; rkoppaka@cdc.gov, 347-396-2847.

Koppaka, Ram. From *MMWR: Morbidity & Mortality Weekly Report,* May 20, 2011, pp. 619–623. Published by Centers for Disease Control. http://www.cdc.gov/mmwr/

UNIT 8

Health Care and the Health Care System

Unit Selections

Learning Outcomes

After reading this Unit, you will be able to:

- Describe what can be done to help reduce health care costs.

- Discuss whether individuals without health insurance die earlier than those who are insured.

- Distinguish whether quality health care is a right or a privilege.

- Explain whether health care is just another commodity.

- Discuss the failure of current health care price controls.

Student Website
www.mhhe.com/cls

Internet References

American Medical Association (AMA)
　　www.ama-assn.org
MedScape: The Online Resource for Better Patient Care
　　www.medscape.com

Americans are healthier today than they have been at any time in this nation's history. Americans suffer more illness today than they have at any time in this nation's history. Which statement is true? They both are, depending on the statistics you quote. According to longevity statistics, Americans are living longer today and, therefore, must be healthier. Still, other statistics indicate that Americans today report twice as many acute illnesses as did our ancestors 60 years ago. They also report that their pain lasts longer. Unfortunately, this combination of living longer and feeling sicker places additional demands on a health care system that, according to experts, is already in a state of crisis.

Despite the clamor about the problems with our health care system, if you can afford it, then the American health care system is one of the best in the world. However, being the best does not mean that it is without problems. Each year, more than half a million Americans are injured or die due to preventable mistakes made by medical care professionals. In addition, countless unnecessary tests are preformed that not only add to the expense of health care, but may actually place the patient at risk. Reports such as these fuel the fire of public skepticism toward the quality of health care that Americans receive. While these aspects of our health care system indicate a need for repair, they represent just the tip of the iceberg.

While choices in health care providers are increasing, paying for services continues to be a challenge as medical costs continue to rise. Why have health care costs risen so much? The answer to this question is multifaceted and includes such factors as physicians' fees, hospital costs, insurance costs, pharmaceutical costs, malpractice, advanced technology, and health fraud. It could be argued that while these factors operate within any health care system, the lack of a meaningful form of outcomes assessment has permitted and encouraged waste and inefficiency within our system. Ironically, one of the major factors for the rise in the cost of health care is our rapidly expanding aging population—tangible evidence of an improving health care delivery system. This is obviously one factor that we hope will continue to rise. Another significant factor that is often overlooked is the constantly expanding boundaries of health care. It is somewhat ironic that as our success in treating various disorders has expanded, so has the domain of health care, and often into areas where previously health care had little or no involvement.

Traditionally, Americans have felt that the state of their health was largely determined by the quality of the health care available to them. This attitude has fostered an unhealthy dependence upon doctors and the health care system and contributed to the skyrocketing costs. It should be obvious by now that while there is no simple solution to our health care problems, we would all be a lot better off if we accepted more personal responsibility for our health. While this shift would help ease the financial burden of health care, it might necessitate a more responsible coverage of medical news in order to educate and enlighten the public on personal health issues.

Currently the United States is the only developed nation without universal coverage or national health insurance. According to the Census Bureau, the number of people who lacked health insurance is close to 50 million or about 16.3% of the

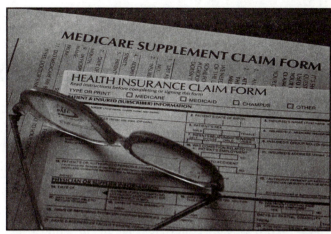

© Kent Knudson/PhotoLink/Getty Images

population. The majority of the uninsured include foreign-born residents, young adults ages 19 to 25, and low-income families with an annual household income of less than $25,000. Much of the declines in insured rates in recent years can be attributed to the loss of employer-provided coverage, which fell amid sustained unemployment and as employers continued to cut back on benefits. To help the millions of Americans without health insurance, ObamaCare, more formally known as "The Patient Protection and Affordable Care Act," was passed by Congress on March 21, 2010, and signed into federal law by President Barack Obama on March 23, 2010. The centerpiece of ObamaCare is the individual mandate, a provision that makes it mandatory for every citizen to purchase private health insurance beginning in 2014. The act is controversial and there have been attempts to repeal it.

Four articles were chosen for this unit and include topics such as health care costs, health insurance, and the need for universal health coverage for all Americans. Jonathan Gruber in "The Cost Implications of Health Care Reform" discusses the number of Americans who are uninsured and the problems they face. As the number continues to rise, Gruber calls for the government to address the cost concerns related to health care reform. He believes that universal coverage will not only insure all Americans, but it will also impact the cost of health care. Gruber also believes that costs continue to rise due to the blockage of price controls by the pharmaceutical industry. Two related articles, "In Dire Health" and "Medicare Whac-A-Mole" discuss the current U.S. health care system. In the former, the author addresses the need for a tax-supported universal access to health care that would improve health care and be less expensive than our current system. In the latter, the need to transform our current health care appears to be the only way to manage the rise in costs. In "Myth Diagnosis", author Megan McArdle discusses the myth that the uninsured are more likely to die than those with health insurance. She maintains that the uninsured have more health risks since they're more likely to be poor, smokers, less educated, obese and unemployed, all factors that increase the likelihood of poor health.

The Cost Implications of Health Care Reform

JONATHAN GRUBER, PH.D.

On March 23, 2010, President Barack Obama signed into law the most significant piece of U.S. social policy legislation in almost 50 years. There is little disagreement over the premise that the Patient Protection and Affordable Care Act (ACA) will dramatically expand health insurance coverage. But there is concern about its implications for health care costs. These concerns have been heightened by a recent report from the actuary at the Centers for Medicare and Medicaid Services (CMS), which shows that health care reform will cause an expansion of national health care expenditures.

The ACA includes a major investment in the affordability of health insurance for low-income families: under the law, all individuals with family incomes below 133% of the poverty line (i.e., below about $30,000 for a family of four) are eligible for free public insurance, and there are tax credits to help make health insurance affordable for families with incomes of up to 400% of the poverty level. At the same time, the ACA incorporates a number of fund-raising mechanisms, including a reduction in the overpayment to Medicare Advantage insurers, a reduction in the update factor for Medicare hospital reimbursement, an increase in the Medicare tax (and extension to unearned income) for high-income families, an assessment on employers whose employees use subsidies rather than employer-sponsored insurance, and the "Cadillac tax" (an assessment on the highest-cost insurance plans). The Congressional Budget Office estimates that these revenue increases will exceed the new spending, reducing the federal deficit by more than $100 billion in the first decade and more than $1 trillion in the second decade.[1]

Some have questioned the likelihood of this deficit reduction, claiming, for example, that the numbers are "front loaded" because some of the revenue-raising mechanisms begin before 2014, whereas the majority of spending doesn't start until after 2014. But the trend under the law will actually be toward larger deficit reduction over time; indeed, the reduction in the deficit is expected to increase in the last 2 years of the budget window. The cuts in spending and increases in taxes are actually "back-loaded," with the revenue increases rising faster over time than the spending increases, so that this legislation improves our nation's fiscal health more and more over time.[1]

Others have raised the possibility that the cuts that provide much of this financing will never take place, and they point to the physician-payment cuts required by the Balanced Budget Act of 1997, which have been repeatedly delayed by Congress. But as Van de Water and Horney have highlighted,[2] Congress has passed many Medicare cuts during the past 20 years, and the physician-payment cut is the only one that has not taken effect.

With U.S. health care spending already accounting for 17% of the gross domestic product (GDP) and growing, there is also concern about policies that increase this spending. And, as the CMS actuary points out, the ACA will increase national health care expenditures. At the peak of its effect on spending, in 2016, the law will increase health care expenditures by about 2%; by 2019, the ACA-related increase will be 1%, or 0.2% of the GDP.

However, these increases are quite small relative to the gains in coverage under the new law. There are currently 220 million insured Americans, and the CMS predicts that 34 million more will be insured by 2019. The agency also estimates that without this reform, health care costs would grow by 6.6% per year between 2010 and 2019. So we'll be increasing the ranks of the insured by more than 15% at a cost that is less than one sixth of 1 year's growth in national health care expenditures.

Alternatively, consider the fact that under this legislation, by 2019, the United States will be spending $46 billion more on medical care than we do today. In 2010 dollars, this amounts to only $800 per newly insured person—quite a low cost as compared (for example) with the $5,000 average single premium for employer-sponsored insurance.[3]

U.S. spending on health care is very high and a source of great concern, but it is the growth rate of medical spending, not the level of spending, that ultimately determines our country's financial well-being. If current trends persist, we will be spending an unsustainable 38% of our GDP on health care by 2075, as the growth rate of health care costs continues to outstrip the growth rate of the overall economy. In this environment, whether annual health care costs rise or fall by 1% or even 5% is irrelevant—all we do is move the day of reckoning less than 1 year closer or farther away. Clearly, the key to the long-term viability of our health care system is to lower the rate of cost growth, often referred to as "bending the cost curve."

On this count, the CMS actuary's news is good: although the ACA will boost medical spending somewhat, its incremental impact on spending will decrease over time (from 2% in 2016 to 1% in 2019). These declining estimates imply that by the second decade, the ACA will have reduced national health care spending. This effect is due to provisions such as the Cadillac tax, for which the definition of a high-cost plan is indexed to the growth in overall prices in the economy, not to the (higher) growth in health insurance premiums. As a result, an increasing proportion of plans will be taxed, and more people will shift into lower-cost insurance options in order to avoid paying the tax, thus reducing national health care expenditures.

Yet the real question concerns how far the ACA will go in slowing cost growth. There is great uncertainty, mostly because there is such uncertainty in general about how to control the rate of growth in health care costs. There is no shortage of good ideas for ways of doing so, ranging from reducing consumer demand for health care services, to reducing payments to health care providers, to reorganizing the payment for and delivery of care, to promoting cost-effectiveness standards in care delivery, to reducing pressure from the threat of medical malpractice claims. There is, however, a shortage of evidence regarding which approaches will actually work—and therefore no consensus on which path is best to follow.

Given this uncertainty, it is best to cautiously pursue many different approaches toward cost control and study them to see which ones work best. That is exactly the approach taken in the ACA, which includes provisions to reduce consumer demand through the Cadillac tax, to reduce provider payments by appointing a depoliticized board to make up-or-down recommendations to Congress on changes to Medicare's provider payments, to run dozens of pilots to test various approaches to revamping provider-payment incentives and organizational structure, to invest hundreds of millions of dollars in new comparative-effectiveness research, and to launch pilot programs to assess the impact of various reorganizations of the medical malpractice process. None of these is guaranteed to work, but together they represent a significant step toward fundamental cost control.

In summary, analysis by both the Congressional Budget Office and the CMS actuary show that the ACA will substantially reduce the federal deficit, only slightly increase national medical spending (despite an enormous expansion in insurance coverage), begin to reduce the growth rate of medical spending, and introduce various new initiatives that may lead to more fundamental reductions in the long-term rate of health care cost growth. The ACA will not solve our health care cost problems, but it is a historic and cost-effective step in the right direction.

Notes

1. Letter from Douglas W. Elmendorf to House Speaker Nancy Pelosi, March 18, 2010. (Accessed May 6, 2010, at http://www.cbo.gov/ftpdocs/113xx/doc11355/hr4872.pdf.)

2. Van de Water PN, Horney JR. Health reform will reduce the deficit: charges of budgetary gimmickry are unfounded. Washington, DC: Center on Budget and Policy Priorities, March 25, 2010. (Accessed May 6, 2010, at http://www.cbpp.org/cms/index.cfm?fa=view&id=3134.)

3. Employer health benefits: 2009 annual survey. Washington, DC: Henry J. Kaiser Family Foundation, 2009.

Critical Thinking

1. Describe the relationship between medical technology and health care costs.

2. What can you as an individual do to help reduce health care costs? Give specific actions that can be taken.

3. Other than technology, why are health care costs increasing so rapidly?

Myth Diagnosis

Everyone knows that people without health insurance are more likely to die. But are they?

Megan McArdle

Outside of the few states where it is illegal to deny coverage based on medical history, I am probably uninsurable. Though I'm in pretty good health, I have several latent conditions, including an autoimmune disease. If I lost the generous insurance that I have through *The Atlantic,* even the most charitable insurer might hesitate to take me on.

So I took a keen interest when, at the fervid climax of the health-care debate in mid-December, a *Washington Post* blogger, Ezra Klein, declared that Senator Joseph Lieberman, by refusing to vote for a bill with a public option, was apparently "willing to cause the deaths of hundreds of thousands" of uninsured people in order to punish the progressives who had opposed his reelection in 2006. In the ensuing blogstorm, conservatives condemned Klein's "venomous smear," while liberals solemnly debated the circumstances under which one may properly accuse one's opponents of mass murder.

But aside from an exchange between Matthew Yglesias of the Center for American Progress and Michael Cannon of the Cato Institute, few people addressed the question that mattered most to those of us who cannot buy an individual insurance policy at any price—the question that was arguably the health-care debate's most important: Was Klein (not to mention other like-minded editorialists who cited similar numbers) *right?* If we lost our insurance, would this gargantuan new entitlement really be the only thing standing between us and an early grave?

Perhaps few people were asking, because the question sounds so stupid. Health insurance buys you health care. Health care is supposed to save your life. So if you don't have someone buying you health care . . . well, you can complete the syllogism.

Last year's national debate on health-care legislation tended to dwell on either heart-wrenching anecdotes about costly, unattainable medical treatments, or arcane battles over how many people in the United States lacked insurance. Republicans rarely plumbed the connection between insurance and mortality, presumably because they would look foolish and heartless if they expressed any doubt about health insurance's benefits. It was politically safer to harp on the potential problems of government interventions—or, in extremis, to point out that more than half the uninsured were either affluent, lacking citizenship, or already eligible for government programs in which they hadn't bothered to enroll.

Even Democratic politicians made curiously little of the plight of the uninsured. Instead, they focused on cost control, so much so that you might have thought that covering the uninsured was a happy side effect of really throttling back the rate of growth in Medicare spending. When progressive politicians or journalists did address the disadvantages of being uninsured, they often fell back on the same data Klein had used: a 2008 report from the Urban Institute that estimated that about 20,000 people were dying every year for lack of health insurance.

But when you probe that claim, its accuracy is open to question. Even a rough approximation of how many people die because of lack of health insurance is hard to reach. Quite possibly, lack of health insurance has no more impact on your health than lack of flood insurance.

Part of the trouble with reports like the one from the Urban Institute is that they cannot do the kind of thing we do to test drugs or medical procedures: divide people randomly into groups that do and don't have health insurance, and see which group fares better. Experimental studies like this would be tremendously expensive, and it's hard to imagine that they'd attract sufficient volunteers. Moreover, they might well violate the ethical standards of doctors who believed they were condemning the uninsured patients to a life nasty, brutish, and short.

So instead, researchers usually do what are called "observational studies": they take data sets that include both insured and uninsured people, and compare their health outcomes—usually mortality rates, because these are unequivocal and easy to measure. For a long time, two of the best studies were Sorlie et al. (1994), which used a large sample of census data from 1982 to 1985; and Franks, Clancy, and Gold (1993), which examined a smaller but richer data set from the National Health and Nutrition Examination Survey, and its follow-up studies, between 1971 and 1987. The Institute of Medicine used the math behind these two studies to produce a 2002 report on an increase in illness and death from lack of insurance; the Urban Institute, in turn, updated those numbers to produce the figure that became the gold standard during the debate over healthcare reform.

The first thing one notices is that the original studies are a trifle elderly. Medicine has changed since 1987; presumably, so has the riskiness of going without health insurance.

Moreover, the question of who had insurance is particularly dodgy: the studies counted as "uninsured" anyone who lacked insurance in the initial interview. But of course, not all of those people would have stayed uninsured—a separate study suggests that only about a third of those who reported being uninsured over a two-year time frame lacked coverage for the entire period. Most of the "uninsured" people probably got insurance relatively quickly, while some of the "insured" probably lost theirs. The effect of this churn could bias your results either way; the inability to control for it makes the statistics less accurate.

The bigger problem is that the uninsured generally have more health risks than the rest of the population. They are poorer, more likely to smoke, less educated, more likely to be unemployed, more likely to be obese, and so forth. All these things are known to increase your risk of dying, independent of your insurance status.

There are also factors we can't analyze. It's widely believed that health improves with social status, a quality that's hard to measure. Risk-seekers are probably more likely to end up uninsured, and also to end up dying in a car crash—but their predilection for thrills will not end up in our statistics. People who are suspicious of doctors probably don't pursue either generous health insurance or early treatment. Those who score low on measures of conscientiousness often have trouble keeping jobs with good health insurance—or following complicated treatment protocols. And so on.

The studies relied upon by the Institute of Medicine and the Urban Institute tried to control for some of these factors. But Sorlie et al.—the larger study—lacked data on things like smoking habits and could control for only a few factors, while Franks, Clancy, and Gold, which had better controls but a smaller sample, could not, as an observational study, categorically exclude the possibility that lack of insurance has no effect on mortality at all.

The possibility that no one risks death by going without health insurance may be startling, but some research supports it. Richard Kronick of the University of California at San Diego's Department of Family and Preventive Medicine, an adviser to the Clinton administration, recently published the results of what may be the largest and most comprehensive analysis yet done of the effect of insurance on mortality. He used a sample of more than 600,000, and controlled not only for the standard factors, but for how long the subjects went without insurance, whether their disease was particularly amenable to early intervention, and even whether they lived in a mobile home. In test after test, he found no significantly elevated risk of death among the uninsured.

This result is not, perhaps, as shocking as it seems. Health care heals, but it also kills. Someone who lacked insurance over the past few decades might have missed taking their Lipitor, but also their Vioxx or Fen-Phen. According to one estimate, 80,000 people a year are killed just by "nosocomial infections"—infections that arise as a result of medical treatment. The only truly experimental study on health insurance, a randomized study of almost 4,000 subjects done by Rand and concluded in 1982, found that increasing the generosity of people's health insurance caused them to use more health care, but made almost no difference in their health status.

> **Health care heals, but it also kills. Someone who lacked insurance over the past decade might have missed taking Lipitor, but also Vioxx or Fen-Phen.**

If gaining insurance has a large effect on people's health, we should see outcomes improve dramatically between one's early and late 60s. Yet like the Kronick and Rand studies, analyses of the effect of Medicare, which becomes available to virtually everyone in America at the age of 65, show little benefit. In a recent review of the literature, Helen Levy of the University of Michigan and David Meltzer of the University of Chicago noted that the latest studies of this question "paint a surprisingly consistent picture: Medicare increases consumption of medical care and may modestly improve self-reported health but has no effect on mortality, at least in the short run."

Of course, that might be an indictment of programs like Medicare and Medicaid. Indeed, given the uncertainties about their impact on mortality rates—uncertainties that the results from Sorlie et al. don't resolve—it's possible that, by blocking the proposed expansion of health care through Medicare, Senator Lieberman, rather than committing the industrial-scale slaughter Klein fears, might not have harmed anyone at all. We cannot use one study to "prove" that having government insurance is riskier than having none. But we also cannot use a flawed and conflicting literature to "prove" that Lieberman was willing to risk the deaths of hundreds of thousands. Government insurance should have some effect, but if that effect is not large enough to be unequivocally evident in the data we have, it must be small.

Even if we did agree that insurance rarely confers significant health benefits, that would not necessarily undermine the case for a national health-care program. The academics who question the mass benefits of expanding coverage still think that doing so improves outcomes among certain vulnerable subgroups, like infants and patients with HIV. Besides, a national health program has nonmedical benefits. Leaving tens of millions of Americans without health insurance violates our sense of equity—and leaves those millions exposed to the risk of mind-boggling medical bills.

But we should have had a better handle on the case for expanded coverage—and, more important, the evidence behind it—before we embarked on a year-long debate that divided our house against itself. Certainly, we should have had it before Congress voted on the largest entitlement expansion in 40 years. Unfortunately, most of us forgot to ask a fundamental question, because we were certain we already knew the answer. By the time we got around to challenging our assumptions, it was too late to do anything except scream at each other from the sidelines.

Critical Thinking

1. Do individuals without health insurance die earlier than those who are insured? Why or why not?

2. Is quality health care a right or a privilege? Defend your answer.

3. Why do the uninsured typically have more health risks?

MEGAN MCARDLE is *The Atlantic*'s business and economics editor, and the editor of the business channel at theatlantic.com.

In Dire Health

Despite the passage of the Affordable Care Act, the U.S. medical system is near collapse. What will save it is a single-payer system and physicians in group practice.

Arnold S. Relman

Most people assume that insurance is an essential part of the health-care system. Some think it should be provided through public programs like Medicare, while others prefer to see it purchased from private insurance companies, but the majority believe that insurance is needed to help pay the unpredictable and often catastrophic expenses of medical care. That is why so much public policy focuses on extending coverage to as many people as possible and controlling its cost. I think this emphasis on insurance is mistaken. We would have a much better and more affordable health-care system if the reimbursement of medical expenses through public or private insurance plans was replaced by tax-supported universal access to comprehensive care, without bills for specific services and without insurance plans to pay those bills.

Insurance is not simply a mechanism for spreading financial risks and paying for medical care. Because it usually tries to limit payments to providers, insurance often is an intrusive third party in the doctor-patient relationship and, particularly with private insurance, restricts the freedom of doctors and patients to select the services, specialists, and facilities they want to use. At the same time, insurance coverage tends to encourage the "moral hazard" of overuse of elective services, by reducing patients' awareness of costs and limiting their out-of-pocket expenditures. Furthermore, all insurance plans have administrative expenses, and most private plans take profits that add to the cost of their premiums. The billing and collecting operations that are an integral part of any insured health system are a major expense for doctors and hospitals as well. Billing and collecting through insurance also offer abundant opportunities for fraud and abuse, which skim off as much as 5 percent to 10 percent of the total expenditure on health care.

For-profit insurance companies, which control most of the private market, are the greatest problem. They have a direct conflict of interest with their customers, because a plan's net income is increased by avoiding coverage of patients with serious illnesses (who, of course, are most in need of insurance), restricting access to services, and limiting coverage of expensive medical conditions. Provisions in the new Affordable Care Act, which take effect in 2014, will prevent private insurers from denying or dropping coverage because of illness, but the act will also put many more people into for-profit insurance plans, which will still be permitted to raise premiums. According to the Centers for Medicare and Medicaid Services, the business costs and profits of these plans currently take more than $150 billion from their premiums before paying for medical services and are projected to increase more rapidly than national expenditures on health care. Additionally, the private insurance industry adds costs to doctors and hospitals that must spend tens of billions in billing and collecting from multiple plans, each with its own rules and regulations.

Apologists for the for-profit insurance industry claim that its high overhead costs are justified by greater control of providers' charges, the provision of preventive services, and the promotion of the quality of medical care. No credible evidence supports these claims. The rapid turnover of membership in private plans makes continuity of oversight by insurers nearly impossible and limits the effectiveness of preventive and quality-promoting programs. Despite insurers' efforts to control costs in the private sector, they continue to rise more rapidly than in public programs.

The private insurers' "managed care" plans did stabilize the costs of care in the private sector for a few years in the mid-1990s by limiting patients' choices of physicians and hospitals, monitoring physicians' recommendations of expensive procedures, and reducing elective hospitalizations. However, a backlash from patients and physicians forced the plans to change these tactics, which were seen as an intrusion into the practice of medicine. By the end of the decade, private health costs had resumed their rapid rise. Private for-profit health insurance has now grown into a huge industry that exerts a powerful self-serving influence on national health policy.

Public insurance through Medicare also has its problems. Although its overhead costs (less than 5 percent of expenditures) are much lower than those of private insurance (about 15 percent to 25 percent of expenditures), it also encourages overuse of elective services. Medicare also struggles with constantly rising expenditures. According to the Congressional Budget Office, the program's costs will almost double over the next decade. The increase has caused a federal budget crisis requiring urgent efforts at cost control. Payments to hospitals are being cut, and more medical costs are being shifted to Medicare beneficiaries. Provisions in the Affordable Care Act authorize trials of new forms of payment and new organizations of physicians and hospitals to receive these payments (accountable-care organizations). The administration of these trials, though, will require so much new bureaucracy that their number will be severely limited—even if Republican opposition in Congress doesn't block their implementation. Most experts think that without major reforms, Medicare's rising costs will not be sustainable much longer, but there is little agreement on what reforms will rescue the program or whether any of the proposed cost—saving measures will succeed.

There is, however, a practical alternative to health insurance and the fee-for-service system with which it is usually associated: a not-for-profit system in which a public single payer provides universal access to comprehensive private care delivered by primary-care physicians cooperating with medical specialists in group-practice arrangements. Like health systems based on insurance, this system would not require that patients have much "skin in the game" and therefore might pose a moral hazard that would lead to overuse of elective services. However, unlike insurance-based systems, physicians would be paid by salary rather than fee-for-service, so it would give physicians no financial incentive to recommend unnecessary procedures. Each group's management would determine and pay salaries, under federal regulations that would cap the fraction of the group's budget allocated to salaries but would allow management to determine individual compensation. Furthermore, in this insurance-free system, primary-care physicians trained to avoid unneeded care would counsel patients.

Successful examples already exist of systems that are based on a single payer and group practice centered on

primary care. They are self-insured, not-for-profit staff-model HMOs such as Kaiser Foundation health plans, Geisinger Health Plan, and the plan designed by and for the New York hotel and restaurant workers' union. In self-insured plans, there is no third-party insurer to pay the charges; these plans assume the insurance risk of providing their members with the medical care for which they contract. These plans support a multispecialty group practice that provides a specified range of comprehensive medical services. Their members usually choose a primary-care physician in the group who directs their treatment and refers them to specialist colleagues and other personnel in the group as needed. Some plans have no bills for individual services; others charge small token fees for each visit. Evidence shows that plans like these deliver quality, cost-effective care.

The recently reorganized Veterans Affairs medical-care system is an example of a single-payer system that provides comprehensive care by teams of salaried physicians without insurance reimbursement.

The recently reorganized Veterans Affairs medical-care system, once viewed unfavorably, now is often cited as another example of a single-payer system that provides comprehensive care by teams of salaried physicians and other health professionals, without insurance reimbursement. The federal government funds the program, but its patients contribute modest payment for some services.

In the system I envision, there would be no bills, although there might be small token fees at the point of service to discourage overuse for trivial complaints. Regulated private accountable-care organizations of salaried physicians that delivered the treatment would be responsible for staying within budgetary limits set by the agency that paid them on a per-capita basis. Physician groups would be nonprofit; low-cost public reinsurance would compensate them for any losses due to caring for extremely sick patients. Net income could not be used to enhance salaries or make capital improvements but could be applied to upgrading patient services. Physician groups could be expected to pay hospital costs, or hospitals could be separately paid by the single payer, but all hospital charges would be regulated.

Congress would not have a separate health-care system. Everyone, including legislators and government officials, would be in the system and would pay their share of the progressive, designated health-care tax that supported the program. This would, among other things, prevent legislative underfunding. People would be free to choose their primary-care physician and physician group and could change doctors and group membership as they wished. They would also be free to pay for any medical services they might choose outside the publicly funded program.

The envisioned system would be much less expensive than the hodgepodge we now have, because the profits and overhead costs of private insurance would be gone. Without bills, there would be little or no fraud and abuse and less administrative hassle. Without fee-for-service, physicians would have no incentives for unnecessary elective services. And with medical care based on non-profit groups of cooperating specialists centered on primary-care physicians, there would be good reason to expect services to be efficient and of high quality.

Given what we know about the added costs of private insurance and given informed estimates of the costs of fraudulent billing and of unnecessary and duplicated services, a conservative guess of the total savings from eliminating these problems might be one-third or more of the entire cost of medical care. In any case, these savings would amount to many hundreds of billions—far more than enough to pay for the cost of providing good care for everyone. A reformed system based on group practice could also reduce the cost of defensive medicine (procedures done in response to concerns about malpractice liability). This would probably add a substantial amount to the projected savings. The federal government would have ultimate control over rising costs, because it would set the rate of the designated, progressive tax that funded the entire system and would thereby determine how much could be spent on health care each year. At the beginning of reform, the health tax would presumably collect an amount close to the current total cost of health care. Subsequent tax rates would reflect the new system's needs and its savings.

Converting the present system to the one I have proposed would require a sea change in public opinion and government policy and would also need the support of most of the medical profession. To say the least, it would be a long and difficult process that would be bitterly opposed by the private insurance industry and its friends and by all those who fear a "government takeover" and cling to the groundless belief that the free market can best govern the health-care system. Nevertheless, there are reasons I believe this transformation has at least a chance of becoming reality.

First, physicians are flocking to join group practices in great numbers, and this could be the beginning of a major national reorganization of medical care. About 200,000 physicians (approximately 25 percent to 30 percent of all those in practice) are now employed by multispecialty groups owned by physicians or by hospitals, and this number is increasing by about 10 percent annually. Most of these groups pay their physicians at least a partial salary—only a few pay full salaries. The majority, though, still receive payment from insurance plans on a fee-for-service basis.

A rapidly growing fraction of practicing physicians are beginning to see the advantages to themselves and their patients of organized group practice with partial or full salaries. At the same time, the traditional conservatism of doctors seems to be changing. If this trend continues—and I believe it is being accelerated by the increasing number of women in medicine, who tend to favor group practice and health-care reform—we may see physicians and many medical societies urging basic reforms that would include a single-payer system. Women will soon represent half of all practicing physicians, and their attitudes will influence the profession, patients, and the general public. Legislators, now largely responsive to the financial inducements of lobbyists and vested interests, might begin to appreciate that they need votes even more than money and might become more receptive to proposals for reform that their constituents widely support.

The private health-insurance industry would be a formidable opponent of the reforms I propose, and its position would be supported by those who worry about the many thousands of jobs that might be lost if this industry were to disappear. However, a huge compensating gain in jobs could result from the expansion of employment in businesses that would no longer have to pay the ever-increasing costs of their employees' health insurance. Because health benefits were originally given to employees in lieu of salary increases, employers should be expected to share their savings with their employees in the form of increased wages to help them pay their health-care tax. However, if the new system reduced health-care costs and controlled their rate of rise as much as expected, both employers and employees would benefit.

Private insurers would not be appeased by these developments but might be satisfied if the industry's investors were compensated for their equity interests. Some of the health-care-tax receipts could be used for this purpose over a period of time, perhaps by issuing government bonds to investors in exchange for stock in the private insurance companies.

The phasing-out of private insurance could also be accomplished through competition from a government program. Medicare coverage could be offered to those under age 65 as an alternative to private insurance in decade-by-decade steps. This would allow time for physicians to develop their group-practice arrangements and for the government to carry out trials of capitated payment to groups (that is, payment on a per-capita basis for comprehensive care). To control costs, capitated payments would ultimately have to replace Medicare's current fee-for-service arrangement, and this would mean a change in the way most Medicare beneficiaries receive their care. Instead of being subsidized by government to obtain health care on a fee-for-service basis, beneficiaries would be expected to select a group practice in a system that would meet all their medical needs at a cost no more—and probably less—than they would pay for Medicare coverage. Opponents of reform would nevertheless claim this abandons entitlements for the elderly, so it would take a lot of public education—and the medical profession's reassurance—to convince Medicare beneficiaries that they would be much better off in the new system.

Experiments at the state level could facilitate national conversion to a single-payer system. Vermont recently passed legislation to establish such a system and is working toward reorganizing the delivery of medical care. As economic pressures for reform continue to grow, other states may follow. The Hawaii Legislature is considering a universal health system, and Massachusetts is looking at replacing fee-for-service with some form of global payment. The success of state experiments like these would embolden the federal government to act on a national level.

I do not underestimate the complexity of the changes I am proposing. The odds against it are daunting. Congress might not even begin to debate major reform until the health system is near collapse. But what seems clear is that the best—possibly the only—hope for achieving universal, affordable care lies in the eventual elimination of private insurance and fee-for-service payment and in the creation of a tax-supported system based on group practice. Although this proposal makes good medical, social, and economic sense, its ultimate fate will be decided in the political arena. It cannot become a reality without an informed and aroused public bolstered by the medical profession's strong support for the reform.

Critical Thinking

1. According to the author, why is universal coverage the more affordable health care option?
2. Why does the author also believe that a tax-supported system involving doctors in a group practice is the best way to provide health care?
3. Why do many people oppose national health insurance?

ARNOLD S. RELMAN is a professor emeritus of medicine and social medicine at Harvard Medical School and the former editor of *The New England Journal of Medicine*.

Relman, Arnold S.. Reprinted with permission from *The American Prospect*, by Relman, Arnold S., January/February 2012, pp. 34–37. http://www.prospect.org. *The American Prospect*, 1710 Rhode Island Avenue, NW, 12th Floor, Washington, DC 20036. All rights reserved.

Medicare Whac-A-Mole

Why health care price controls always fail.

PETER SUDERMAN

House Republicans, you may have heard, are trying to "end Medicare as we know it." And well they should—Medicare as we know it is the nation's biggest fiscal disaster. For years members of Congress and the executive branch have been trying, and failing, to find ways to restrain the growth of government health spending on seniors. Medicare is a $500 billion program on track to become a $1 trillion program before hitting insolvency in 2024, even under the rosiest projections. The program looms as a threat not only to itself but to the budgetary health of the nation. It is the single largest driver of long-term federal debt.

Despite the potential campaign effectiveness of the political charge that Republicans want to gut Medicare, President Barack Obama has positioned himself as a willing butcher of his own party's sacred cow. "We have to tackle entitlements" to control the federal debt, the president said in June, and "Medicare has to bear a greater part of the burden." Over the summer, Obama signed a debt deal with Republicans that allowed for a 2 percent cut to Medicare spending should a bipartisan deficit committee fail to come up with savings. In September he endorsed $248 billion in Medicare cuts as part of his own debt reduction proposal.

The cuts Obama proposed were not part of a fundamental Medicare overhaul, but they were cuts all the same. "Despite what some in my own party have argued," he said, "I believe that we need to make some modest adjustments to programs like Medicare to ensure that they're still around for future generations." Obama claimed he was open to reforms that would bring down the cost of Medicare, "not by shifting those costs to seniors but rather by actually reducing those costs."

"Actually reducing" the cost of Medicare has long represented the biggest pot of gold at the end of the public policy rainbow. It is treasure that Obama has been promising to deliver since early in his presidency. "If we do nothing to slow these skyrocketing costs," he said in 2009, "we will eventually be spending more on Medicare and Medicaid than every other government program combined. Put simply, our health care problem is our deficit problem. Nothing else even comes close....We know we must reform this system. The question is how."

So what innovative solution does Obama propose to begin fixing America's biggest fiscal problem? Simple: He would change the way providers are paid for Medicare's services. Pay less, spend less. Right? It is so obvious that one might wonder why it hasn't been tried before. The answer is that it has—many, many times.

It is often said that you can't put a price on health. But for decades that is exactly what the federal government has attempted. Since the birth of the entitlement, a parade of legislators and bureaucrats has been playing billion- and trillion-dollar games of Whac-A-Mole with Medicare, knocking down spending with an elaborately constructed set of technocratic payment schemes in one area only to see it rise back up in some other part of the system. Obama is merely proposing to try it one more time.

All-You-Can-Eat Health Care

When Medicare, the federally run health care financing system for Americans who are 65 or older, passed in 1965, supporters knew the program would be expensive. Its lack of cost controls was the price of passage. Wilbur Cohen, a top health bureaucrat dubbed "The Man Who Built Medicare" by *Medical World News*, admitted that "the sponsors of Medicare, including myself, had to concede in 1965 that there would be no real controls over hospitals and physicians. I was required to promise before the final vote in the executive session of the House Ways and Means Committee that the federal agency would exercise no control."

Indeed, that promise was explicitly built into the legislation, which declared that "nothing in this title shall be construed to authorize any Federal officer or employee to exercise any supervision or control over the practice of medicine or the manner in which medical services are provided ... or to exercise any supervision or control over the administration or operation of any such [health-care] institution, agency, or person." In other words, no rationing, no death panels. As Richmond University political scientist Rick Mayes explained in a 2007 essay for the *Journal of the History of Medicine*, Medicare was inaugurated with "a reimbursement system that neither imposed limits nor required outside approval." As a result, "unrestricted cost reimbursement became the modus operandi for financing American medical care."

Even then, the program's supporters grossly underestimated how expensive the program would be. The House Ways and Means Committee projected that 95 percent of the elderly would enroll in the program's doctor insurance component during 1967, its first year of operation. That estimate proved accurate. But the committee also projected that total costs for the first year would run no more than $1.3 billion. Total spending in the first year instead ran a whopping $4.6 billion.

As the program continued, its true costs rapidly departed even further from initial expectations. The committee had projected that hospital spending would amount to just $3.1 billion in 1970. Instead it was $7.1 billion. Hospital spending in 1975, initially expected to be around $4.2 billion, was actually $15.6 billion. The estimates were off because they didn't account for the increase in demand spurred by the program's offer of essentially unlimited benefits.

This was a new problem for America. "Prior to Medicare," explains John Goodman, president of the National Center for Policy Analysis and a frequent contributor to the health policy journal Health Affairs, "we maintained a system that took up a reasonable percentage of the national income," holding more or less steady at 5 percent of GDP. But after Medicare, he says, the country "began to have health inflation that has never quit."

Coincidence? Not at all. Medicare was a major contributor to the problem. For beneficiaries, it transformed the health care system into a generously subsidized, all-you-can-eat buffet. For providers, it offered a steady revenue stream that they used to rapidly build out expensive new services. In 2007 MIT economist Amy Finkelstein published a paper estimating that the introduction of Medicare accounted for a 23 percent increase in total hospital expenditures between 1965 and 1970, with an even larger effect in the subsequent five years.

Part of the problem was that the program served up its smorgasbord all at once. On July 1, 1966—Medicare's very first day of operation—19 million individuals were instantly eligible for its benefits. Not one of them had ever paid a dime to directly support the program, but they collected full benefits anyway. That situation was at odds with the way the program had been sold, which was not as an entitlement but as a government-managed savings mechanism. When President John F. Kennedy outlined his original vision of the program, he declared, "We're not asking for anybody to hand this out—we are asking for a chance for the people who will receive the benefit to earn their way." In reality, when the program began, it was pure handout.

Seniors got the medical benefits, but doctors got the money. The payment system offered doctors and hospitals essentially unrestricted payments. Providers invoiced their expenses, and the government paid. The system gave doctors and hospitals both license and incentive to spend—and spend and spend and spend. Which is exactly what they did.

By 1970 the Senate was circulating memos examining ways to tamp down runaway Medicare spending growth. A set of 1972 amendments to Social Security included some unsophisticated attempts to cut Medicare payments, but hospital inflation

continued to spiral upward, as did public concern about the issue. Hospital costs were growing at roughly twice the general inflation rate; between 1974 and 1977, total government spending on health care doubled.

Control Payments, Control Spending?

Medicare didn't just drive spending upward; it also made health spending a government problem. With polls showing that the rapidly rising cost of health care was one of America's top three policy concerns, elected officials took notice. And President Jimmy Carter came to believe that controlling payments was the best way to exert influence on the system.

In April 1977, Carter introduced a proposal to put strict limits on reimbursements to hospitals, which were believed to be a key driver of health care inflation. After years in which spending grew by an average of 15 percent, Carter wanted to impose a ceiling of 9 percent. Because he was responding to concerns about escalating costs across the medical sector, his plan imposed a federal cap on spending growth for both public and private payers. Rather than a single-payer system, it was a variation known as "all-payer."

But Carter's plan faced intense opposition from the American Hospital Association (AHA). The AHA successfully killed cost-control legislation twice under Carter by convincing a group of conservative Democrats that hospitals could control costs voluntarily. But the AHA's members failed to hold up their end of the political bargain. As President Ronald Reagan took office, hospital inflation continued to balloon, growing 13 percent in 1980 and 18 percent in 1981. Voluntary restraint, it turned out, was no match for the temptation of nearly unlimited federal funds.

In 1982 Reagan responded with the Tax Equity and Fiscal Responsibility Act (TEFRA), which, among other things, would have imposed strict new limits on Medicare payments. The law ditched Carter's "all-payer" idea and addressed public programs only.

The idea was to encourage cost-effective treatment by paying providers on a per-patient rather than fee-for-service basis. But TEFRA was intended more as a negotiating tactic than an actual reform. As David G. Smith, currently a professor emeritus of political science at Swarthmore College, points out in his 1992 book *Paying for Medicare: The Politics of Reform,* TEFRA was "designed to help the hospitals perceive the desirability" of reform. It wasn't an overhaul; it was a threat.

Hospitals got the message and relented, dropping their opposition to a new payment system. In less than two months, Congress approved a system of standardized payments that paid a flat rate per case and allowed federal officials to determine hospital payment rates in advance. Reagan administration staffers convinced themselves the reform was market-based because standardized prices rewarded more efficient providers, but there was no mistaking the system's fundamental element: bureaucratic price setting.

The only question was how the bureaucrats would decide what to charge. A robust system would need to create enough diagnostic groups to contain every possible patient and every possible diagnosis. That meant creating categories, and lots of them.

Think of a filing cabinet with hundreds of drawers, each labeled according to a particular category of medical diagnosis. These are Medicare's diagnosis-related groups (DRGs), and every hospital patient is assigned to one. After that, prices are set based on the average cost of everything in the drawer. Anything from drawer number 707—major male pelvic procedures—gets one price. Anything from drawer number 385—inflammatory bowel disorders—gets another price. What if a treatment ends up costing far more or less than the assigned price? The theory is that it doesn't matter, since everything averages out in the end. Everything is covered; everything has a code and a category.

Or at least it's supposed to. When the system was launched in 1983, there were 500 DRG codes. But like so many bureaucratic systems, this one grew larger and more complex over time. By 2010 there were almost 750 DRG codes. No matter how narrowly and meticulously Medicare's bureaucrats organized their files, they were always forced into an implicit admission of defeat in their quest to create an all-encompassing system. Each revision of the DRGs left a junk drawer-labeled "ungroupable"—at the very end.

Leave the Hospital, Go to the Doctor

Did the Reagan administration's price controls restrain Medicare spending? Within hospitals, yes. But the system had an unintended consequence: Hospitals, paid according to the diagnostic drawers their patients fit in rather than according to their own rates, were given an incentive to cycle through patients much faster. As a result, hospital stay lengths dropped dramatically, and so did inpatient hospital spending. A RAND Corporation study published in 1992 found that the new payment system reduced the length of hospital stays by an average of 24 percent.

Quicker discharges often meant sicker discharges. Where do sick patients who have been discharged from the hospital go? To doctor's offices, outpatient hospital services, or, in the case of seniors, nursing homes, none of which was covered under the new payment scheme. That's where the spending went too. Starting in 1983, outpatient hospital spending rose at three times the rate of inpatient spending. And according to a 2003 World Health Organization review of U.S. health policy, the savings generated by shorter hospital stays were offset by increased spending on nursing home and outpatient care. Throughout the 1980s, Medicare spending on physician payments grew an average of 13.7 percent—7 percent faster than all other services. By 1990 total Medicare payments to physicians had blown up to two and a half times what they were a decade earlier.

So by the mid-1980s, policy makers were hunting for yet another payment reform. This time physician payments would be the target. Whack one mole, another one pops up.

In 1985 Congress commissioned a review of the DRG system. But rather than stick to a retrospective, the authors of the report expanded its scope, using it as an opportunity to push for expanded physician price controls. The theory was that DRGs, focusing only on hospital payments, hadn't gone far enough. According to Smith's Medicare history, the authors of the review believed "the most viable approach . . . was to aim at increasingly global control of physician payments." A program passed on a promise to avoid control of the medical system was now looking to control its entire payment structure.

Who was behind this push for global control? Joseph Antos, an American Enterprise Institute health policy scholar who served as a senior economist in the Reagan administration—a role he describes as the "designated health and everything else person"—attended many senior staff meetings during which the new system was drawn up. "This was a group that consisted of high-level people, often political appointees from all sorts of different agencies," Antos tells me. "I don't think many of them were health policy experts. I know none of them were economists."

The system they were planning would become known as the resource-based relative value scale, or RBRVS. It attempted to divide physician's services into roughly equal work units and make payments accordingly. The assorted high-level officials had a naive confidence in their ability to accurately align the amount of work that went into a procedure with the amount of payment a physician received. "They knew that there was a problem paying physicians," Antos says. "They thought they knew what the problem was. This was going to be a new system that was going to rationalize the old system."

Antos, the only economist in the group, wasn't so sure. And so he began to ask questions: "How does the government know what the relative values should be? How is this related to any market-clearing process that anybody's ever known?" One idea was to set prices by committee. Antos pointed out that "asking committees of doctors to guess how much work is involved in something is the same thing as just setting prices."

In an October 2010 essay for *The American,* Antos described the initial plan as being "based on academic theory with its roots in the Soviet Union." Just as the Soviets made all economic decisions—how many tanks to build, how many jackets to sew, how much food to produce—through central planning, the RBRVS system is an effort to centrally plan medical prices. But as in the Soviet Union, those prices are not informed by market-based signals, which are generated by the interaction of supply, demand, and willingness to pay. In particular, the RBRVS system ignores how much value a patient receives from a service.

Thanks at least in part to Antos's questions, 1986 came and went with no major overhaul of the physician reimbursement system. But Antos eventually left for a new post. And in 1988 researchers at Harvard University finalized a study that would bring a modified form of prospective payment to physicians. In December 1989, as part of an omnibus budget proposal, President George H.W. Bush signed the RBRVS system into law. It would take effect in January of 1992.

Antos, who eventually transitioned to a senior position at the Health Care Financing Administration (HCFA, now the Centers for Medicare & Medicaid Services within the Department of Health and Human Services), was put in charge of implementing the system—not in spite of his skepticism but because of it. "I had a long connection to it, so I understood it," he says. "And [HCFA Administrator Gail Wilensky] didn't mind that I was against it, because she was an economist and also agreed that it wasn't going to work."

The Socialist Calculation Problem

Why would an economist be so skeptical of the system? Even from a purely technocratic perspective, it is an enormous challenge. Antos warns of the "technical difficulty of creating a prospective payment system that wouldn't totally screw everything up."

But the problem goes deeper than that. Medicare's twin payment schemes are inevitably beset by what George Mason University economist Arnold Kling calls "the socialist calculation problem." The bureaucrats in charge of setting prices have to come up with a rational basis for the prices they set. They have to be justified, somehow, which is where the complex rate-setting formulas come into play. But without price signals, the result is almost always an arbitrary formula based on a limited, imperfect set of factors. When all is said and done, says Kling, "it's just a made-up formula. It has to be."

The other problem is that any payment system inevitably ends up being manipulated by savvy payees. "You price on the basis of one thing, but then people optimize their behavior to that thing," says Kling. In a sense this is the primary job of health care administrators: to understand payment systems and squeeze every possible dollar out of them.

In the wake of the two payment reforms, hospitals began to manipulate the system through "upcoding"—systematically shifting patients into higher-paying DRGs. Research by economists at Dartmouth University suggests that during the early 1990s, hospital administrators figured out ways to substantially increase the number of Medicare cases they billed to higher-paying DRGs. Payment games continue today. In October the Senate Finance Committee released a report accusing several large home health care companies of abusing Medicare's payment rules by pushing employees to perform extra therapy visits, thereby qualifying for Medicare bonus payments, even when those visits weren't strictly necessary. But for many health care providers, that's the business. Hospital administrators "are people whose job it is to game the system," Kling says. "They know every little detail of the rules."

Playing by the rules, and getting the most out of them, becomes the focus. Over time, the rules cease to guide the game and instead become the purpose of the game. Activities that are coded and paid for become the activities that providers do the most. The system encourages covered procedures, such as surgeries and child delivery, while discouraging doctors from

spending time in nonpaid activities such as emailing patients or monitoring health data collected electronically at home by the patient. The provision of care bends to fit the shape, however quirky, of the payment rules.

Which may explain why controlling physician payments failed to restrain the growth of Medicare spending. As Antos expected, the system did not work. The RBRVS system took effect in 1992. By 1997 Congress had the mole mallet out once again.

The Unsustainable Growth Rate

The RBRVS system included a mechanism, known as the volume performance standard, aimed at preventing doctors from gaming the standardized payments by increasing the number of cases they processed. If total physician spending increased, fees went down. If total physician spending decreased, the fees went up. The problem was that the formula was based on historical trends in volume, which had been rising for years. But in the mid 1990s, that trend unexpectedly slowed, leading to substantial increases in Medicare's physician fees.

Under President Bill Clinton, a Republican Congress tried out a new payment mechanism intended to control volume as part of the 1997 Balanced Budget Act. It tied payments to the size of the economy in the hope of controlling inflationary spending by keeping costs per patient from rising faster than GDP. If total spending on physician reimbursements stayed under the spending target, fees would go up. If reimbursements exceeded the target, fees would go down.

For a few years, payments to providers rose as planned, and spending stayed within budgetary targets. But like previous payment reforms, the Clinton-era "sustainable growth rate" (SGR) formula put pressure on one part of the system, shifting costs elsewhere. Douglas Holtz-Eakin, a former director of the Congressional Budget Office, argues that the formula has two major flaws: First, it targets only one component of Medicare—physician spending—rather than the program as a whole. Second, despite its goal, it does not really control volume. "Congress failed to understand that physicians respond to incentives," he says. Lower reimbursements inevitably result in more services being performed. "Cut rates, they will respond." Rather quickly, the system started to break down. As the journal Health Affairs dryly noted in a recent primer on the issue, "The expectation that this payment system would control spending was not realized."

That was not entirely the fault of SGR. Legislators in Congress did not let their own system work. The reform allowed for payment reductions in order to keep spending in line with the economy. But in the booming 1990s, when the law was passed, most policymakers never expected that payments would ever fall. As long as GDP grew and payments rose in response, the system worked mostly as planned. But in 2002 the formula called for a 5 percent reimbursement cut to keep payments in line with the flagging, post-tech bubble economy.

Congress allowed the cut to take effect, but doctors weren't happy. The grumbling was loud enough that when the formula called for another cut in 2003, Congress overrode it and voted to institute a small reimbursement hike. Since then that pattern has held: Each year the SGR has called for a reimbursement cut, and each year—sometimes multiple times a year—Congress, ever susceptible to outside influence, has instead voted to delay the cut though a temporary patch, now known widely as "the doc fix."

The lack of congressional fortitude has created additional headaches for doctors and patients. Although doctors took a pay cut only once, the temporary nature of the extensions still means that Medicare payments are riddled with uncertainty. Almost everyone—doctors and policy makers alike—assumes the cuts will never go through. But they don't know for sure. That makes doctors wary of relying too much on Medicare payments, which already lag behind the rates paid by private insurers. As a result, some are reducing the number of new Medicare patients they see, while others are dropping out of the program entirely. A 2010 survey by the Texas Medical Association found that 100 to 200 doctors in the state were giving up on Medicare each year. The SGR's unlikely but persistent threat of dramatic fee cuts has made it harder for seniors to obtain health care.

Doctors, led by the American Medical Association, have escaped those big cuts so far. But lobbying pressure to override the programmatic cuts has exacerbated the long-term problem. When Congress replaced a scheduled reduction in 2004 and 2005 with a 1.5 percent increase, it did not bother to change the long-term spending target. Consequently, the SGR called for even bigger cuts down the road to make up for the short-term hikes. As the overrides have mounted over the years, so have the cuts called for by the formula. There is now an enormous chasm between what physicians who accept Medicare are supposed to be paid under the SGR and what they are actually paid.

In December 2010, congressional leaders announced a tentative deal to pay for a one-year extension of the doc fix by trimming funding for the first year of ObamaCare's insurance subsidies. But time is running out. By the formula's reckoning, doctors face as much as a 29.5 percent cut at the beginning of 2012. Depending on how long Congress continues to delay the cuts, an even steeper reduction looms in the future—an estimated 40 percent if the charade continues until 2014.

Abolishing the SGR entirely, as many doctors would like, could cost up to $370 billion over a decade, according to the Congressional Budget Office (CBO). But the Obama administration, despite cutting more than $500 billion in Medicare payments to pay for the president's health care overhaul, and despite calling for another $248 billion in Medicare reductions as part of his debt reduction plan, has paid little attention to the problem. In February 2011, Health and Human Services Secretary Kathleen Sebelius told members of Congress that the administration thinks the doc fix is "very important to do." Early drafts of the health care overhaul included a doc fix. But in the end, Democrats chose to use the law's Medicare cuts to pay for expanded coverage rather than to stabilize physician payments. An administration budget proposal this year also called for the doc fix to be fully paid for. How? The administration won't say. Instead, it has offered up enough money to extend the doc fix for just two years—and then only by reducing the rate of

Medicare spending growth over a full decade. This is rather like a lifelong two-pack-a-day smoker promising to quit next year, then spending the money he'll "save" on cigarettes over the course of the year at a bar that evening.

But the SGR puts Republicans in a tough spot too. CBO projections, based on current law, assume that the SGR's scheduled cuts will take effect. Few Republicans want to be seen as advocating what the CBO will count as hundreds of billions in additional Medicare spending. But neither do GOP legislators want to be seen as advocating a nearly 30 percent reduction in physician reimbursements, which will further reduce seniors' access to doctors.

Medicare's resident technocrats have been somewhat more forthcoming with proposals. In October, the Medicare Payment Advisory Commission, a 17-member panel of experts that advises Congress about how to structure the program's reimbursements, voted to recommend a decade-long doc fix. Its proposal, which can't go into effect without congressional approval, would cut specialist rates by 5.9 percent annually for three years while freezing primary care reimbursements. But this plan pays for only $100 billion or so of the 10-year cost; the remaining $200 to $300 billion would come from cuts in payments to hospitals, drug makers, acute care facilities, and other providers. Provider groups immediately launched an aggressive opposition campaign; given Congress's historical reluctance to let doctors take a hit, it seems unlikely that this proposal will succeed where others have failed.

Holtz-Eakin, the former CBO director, argues that members of Congress need to recognize that the cost of recurrent SGR overrides is already built into the system. "We've already really committed to spending this money," he says. After accepting that reality, he says, Congress should move to a new system that puts the entire Medicare program on a budget and turns control of that budget over to individual seniors. "It's the first step that's killing everyone, though," he says. "No politician wants to be seen as adding $300 or $400 billion to the deficit."

The second step won't be easy either. In April, House Republicans voted for a budget plan authored by House Budget Committee Chairman Paul Ryan (R-Wis.) that would have transformed Medicare from an essentially unlimited program, committed to endless spending, into a premium support system that would allow seniors to buy regulated plans from private insurers. Democrats spent the following months accusing House Republicans of having voted to "end Medicare as we know it," a line that many promised to repeat all the way up to the 2012 election. But according to Antos, the American Enterprise Institute health policy expert, transforming the system is the only way to escape the flaws of SGR and other price controls. "If you leave the structure of Medicare alone," he says, "you cannot solve the problem."

ObamaCare and Medicare

Obama didn't transform the system so much as double down on its faults. Much like the introduction of Medicare, ObamaCare extends subsidized insurance coverage to millions of people, a move that is likely to spur additional demand.

It also starts a new round of price-control Whac-A-Mole via yet another mechanism designed to rein in Medicare spending. The Independent Payment Advisory Board (IPAB), an ostensibly independent 15-member panel, is charged with reviewing Medicare spending each year and making recommendations to Congress aimed at keeping costs below a threshold based on inflation in both the health care sector and the economy as a whole. Most of the board's recommendations are likely to address reimbursement rates. Those changes will take effect unless Congress votes them down and approves an alternative savings plan.

The board's boosters have great hopes that it will finally control the growth of Medicare. But the program's own number crunchers have less confidence. In May 2011, Medicare's actuary and its director of cost estimates warned that "it is doubtful that Medicare providers can take steps to keep their cost growth within the bounds imposed by these price limitations, year after year, indefinitely." Over time, they said, the new "price constraints would become unsustainable," noting that ObamaCare's payment updates likely would result in 15 percent of hospitals, home health agencies, and nursing facilities operating at negative margins by the end of the decade.

The current head of the CBO, Douglas Elmendorf, also seems wary. In the summer of 2009, when IPAB was first discussed, Elmendorf wrote a letter to Congress that said "in CBO's judgment, the probability is high that no savings would be realized . . . but there is also a chance that substantial savings might be realized"—a polite way of signaling minimal confidence in the board's ability to cut costs.

That suggestion was affirmed the following summer, just months after ObamaCare was enacted, when Elemen-dorf released the CBO's long-term budget outlook. In the alternative fiscal scenario, which is based not on current law but on the CBO's best guess as to how legislation will change and evolve, Elmendorf assumed ObamaCare would fail to achieve its intended Medicare savings. The CBO's mission does not include making policy recommendations. But it was hard to read the CBO's report as anything other than an implicit jab at the notion of relying on an independent advisory board to control costs.

And why shouldn't the CBO—or anyone else—be skeptical? Congress has not given up the game of Whac-A-Mole. It has merely assigned an independent committee to play for it. The board will face the same problems that price controllers have always faced: Without market signals, prices are inherently arbitrary. It's the socialist calculation problem all over again. There is no way for policy makers to avoid it—except, of course, by refusing to play the price-setting game at all.

At this point, that does not seem likely. Although it was passed based on an explicit promise not to control the practice of medicine, Medicare is now defined by its many payment processes, which exert substantial influence on how doctors and hospitals treat patients. "Medicare screws up the American medical system, period," says Holtz-Eakin. It does so not by telling doctors what to do but by deciding what to pay. He who controls the price, controls the system.

Medicare is a $500 billion program on track to become a $1 trillion program before hitting insolvency in 2024, even under the rosiest projections. The program imperils the budgetary health of the nation.

Pay less for Medicare, spend less. Right? It is so obvious that one might wonder why it hasn't been tried before. The answer is that it has—many, many times.

Hospital administrators "are people whose job it is to game the system," says economist Arnold Kling. "They know every little detail of the rules."

"If you leave the structure of Medicare alone," says former Reagan administration health care official Joseph Antos, "you cannot solve the problem."

Critical Thinking

1. Why does the author perceive the American health care system to be a failure?

2. Describe the American Enterprise's health care policy and explain why it would be successful.

3. Why have health care price controls not been effective? Explain.

Suderman, Peter. From *Reason Magazine*, January 2012. Copyright © 2012 by Reason Foundation, 3415 S. Sepulveda Blvd., Suite 400, Los Angeles, CA 90034. www.reason.com

UNIT 9

Consumer Health

Unit Selections

Learning Outcomes

After reading this Unit, you will be able to:

- Distinguish whether vaccination is more dangerous than getting the disease prevented by the vaccine.

- Explain why some parents opt out of vaccinating their children.

- Describe medical tourism.

- Discuss the risks versus benefits of medical tourism.

- Discuss why the number of bed bug infestations has been increasing.

- Address the means of eradicating bed bugs.

- List the steps you should take to prevent food-borne illness while processing meat and produce at home.

- Discuss what consumers should look for when choosing health insurance.

- Distinguish between adequate and inadequate health care coverage.

- Distinguish between the advantages and disadvantages of cybermedicine.

- Discuss why obesity plays a role in getting adequate health care.

Student Website

www.mhhe.com/cls

Internet References

FDA Consumer Magazine
www.fda.gov/fdac
Global Vaccine Awareness League
www.gval.com

For many people the term *consumer health* conjures up images of selecting health care services and paying medical bills. While these two aspects of health care are indeed consumer health issues, the term *consumer health* encompasses all consumer products and services that influence the health and welfare of people as well as the ability to understand and use health care products wisely and appropriately. A definition this broad suggests that almost everything we see or do may be construed to be a consumer health issue. In many ways consumer health is an outward expression of our health-related behaviors and decision-making processes, and as such, is based on our desire to make healthy choices, be assertive, and be in possession of accurate information on which to base our decisions. The health-conscious consumer seeks to be as informed as possible when making dietary and medical decisions—but the best intentions come to no avail when consumers base their decisions on inaccurate information, old beliefs, or media hype that lacks a scientific base. Knowledge (based on accurate information) and critical thinking are the key elements required to become proactive in managing your daily health concerns.

In the report Healthy People 2010, the U.S. Department of Health and Human Services included improved consumer health literacy as an objective and identified health literacy as an important component of health communication, medical product safety, and oral health. Health literacy is defined in Healthy People 2010 as "The degree to which individuals have the capacity to obtain, process, and understand basic health information and services needed to make appropriate health decisions."

Health literacy includes the ability to understand instructions on prescription drug bottles, appointment slips, medical education brochures, doctor's directions and consent forms, and the ability to negotiate complex health care systems. Health literacy is not simply the ability to read. It requires a complex group of reading, listening, analytical, and decision-making skills, and the ability to apply these skills to health situations.

Health literacy varies by context and setting and is not necessarily related to years of education or general reading ability. A person who functions adequately at home or work may have marginal or inadequate literacy in a health care environment. With the move towards a more "consumer-centric" health care system as part of an overall effort to improve the quality of health care and to reduce health care costs, individuals need to take an even more active role in health care related decisions. To accomplish this people need strong health information skills.

Seven articles were chosen for this unit and address several issues including vaccine refusal, medical tourism, bed bugs, contaminated food, hazardous health plans, cybermedicine, and the challenges obese individuals face with the health care system. While being overweight may increase the risk for certain health problems, how much a person weighs may also affect the quality of health care that he or she receives. Ginny Graves addresses this issue in " The *Surprising Reason* Why Heavy Isn't Healthy." Accessing a health provider can sometimes be challenging. To facilitate this, many doctors now communicate with their patients through online medical consultations. While this does give patients access, it's unclear if cybermedicine is an acceptable substitute for a face-to-face office visit. It also

© Stockbyte/Getty Images

discriminates against those without computer access. Regina A. Bailey discusses this issue in "Cybermedicine: What You Need to Know." In "Vaccine Refusal, Mandatory Immunization, and the Risks of Vaccine-Preventable Diseases," author Saad B. Omer et al. discusses the risk versus benefit of vaccination. There is a growing number of children in the United States who are not vaccinated against childhood diseases. Their parents have opted to forgo immunization due to their belief that vaccines are more dangerous than the measles, whooping cough, polio, and other diseases they prevent. This has caused an increase in disease reports among children.

Consumer Reports covers the adequacy of many health insurance plans in "Hazardous Health Plans." Another consumer health issue is addressed by Lorene Burkhart and Lorna Gentry in "Medical Tourism: What You Should Know." During the past few years, nearly a half million Americans went overseas for medical and dental treatment—a number that's expected to rise. These travelers find that the costs of many treatments are much lower than in the United States, and they can also seek those treatments that are not yet available back home. These days, travelers within the United States may come home with more than they bargained for, as described by Rebecca Berg in "Bed Bugs: The Pesticide Dilemma." While pesticide-resistant bed bugs don't appear to cause disease with their bites, they invade beds, interfere with sleep, and can affect people emotionally. Pesticides used to control them however, may pose health risks. The final article reviews the evidence that even though animal foods are more likely to be contaminated, there has been an increase of food-borne illness from fruit and vegetable consumption. Mark Fischetti discusses this issue in "Is Your Food Contaminated?"

Vaccine Refusal, Mandatory Immunization, and the Risks of Vaccine-Preventable Diseases

Saad B. Omer et al.

Vaccines are among the most effective tools available for preventing infectious diseases and their complications and sequelae. High immunization coverage has resulted in drastic declines in vaccine-preventable diseases, particularly in many high- and middle-income countries. A reduction in the incidence of a vaccine-preventable disease often leads to the public perception that the severity of the disease and susceptibility to it have decreased.[1] At the same time, public concern about real or perceived adverse events associated with vaccines has increased. This heightened level of concern often results in an increase in the number of people refusing vaccines.[1,2]

In the United States, policy interventions, such as immunization requirements for school entry, have contributed to high vaccine coverage and record or near-record lows in the levels of vaccine-preventable diseases. Herd immunity, induced by high vaccination rates, has played an important role in greatly reducing or eliminating continual endemic transmission of a number of diseases, thereby benefiting the community overall in addition to the individual vaccinated person.

Recent parental concerns about perceived vaccine safety issues, such as a purported association between vaccines and autism, though not supported by a credible body of scientific evidence,[3-8] have led increasing numbers of parents to refuse or delay vaccination for their children.[9,10] The primary measure of vaccine refusal in the United States is the proportion of children who are exempted from school immunization requirements for nonmedical reasons. There has been an increase in state-level rates of nonmedical exemptions from immunization requirements.[11] In this article, we review the evidentiary basis for school immunization requirements, explore the determinants of vaccine refusal, and discuss the individual and community risks of vaccine-preventable diseases associated with vaccine refusal.

Evolution of U.S. Immunization Requirements

Vaccination was introduced in the United States at the turn of the 19th century. The first U.S. law to require smallpox vaccination was passed soon afterward, in 1809 in Massachusetts, to prevent and control frequent smallpox outbreaks that had substantial health and economic consequences.[12–14] Subsequently, other states enacted similar legislation.[13] Despite the challenges inherent in establishing a reliable and safe vaccine delivery system, vaccination became widely accepted as an effective tool for preventing smallpox through the middle of the 19th century, and the incidence of smallpox declined between 1802 and 1840.[15] In the 1850s, "irregular physicians, the advocates of unorthodox medical theories,"[16] led challenges to vaccination. Vaccine use decreased, and smallpox made a major reappearance in the 1870s.[15] Many states passed new vaccination laws, whereas other states started enforcing existing laws. Increased enforcement of the laws often resulted in increased opposition to vaccination. Several states, including California, Illinois, Indiana, Minnesota, Utah, West Virginia, and Wisconsin, repealed compulsory vaccination laws.[15] Many other states retained them.

In a 1905 landmark case, *Jacobson v. Massachusetts,* which has since served as the foundation for public health laws, the U.S. Supreme Court endorsed the rights of states to pass and enforce compulsory vaccination laws.[17] In 1922, deciding a case filed by a girl excluded from a public school (and later a private school) in San Antonio, Texas, the Supreme Court found school immunization requirements to be constitutional.[18] Since then, courts have been generally supportive of the states' power to enact and implement immunization requirements.

Difficulties with efforts to control measles in the 1960s and 1970s ushered in the modern era of immunization laws in the United States.[12] In 1969, a total of 17 states had laws that required children to be vaccinated against measles before entering school, and 12 states had legally mandated requirements for vaccination against all six diseases for which routine immunization was carried out at the time.[13] During the 1970s, efforts were made to strengthen and strictly enforce immunization laws.[12,13] During measles outbreaks, some state and local health officials excluded from school those students who did not comply with immunization requirements, resulting in minimal backlash, quick improvement in local coverage, and control of outbreaks.[19–22] Efforts by the public health community and other immunization advocates to increase measles vaccine coverage among school-age children resulted in enforcement of immunization requirements for all vaccines and the introduction of such requirements in states that did not already have them. By the beginning of the 1980s, all 50 states had school immunization requirements.

Recent School Immunization Requirements

Because laws concerning immunization are state-based, there are substantial differences in requirements across the country. The requirements from state to state differ in terms of the school grades covered, the vaccines included, the processes and authority used to introduce new vaccines, reasons for exemptions (medical reasons, religious reasons, philosophical or personal beliefs), and the procedures for granting exemptions.[23]

State immunization laws contain provisions for certain exemptions. As of March 2008, all states permitted medical exemptions from school immunization requirements, 48 states allowed religious exemptions, and 21 states allowed exemptions based on philosophical or personal beliefs.[23] Several states (New York, Arkansas, and Texas) have recently expanded eligibility for exemptions.

Secular and Geographic Trends in Immunization Refusal

Between 1991 and 2004, the mean state-level rate of nonmedical exemptions increased from 0.98 to 1.48%. The increase in exemption rates was not uniform.[11] Exemption rates for states that allowed only religious exemptions remained at approximately 1% between 1991 and 2004; however, in states that allowed exemptions for philosophical or personal beliefs, the mean exemption rate increased from 0.99 to 2.54%.[11]

Like any average, the mean exemption rate presents only part of the picture, since geographic clustering of nonmedical exemptions can result in local accumulation of a critical mass of susceptible children that increases the risk of outbreaks. There is evidence of substantial geographic heterogeneity in nonmedical-exemption rates between and within states.[24] For example, in the period from 2006 through 2007, the state-level nonmedical-exemption rate in Washington was 6%; however, the county-level rate ranged from 1.2 to 26.9%.[25] In a spatial analysis of Michigan's exemption data according to census tracts, 23 statistically significant clusters of increased exemptions were identified.[26] Similar heterogeneity in exemption rates has been identified in Oregon[27] and California (unpublished data).

The reasons for the geographic clustering of exemptions from school vaccination requirements are not fully understood, but they may include characteristics of the local population (e.g., cultural issues, socioeconomic status, or educational level), the beliefs of local health care providers and opinion leaders (e.g., clergy and politicians), and local media coverage. The factors known to be associated with exemption rates are heterogeneity in school policies[28] and the beliefs of school personnel who are responsible for compliance with the immunization requirements.[29]

Instead of refusing vaccines, some parents delay vaccination of their children.[30–32] Many parents follow novel vaccine schedules proposed by individual physicians (rather than those developed by expert committees with members representing multiple disciplines).[32,33] Most novel schedules involve administering vaccines over a longer period than that recommended by the Advisory Committee on Immunization Practices and the American Academy of Pediatrics or skipping the administration of some vaccines.

Individual Risk and Vaccine Refusal

Children with nonmedical exemptions are at increased risk for acquiring and transmitting vaccine-preventable diseases.[34,35] In a retrospective cohort study based on nationwide surveillance data from 1985 through 1992, children with exemptions were 35 times as likely to contract measles as nonexempt children (relative risk, 35; 95% confidence interval [CI], 34 to 37).[34] In a retrospective cohort study in Colorado based on data for the years 1987 through 1998, children with exemptions, as compared with unvaccinated children, were 22 times as likely to have had measles (relative risk, 22.2; 95% CI, 15.9 to 31.1) and almost six times as likely to have had pertussis (relative risk, 5.9; 95% CI, 4.2 to 8.2).[35] Earlier data showed that lower incidences of measles and mumps were associated with the existence and enforcement of immunization requirements for school entry.[12,36–38]

The consequences of delayed vaccination, as compared with vaccine refusal, have not been studied in detail. However, it is known that the risk of vaccine-preventable diseases and the risk of sequelae from vaccine-preventable diseases are not constant throughout childhood. Young children are often at increased risk for illness and death related to infectious diseases, and vaccine delays may leave them vulnerable at ages with a high risk of contracting several vaccine-preventable diseases. Moreover, novel vaccine schedules that recommend administering vaccines over a longer period may exacerbate health inequities, since parents with high socioeconomic status are more likely to make the extra visits required under the alternative schedules than parents with low socioeconomic status.[39]

Clustering of Vaccine Refusals and Community Risk

Multiple studies have shown an increase in the local risk of vaccine-preventable diseases when there is a geographic aggregation of persons refusing vaccination. In Michigan, significant overlap between geographic clusters of nonmedical exemptions and pertussis clusters was documented.[26] The odds ratio for the likelihood that a census tract included in a pertussis cluster would also be included in an exemptions cluster was 2.7 (95% CI, 2.5 to 3.6) after adjustment for demographic factors.

In Colorado, the county-level incidence of measles and pertussis in vaccinated children from 1987 through 1998 was associated with the frequency of exemptions in that county.[35] At least 11% of the nonexempt children who acquired measles were infected through contact with an exempt child.[35] Moreover, school-based outbreaks in Colorado have been associated with increased exemption rates; the mean exemption rate among schools with outbreaks was 4.3%, as compared with 1.5% for the schools that did not have an outbreak (P = 0.001).[35]

High vaccine coverage, particularly at the community level, is extremely important for children who cannot be vaccinated, including children who have medical contraindications to vaccination and those who are too young to be vaccinated. These groups are often more susceptible to the complications of infectious diseases than the general population of children and depend on the protection provided by the vaccination of children in their environs.[40–42]

Vaccine Refusal and the Recent Increase in Measles Cases

Measles vaccination has been extremely successful in controlling a disease that previously contributed to considerable morbidity and mortality. In the United States, the reported number of cases dropped from an average of 500,000 annually in the era before vaccination (with reported cases considered to be a fraction of the estimated total, which was more than 2 million) to a mean of 62 cases per year from 2000 through 2007.[43–45] Between January 1, 2008, and April 25, 2008, there were five measles outbreaks and a total of 64 cases reported.[45] All but one of the persons with measles were either unvaccinated or did not have evidence of immunization. Of the 21 cases among children and adolescents in the vaccine-eligible age group (16 months to 19 years) with a known reason for nonvaccination, 14, or 67%, had obtained a nonmedical exemption and all of the 10 school-age children had obtained a nonmedical exemption.[45] Thirteen cases occurred in children too young to be vaccinated, and in more than a third of the cases (18 of 44) occurring in a known transmission setting the disease was acquired in a health care facility.[45]

Outbreaks of vaccine-preventable disease often start among persons who refused vaccination, spread rapidly within unvaccinated populations, and also spread to other subpopulations. For example, of the four outbreaks with discrete index cases (one outbreak occurred by means of multiple importations) reported January through April 2008, three out of four index cases occurred in people who had refused vaccination due to personal beliefs; vaccination status could not be verified for the remaining cases.[45,46] In Washington State, a recent outbreak of measles occurred between April 12, 2008, and May 30, 2008, involving 19 cases. All of the persons with measles were unimmunized with the exception of the last case, a person who had been vaccinated. Of the other 18 cases, 1 was an infant who was too young to be vaccinated, 2 were younger than 4 years of age, and the remaining 15 were of school age (unpublished data).

Who Refuses Vaccines and Why

Using data from the National Immunization Survey for the period from 1995 through 2001, Smith et al. compared the characteristics of children between the ages of 19 and 35 months who did not receive any vaccine (unvaccinated) with the characteristics of those who were partially vaccinated (undervaccinated).[47] As compared with the undervaccinated children, the unvaccinated children were more likely to be male, to be white, to belong to households with higher income, to have a married mother with a college education, and to live with four or more children.[47] Other studies have shown that children who are unvaccinated are likely to belong to families that intentionally refuse vaccines, whereas children who are undervaccinated are likely to have missed some vaccinations because of factors related to the health care system or sociodemographic characteristics.[48–51]

In a case–control study of the knowledge, attitudes, and beliefs of parents of exempt children as compared with parents of vaccinated children, respondents rated their views of their children's vulnerability to specific diseases, the severity of these diseases, and the efficacy and safety of the specific vaccines available for them. Composite scores were created on the basis of these vaccine-specific responses. As compared with parents of vaccinated children, significantly more parents of exempt children thought their children had a low susceptibility to the diseases (58% vs. 15%, P < 0.05), that the severity of the diseases was low (51% vs. 18%, P < 0.05), and that the efficacy and safety of the vaccines was low (54% vs. 17% for efficacy and 60% vs. 15% for safety, P < 0.05 for both comparisons).[52] Moreover, parents of exempt children were more likely than parents of vaccinated children both to have providers who offered complementary or alternative health care and to obtain information from the Internet and groups opposed to aspects of immunization.[52] The most frequent reason for nonvaccination, stated by 69% of the parents, was concern that the vaccine might cause harm.[52]

Other studies have also reported the importance of parents' concerns about vaccine safety when they decide against vaccination.[53–56] A national survey of parents from 2001 through 2002 showed that although only 1% of respondents thought vaccines were unsafe, the children of these parents were almost three times as likely to not be up to date on recommended vaccinations as the children of parents who thought that vaccines were safe.[54] In a separate case–control study with a national sample, underimmunization was associated with negative perceptions of vaccine safety (odds ratio, 2.0; 95% CI, 1.2 to 3.4).[55] And in another case–control study, Bardenheier et al. found that although concerns regarding general vaccine safety did not differ between the parents of vaccinated children and the parents of undervaccinated or unvaccinated children, more than half of the case and control parents did express concerns about vaccine safety to their child's health care provider.[57] Moreover, parents of undervaccinated or unvaccinated children were more likely to believe that children receive too many vaccines.[57]

The Role of Health Care Providers

Clinicians and other health care providers play a crucial role in parental decision making with regard to immunization. Health care providers are cited by parents, including parents of unvaccinated children, as the most frequent source of information about vaccination.[52]

In a study of the knowledge, attitudes, and practices of primary care providers, a high proportion of those providing care for children whose parents have refused vaccination and those providing care for appropriately vaccinated children were both found to have favorable opinions of vaccines.[58] However, those providing care for unvaccinated children were less likely to have confidence in vaccine safety (odds ratio, 0.37; 95% CI, 0.19 to 0.72) and less likely to perceive vaccines as benefitting individuals and communities.[58] Moreover, there was overlap between clinicians' unfavorable opinions of vaccines and the likelihood that they had unvaccinated children in their practice.[58]

There is evidence that health care providers have a positive overall effect on parents' decision making with regard to vaccination of their children. In a study by Smith et al., parents who reported that their immunization decisions were influenced by their child's health care provider were almost twice as likely to consider vaccines safe as parents who said their decisions were not influenced by the provider.[59]

In focus-group discussions, several parents who were not certain about vaccinating their child were willing to discuss their immunization concerns with a health care provider and wanted the provider to offer information relevant to their specific concerns.[56] These findings highlight the critical role that clinicians can play in explaining the benefits of immunization and addressing parental concerns about its risks.

Clinicians' Response to Vaccine Refusal

Some clinicians have discontinued or have considered discontinuing their provider relationship with families that refuse vaccines.[60,61] In a national survey of members of the American Academy of Pediatrics, almost 40% of respondents said they would not provide care to a family that refused all vaccines, and 28% said they would not provide care to a family that refused some vaccines.[61]

The academy's Committee on Bioethics advises against discontinuing care for families that decline vaccines and has recommended that pediatricians "share honestly what is and is not known about the risks and benefits of the vaccine in question."[62] The committee also recommends that clinicians address vaccine refusal by respectfully listening to parental concerns, explaining the risk of nonimmunization, and discussing the specific vaccines that are of most concern to parents.[62] The committee advises against more serious action in a majority of cases: "Continued refusal after adequate discussion should be respected unless the child is put at significant risk of serious harm (e.g., as might be the case during an epidemic). Only then should state agencies be involved to override parental discretion on the basis of medical neglect."[62]

Policy-Level Determinants of Vaccine Refusal

Immunization requirements and the policies that ensure compliance with the requirements vary considerably among the states; these variations have been associated with state-level exemption rates.[11,63] For example, the complexity of procedures for obtaining exemption has been shown to be inversely associated with rates of exemption.[63] Moreover, between 1991 and 2004, the mean annual incidence of pertussis was almost twice as high in states with administrative procedures that made it easy to obtain exemptions as in states that made it difficult.[11]

One possible way to balance individual rights and the greater public good with respect to vaccination would be to institute and broaden administrative controls. For example, a model law proposed for Arkansas suggested that parents seeking nonmedical exemptions be provided with counseling on the hazards of refusing vaccination.[64]

States also differ in terms of meeting the recommendations for age-appropriate coverage for children younger than 2 years of age.[65] School immunization requirements ensure completion by the time of school entry, but they do not directly influence the timeliness of vaccination among preschoolers. However, there is some evidence that school immunization laws have an indirect effect on preschool vaccine coverage. For example, varicella vaccine was introduced in the United States in 1995 and has played an important role in reducing the incidence of chickenpox.[66] In 2000, states that had implemented mandatory immunization for varicella by the time of school entry had coverage among children 19 to 35 months old that was higher than the average for all states. Having an immunization requirement could be an indicator of the effectiveness of a state's immunization program, but the effect of school-based requirements on coverage among preschoolers cannot be completely discounted.

Conclusions

Vaccine refusal not only increases the individual risk of disease but also increases the risk for the whole community. As a result of substantial gains in reducing vaccine-preventable diseases, the memory of several infectious diseases has faded from the public consciousness and the risk–benefit calculus seems to have shifted in favor of the perceived risks of vaccination in some parents' minds. Major reasons for vaccine refusal in the United States are parental perceptions and concerns about vaccine safety and a low level of concern about the risk of many vaccine-preventable diseases. If the enormous benefits to society from vaccination are to be maintained, increased efforts will be needed to educate the public about those benefits and to increase public confidence in the systems we use to monitor and ensure vaccine safety. Since clinicians have an influence on parental decision making, it is important that they understand the benefits and risks of vaccines and anticipate questions that parents may have about safety. There are a number of sources of information on vaccines that should be useful to both clinicians and parents (e.g., Appendix 1 in the fifth edition of *Vaccines,* edited by Plotkin et al.; the list of Web sites on vaccine safety posted on the World Health Organization's Web site; and the Web site of the National Center for Immunization and Respiratory Diseases).[67–69]

References

1. Chen RT, Hibbs B. Vaccine safety: current and future challenges. *Pediatr Ann* 1998;27:445–55.

2. Chen RT, DeStefano F. Vaccine adverse events: causal or coincidental? *Lancet* 1998;351:611–2.

3. DeStefano F. Vaccines and autism: evidence does not support a causal association. *Clin Pharmacol Ther* 2007;82:756–9.

4. Doja A, Roberts W. Immunizations and autism: a review of the literature. *Can J Neurol Sci* 2006;33:341–6.

5. Fombonne E, Cook EH. MMR and autistic enterocolitis: consistent epidemiological failure to find an association. *Mol Psychiatry* 2003;8:133–4.

6. Fombonne E. Thimerosal disappears but autism remains. *Arch Gen Psychiatry* 2008;65:15–6.

7. Schechter R, Grether JK. Continuing increases in autism reported to California's developmental services system: mercury in retrograde. *Arch Gen Psychiatry* 2008;65:19–24.

8. Thompson WW, Price C, Goodson B, et al. Early thimerosal exposure and neuropsychological outcomes at 7 to 10 years. *N Engl J Med* 2007;357:1281–92.

9. Offit PA. Vaccines and autism revisited—the Hannah Poling case. *N Engl J Med* 2008;358:2089–91.

10. Smith MJ, Ellenberg SS, Bell LM, Rubin DM. Media coverage of the measles-mumps-rubella vaccine and autism controversy and its relationship to MMR immunization rates in the United States. *Pediatrics* 2008;121(4):e836–e843.

11. Omer SB, Pan WK, Halsey NA, et al. Nonmedical exemptions to school immunization requirements: secular trends and association of state policies with pertussis incidence. *JAMA* 2006;296:1757–63.

12. Orenstein WA, Hinman AR. The immunization system in the United States—the role of school immunization laws. *Vaccine* 1999;17:Suppl 3:S19–S24.

13. Jackson CL. State laws on compulsory immunization in the United States. *Public Health Rep* 1969;84:787–95.

14. Colgrove J, Bayer R. Could it happen here? Vaccine risk controversies and the specter of derailment. *Health Aff* (Millwood) 2005;24:729–39.

15. Kaufman M. The American anti-vaccinationists and their arguments. *Bull Hist Med* 1967;41:463–78.

16. Stern BJ. Should we be vaccinated? A survey of the controversy in its historical and scientific aspects. New York: Harper & Brothers, 1927:93–109.

17. Jacobson v. Massachusetts, 197 U.S. 11 (1905).

18. Zucht v. King, 260 U.S. 174 (Nov. 13, 1922).

19. Middaugh JP, Zyla LD. Enforcement of school immunization law in Alaska. *JAMA* 1978;239:2128–30.

20. Lovejoy GS, Giandelia JW, Hicks M. Successful enforcement of an immunization law. *Public Health Rep* 1974;89:456–8.

21. Fowinkle EW, Barid S, Bass CM. A compulsory school immunization program in Tennessee. *Public Health Rep* 1981;96:61–6.

22. Measles—Florida, 1981. MMWR Morb Mortal Wkly Rep 1981;30:593–6.

23. Vaccine Exemptions. Johns Hopkins Bloomberg School of Public Health—Institute for Vaccine Safety, 2008. (Accessed April 16, 2009, at www.vaccinesafety.edu/ccexem.htm.)

24. National Center for Immunization and Respiratory Diseases. School and childcare vaccination surveys. May 2007. (Accessed April 13, 2009, at www.cdc.gov/vaccines/stats-surv /schoolsurv/default.htm.)

25. School Status Data Reports. Washington State Department of Health, 2009. (Accessed April 16, 2009, at //www.doh.wa.gov /cfh/Immunize/schools/schooldatarprts.htm.)

26. Omer SB, Enger KS, Moulton LH, Halsey NA, Stokley S, Salmon DA. Geographic clustering of nonmedical exemptions to school immunization requirements and associations with geographic clustering of pertussis. *Am J Epidemiol* 2008;168:1389–96.

27. Attitudes, networking and immunizations in a community with a high rate of religious exemptions. Presented at the 37th National Immunization Conference, Chicago, March 17–20, 2003. Abstract.

28. Salmon DA, Omer SB, Moulton LH, et al. Exemptions to school immunization requirements: the role of school-level requirements, policies, and procedures. *Am J Public Health* 2005;95:436–40. [Erratum, Am J Public Health 2005;95:551.]

29. Salmon DA, Moulton LH, Omer SB, et al. Knowledge, attitudes, and beliefs of school nurses and personnel and associations with nonmedical immunization exemptions. *Pediatrics* 2004;113(6):e552–e559.

30. Luman ET, Barker LE, Shaw KM, McCauley MM, Buehler JW, Pickering LK. Timeliness of childhood vaccinations in the United States: days undervaccinated and number of vaccines delayed. *JAMA* 2005;293:1204–11.

31. Luman ET, Shaw KM, Stokley SK. Compliance with vaccination recommendations for U.S. children. *Am J Prev Med* 2008;34:463–70. [Erratum, Am J Prev Med 2008:35:319.]

32. Cohen E. Should I vaccinate my baby? Cable News Network. 2008. (Accessed April 13, 2009, at www.cnn.com/2008 /HEALTH/family/06/19/ep.vaccines/index.html.)

33. Sears R. Dr. Bob's blog categories: alternative vaccine schedule. (Accessed April 13, 2009, at http://askdrsears.com/ thevaccinebook/labels/Alternative%20Vaccine%20Schedule .asp.)

34. Salmon DA, Haber M, Gangarosa EJ, Phillips L, Smith NJ, Chen RT. Health consequences of religious and philosophical exemptions from immunization laws: individual and societal risk of measles. *JAMA* 1999;282:47–53. [Erratum, JAMA 2000;283:2241.]

35. Feikin DR, Lezotte DC, Hamman RF, Salmon DA, Chen RT, Hoffman RE. Individual and community risks of measles and

pertussis associated with personal exemptions to immunization. *JAMA* 2000;284:3145–50.

36. Measles—United States. MMWR Morb Mortal Wkly Rep 1977;26:109–11.

37. Robbins KB, Brandling-Bennett D, Hinman AR. Low measles incidence: association with enforcement of school immunization laws. *Am J Public Health* 1981;71:270–4.

38. van Loon FP, Holmes SJ, Sirotkin BI, et al. Mumps surveillance—United States, 1988–1993. *MMWR CDC Surveill* 1995;44:1–14.

39. Williams IT, Milton JD, Farrell JB, Graham NM. Interaction of socioeconomic status and provider practices as predictors of immunization coverage in Virginia children. *Pediatrics* 1995;96:439–46.

40. Bisgard KM, Pascual FB, Ehresmann KR, et al. Infant pertussis: who was the source? *Pediatr Infect Dis J* 2004;23:985–9.

41. Deen JL, Mink CA, Cherry JD, et al. Household contact study of Bordetella pertussis infections. *Clin Infect Dis* 1995;21:1211–9.

42. Poehling KA, Talbot TR, Griffin MR, et al. Invasive pneumococcal disease among infants before and after introduction of pneumococcal conjugate vaccine. *JAMA* 2006;295:1668–74.

43. Bloch AB, Orenstein WA, Stetler HC, et al. Health impact of measles vaccination in the United States. *Pediatrics* 1985;76:524–32.

44. Orenstein WA, Papania MJ, Wharton ME. Measles elimination in the United States. *J Infect Dis* 2004;189:Suppl 1:S1–S3.

45. Measles—United States, January 1–April 25, 2008. MMWR Morb Mortal Wkly Rep 2008;57:494–8.

46. Update: measles—United States, January–July 2008. MMWR Morb Mortal Wkly Rep 2008;57:893–6.

47. Smith PJ, Chu SY, Barker LE. Children who have received no vaccines: who are they and where do they live? *Pediatrics* 2004;114:187–95.

48. Allred NJ, Wooten KG, Kong Y. The association of health insurance and continuous primary care in the medical home on vaccination coverage for 19- to 35-month-old children. *Pediatrics* 2007;119:Suppl 1:S4–S11.

49. Daniels D, Jiles RB, Klevens RM, Herrera GA. Undervaccinated African-American preschoolers: a case of missed opportunities. *Am J Prev Med* 2001;20:Suppl:61–68.

50. Luman ET, McCauley MM, Shefer A, Chu SY. Maternal characteristics associated with vaccination of young children. *Pediatrics* 2003;111:1215–8.

51. Smith PJ, Santoli JM, Chu SY, Ochoa DQ, Rodewald LE. The association between having a medical home and vaccination coverage among children eligible for the Vaccines for Children program. *Pediatrics* 2005;116:130–9.

52. Salmon DA, Moulton LH, Omer SB, Dehart MP, Stokley S, Halsey NA. Factors associated with refusal of childhood vaccines among parents of school-aged children: a case-control study. *Arch Pediatr Adolesc Med* 2005;159:470–6.

53. Humiston SG, Lerner EB, Hepworth E, Blythe T, Goepp JG. Parent opinions about universal influenza vaccination for infants and toddlers. *Arch Pediatr Adolesc Med* 2005;159:108–12.

54. Allred NJ, Shaw KM, Santibanez TA, Rickert DL, Santoli JM. Parental vaccine safety concerns: results from the National Immunization Survey, 2001–2002. *Am J Prev Med* 2005;28:221–4.

55. Gust DA, Strine TW, Maurice E, et al. Underimmunization among children: effects of vaccine safety concerns on immunization status. *Pediatrics* 2004;114(1):e16–e22.

56. Fredrickson DD, Davis TC, Arnould CL, et al. Childhood immunization refusal: provider and parent perceptions. *Fam Med* 2004;36:431–9.

57. Bardenheier B, Yusuf H, Schwartz B, Gust D, Barker L, Rodewald L. Are parental vaccine safety concerns associated with receipt of measles-mumps-rubella, diphtheria and tetanus toxoids with acellular pertussis, or hepatitis B vaccines by children? *Arch Pediatr Adolesc Med* 2004;158:569–75.

58. Salmon DA, Pan WK, Omer SB, et al. Vaccine knowledge and practices of primary care providers of exempt vs. vaccinated children. *Hum Vaccin* 2008;4:286–91.

59. Smith PJ, Kennedy AM, Wooten K, Gust DA, Pickering LK. Association between health care providers' influence on parents who have concerns about vaccine safety and vaccination coverage. *Pediatrics* 2006;118(5):e1287–e1292.

60. Freed GL, Clark SJ, Hibbs BF, Santoli JM. Parental vaccine safety concerns: the experiences of pediatricians and family physicians. *Am J Prev Med* 2004;26:11–4.

61. Flanagan-Klygis EA, Sharp L, Frader JE. Dismissing the family who refuses vaccines: a study of pediatrician attitudes. *Arch Pediatr Adolesc Med* 2005;159:929–34.

62. Diekema DS. Responding to parental refusals of immunization of children. *Pediatrics* 2005;115:1428–31.

63. Rota JS, Salmon DA, Rodewald LE, Chen RT, Hibbs BF, Gangarosa EJ. Processes for obtaining nonmedical exemptions to state immunization laws. *Am J Public Health* 2001;91:645–8.

64. Salmon DA, Siegel AW. Religious and philosophical exemptions from vaccination requirements and lessons learned from conscientious objectors from conscription. *Public Health Rep* 2001;116:289–95.

65. Luman ET, Barker LE, McCauley MM, Drews-Botsch C. Timeliness of childhood immunizations: a state-specific analysis. *Am J Public Health* 2005;95:1367–74.

66. Seward JF, Watson BM, Peterson CL, et al. Varicella disease after introduction of varicella vaccine in the United States, 1995–2000. *JAMA* 2002;287:606–11.

67. Wexler DL, Anderson TA. Websites that contain information about immunization. In: Plotkin S, Orenstein WA, Offit PA, eds. Vaccines. 5th ed. Philadelphia: Saunders, 2008:1685–90.

68. Vaccine safety websites meeting credibility and content good information practices criteria. Geneva: World Health Organization, September 2008.

69. National Center for Immunization and Respiratory Diseases. Centers for Disease Control and Prevention, 2009. (Accessed April 16, 2009, at www.cdc.gov/ncird/.)

Critical Thinking

1. Is vaccination more dangerous than getting the disease prevented by the vaccine?

2. Why do some parents refuse to have their children vaccinated? Are their reasons valid?

3. Should parents be forced to have their children vaccinated? Why or why not?

From the Hubert Department of Global Health, Rollins School of Public Health (S.B.O.), and the Emory Vaccine Center (S.B.O., W.A.O.), Emory University, Atlanta; the Department of International Health (S.B.O., D.A.S., N.H.) and the Institute for Vaccine Safety (N.H.), Johns Hopkins Bloomberg School of Public Health, Baltimore; the National Vaccine Program Office, Department of Health and Human Services, Washington, DC (D.A.S.); and Maternal and Child Health Assessment, Washington State Department of Health, Olympia (M.P.D.). Address reprint requests to Dr. Omer at the Hubert Department of Global Health, Rollins School of Public Health, Emory University, 1518 Clifton Rd. NE, Atlanta, GA 30322, or at somer@emory.edu.

Dr. Salmon reports serving on the Merck Vaccine Policy Advisory Board; Dr. Orenstein, receiving research funds from Novartis, Merck, and Sanofi Pasteur and a training grant from the Merck Foundation and serving on data and safety monitoring boards associated with GlaxoSmithKline and Encorium; and Dr. Halsey, receiving research funds from Wyeth and Berna, lecture fees from Sanofi, and payments for testimony to the Department of Justice regarding several vaccine compensation cases and serving on data and safety monitoring committees associated with Novartis and Merck. No other potential conflict of interest relevant to this article was reported.

We thank Tina Proveaux of the Johns Hopkins Bloomberg School of Public Health for reviewing an earlier version of the manuscript and Dr. Jane Seward of the Centers for Disease Control and Prevention for providing input on new measles cases.

Medical Tourism: What You Should Know

From international outsourcing to in-home visits, doctors and patients are reinventing the way medicine is viewed and practiced at home and around the world.

LORENE BURKHART AND LORNA GENTRY

In 2006, West Virginia lawmaker Ray Canterbury made headlines across the country when he introduced House Bill 4359, which would allow enrollees in the state government's health plan to travel to foreign countries for surgery and other medical services. In fact, not only would the bill allow for such a choice, it encourages it; those choosing to go to an approved foreign clinic for a procedure covered by the plan would have all of their medical and travel expenses (including those of one companion) paid, plus be given 20 percent of the savings they racked up by having the procedure done overseas, rather than here at home.

Canterbury's bill drew attention to a growing international boom in medical tourism—an industry with special appeal for many of America's 61 million uninsured or underinsured citizens. At prices as much as 80 to 90 percent lower than those here, hospitals in countries such as Costa Rica, Thailand, India, and the Philippines offer a wide range of healthcare procedures in accommodations equal to or even better than their American counterparts. Some estimate that 500,000 Americans went overseas for medical treatment in 2006 alone, and that medical tourism could become a $40 billion industry by 2010.

Overseas Surgery? What You Should Know

According to Canterbury and other proponents of medical service outsourcing, the idea is all about competition. Proponents believe the rate of healthcare inflation in this country, at almost four times the rate of overall inflation, has placed an unsustainable burden on the American economy.

"The best way to solve this problem is to rely on market forces," Canterbury writes. "My bills are designed to force domestic healthcare companies to compete for our business."

It's hard to argue with the economics of medical outsourcing. According to MedicalTourism.com, the cost of typical heart bypass surgery in the United States is $130,000. The same operation is estimated to cost approximately $10,000 in India, $11,000 in Thailand, and $18,500 in Singapore. A $43,000 hip replacement in an American hospital could be performed for $9,000 in India, or for $12,000 in either Thailand or Singapore. Even adding the costs of travel and lodging, consumers stand to save real money by traveling overseas for these and many other types of routine surgery, including angioplasties, knee replacements, and hysterectomies.

Of course, many people have serious concerns about the idea of shopping overseas for invasive medical procedures. What about the quality of the service? Followup care? And what happens if something goes terribly wrong? Those backing the business—including employers and lawmakers desperately seeking ways to cut the cost of employer-sponsored medical care—are quick to answer these concerns.

Most of the foreign medical facilities courting Western tourists are state-of-the-art facilities that offer luxurious accommodations and individual around-the-clock nursing attention. Thailand's Bumrungrad Hospital, for example, offers five-star hotel quality rooms, a lobby that includes Starbucks and other restaurants, valet parking, an international staff and interpreters, a travel agent, visa desk, and a meet-and-greet service at Bangkok's Suvarnabhumi Airport. In a 2007 report broadcast on NPR, an American woman told how when her doctor in Alaska announced that she needed double knee replacements at a cost of $100,000, she replied that she couldn't afford the treatment. Her doctor recommended that she wait four years, when she would be eligible for Medicare. Instead, the woman opted for treatment at Bumrungrad, where the two knee replacements cost $20,000 (including the services of two physicians, an anesthesiologist, and physical therapy), and she was able to recover in the hospital's luxurious surroundings with her husband at her side. Her husband, who underwent surgery in the United States the previous year, couldn't believe the amount of attention his wife received from her doctors and nurses, whom he said were in almost constant attendance.

Why is all of this lavish treatment and high-quality care so much cheaper abroad than here? We only need to look at all of the other services the United States has outsourced in the past decade to find the first part of the answer to that question: In places like Thailand and India—two popular destinations for cardiac, orthopedic, and cosmetic surgery—salaries are much lower than in the United States. Further, most services are provided under one roof, and patients select and pay for their medical services up front—no insurance billing. Medical malpractice liability insurance and claims caps in some foreign countries also help keep costs down.

But how safe are foreign medical facilities? Bumrungrad Hospital is accredited by the Joint Commission International (the same organization that accredits U.S. hospitals) and has over 200 U.S. board-certified physicians. And that hospital isn't unique in the world of international medicine. Increasing numbers of medical tourism facilities are staffed by American- and European-trained physicians and backed by well-funded research facilities. Dubai, already a luxury travel destination, is preparing to enter the business of international medical practice and research in a very serious way. Its 4.1 million square-foot Dubai Healthcare City is slated to open in 2010 and will offer academic medical research facilities, disease treatment, and wellness services backed by the oversight of a number of international partners, including a new department of the Harvard School of Medicine.

Good News for Patients Might Be Bad News for U.S. Hospitals

Most baby boomers love to travel, and many are only too happy to combine foreign travel experiences with low-cost and high-value medical procedures. And many insurance companies are eyeing medical outsourcing, too, as a way to cut costs for both enrollees and their employers. Blue Cross/Blue Shield of South Carolina, for example, has begun working with Bumrungrad to provide overseas alternatives for healthcare to its members.

Of course, one or two horrific medical mishaps alone could seriously damage the medical tourism industry. Most foreign countries don't support malpractice litigation to the extent that we do in the United States, and fears of the "what ifs" are keeping many private individuals and organizations from plunging in until they have a few more years to observe the medical outsourcing industry in action. For now, however, foreign medical facilities are eager to maintain standards high enough to avoid any claims of malpractice. And many Americans with our fondness for bargains and luxury are more than willing to give those facilities an opportunity to prove their worth.

Medical tourism is good news for patients, but it could pose consequences for America's already-ailing hospital system. If patients travel to foreign lands to avoid pricey surgeries at home, what kind of financial "hit" will American hospitals face? At 2007's International Medical Tourism Conference in Las Vegas, hospital physicians and administrators from around the globe

gathered to discuss the issues surrounding medical tourism and its impact on the healthcare industry. In an interview about the conference, Sparrow Mahoney, chief executive officer of MedicalTourism.com and conference co-chair, admitted that American medical facilities are now in direct competition with their foreign competitors. "Hospitals will feel a pinch," she said.

Yes, We Make House Calls

All of us have experienced the frustrating and sometimes frightening wait for medical care that we desperately need. We have a raging fever and are told that the doctor can see us in three days. If we choose instead to go to the emergency room of a nearby hospital, we may wait for hours in a roomful of equally ill and distressed people with their impatient spouses, parents, or screaming children, and the constant chiming of cell phones. If our doctor agrees to "work us in," we're faced with an only slightly less daunting process, requiring what might be an hour or so wait. When we finally see a doctor, we're rushed through a few minutes of evaluation, given a prescription, and sent on our way—typically worn out and much worse for the wear of the experience.

But many Americans are opting out of this tribal experience and choosing instead to pay an annual fee (typically, $3,000 to $30,000 above insurance costs) to retain the personalized, private care of a family physician. The "boutique" healthcare movement began in the early 1990s in Seattle, Washington, and has since spread to urban areas around the nation. Instead of waiting days, weeks, or even months for an appointment that fits the doctor's schedule, members of these plans schedule medical visits at their convenience.

Need a house call? Not a problem with most boutique or "concierge" plans. Members have their doctor's cell phone number and can simply call to arrange for the doctor to come to their home. If a plan member needs to see a specialist or go to the emergency room, he or she is accompanied by a plan physician—and no rushing through appointments.

Although many primary care physicians have caseloads of as many as 3,000 to 5,000 patients, doctors in boutique plans might have no more than a few hundred patients under their care; Seattle retainer medicine pioneer MD^2 (pronounced "MD Squared") limits its doctor loads to no greater than 50 patients.

Some retainer plans require that members also carry insurance, while others refuse to process insurance payments at all. In a 2005 report on boutique medicine by CBS5 News in California, one doctor complained that he had lost patience with insurance companies that require reams of tedious paperwork and billing regulations, then reimburse at 20 percent of his billing rate. "I went to medical school to be a doctor and take care of patients," says Dr. Jordan Shlain of the San Francisco group On Call. "I didn't take one class on billings, on insurance company shenanigans and the HMO grip."

Although some concierge medical services charge fees aimed squarely at the middle class, most admit that their fees put them out of the range of many people. FirstLine Personal Health Care, in Indianapolis, charges members an annual retainer of a few thousand dollars in return for 24-hour access to one of the plan's doctors, unlimited office visits, and a small keychain hard drive loaded with their medical records. Even though their fees are modest in comparison with some concierge medical services, FirstLine doctors Kevin McCallum and Timothy Story know that many patients they saw prior to forming the service won't be able to afford membership.

Like other doctors around the country, however, McCallum and Story believe that retainer medicine offers the only option for family medicine doctors trying to escape the grinding demands of escalating practice costs and patient caseloads. With many family physicians around the country retiring early and medical students avoiding the low pay and high demands of a typical family practice, retainer-fee medical groups might be the most viable way to keep the "good old family doctor" in business.

We have yet to see what will happen when the average American is financially excluded from most family medicine clinics and groups—a fate that may occur in the not-so-distant future. Dr. Kevin Grumbach of the University of California at San Francisco was in family practice for more than 20 years and now worries that the rush to boutique medical services is threatening our nation's system of medical care.

"I have grave concerns," he told the CBS5 news reporter, "that . . . we are as a profession abandoning the need of the vast majority of Americans . . . . It's the middle class people that are increasingly left behind in an increasingly inequitable system."

Critical Thinking

1. What is medical tourism?
2. Distinguish between the risks and benefits of medical tourism.
3. What motivates people to obtain medical care abroad?

Bed Bugs: The Pesticide Dilemma

REBECCA BERG

"Six different companies have now found them in movie theaters," said Michael Potter, professor of entomology at the University of Kentucky.

Potter works with pest control companies and their customers all over the country. Asked where bed bugs are cropping up, he rattled off a list that included everything from single-family homes to hospitals, libraries, schools ("obviously dormitories," he noted), and modes of transportation. The problem is particularly daunting in apartment buildings since people frequently move in and out with all their belongings.

"It's bad and getting worse," he said. "It's almost like an epizootic or a pandemic where somebody coughs and six more people get it."

He is not alone in sounding the alarm.

"I don't think we've hit anywhere near the peak," observed Jack Marlowe, president of Eden Advanced Pest Technologies. Eden Commercial I.P.M. Consultant Cody Pace, who was on the same call, added that before World War II, one in three homes were infested with bed bugs. "People dealt with it, and it was part of life. . . . I hope it doesn't get to the point where we're all just living with bed bugs."

A Logistical Nightmare

They are small. They can hide in any crack or crevice. (Think furniture joints, floorboards, baseboards, box springs, picture frames, closets full of clothing, personal belongings of almost any sort.) The early stages of infestations are hard to spot.

They can spread from room to room through duct work or false ceilings. They can be transported from venue to venue on clothing and belongings.

Their eggs are even smaller and almost transparent. They are attached to surfaces by means of a sticky substance.

You can't reduce infestations the way you might with cockroaches, by cleaning up food scraps, depriving them of shelter, and putting out bait. "You *are* their meal," said Elizabeth Dykstra, public health entomologist for the Zoonotic Disease Program of the Washington State Department of Health (WDOH).

And, she said, they can survive up to 18 months without a meal.

They have a history of developing resistance to pesticides. Potter and colleagues' research has shown widespread resistance to the pyrethroid insecticides that are currently the standard treatment (Romero, Potter, & Haynes, 2007).

They have idiosyncratic tastes—they're attracted by the heat and carbon dioxide that sleeping people generate, and they will feed only through a membrane. That means significant logistical challenges for trapping and baiting. (A Rutgers University Web page provides information on devising traps out of cat food bowls and dry ice—but only for diagnostic purposes. See njaes.rutgers.edu/pubs/publication .asp?pid=FS1117.)

None of the experts *JEH* spoke with saw any prospect of the bed bug problem spontaneously lessening in coming years.

Solutions from the Last Time Around

For half a century now, most Americans haven't had to worry about bed bugs. The problem previously reached its height in the 1920s and 1930s. Bed bugs had spread from port areas to major cities and eventually reached less populated rural areas.

Through the '40s and '50s, populations of the pest declined, primarily because DDT was widely available. Consumers could, for instance, buy DDT bug bombs in grocery stores. By the time bed bugs began developing resistance to DDT—which, inevitably, they did—organophosphates like diazinon and malathion were being used to clear up remaining infestations.

Larry Treleven, whose family has been in the pest control business for 84 years, said that his father and grandfather used to fumigate used furniture in their vaults. State laws required that the furniture be tagged as fumigated before it could be resold.

It was a different way of life, according to Potter. When people traveled, they knew to check their beds. When children came back from summer camp, their clothes and bedding had to be checked. He wondered whether people these days are prepared to exercise that kind of vigilance.

"And," he said, "people have a lot more clutter today, a lot more *stuff*. Which makes bed bug elimination more difficult."

Today, the hazards of pesticide treatment are also more widely recognized. Pesticide treatment options have narrowed for other reasons. DDT, for instance, is now illegal in the United States (U.S. Environmental Protection Agency [U.S. EPA], 1972). Besides, toward the end of the last epidemic, it had lost much of its effectiveness because bed bugs had developed resistance to it. Then other chemicals such as lindane and the organophosphates diazinon and malathion were used to mop up.

The Propoxur Proposal

On October 21, 2009, Matt Beal, acting chief of the Plant Industry Division of the Ohio Department of Agriculture (ODA), submitted a Section 18 request to the U.S. Environmental Protection Agency (U.S. EPA). The request was for an emergency exemption that would allow a pesticide called propoxur to be used by pest control professionals for treatment of bed bugs.

"For reasons nobody fully understands," Potter told *JEH*, "Ohio is really getting hammered."

Mystery Pesticide

Propoxur is a carbamate pesticide with a murky regulatory history. Currently it is used in some ant and cockroach baits, insecticidal strips, shelf paper, and pet collars. Although it is also labeled for use as a crack-and-crevice spray in food-handling establishments, U.S. EPA does not currently permit its use in locations where children may be present. That means no use in residential buildings and hotels.

But there's a loophole: products that were already in the channels of trade when current prohibitions went into effect may still be labeled for now prohibited uses. Strictly speaking, Beal said, use of those products is still legal. "The label is the law," as Jennifer Sievert, public health advisor for the WDOH Pesticide Program, put it. Indeed, because some of the labels allow consumers to use the product indoors, the permission that ODA is seeking (which would make propoxur available only to pest control professionals) would actually be *more* restrictive than the law as it now stands. That circumstance, according to Beal, has been a factor in the choice of propoxur for the Section 18 exemption request.

Of course, legality is not synonymous with safety. In 1988, U.S. EPA considered conducting a Special Review of propoxur "because of the potential carcinogenic risks to pest control operators and the general public during indoor and outdoor applications and risks to occupants of buildings treated with propoxur products" (U.S. EPA, 1997a, 1997b). In 1995, the agency decided *not* to initiate the Special Review because "the uses which posed the greatest concern had been eliminated through voluntary cancellation or label amendment" (U.S. EPA, 1997b). And in 2007, at the request of the registrant, it issued a final order terminating indoor use, according to the U.S. EPA document *Risk Management Decisions for Individual N-methyl Carbamate Pesticides* (U.S. EPA, 2007).

Sievert interprets that history to mean that propoxur was withdrawn because of evidence suggesting it was not safe. Potter interprets the withdrawal as a business decision; he believes that the cost of refuting challenges to its safety would have been more than the product was worth to its manufacturers. Either way, there are now some gaps in the data on health effects.

U.S. EPA has placed propoxur in Toxicity Category II (the second-highest category) for oral exposure and Toxicity Category III for dermal and inhalation exposures. Propoxur is also classed as a "probable human carcinogen."

Why Propoxur?

A couple of years ago, Potter and colleagues at the University of Kentucky decided to test some older insecticides and compare their efficacy to that of pyrethroids. They tested propoxur and chlorpyrifos (an organophosphate) on five populations of bed bugs collected from the field. Four of those populations had proved to be highly resistant to pyrethroids. Both pesticides killed 100% of all populations within 24 hours—"and frankly," Potter told *JEH*, "within an *hour.*"

Ohio is not making its request in a vacuum. Beal has worked on this issue not only with Potter, but also with the Association of Structural Pest Control Regulatory Officials (ASPCRO). There were also some preliminary conversations with U.S. EPA, he said, and "there's a multitude of other states awaiting this decision."

What about the safety concerns? Beal told *JEH*: "Basically, our role here is that we have a serious situation at hand. . . . We feel that it's a reasonable request to ask the agency to take a look at this. Certainly I'm not a toxicologist, I'm not a physician. I'm in the area of pesticide regulation. So we felt it was a reasonable request."

Does that mean ODA is putting this request out as an open question to U.S. EPA? In other words, the gist is not: We think it's safe, and we definitely want to use it? Rather, the gist is: Will you check this out and see if it's safe?

"Exactly," Beal said. "That's what the process is."

What if U.S. EPA says no, it's not safe? Is there a plan B?

"That is an interesting dilemma," he said. "Then we stand back and we keep talking amongst the ASPCRO states. We talk with the professional management folks—the pest management professionals—and try to see if there are any other avenues for us to go down. Fortunately, we're not at that point right now."

Contra

Early this year, Dykstra and Sievert submitted the following comment to U.S. EPA: "We do not support the proposed health exemption request from the Ohio Department of Agriculture to use the pesticide propoxur . . . to treat indoor residential single or multiple unit dwellings, apartments, hotels, motels, office buildings, modes of transportation, and commercial industrial buildings to control bed bugs." They cited research showing that the pesticide "remains detectable in indoor air weeks after initial application" and that "use of propoxur exposes the developing fetus in pregnant women to the chemical."

Carbamate pesticides, of which propoxur is one, are neurotoxins. Like organophosphates, they inhibit cholinesterase, although poisoning with carbamates is more easily reversed with treatment, and there is a "greater span between symptom-producing and lethal doses," according to Reigart and Roberts's *Recognition and Management of Pesticide Poisonings* (Reigart & Roberts, 1999). Serious overexposure can cause death

Propoxur and the Regulatory Process: Information from U.S. EPA

In response to *JEH*'s request for an interview, U.S. EPA sent the following written statement about the regulatory history of propoxur and the process the agency is following in determining whether to grant ODA's Section 18 request:

Section 18 of Federal Insecticide, Fungicide, and Rodenticide Act (FIFRA) authorizes EPA to allow an unregistered use of a pesticide for a limited time if EPA determines that an emergency condition exists. EPA's review process for a Section 18 includes determining whether the use meets the applicable safety standard as well as whether the unregistered use meets the criterion of being an emergency. See www.epa.gov/opprd001/section 18/for more information.

Propoxur is currently registered for use as follows:

- Indoor sprays in commercial buildings including food handling establishments to control roaches, ants, beetles, bees, etc. Labels explicitly exclude sprays in locations where children may be present (so no use in hotels, residential buildings, libraries, daycare facilities, schools). In food handling establishments, the use is restricted to crack and crevice application. Note that products in the channels of trade currently before the most recent labeling requirements may still be labeled for indoor residential use.
- Granular and gel baits for ants and cockroaches, some enclosed in bait stations.
- Impregnated insecticidal strips and shelf paper, to control cockroaches, bees, wasps, ants, etc.
- Pet collars to control fleas and ticks. Some are combination products with other active ingredients.

Information about historical use/regulation is available in the Propoxur Reregistration Eligibility Decision (1997), which can be accessed at www.epa.gov/pesticides/reregistration/propoxur/.

by cardiorespiratory depression. Early symptoms include malaise, sweating, muscle weakness, headache, dizziness, and gastrointestinal symptoms. Other symptoms of acute toxicity are coma, hypertension, trouble breathing, blurred vision, lack of coordination, twitching, and slurring of speech.

The biggest concern is with chronic (or acute) exposure to small children and developing fetuses, according to Wayne Clifford, who manages the Pesticide Illness and Zoonotics Disease Surveillance and Prevention program in WDOH's Office of Environmental Health. Children are not small adults, he reminded *JEH;* their neurological pathways are developing. "There's so much going on there biologically that *isn't* happening in full-grown adults, and they are much more sensitive. That's the primary population that we're trying to protect."

But the fact that propoxur is classed as a probable carcinogen is of concern for people of any age.

Dykstra and Sievert think pest control professionals should pursue alternative treatments. Such treatments might not, Dykstra acknowledged, completely eliminate the problem. But they would reduce it to tolerable levels.

"Instead of poisoning yourself or your children or whoever lives in the house," Sievert said. "That's really being played down here by propoxur proponents. In fact, there's basically no mention of it, that I can see."

Other Options

Marlowe of Eden Advanced Pest Technologies told *JEH* he is not a "fan" of the Ohio request: "From a *business* standpoint, it seems like we're headed in the wrong direction, to use a product like that around people's beds and in their bedrooms." Pesticides in sleeping quarters, he noted, are a potential liability for a company: "Even if it was made available to us, I'd probably stay with some of the other, lighter chemistries that we already have in the toolbox."

Eden uses steam heat to kill bedbugs, in combination with cedar oil and some other essential oils. Since these methods kill bed bugs only upon direct contact, Eden also applies diatomaceous earth to cracks, crevices, and any area bed bugs might be likely to crawl across. Diatomaceous earth abrades the exoskeleton, so that bodily fluids leak out and the insect eventually dries up.

Everyone agreed that diatomaceous earth is effective and that it shares an important advantage with propoxur: the ability to act residually. That is, it will act on any bugs not killed by direct-contact treatments, as well as on any bugs that get reintroduced after a treatment. A drawback, however, is that it works slowly. Potter also noted that application is tricky because it requires an extremely fine dusting, and applicators are not readily available to consumers. Pest control professionals have to be called in, and that means expense. Of course, the same would also be true of propoxur.

Another alternative, used by Treleven's company, Sprague Pest Solutions, is volumetric heating, which involves "superheating" an entire room to around 140F. Probes are used to ensure that the internal temperatures of objects in the room also reach temperatures high enough to kill the bugs. In addition, Sprague has dogs trained to sniff out any bed bugs that might remain. Unfortunately, this approach is expensive. The cost of equipping a single pest control team with a heater and generator approaches $50,000, and the setup and breakdown work make treatment an all-day, labor-intensive affair. Treleven estimated that treating a 1,700 square foot townhouse could cost a couple thousand dollars. Any conjoined units might then also have to be treated. Room-by-room treatment of multi-unit buildings could be a daunting prospect.

Treleven does recommend heat, combined with diatomaceous earth and canine detection, as a first, best treatment choice. But, he said, "If they can't afford the heating and the alternatives and things, it would be nice to have propoxur. I mean, I'm not going to lie to you. Because it is an alternative that would work."

Conclusion

In the case of bed bugs, none of the options are ideal. All can take a bite, figuratively speaking, out of someone's life.

Let's start with pesticides. Cancer risk, developmental detriments, and central nervous system effects can all subtract from longevity, fruitfulness, and life satisfaction. According to U.S. EPA's *R.E.D. Facts,* a reference dose (RfD) of 0.004 mg/kg/day is not expected to cause adverse effects over a 70-year lifetime (U.S. EPA, 1997). But as Clifford of WDOH put it, "there is not really a safe level of exposure to a carcinogen," because effects are cumulative and people may have exposures from other sources, such as residue on food. Propoxur treatments in areas where people sleep could entail extended exposures, especially since the pesticide has been demonstrated to volatilize in the air and be absorbed into the blood weeks after application (Whyatt et al., 2003).

But absent an effective pesticide, the need for relentless vigilance just as assuredly takes a bite out of life. Potter told *JEH* that he's had residents call him in tears when infestations have persisted after months of vigilant laundering and vacuuming. Added to the many stresses contemporary Americans already face, that kind of constant pressure can have a cumulative effect. Nor is money a negligible concern: the need for repeated expensive treatments can further contribute to financial insecurity—which in turn has its own, well-documented, health impacts.

Individual consumers could well come to different conclusions depending on personal circumstances, and making propoxur available could add to their choices.

But there are a couple of problems with casting this issue as a straightforward risk-benefit decision for individuals.

First, the impacts of neurotoxins on developing brains are difficult to sort out, much less document and quantify—which doesn't mean they're not happening. As Colborn writes: "Unlike obvious birth defects, most developmental effects cannot be seen at birth or even later in life. Instead, brain and nervous system disturbances are expressed in terms of how an individual behaves and functions, which can vary considerably from birth through adulthood" (2006, p.10).

Second, there's the question of whose risk and whose benefit. It's one thing for homeowners to weigh risks and benefits on their own and their families' behalf. Apartment buildings and other rental properties represent a different scenario. How many landlords, given the choice between repeated expensive heat treatments and a quick, inexpensive treatment with a U.S EPA approved pesticide, can be expected to choose the former? Perhaps a few. But it seems likely that in most cases, the decision will be a foregone conclusion. In the end, apartment dwellers could be subject, involuntarily and perhaps unknowingly, to extended exposures.

Nobody *JEH* interviewed thinks propoxur holds all the answers. ODA's exemption request is just a way of looking for something to, as Beal said, "help us through this critical time right now that we're seeing until something else further down the road can be developed to try to take care of the problem."

But will something else be developed "down the road"? Or will propoxur simply become the default treatment—at least until bed bugs develop resistance to it, too?

References

Colborn, T. (2006). A case for revisiting the safety of pesticides: A closer look at neurodevelopment. *Environmental Health Perspectives,* 114(1), 10-17.

Reigart, J.R., & Roberts, J.R. (1999). *Recognition and management of pesticide poisonings* (5th ed.). Washington, DC: U.S. EPA. Retrieved March 3, 2010, from www.epa.gov/pesticides/safety / healthcare/handbook/Chap05.pdf

Romero, A., Potter, M.F., & Haynes, K.F. (2007, July). Insecticide-resistant bed bugs: Implications for the industry. *Pest Control Technology.* Retrieved April 6, 2010, from www.pctonline.com /Article.aspx?article%5fid=37916

U.S. Environmental Protection Agency. (1972). *DDT ban takes effect.* Retrieved April 5, 2010, from www.epa.gov/history/topics /ddt/01.htm

U.S. Environmental Protection Agency. (1997a). *Reregistration eligibility decision (RED): Propoxur.* Retrieved April 5, 2010, from www.epa.gov/oppsrrd1/REDs/2555red.pdf

U.S. Environmental Protection Agency. (1997b). *R.E.D. facts: Propoxur* (U.S. EPA document # EPA-738-F-97-009). Retrieved April 5, 2010, from www.epa.gov/oppsrrd1/REDs /factsheets/2555fact.pdf

U.S. Environmental Protection Agency. (2007). *Risk management decisions for individual N-methyl carbamate pesticides.* Retrieved April 3, 2010, from epa.gov/oppsrrd1/cumulative /carbamate_ risk_mgmt.htm#propoxur

Whyatt, R.M., Barr, D.B., Camann, D.E., Kinney, P.L., Barr, J.R., Andrews, H.F., Hoepner, L.A., Garfinkel, R., Hazi, Y., Reyes, A., Ramirez, J., Cosme, Y., & Perera, F.P. (2003). Contemporary-use pesticides in personal air samples during pregnancy and blood samples at delivery among urban minority mothers and newborns. *Environmental Health Perspectives,* 111(5), 749–756.

Critical Thinking

1. What are the health risks associated with bed bugs?
2. Why might the use of pesticides cause health concerns?
3. Why have bed bugs increased in recent years? What practices have contributed to the increase?

From *Journal of Environmental Health,* June 2010, pp. 32–35. Copyright © 2010 by National Environmental Health Association. Reprinted by permission.

Is Your Food Contaminated?

New approaches are needed to protect the food supply.

MARK FISCHETTI

Given the billions of food items that are packaged, purchased and consumed every day in the U.S., let alone the world, it is remarkable how few of them are contaminated. Yet since the terrorist attacks of September 11, 2001, "food defense" experts have grown increasingly worried that extremists might try to poison the food supply, either to kill people or to cripple the economy by undermining public confidence. At the same time, production of edible products is becoming ever more centralized, speeding the spread of natural contaminants, or those introduced purposely, from farms or processing plants to dinner tables everywhere. Mounting imports pose yet another rising risk, as recent restrictions on Chinese seafood containing drugs and pesticides attest.

Can the tainting of what we eat be prevented? And if toxins or pathogens do slip into the supply chain, can they be quickly detected to limit their harm to consumers? Tighter production procedures can go a long way toward protecting the public, and if they fail, smarter monitoring technologies can at least limit injury.

Tighten Security

Preventing a terrorist or a disgruntled employee from contaminating milk, juice, produce, meat or any type of comestible is a daunting problem. The food supply chain comprises a maze of steps, and virtually every one of them presents an opportunity for tampering. Blanket solutions are unlikely because "the chain differs from commodity to commodity," says David Hennessy, an economics professor at Iowa State University's Center for Agricultural and Rural Development. "Protecting dairy products is different from protecting apple juice, which is different from protecting beef."

Even within a given supply chain there are few technology-based quick fixes. Preventing contamination largely comes down to tightening physical plant security and processing procedures at every turn. Each farmer, rancher, processor, packager, shipper, wholesaler and retailer "has to identify every possible vulnerability in the facility and in their procedures and close up every hole," says Frank Busta, director of the National Center for Food Protection and Defense at the University of Minnesota. The effort begins with standard facility access controls, which Busta often refers to as "gates, guns and guards," but extends to thoroughly screening employees and carefully sampling products at all junctures across the facility at all times.

That advice seems sound, of course, but the challenge for operators is how best to button down procedures. Several systems for safeguarding food production have been rolled out in recent years. Though these are not required by any regulatory agency, Busta strongly recommends that producers implement them. In the U.S., that impetus has been made stronger by legislation such as the 2002 Bioterrorism Act and a 2004 presidential directive, both of which require closer scrutiny of ingredient suppliers and tighter control of manufacturing procedures.

The primary safeguard systems Busta recommends borrow from military practices. The newest tool, which the FDA and the U.S. Department of Agriculture are now promoting, carries the awkward name of CARVER + Shock. It is being adapted from Defense Department procedures for identifying a military service's greatest vulnerabilities. "CARVER + Shock is essentially a complete security audit," says Keith Schneider, associate professor at the University of Florida's department of food science and human nutrition. The approach analyzes every node in the system for factors that range from the likely success of different kinds of attacks to the magnitude of public health, economic and psychological effects (together, the "shock" value) that a given type of infiltration could cause.

Track Contaminants

No matter how tightly procedures are controlled, determined perpetrators could still find ways to introduce pathogens or poisons. And natural pathogens such as salmonella are always a

Detect, Track and Trace

If a natural pathogen, or a perpetrator, contaminates food, lives will be saved if the tainted product can be quickly detected, then traced back to its point of origin so the rest of the batch can be tracked down or recalled. The following technologies, in development, could help:

- **Microfluidic Detectors**—Botulinum bacteria produce the most poisonous toxin known. They and similar agents, such as tetanus, could be detected during food processing by microfluidic chips—self-contained diagnostic labs the size of a finger. The University of Wisconsin–Madison is crafting such a chip, lined with antibodies held in place by magnetic beads, that could detect botulism during milk production. The chip could sample milk before or after it was piped into tanker trucks that leave the dairy and before or after it was pasteurized at a production plant. Other chips could detect other toxins at various fluid-processing plants, such as those that produce apple juice, soup or baby formula.

- **Active Packaging**—*E. coli,* salmonella and other pathogens could be detected by small windows in packaging, such as the cellophane around meat or the plastic jar around peanut butter. The "intelligent" window would contain antibodies that bind to enzymes or metabolites produced by the microorganism, and if that occurred the patch would turn color. The challenge is to craft the windows from materials and reactants that can safely contact food. Similar biosensors could react if the contents reached a certain pH level or were exposed to high temperature, indicating spoilage. And they could sense if packaging was

tampered with, for example, by reacting to the pressure imposed by a syringe or to oxygen seeping in through a puncture hole.

- **RFID Tags**—Pallets or cases of a few select foods now sport radio-frequency identification (RFID) tags that, when read by a scanner, indicate which farm or processing plant the batch came from. Future tokens that are smaller, smarter and cheaper could adorn individual packages and log every facility they had passed through and when. The University of Florida is devising tags that could be read through fluid (traditional designs cannot) and thus could be embedded inside the wall of sour cream or yogurt containers. The university is also developing active tags that could record the temperatures a package had been exposed to.

- **Edible Tags**—Manufacturers often combine crops from many growers, such as spinach leaves, into a retail package, so tags affixed to bags might not help investigators track contamination back to a specific source. ARmark Authentication Technologies can print microscopic markers that indicate site of origin directly onto a spinach leaf, apple or pellet of dog food using a spray made from edible materials such as cellulose, vegetable oil or proteins. Also, the tiny size would be hard for terrorists to fake, making it harder for them to sneak toxin-laced counterfeit foods past inspectors and into the supply. As an alternative, DataLase can spray citrus fruits or meats with an edible film in a half-inch-diameter patch that is then exposed to a laser beam that writes identification codes within the film.

concern. Detecting these agents, tracing them back to the spot of introduction, and tracking which grocery stores and restaurants ended up with tainted products are therefore paramount. Putting such systems in place "is just as important as prevention," Schneider says.

Here new technology does play a major role, with various sensors applied at different points along the chain. "You can't expect one technology to counter all the possible taintings for a given food," notes Ken Lee, chairman of Ohio State University's department of food science and technology.

A variety of hardware is being developed [see box on top of this page], although little has been deployed commercially thus far. Radio-frequency identification (RFID) tags are furthest along, in part because the Defense Department and Wal-Mart have required their main suppliers to attach the tokens to pallets or cases of foodstuffs. The Metro AG supermarket chain in Germany has done the same. The ultimate intent is for automated readers to scan the tags at each step along the supply chain—from farm, orchard, ranch or processor, through

packaging, shipping and wholesale—and to report each item's location to a central registry. That way if a problem surfaces, investigators can quickly determine where the batch originated and which stores or facilities might have received goods from that batch and when. Retailers can also read the tags on their items to see if they have received a product later identified as suspicious.

As RFID tags get smaller and cheaper, they will be placed directly on individual items—on every bag of spinach, jar of peanut butter, container of shrimp and sack of dog food. "That way if a recall is issued, the items can be found as they run past a scanner at the checkout counter," says Jean-Pierre Émond, professor of agricultural and biological engineering at the University of Florida.

Universities and companies are developing all kinds of other tags, some that are very inexpensive and others that cost more but supply extensive information. Some tokens, for example, can sense if food has been exposed to warm temperatures and thus might be more likely to harbor *Escherichia coli* or

Intentional Poisonings

U.S., 1984,
salmonella in salad bars, by Rajneeshees cult,
751 sickened

China, 2002,
rat poison in breakfast foods, by competitor to the vendor,
400 sickened, over 40 killed

U.S., 2002,
nicotine sulfate in ground beef, by disgruntled worker,
111 sickened

salmonella. Other tags could track how long items spent in transit from node to node in the supply chain, which could indicate unusually long delays that might raise suspicion about tampering. So-called active packaging could detect contamination directly and warn consumers not to eat the product they are holding.

The big impediment for any marker, of course, is the price. "Right now it costs 25 cents to put an RFID tag on a case of lettuce," Émond notes. "But for some growers, that equals the profit they're going to make on that case."

To be embraced widely, therefore, he says tags will have to provide additional value to suppliers or buyers. His university has been conducting an ongoing project with Publix Super Markets and produce suppliers in Florida and California to assess the possibilities. In initial trials, tags tracked crates and pallets that were shipped from the growers to several of Publix's distribution centers. Information gleaned from scanning tags at various points was available to all the companies via a secure Internet site hosted by VeriSign, the data security firm. The compilation allowed the participants to more quickly resolve order discrepancies, to log how long food sat idle, and to reveal ways to raise shipping efficiency. The group plans to extend the test to retail stores.

The U.S. imports 50 percent more food than it did just five years ago.

Control Suppliers

Costs will not drop until new technologies are widely deployed, but food defense analysts say adoption is unlikely to occur until clear, streamlined regulations are enacted. That prospect, in turn, will remain remote until the highest levels of government are reformed. "There are more than a dozen different federal agencies that oversee some aspect of food safety," Lee points out, noting that simple coordination among

Making Imports Safer

Alarming warnings about Chinese products in recent months have shown how dangerous imported edibles can be. In March some 100 brands of pet food were recalled after they were found to contain melamine, a toxic chemical used as a cheap replacement for wheat gluten. Then in June the U.S. Food and Drug Administration issued alerts about five types of seafood that contained antibiotic residues, pesticides and salmonella.

After the seafood scare, Senator Charles Schumer of New York declared that the federal government should establish an import czar. He blamed poor control of imports on a lack of inspection and poor regulation, telling the *Washington Post* that "neither the Chinese or American government is doing their job."

Regardless of how safe domestic production is, "imports are our Achilles' heel," says Ken Lee, chairman of Ohio State University's department of food science and technology. "There is no global food regulator. If the Chinese want to put an adulterant into food, they can do it until they get caught. I'll wager it will happen again, because it's driven by the profit motive."

Realistically, no technology can ensure that imports are safe. The food in every shipping container entering a U.S. port or border crossing could be pulled and irradiated, and some comestibles such as spices are already processed this way. But industry says the step would add significant cost for producers and shipping delays for middlemen. And the public continues to be wary of the technology. Furthermore, although irradiation would kill pathogens, it would have no effect on poisons or adulterants.

Inspecting all incoming food would also require vast increases in FDA and U.S. Department of Agriculture budgets; the agencies currently inspect a meager 1 percent of imports. As a partial alternative, in June the FDA said it intended to conduct more inspections of products from countries it deems to have poorer food-safety controls, such as China, offset by fewer inspections of products from countries with stronger standards, such as Britain and Canada. The agency also said it might require importers and U.S. manufacturers that use imported ingredients to provide more detailed information about production processes at foreign suppliers.

The best recourse, Lee says, is for companies to insist that suppliers impose strict standards and that the companies send inspectors overseas to verify compliance. Other experts agree, adding that government edicts are not as effective. "Too often import requirements are used as trade barriers, and they just escalate," says David Hennessy, an economics professor at Iowa State University. "The food companies themselves have a lot to lose, however. When they source a product in a country, they ought to impose tough procedures there."

—M.F.

The Vigilant Kitchen

If contaminated food does make it into your grocery bag, smart appliances could still prevent it from reaching your mouth. Innovations that could reach commercial introduction are described here by Ken Lee of Ohio State University. "None of this technology would be visually obtrusive," he says, "and all of it would be easy to clean."

Pulsed Light

When homeowners are asleep, fixtures underneath cabinets emit pulses of ultraviolet light that kill germs on counter-tops and other surfaces.

Microwave

An infrared sensor gauges internal food temperature and compares it with safety guidelines, indicating when the proper value has been reached. Instead of entering a cooking time, a user enters the food type or target temperature.

Refrigerator

A built-in reader scans RFID tags on food and checks for recalls over a wireless Internet connection. (A homeowner could hold nonrefrigerator items under it, too.) The reader also notes expiration dates written into the tags and tracks when containers such as milk cartons are removed and put back, to see if they have been out for too long and therefore might be spoiled. A red light warns of trouble.

them is difficult enough, and efficient approval of sensible requirements is even harder to come by. The FDA regulates pizza with cheese on it, but the USDA regulates pizza if it has meat on it, quips Jacqueline Fletcher, professor of entomology

and plant pathology at Oklahoma State University. "The requirements for organic farmers are different from those for nonorganic farmers."

Spurred by recent recalls, members of Congress have called for streamlining the regulation system. Illinois Senator Richard Durbin and Connecticut Representative Rosa DeLauro are advocating a single food-safety agency, but turf wars have hampered any progress toward that goal.

Concerned that more effective government is a long shot, experts say the responsibility for improved vigilance falls largely on food suppliers. "The strongest tool for stopping intentional contamination is supply-chain verification," says Shaun Kennedy, deputy director of the National Center for Food Protection and Defense. That means a brand-name provider such as Dole or a grocery store conglomerate such as Safeway must insist that every company involved in its supply chain implement the latest security procedures and detection, track and trace technologies or be dropped if it does not. The brand company should also validate compliance through inspections and other measures. The impetus falls on the brand-name provider because it has the most to lose. If a natural or man-made toxin is found in, say, a bag of Dole spinach or a container of Safeway milk, consumers will shun that particular label. "If a brand-name company wants to protect its products," Kennedy says, "it should validate every participant in the chain, all the way back to the farm."

Critical Thinking

1. What are the risks associated with eating contaminated food?

2. What can be done to reduce this risk?

3. Is the government doing enough to keep the food supply safe? Discuss.

Hazardous Health Plans

Coverage gaps can leave you in big trouble.

Many people who believe they have adequate health insurance actually have coverage so riddled with loopholes, limits, exclusions, and gotchas that it won't come close to covering their expenses if they fall seriously ill, a *Consumer Reports* investigation has found.

At issue are so-called individual plans that consumers get on their own when, say, they've been laid off from a job but are too young for Medicare or too "affluent" for Medicaid. An estimated 14,000 Americans a day lose their job-based coverage, and many might be considering individual insurance for the first time in their lives.

But increasingly, individual insurance is a nightmare for consumers: more costly than the equivalent job-based coverage, and for those in less-than-perfect health, unaffordable at best and unavailable at worst. Moreover, the lack of effective consumer protections in most states allows insurers to sell plans with "affordable" premiums whose skimpy coverage can leave people who get very sick with the added burden of ruinous medical debt.

Just ask Janice and Gary Clausen of Audubon, Iowa. They told us they purchased a United Healthcare limited benefit plan sold through AARP that cost about $500 a month after Janice lost her accountant job and her work-based coverage when the auto dealership that employed her closed in 2004.

"I didn't think it sounded bad," Janice said. "I knew it would only cover $50,000 a year, but I didn't realize how much everything would cost." The plan proved hopelessly inadequate after Gary received a diagnosis of colon cancer. His 14-month treatment, including surgery and chemotherapy, cost well over $200,000. Janice, 64, and Gary, 65, expect to be paying off medical debt for the rest of their lives.

For our investigation, we hired a national expert to help us evaluate a range of real policies from many states and interviewed Americans who bought those policies. We talked to insurance experts and regulators to learn more. Here is what we found:

- Heath insurance policies with gaping holes are offered by insurers ranging from small companies to brand-name carriers such as Aetna and United Healthcare. And in most states, regulators are not tasked with evaluating overall coverage.
- Disclosure requirements about coverage gaps are weak or nonexistent. So it's difficult for consumers to figure out in advance what a policy does or doesn't cover, compare plans, or estimate their out-of-pocket liability for a medical catastrophe. It doesn't help that many people who have never been seriously ill might have no idea how expensive medical care can be.
- People of modest means in many states might have no good options for individual coverage. Plans with affordable premiums can leave them with crushing medical debt if they fall seriously ill, and plans with adequate coverage may have huge premiums.
- There are some clues to a bad policy that consumers can spot. We tell you what they are, and how to avoid them if possible.
- Even as policymakers debate a major overhaul of the health-care system, government officials can take steps now to improve the current market.

Good Plans vs. Bad Plans

We think a good health-care plan should pay for necessary care without leaving you with lots of debt or high out-of-pocket costs. That includes hospital, ambulance, emergency-room, and physician fees; prescription drugs; outpatient treatments; diagnostic and imaging tests; chemotherapy, radiation, rehabilitation and physical therapy; mental-health treatment; and durable medical equipment, such as wheelchairs. Remember, health insurance is supposed to protect you in case of a catastrophically expensive illness, not simply cover your routine costs as a generally healthy person. And many individual plans do nowhere near the job.

For decades, individual insurance has been what economists call a "residual" market—something to buy only when you have run out of other options. The problem, according to insurance experts we consulted, is that the high cost of treatment in the U.S., which has the world's most expensive health-care system, puts truly affordable, comprehensive coverage out of the reach of people who don't have either deep pockets or a generous employer. Insurers tend to provide this choice: comprehensive coverage with a high monthly premium or skimpy coverage at a low monthly premium within the reach of middle- and low-income consumers.

More consumers are having to choose the latter as they become unemployed or their workplace drops coverage. (COBRA, the federal program that allows former employees to continue with the insurance from their old job by paying the full monthly premium, often costs $1,000 or more each month for family coverage. The federal government is temporarily subsidizing 65 percent of those premiums for some, but only for a maximum of nine months.) *Consumer Reports* and others label as "junk insurance" those so-called affordable individual plans with huge coverage gaps. Many such plans are sold throughout the nation, including policies from well-known companies.

Decent insurance covers more than just routine care.

Aetna's Affordable Health Choices plans, for example, offer limited benefits to part-time and hourly workers. We found one such policy that covered only $1,000 of hospital costs and $2,000 of out-patient expenses annually.

The Clausens' AARP plan, underwritten by insurance giant United Health Group, the parent company of United Healthcare, was advertised as "the essential benefits you deserve. Now in one affordable plan." AARP spokesman Adam Sohn said, "AARP has been fighting for affordable, quality health care for nearly a half-century, and while a fixed-benefit indemnity plan is not perfect, it offers our members an option to help cover some portion of their medical expenses without paying a high premium."

Nevertheless, AARP suspended sales of such policies last year after Sen. Charles Grassley, R-Iowa, questioned the marketing practices. Some 53,400 AARP members still have policies similar to the Clausens' that were sold under the names Medical Advantage Plan, Essential Health Insurance Plan, and Essential Plus Health Insurance Plan. In addition, at least 1 million members are enrolled in the AARP Hospital Indemnity Insurance Plan, Sohn said, an even more bare-bones policy. Members who have questions should first call 800-523-5800; for more help, call 888-687-2277. (Consumers Union, the nonprofit publisher of *Consumer Reports,* is working with AARP on a variety of health-care reforms.)

United American Insurance Co. promotes its supplemental health insurance as "an affordable solution to America's health-care crisis!" When Jeffrey E. Miller, 56, of Sarasota, Fla., received a diagnosis of prostate cancer a few months after buying one of the company's limited-benefit plans, he learned that it would not cover tens of thousands of dollars' worth of drug and radiation treatments he needed. As this article went to press, five months after his diagnosis, Miller had just begun treatment after qualifying for Florida Medicaid. A representative of United American declined to comment on its products.

Even governments are getting into the act. In 2008, Florida created the Cover Florida Health Care Access Program, which Gov. Charlie Crist said would make "affordable health coverage available to 3.8 million uninsured Floridians." But many of the basic "preventive" policies do not cover inpatient hospital treatments, emergency-room care, or physical therapy, and they severely limit coverage of everything else.

7 Signs a Health Plan Might Be Junk

Do Everything in Your Power to Avoid Plans with the Following Features:

Limited benefits. Never buy a product that is labeled "limited benefit" or "not major medical" insurance. In most states those phrases might be your only clue to an inadequate policy.

Low overall coverage limits. Health care is more costly than you might imagine if you've never experienced a serious illness. The cost of cancer or a heart attack can easily hit six figures. Policies with coverage limits of $25,000 or even $100,000 are not adequate.

"Affordable" premiums. There's no free lunch when it comes to insurance. To lower premiums, insurers trim benefits and do what they can to avoid insuring less healthy people. So if your insurance was a bargain, chances are good it doesn't cover very much. To check how much a comprehensive plan would cost you, go to *ehealthinsurance.com,* enter your location, gender, and age as prompted, and look for the most costly of the plans that pop up. It is probably the most comprehensive.

No coverage for important things. If you don't see a medical service specifically mentioned in the policy, assume it's not covered. We reviewed policies that didn't cover prescription drugs or outpatient chemotherapy but didn't say so anywhere in the policy document—not even in the section labeled "What is not covered."

Ceilings on categories of care. A $900-a-day maximum benefit for hospital expenses will hardly make a dent in a $45,000 bill for heart bypass surgery. If you have to accept limits on some services, be sure your plan covers hospital and outpatient medical treatment, doctor visits, drugs, and diagnostic and imaging tests without a dollar limit. Limits on mental-health costs, rehabilitation, and durable medical equipment should be the most generous you can afford.

Limitless out-of-pocket costs. Avoid policies that fail to specify a maximum amount that you'll have to pay before the insurer will begin covering 100 percent of expenses. And be alert for loopholes. Some policies, for instance, don't count co-payments for doctor visits or prescription drugs toward the maximum. That can be a catastrophe for seriously ill people who rack up dozens of doctor's appointments and prescriptions a year.

Random gotchas. The AARP policy that the Clausens bought began covering hospital care on the second day. That seems benign enough, except that the first day is almost always the most expensive, because it usually includes charges for surgery and emergency-room diagnostic tests and treatments.

137

The Wild West of Insurance

Compounding the problem of limited policies is the fact that policyholders are often unaware of those limits—until it's too late.

"I think people don't understand insurance, period," said Stephen Finan, associate director of policy at the American Cancer Society Cancer Action Network. "They know they need it. They look at the price, and that's it. They don't understand the language, and insurance companies go to great lengths to make it incomprehensible. Even lawyers don't always understand what it means."

Case in point: Jim Stacey of Fayetteville, N.C. In 2000, Stacey and his wife, Imelda, were pleased to buy a plan at what they considered an "incredible" price from the Mid-West National Life Insurance Co. of Tennessee. The policy's list of benefits included a lifetime maximum payout of up to $1 million per person. But after Stacey learned he had prostate cancer in 2005, the policy paid only $1,480 of the $17,453 it cost for the implanted radioactive pellets he chose to treat the disease.

"To this day, I don't know what went wrong," Stacey said about the bill.

We sent the policy, along with the accompanying Explanation of Benefit forms detailing what it did and didn't pay, to Karen Pollitz, research professor at the Georgetown University Health Policy Institute. We asked Pollitz, an expert on individual health insurance, to see whether she could figure out why the policy covered so little.

"The short answer is, 'Beats the heck out of me,'" she e-mailed back to us. The Explanation of Benefit forms were missing information that she would expect to see, such as specific billing codes that explain what treatments were given. And there didn't seem to be any connection between the benefits listed in the policy and the actual amounts paid.

Contacted for comment, a spokeswoman for HealthMarkets, the parent company of Mid-West National, referred us to the company website. It stated that the company "pays claims according to the insurance contract issued to each customer" and that its policies "satisfy a need in the marketplace for a product that balances the cost with the available benefit options." The spokeswoman declined to answer specific questions about Stacey's case, citing patient privacy laws.

One reason confusion abounds, Pollitz said, is that health insurance is regulated by the states, not by the federal government, and most states (Massachusetts and New York are prominent exceptions) do not have a standard definition of what constitutes health insurance.

"Rice is rice and gasoline is gasoline. When you buy it, you know what it is," Pollitz said. "Health insurance—who knows what it is? It is some product that's sold by an insurance company. It could be a little bit or a lot of protection. You don't know what is and isn't covered. Nothing can be taken for granted."

How to Protect Yourself

Seek out comprehensive coverage. A good plan will cover your legitimate health care without burdening you with oversized debt.

Want Better Coverage? Try Running for Congress

President Barack Obama says Americans should have access to the kind of health benefits Congress gets. We detail them below. Members of Congress and other U.S. government employees can receive care through the Federal Employees Health Benefits Program. Employees choose from hundreds of plans, but the most popular is a national Blue Cross and Blue Shield Preferred Provider Organization plan. Employee contributions for that plan are $152 per person, or $357 per family, per month.

Plan Features
- No annual or lifetime limits for major services
- Deductible of $300 per person and $600 per family
- Out-of-pocket limit of $5,000 per year with preferred providers, which includes most deductibles, co-insurance, and co-payments

Covered Services
- Inpatient and outpatient hospital care
- Inpatient and outpatient doctor visits
- Prescription drugs
- Diagnostic tests
- Preventive care, including routine immunizations
- Chemotherapy and radiation therapy
- Maternity care
- Family planning
- Durable medical equipment, orthopedic devices, and artificial limbs
- Organ and tissue transplants
- Inpatient and outpatient surgery
- Physical, occupational, and speech therapy
- Outpatient and inpatient mental-health care

"The idea of 'Cadillac' coverage vs. basic coverage isn't an appropriate way to think about health insurance," said Mila Kofman, Maine's superintendent of insurance. "It has to give you the care you need, when you need it, and some financial security so you don't end up out on the street."

What you want is a plan that has no caps on specific coverages. But if you have to choose, pick a plan offering unlimited coverage for hospital and outpatient treatment, doctor visits, drugs, and diagnostic and imaging tests. When it comes to lifetime coverage maximums, unlimited is best and $2 million should be the minimum. Ideally, there should be a single deductible for everything or, at most, one deductible for drugs and one for everything else. And the policy should pay for 100 percent of all expenses once your out-of-pocket payments hit a certain amount, such as $5,000 or $10,000.

If you are healthy now, do not buy a plan based on the assumption that you will stay that way. Don't think you can safely

The Real Cost of Illness Can Be Staggering . . .

Few Americans realize how much care costs. Coverage gaps can leave you in debt.

Condition	Treatment	Total Cost
Late-stage colon cancer	124 weeks of treatment, including two surgeries, three types of chemotherapy, imaging, prescription drugs, hospice care.	$285,946
Heart attack	56 weeks of treatment, including ambulance, ER workup, angioplasty with stent, bypass surgery, cardiac rehabilitation, counseling for depression, prescription drugs.	$110,405
Breast cancer	87 weeks of treatment, including lumpectomy, drugs, lab and imaging tests, chemotherapy and radiation therapy, mental-health counseling, and prosthesis.	$104,535
Type 2 diabetes	One year of maintenance care, including insulin and other prescription drugs, glucose test strips, syringes and other supplies, quarterly physician visits and lab, annual eye exam.	$5,949

. . . and Out-of-Pocket Expenses Can Vary Widely

With its lower premium and deductible, the California plan at right would seem the better deal. But because California, unlike Massachusetts, allows the sale of plans with large coverage gaps, a patient there will pay far more than a Massachusetts patient for the same breast cancer treatments, as the breakdown below shows.

Massachusetts Plan	California Plan
Monthly premium for any 55-year-old: $399	**Monthly premium for a healthy 55-year-old:** $246
Annual deductible: $2,200	**Annual deductible:** $1,000
Co-pays: $25 office visit, $250 outpatient surgery after deductible, $10 for generic drugs, $25 for nonpreferred generic and brand name, $45 for nonpreferred brand name	**Co-pays:** $25 preventive care office visits
	Co-insurance: 20% for most covered services
Co-insurance: 20% for some services	**Out-of-pocket maximum:** $2,500, includes hospital and surgical co-insurance only.
Out-of-pocket maximum: $5,000, includes deductible, co-insurance, and all co-payments	**Exclusions and limits:** Prescription drugs, most mental-health care, and wigs for chemotherapy patients not covered. Outpatient care not covered until out-of-pocket maximum satisfied from hospital/surgical co-insurance.
Exclusions and limits: Cap of 24 mental-health visits, $3,000 cap on equipment	
Lifetime benefits: Unlimited	**Lifetime benefits:** $5 million

Service and Total Cost	Patient Pays	Patient Pays
Hospital	$0	$705
Surgery	$981	$1,136
Office visits and procedures	$1,833	$2,010
Prescription drugs	$1,108	$5,985
Laboratory and imaging tests	$808	$3,772
Chemotherapy and radiation therapy	$1,987	$21,113
Mental-health care	$950	$2,700
Prosthesis	$0	$350
Total $104,535	$7,668	$37,767

Source: Karen Pollitz, Georgetown University Health Policy Institute, using real claims data and policies. Columns of figures do not add up exactly because all numbers are rounded.

go without drug coverage, for example, because you don't take any prescriptions regularly today. "You can't know in advance if you're going to be among the .01 percent of people who needs the $20,000-a-month biologic drug," said Gary Claxton, a vice president of the nonprofit Kaiser Family Foundation, a health-policy research organization. "What's important is if you get really sick, are you going to lose everything?"

Consider trade-offs carefully. If you have to make a trade-off to lower your premium, Claxton and Pollitz suggest opting for a higher deductible and a higher out-of-pocket limit rather than fixed dollar limits on services. Better to use up part of your retirement savings paying $10,000 up front than to lose your whole nest egg paying a $90,000 medical bill after your policy's limits are exhausted.

What Lawmakers Need to Do Next

Consumers Union, the nonprofit publisher of *Consumer Reports,* has long supported national health-care reform that makes affordable health coverage available to all Americans. The coverage should include a basic set of required, comprehensive health-care benefits, like those in the federal plan that members of Congress enjoy. Insurers should compete for customers based on price and the quality of their services, not by limiting their risk through confusing options, incomplete information, or greatly restricted benefits.

As reform is developed and debated, Consumers Union supports these changes in the way health insurance is presented and sold:

Clear terms. All key terms in policies, such as "out-of-pocket" and "annual deductible," should be defined by law and insurers should be required to use them that way in their policies.

Standard benefits. Ideally, all plans should have a uniform set of benefits covering all medically necessary care, but consumers should be able to opt for varying levels of cost-sharing. Failing that, states should establish a menu of standardized plans, as Medicare does for Medigap plans. Consumers would then have a basis for comparing costs of plans.

Transparency. Policies that insurers currently sell should be posted in full online or available by mail upon request for anyone who wants to examine them. They should be the full, legally binding policy documents, not just a summary or marketing brochure. In many states now, consumers can't see the policy document until after they have joined the plan. At that point, they're legally entitled to a "free look" period in which to examine the policy and ask for a refund if they don't like what they see. But if they turn the policy back in, they face the prospect of being uninsured until they can find another plan.

Disclosure of costs. Every plan must provide a standard "Plan Coverage" summary that clearly displays what is—and more important, is not—covered. The summary should include independently verified estimates of total out-of-pocket costs for a standard range of serious problems, such as breast cancer treatment or heart bypass surgery.

Moreover, reliable information should be available to consumers about the costs in their area of treating various medical conditions, so that they have a better understanding of the bills they could face without adequate health coverage.

With such a high deductible, in years when you are relatively healthy you might never collect anything from your health insurance. To economize on routine care, take advantage of free community health screenings, low-cost or free community health clinics, immediate-care clinics offered in some drugstores, and low-priced generic prescriptions sold at Target, Walmart, and elsewhere.

Look for a plan that doesn't cap your coverage.

If your financial situation is such that you can afford neither the higher premiums of a more comprehensive policy nor high deductibles, you really have no good choices, Pollitz said, adding, "It's why we need to fix our health-care system."

Check out the policy and company. You can, at least, take some steps to choose the best plan you can afford. First, see "7 Signs a Health Plan Might Be Junk" to learn to spot the most dangerous pitfalls and the preferred alternatives.

Use the Web to research insurers you're considering. The National Association of Insurance Commissioners posts complaint information online at www.naic.org.

Entering the name of the company and policy in a search engine can't hurt either. Consumers who did that recently would have discovered that Mid-West National was a subsidiary of HealthMarkets, whose disclosure and claims handling drew many customers' ire. Last year, HealthMarkets was fined $20 million after a multi-state investigation of its sales practices and claims handling.

Don't rely on the salesperson's word. Jeffrey E. Miller, the Florida man whose policy failed to cover much of his cancer treatment, recalls being bombarded with e-mail and calls when he began shopping for insurance. "The salesman for the policy I bought told me it was great, and I was going to be covered, and it paid up to $100,000 for a hospital stay," he said. "But the insurance has turned out to pay very little."

Pollitz advises anyone with questions about their policy to ask the agent and get answers in writing. "Then if it turns out not to be true," she said, "you can complain."

Critical Thinking

1. What should consumers look for when choosing health insurance?
2. What constitutes inadequate health care coverage?
3. Why do you think so many consumers end up with inadequate coverage?

Cybermedicine: What You Need to Know

Regina A. Bailey

Introduction

Physicians are increasingly using the internet to communicate with patients, even providing online medical consultations, also known as cybermedicine. With the simple click of a mouse button a patient can communicate with a physician about an illness, receive a diagnosis and in some situations, obtain a prescription.

However, there are drawbacks, as well. Because regulation of the practice of medicine is governed by states, there is no uniform law regarding the legality of online medical consultations. This may cause problems for physicians trying to maintain licenses in more than one state in order to comply with each state's medical licensing law.

Another barrier to the use of cybermedicine is reimbursement. Although Medicare and Medicaid reimburse for telemedicine services in limited situations, so far they have not allowed for reimbursement of cybermedicine—and it is not yet clear whether they will do so. In addition, only a few private insurers offer reimbursement for cybermedicine.

What is Cybermedicine?

The number of people that use the internet to obtain medical information is growing, with up to 61 percent of all American adults going online for health information.[1] People are also using the internet to communicate with their physicians and to refill prescriptions online. A recent study showed 5.6 percent of women and 4.2 percent of men age 18-64 communicated with a healthcare provider by email and 6.6 percent of women and 5.3 percent of men refilled a prescription online.[2] The number of physicians using the internet is growing, as well. Eighty-six percent of physicians use the internet to access health information.[3] With this growth, there is an increased interest in consulting with a physician via the internet as an alternative to in-office visits. According to a recent PriceWaterhouseCoopers study, 50 percent of respondents stated that they would seek healthcare through online consultations and that email consultations were the

most preferred method, followed by online web-cam/video consultations.[4]

Telemedicine, which is the use of medical information through electronic communication to improve a patient's health status or to provide medical care, has been in use for many years.[5] It primarily involves the interaction of one physician (or other healthcare provider) with another physician in a different location to help diagnose or treat a patient; for example, consulting with a physician at a distant location to obtain treatment advice.[6]

Cybermedicine has grown out of telemedicine and is defined as the communication between a physician and patient by email or online chat services to obtain healthcare information and/or to receive medical services.[7] The greatest difference between telemedicine and cybermedicine is that with the latter, the online physician interacts directly with the patient, and essentially eliminates the middleman. Some cybermedicine is conducted through online services, and some of it is conducted individually between physician and patient, perhaps via an established direct relationship. There is still much confusion about the differences between telemedicine and cybermedicine, and sometimes the terms are used incorrectly or interchangeably.

There are several benefits of cybermedicine. Some proponents argue that it is a less expensive way to provide routine care.[8] For patients who do not have a primary care physician, cybermedicine can be better and more efficient than going to an emergency room—79 percent of emergency room visits are for routine/non-emergency problems, causing a 40 percent increase in wait time for those who need immediate attention in an emergency room.[9] Cybermedicine may also be effective in rural areas that have a shortage of physicians; for example, 180 counties in Texas do not have enough physicians.[10] It is a way for people to communicate with a physician more quickly than allowed under traditional methods; 70 percent of Texas patients cannot get a same-day appointment with their primary care physician.[11] Cybermedicine may be a way to help alleviate the worsening physician shortage problem. It may also be beneficial for people with rare disorders that live far away from physicians who are familiar with such disorders.

There are benefits to the medical community, as well. Physicians that currently use the internet for consultations have noticed increased productivity and a corresponding decrease in the number of phone calls needed, causing less disruption in the practice's daily operations.[12] A recent study at the University of California at Davis showed that physicians who fully implement cybermedicine in their practices can see approximately 11 percent more patients in a day.[13]

There are also particular types of treatment that appear to lend themselves to the use of cybermedicine. For instance, psychotherapy, where there is no physical exam, is appropriate for counseling via webcam; the U.S. Navy has provided behavioral cybermedicine for deployed soldiers with some success.[14]

But diagnosing and treating a patient solely through the internet can have dangerous consequences. Without the ability to examine the patient in person, a physician may miss many important elements that are necessary to the diagnosis. For online consultations conducted via email, the physician is limited to the text of the emails. Although the ability to communicate with the patient is improved with a webcam in that the physician is not limited merely to the patient's typewritten words, the physician is still limited by the inability to obtain more than a visual inspection of the patient, rather than actually conducting a physical exam, which is a critical aspect of assessing patients.[15] Even during a physical exam of a patient which is focused on the patient's chief complaint,[16] the physician takes advantage of information obtained through each of his or her senses (touch, sight, hearing, smell). But with cybermedicine, physicians are stripped of their ability to use some or all of their senses.

The patient also may be less inclined to tell the physician the truth in order to obtain certain services, may not tell the physician about medical conditions that he has and may not tell the physician about medications he is taking. While these situations can occur in a physician's office, they may occur more frequently online given the relative anonymity allowed by the internet.[17] Some cybermedicine services only require that the patient complete a simple questionnaire or form to initiate and/or facilitate the online consultation. Other cybermedicine services, especially those that provide prescriptions, have preselected click-off choices available to the patient via use of a questionnaire with the answers already checked off, and require the patient to physically change the response if the checked off answer is incorrect, making it even easier for the patient to provide misleading information.[18] In addition, the information obtained from these questionnaires may be insufficient for purposes of the physician's making a diagnosis or providing a recommended course of treatment. Thus, this lack of complete information may cause misdiagnosis and inappropriate treatment of the patient's illness.[19]

Another concern is identification verification. Even with face-to-face interactions, there are tremendous problems with medical identity theft; there is an even greater danger for this with cybermedicine. For the most part, the patient need only provide the physician with a credit card number, and possibly health insurance information, to obtain services. But with the informal nature of the internet, someone can easily use someone else's credit card or health insurance to obtain medical services, since there is no way for the doctor to confirm identity.

Similarly, given the lack of oversight of online consultations it would be relatively easy for an unlicensed physician or an individual posing as a physician to conduct online consultations, which can be very dangerous for the patient.[20] In addition, it is possible for a physician not licensed in the state where he is providing services to participate in cybermedicine, which may get the physician in trouble with his state medical board because of violation of state law or terms of his medical license.[21]

Liability for Physicians Participating in Cybermedicine

Cybermedicine raises the issue of potentially greater medical malpractice liability. Although some cybermedicine programs state that they merely offer medical advice, most of them purport to provide diagnosis and treatment of various ailments.

The difficulty in identifying symptoms without actually examining the patient and the potential for inaccuracy contributes to increased liability. Moreover, although to date there have been no malpractice cases involving cybermedicine, when they do arise it is likely that courts will determine that cybermedicine consultations can create a physician-patient relationship and apply traditional malpractice principles accordingly.

Physician-Patient Relationship

Some courts have held that a mere telephone conversation can create a physician-patient relationship if the call provides the patient with information about the course of treatment and if it is foreseeable that the patient would rely on the advice.[22] Cases in which the physician never personally speaks with the patient or only speaks with another physician about the patient have been held to be insufficient to form a physician-patient relationship.[23] But courts have been clear in noting that "the mere fact that a physician does not have direct physical contact with a patient does not preclude the existence of a physician-patient relationship."[24] If a physician-patient relationship can be established by a telephone conversation, a physician-patient relationship can be established through online contact, as well. In fact, there is an even greater likelihood of establishing a physician-patient relationship over the internet. "When a physician accepts an Online Care encounter with a new patient, he or she does so with an initial understanding of the patient medical background and chief complaint and in doing so, is establishing a patient-physician relationship."[25]

Standard of Care

While liability may be established, it is unknown what standard of care should be applied to the services provided. There is no uniform model standard of care in the United States; the relevant standard of care for online consultations varies from state to state. For instance, in Texas, the online physician is held to the same standard of care as a physician conducting an in-office consultation.[26] However, in Hawaii, the online physician is held to a lesser standard of care, the same standard as a physician in a similar, non-face-to-face situation.[27]

Moreover, the standard of care is usually measured by a local standard.[28] However, with cybermedicine, the physician and patients may be in different parts of the country, so it's unclear which standard should apply. It has been argued that there either needs to be a national standard of care to apply to cybermedicine, or that cyber-physicians should be seen as having a separate medical specialty, and therefore a separate standard of care.[29] It is unknown how this will evolve.

Liability Insurance Coverage

Another unanswered question is whether a physician's current liability insurance will cover his/her online interactions.[30] Physicians who become a part of a cybermedicine consulting company will likely receive liability insurance coverage through their employer at no cost.[31] However, it is unclear whether traditional liability insurance policies will include cybermedicine consultation services coverage for doctors providing cybermedicine services outside of cybermedicine companies.

Effectiveness of Disclaimers

Most of the websites that provide online medical consultations have some sort of disclaimer on their website attempting to limit their liability. If the patient fails to read the disclaimer, its effectiveness is suspect. Studies have shown that most online users do not read similar types of information on health websites.[32] Even if the cybermedicine provider uses blanket disclaimers in an attempt to disclaim liability for any and all activities associated with the cybermedicine, such disclaimers may be ineffective in shielding the physician from medical malpractice liability; physicians have been found liable for malpractice even when disclaimers are included.[33] Further, medical malpractice insurance is not likely to cover these activities if the consultations are perceived to be merely a means to provide information rather than the physician's rendering of medical care.[34]

Reimbursement of Cybermedicine Services

Another issue regarding online medical consultations is whether and how the physician will be paid for his/her services. Currently, most cybermedicine services are paid for out-of-pocket.[35] The lack of adequate reimbursement by third party payors for cybermedicine continues to be a barrier to more full-scale adoption of the practice. If physicians will not be reimbursed for providing these services, they have no incentive to participate.

Medicare

The Balanced Budget Act of 1997 ("BBA") authorized partial Medicare reimbursement for telehealth services.[36] Beginning January 1, 1999, Medicare began paying for "teleconsultations" in areas that were identified as rural health professional shortage areas (teleconsultations being defined as consultations between two doctors or healthcare providers at two different sites).[37] Reimbursement in these geographic areas included initial, follow-up, or confirmatory teleconsultations in hospitals, outpatient facilities or medical offices.[38] Because the teleconsultation that Medicare reimburses for is a substitute for a "face-to-face" or in-office consultation, Medicare does require a certain level of interaction between the patient and consulting practitioner during the teleconsultation.[39] The Benefits Improvement and Protection Act of 2000 ("BIPA") expanded teleconsultation reimbursement by providing full reimbursement, rather than partial, but still maintained geographic limitations and restrictions on the telehealth services eligible for reimbursement.[40] Currently, reimbursement is only allowed for certain teleconsultations that occur in Health Professional Shortage Areas ("HPSAs").[41]

To obtain this reimbursement, Medicare requires the use of specific technology defined as interactive telecommunication systems.[42] This includes audio and video equipment that allows two-way, real-time communication between a patient and a physician or other healthcare practitioner.[43] Interactive telecommunication systems do not include telephones, facsimile machines, or email systems.[44] The physician or practitioner at the distant site must be licensed to furnish the service under state law.[45] The medical examination of the patient is performed under the control of the physician or practitioner at the distant site.[46] A telepresenter (a healthcare provider with the patient) is not required unless his presence is deemed medically necessary as determined by the physician or practitioner at the distant site.[47]

Currently, Medicare does not reimburse for cybermedicine services.[48] While BBA and BIPA authorized Medicare reimbursement for telemedicine, Medicare has not extended this to cybermedicine. Although cybermedicine services could arguably fit under the definition of telemedicine and there is a Current Procedural Terminology ("CPT") code for online medical services, Medicare does not value this code and blocks payment for this service.[49]

Medicaid

States are able to obtain waivers of certain Medicaid provisions, giving them greater power and flexibility to allow them to develop new healthcare delivery systems or to allow for implementation of experimental systems in their Medicaid programs.[50] This flexibility has allowed some states the opportunity to deliver telemedicine services to Medicaid patients as a cost-effective alternative to face-to-face medical care.[51] Most states do reimburse for some telemedicine services.[52]

Most state Medicaid programs also provide reimbursement for healthcare-related transportation costs.[53] In order to attempt to save money on transportation costs, a number of states with telemedicine programs entered into collaborations with other state Medicaid programs to develop inter-state telemedicine reimbursement policies as it may be cheaper to have the patient seen at the telemedicine location rather than pay for transportation to a location further away. Currently, twenty-seven state Medicaid programs provide some reimbursement for telehealth services.[54] Like Medicare, however, the state Medicaid programs do not yet reimburse for online medical consultations.

Private Insurance

There are several states (California, Colorado, Georgia, Hawaii, Kentucky, Louisiana, Maine, New Hampshire, Oklahoma, Oregon, Texas and Virginia) that mandate private insurance companies reimburse for telemedicine services.[55] Thirty-eight private insurance programs in twenty-five states currently receive reimbursements from private payors for telemedicine, and over 100 private payors currently reimburse for telemedicine under either a state mandate or a voluntary program.[56] However, it is unclear if the telemedicine state mandate reimbursements also cover cybermedicine consultations.

A few private payer insurance companies have begun to reimburse for cybermedicine consultations on their own initiative. A few years ago, Blue Cross Blue Shield in California, Hawaii, Minnesota, Massachusetts, and Tennessee began to provide reimbursements of $20 to $45 to physicians for online consultations.[57] Group Health, a New York health plan, provides reimbursements for online consultations[58] as does MVP Health Care.[59] As more insurance companies realize that online medical consultations may be cheaper and quicker than in-office visits, they, too, may reimburse physicians for these services.

However, another barrier to reimbursement from private payors is the disclaimers that some websites post. Some of them disclaim any physician-patient relationship, which makes it virtually impossible for the physician to subsequently obtain reimbursement for the provided online interactions.[60] "If the responses are merely informational rather than part of medical care, few health insurance policies are ever likely to pay for such transactions."[61] Alternatively, those individuals whose insurance companies do not reimburse for cybermedicine consultations may submit their receipts to medical flexible spending accounts or health savings accounts for possible reimbursements.[62]

Regulation of Online Consultations

The regulation of cybermedicine varies from state to state. For example, in Texas, cybermedicine consultations are only allowed if the physician and patient have a pre-existing physician-patient relationship. In Hawaii, a pre-existing relationship is not required and patients can obtain a cybermedicine consultation from a doctor that has never met or examined them before. Most laws governing telemedicine are likely to overlap with or address online consultations, but most states do not differentiate or have a separate category for cybermedicine, and some do not have laws covering this area at all.[63]

States have begun to address this issue. In 2009, legislators in Hawaii considered allowing the use of the internet to establish a physician-patient relationship for online medical consultations. Despite testimony by members of the Hawaii Medical Association that online consultations should only be allowed after a physician-patient relationship has been established during a prior in-office visit, Hawaiian legislators passed a law in 2009 allowing the use of telemedicine to establish a physician-patient relationship to evaluate or treat a patient.[64] Over the first six months following the law's enactment, more than 4,000 patients in Hawaii engaged in online consultations with physicians.[65]

The law in Hawaii defines telemedicine as the establishment of a physician-patient relationship through the use of telecommunication services, including real-time video or web conferencing communication or secure web-based communication.[66] Although the law uses the word "telemedicine," what is actually described is not what is traditionally considered telemedicine but is actually cybermedicine. The traditional physical exam is bypassed: "Telemedicine services shall include a documented patient evaluation, including history and a discussion of physical symptoms adequate to establish a diagnosis and to identify underlying conditions or contraindications to the treatment recommended or provided."[67] The standard of care required of physicians engaging in these consultations is lower than that which occurs during a traditional face-to-face/in-office encounter; it is more akin to a situation where an on-call physician covers for another physician in his practice and communicates with the patient over the phone.[68] The law states that issuing a prescription based on an online questionnaire is not acceptable standard of care.[69] The law also requires that the online physician be licensed in Hawaii.[70]

In contrast, Texas' law governing cybermedicine consultations is stricter than Hawaii's law. Title 22, Section 174.4 of the Texas Administrative Code regulates the use of the internet in medical practice.[71] Physicians who utilize the internet for cybermedicine consultations of patients located in Texas are required to ensure that a "proper" physician-patient relationship is established prior to the online interaction, including establishing the identity of the person requesting services, establishing a diagnosis through the use of history, physical exam, diagnostic and laboratory testing, and ensuring the availability of proper follow-up care.[72] The Texas Medical Board has made its position clear that there must be a pre-existing established physician-patient relationship prior to the cybermedicine consultation; "an online or telephone exam [is] inadequate if doctors and patients [have] not met in person and [is] 'not allowed under our rule.'"[73] As noted above, Texas imposes a higher standard of care for cybermedicine consultations than Hawaii does, requiring the same standard of care as in a traditional face-to-face/in-office setting.[74]

The Texas Medical Board has received complaints of adverse events that occur in situations where physicians have treated patients without actually seeing them.[75] Physicians who violate these rules are subject to license suspension or revocation.[76] Sanctions are determined on a case-by-case basis.[77]

Regulation of the practice of medicine has been traditionally reserved to states by the Tenth Amendment, but the nature of telemedicine and online medical consultations is such that the relationship between physician and patient often crosses state, sometimes even national, lines.[78] In addition, the use of the internet has been analogized to other areas of interstate commerce that transmit communication across state lines, for example, transmission of electricity or transportation services.[79] Since cybermedicine consultations can involve the transmission of medical services across state lines, there is a strong argument that it should be regulated under the Commerce Clause.[80]

The lack of uniform state laws may make it difficult for physicians to comply with them. For instance, it would be difficult and expensive for a physician to maintain a license in all 50 states if he desires to electronically consult with any patient in the United States who desires an online consultation.

Possible Solutions to Resolve Regulatory Uncertainty

Since this is an evolving area of the law, it is hoped and expected that the regulatory uncertainty will be addressed in the future. At present there is no one "best" solution.

One solution to the licensing issue may be to change state laws to allow physicians who have a valid full medical license in their respective states to legally practice telemedicine and cybermedicine in the consulting state. Those practicing in the state by virtue of conducting cybermedicine or telemedicine could be subject to the same licensure and disciplinary laws as physicians physically located in the state."[81] An alternative would be to modify current consulting exception laws to include telemedicine and cybermedicine.

Other alternatives could include (1) developing a uniform national licensure system similar to national licensing that is available in the Veterans Administration medical system; (2) developing a uniform national licensure system applicable only to physicians who are participating in online medical consultations; (3) making limited licensing available for those engaging in telemedicine or cybermedicine; or (4) implementing reciprocity agreements between states. "A national licensure system could cure both the inconsistencies in state-to-state requirements and the lack of coordination between state regulatory boards."[82]

Creating a uniform system would make it easier for physicians to obtain and maintain licensure in multiple states, and would also provide a method of monitoring those physicians who are engaging in cybermedicine.

Still, any uniform standard would have to be adopted by each state legislature and then coordinated within the existing state regulatory boards in order to preserve the individual state's right to license physicians in the state.[83] Nursing has uniform licensing, so uniformed licensing for physicians is not a farfetched idea. Because of the increased need for nurses, and the difficulty of obtaining a nursing license in each state, the Interstate Nurse Licensure Compact ("Compact"), a uniformed licensing act, was developed by the National Council of State Boards of Nursing.[84] A nurse who is licensed to practice in a state that has enacted the Compact may practice in any other Compact state without having to obtain a new license.[85] The Compact also provides for cross-state harmonization of standards.[86] "Harmonization of standards may be a palatable means of preserving each state's right to regulate professionals."[87] Currently there are 23 states that have adopted the Compact; adoption is pending in another."[88]

If the country is going to head in the direction of allowing cybermedicine, which seems very likely, it may be best to establish uniform licensing requirements for cybermedicine consultations to allow for harmonizing standards of care and for better, more effective monitoring of doctors engaging in cybermedicine. It wouldn't necessarily be a way to make it easier to engage in online consultations, but would be a better way of monitoring this activity.

Conclusion

Cybermedicine will serve an important part of the future medical practice. These online consultations are an efficient, cost-effective way of enhancing an established physician-patient relationship and for treating certain medical conditions. They should not be a substitute for traditional in-person consultations, but they can be an important way to enhance an established physician-patient relationship.

In order to fully use cybermedicine to its full potential, issues regarding its regulation and its reimbursement will need to be explored and resolved. Seeing the development of this technology and the laws governing it promises to be quite intriguing.

Endnotes

1. Susannah Fox and Sydney Jones, *The Social Life of Health Information,* PEW INTERNET AND AMERICAN LIFE PROJECT 4 (June 2009), *available at* www.pewinternet.org/~/media//Files /Reports/2009/PIP_Health_2009.pdf.

2. Robin A. Cohen and Barbara Strussman, *Health Information Technology Use Among Men and Women Aged 18-64: Early Release of Estimates From the National Health Interview Survey, January-June 2009,* CDC's National Center for Health Statistics 1 (February 2010), *available at* www.cdc.gov/nchs /data/hestat/healthinfo2009/healthinfo2009.pdf.

3. Pamela Lewis Dolan, *86% of physicians use Internet to access health information,* AMERICAN MEDICAL NEWS, (Jan. 4, 2010), *available at* www.ama-assn.org/amednews/2010/01/04 /bisc0104.htm.

4. Michael Thompson, ET AL., *Focusing on Healthcare Value,* PriceWaterhouseCoopers (July 2009), available at www.pwc .com/us/en/view/issue-12/focusing-on-healthcare-value-pg5 .jhtml.

5. American Telemedicine Association, *Telemedicine Defined (2010), available at* www.americantelemed.org/i4a/pages /index.cfm?pageid=3333; Kip Poe, *Telemedicine Liability: Texas and Other States Delve into the Uncertainties of Health Care Delivery via Advanced Communications Technology,* THE REVIEW OF LITIGATION (July 1, 2001) *available at* www.allbusiness.com/technology/telecommunications -conferencing/919240-1.html.

6. Nicolas P. Terry, *Prescriptions Sans Frontières (Or How I Stopped Worrying About Viagra On The Web But Grew Concerned About The Future Of Healthcare Delivery),* 4 YALE JOURNAL OF HEALTH POLICY, LAW & ETHICS. 183, 185 (Summer 2004).

7. Julie Reed, *Cybermedicine: Defying and Redefining Patient Standards of Care,* 37 INDIANA LAW REVIEW 845, 850 (2004). John D. Blum, *Internet Medicine and the Evolving Legal Status of the Physician-Patient Relationship,* 24 JOURNAL OF LEGAL MEDICINE 413 (2004).

8. Claire Miller, *The Virtual Visit May Expand Access to Doctors,* THE NEW YORK TIMES, December 20, 2009, *available at* www.nytimes.com/2009/12/21/technology/start-ups/21doctors .html?_r=1.

9. *Id.*

10. *Id.*

11. *Id.*

12. Ken Ortolon, *Going Online: Texas Health Plans May Soon Pay for Online Patient Encounters,* TEXAS MEDICINE, (March 2007), *available at* www.texmed.org/Template.aspx?id=5540.

13. *Id.*

14. In 1997, during a six-month deployment to the Persian Gulf, the U.S. Navy used cybermedicine for psychiatric consultations on board the *USS George Washington.* Marc Dielman, *Ohio Psychological Association Communications & Technology Committee Members,* TELEPSYCHOLOGY GUIDELINES 12 (April 12, 2009), *available at* www .ohpsych.org/resources/1/files/Comm%20Tech%20Committee /OPA%20Telepsychology%20Guidelines-Revised.pdf. James, *Behavioral Telehealth: Using Telemedicine to Expand Behavioral Medicine Services,* JOURNAL OF HEALTHCARE INFORMATION MANAGEMENT, (1999), *available at* www.himss .org/content/files/jhim/13-4/him13403.pdf.

15. LYNN BICKLEY, BATES GUIDE TO PHYSICAL EXAMINATION AND HISTORY TAKING 10-13 (2003).

16. *Id.* at 9 and 68.

17. Jeremy Hochberg, *Nailing Jell-o to a Wall: Regulating Internet Pharmacies,* 37 JOURNAL OF HEALTH LAW 445, 451-452 (2004).

18. Bernard Bloom, *Internet Availability of Prescription Pharmaceuticals to the Public,* 131 ANN INTERN MED 830,832 (1999); *see also,* Hochberg, *supra* note 17.

19. "Moreover, the consulting cyberdoctor is left to rely on the medical history that is supplied by the patient, which may be incomplete or falsified in order to obtain a desired treatment," Shira D. Weiner, *Mouse-To-Mouse Resuscitation: Cybermedicine and The Need For Federal Regulation,* 23 CARDOZO LAW REVIEW 1107, 1118 (2002), citing Jane E. Brody, *On-Line Health Care for the Savvy Surfer,* N.Y. Times, Aug. 31, 1999, at F6.

20. Ranney Wiesemann, *On-Line Or On-Call? Legal And Ethical Challenges Emerging In Cybermedicine* 43 ST. LOUIS UNIVERSITY LAW JOURNAL 1119, 1147-8 (2009).

21. *Id.*

22. Bienz v. Cent. Suffolk Hosp., 163 A.D.2d 269, 270, 557 N.Y.S.2d 139 (1990), *McKinney v. Schlatter,* 118 Ohio App.3d 328, 692 N.E.2d 1045, 1050-51 (1997), Cogswell by *Cogswell v. Chapman, 249 A.D.2d 865, 672 N.Y.S.2d 460, 462 (N.Y. App. Div. 1998); Lownsbury v. VanBuren, 94 Ohio St. 3d 231, 2002 Ohio 646, 762 N.E.2d 354, 360 (Ohio 2002).*

23. *Id.*

24. *Id.* at 1123-4 (2002), citing *Dougherty v. Gifford,* 826 S.W.2d 668, 674-75 (Tex. App. 1992).

25. *National Working Group, Online Care: Provider Considerations for the Practice of Online Care,* www.americanwell.com /providerConsiderationsForThePracticeOfOnlineCare.pdf (last accessed May 1, 2010).

26. 22 TEX. ADMIN. CODE §174.4 (b) (2010).

27. 25 HRS § 453-1.3 (d)(2010).

28. 3-12 Hooper Lundy & Bookman, TREATISE ON HEALTH CARE LAW § 12.04 (Matthew Bender, Rev. Ed.).

29. Kelly Gelien, *Are Online Medical Consultations a prescription for trouble?* 66 BROOKLYN L. REV. 209, 250-252, (SPRING 2000).

30. Ronald Scott, *Cybermedicine and Virtual Pharmacies,* 103 WEST VIRGINIA LAW REVIEW 407, 453, 457 (2001).

31. Crystal Conde, *Web Consults: TMB Leery of Treating Patients Online,* 106(3) TEXAS MEDICINE 16, 20 (March 2010).

32. California HealthCare Foundation & Internet Healthcare Coalition, *Ethics Survey of Consumer Attitudes about Health Web Site* 8, (January 2000), *available at* www.chcf.org /~media/Files/PDF/S/surveyreport.pdf. (Study showed that only 14% of online health seekers 'always' read sites' privacy and ethics statements, 21% read them 'often,' 36% read them sometimes, and 29% 'rarely' or 'never' read them at all).

33. Patti Dobbins, *Comment: Provision Of Legal And Medical Services On The Internet: Licensure And Ethical Considerations,* 3 NORTH CAROLINA JOURNAL OF LAW & TECHNOLOGY 353 (2002).

34. Scott, *supra,* at 456.

35. Jonnelle Marte, *Doctor is In-Online,* WSJ.com (August 9, 2009).

36. The Center for Telemedicine Law, *Telemedicine Reimbursement Report* 2 (October 2003), *available at* ftp://ftp.hrsa.gov /telehealth/licen.pdf. *See also* The Balanced Budget Act of 1997, Pub.L. 105-33, 111 Stat. 251.

37. U.S. Health Resources and Services, *First Steps of Telemedicine Reimbursement* (December 1998), *available at* www.hrsa.gov /telehealth/pubs/reimb.htm#site.

38. *Id.*

39. *Id.*

40. *Telemedicine Reimbursement Report, supra.*

41. HPSAs are defined as a rural or urban area which the Secretary of Health and Human Services determines has a health manpower shortage and which is not reasonably accessible to an adequately served area, a population group which the Secretary determines has such a shortage, or a public or nonprofit private medical facility or other public facility which the Secretary determines has such a shortage. 42 C.F.R. § 410.78 (a)(1)(A) (2010).

42. "General rule. Medicare Part B pays for office and other outpatient visits, professional consultation, psychiatric diagnostic interview examination, individual psychotherapy, pharmacologic management, end stage renal disease related services included in the monthly capitation payment (except for one visit per month to examine the access site), and individual medical nutrition therapy furnished by an interactive telecommunications system if the following conditions are met: (1) The physician or practitioner at the distant site must be licensed to furnish the service, (2) The physician or practitioner at the distant site who is licensed under State law to furnish a covered telehealth service described in this section may bill, and receive payment for, the service when it is delivered via a telecommunications system." 42 C.F.R. § 410.78 (b) (2010).

43. 42 C.F.R. § 410.78 (a)(3)(2010).

44. "Interactive telecommunications system means multimedia communications equipment that includes, at a minimum, audio and video equipment permitting two-way, realtime interactive communication between the patient and distant site physician or practitioner. Telephones, facsimile machines, and electronic mail systems do not meet the definition of an interactive telecommunications system." *Id.*

45. 42 C.F.R. § 410.78 (b)(1) (2010).

46. 42 C.F.R. § 410.78 (b)(5) (2010).

47. 42 C.F.R. § 410.78 (c) (2010).

48. Ray Painter, *Medicare Final Rule,* UROLOGY TIMES (December 7, 2007), *available at* http://urologytimes.modernmedicine .com/urology times/Coding+and+Reimbursement/Medicare -final-rule-Little-good-news-for-urologist/ArticleStandard /Article/detail/475195. "CPT now includes a code for online E&M service (99444). However, Medicare has chosen not to value this code and also considers this a bundled service, blocking payment for this service as well." *See also,* Sherri Porter, New, Revised CPT Codes Target Online, Telephone Services, AAFP NEWS (February 29, 2008), *available at* www .aafp.org/online/en/home/publications/news/news-now/practice -management/20080229cptcodes.html. "At the present time, Medicare does not pay for any of these codes."

49. *Id. See also,* American Medical Association, *CPT Process, How a Code Becomes a Code, available at* www.ama-assn.org /ama/no-index/physician-resources/3882.shtml. CPT codes are developed, published, updated, and licensed by the American Medical Association. Medicare, Medicaid, and a majority of private healthcare payors require providers to submit CPT codes on claims for services.

50. *Id.*

51. "Under sections 1915(b) and 1115 of the Social Security Act, these waivers allow states to develop innovative health care delivery or reimbursement systems and allow for statewide health care reform experimental systems without increasing costs." *Id.*

52. *Id.*

53. *Telemedicine Reimbursement Report, supra* note 51, at 2.

54. *Id.*

55. Under the statute in Virginia, telemedicine services that are reimbursed include the use of interactive audio, video or other electronic media used for diagnosis, consultation or treatment. It does not include services provided through audio-only telephone, email or fax. Chris Silva, *Telemedicine Coverage Now Mandated in Virginia,* AMA NEWS (April 26, 2010). S*ee also* Telemedicine Reimbursement Report, *supra note 51,* at 7.

56. *Id.*

57. Tyler Chin, *Insurers still weighing pay for online consultations. Plans are considering continuing or expanding programs to reimburse for Web visits on a regular basis.* AMERICAN MEDICAL NEWS (July 1, 2002), *available at* www.ama-assn .org/amednews/2002/07/01/bisb0701.htm; *see also,* Ken Terry, *MN Blues Launch Online Physician Consults,* HEALTH CARE ANALYSIS (April 14, 2009), *available at* http://m.industry .bnet.com/healthcare/1000538/minnesota-blues-launch-online -physician-consults/; *see also,* Marianne Kolbasuk McGee, *E-visits Begin to Pay off for Physicians,* INFORMATION WEEK (May 31, 2004), *available at* www.informationweek.com/news /global-cio/showArticle.jhtml?articleID=21400367.

58. McGee, *supra.*

59. Will Engle, *MVP Health Care will begin reimbursing its network of more than 22,000 physicians for Web-based consultations with patients covered through most of its benefit plans.* HEALTH DATA MANAGEMENT, (October 20, 2009), *available at* http://telemed.org/legal/news.asp.

60. Scott, *supra,* at 456.

61. *Id.,* citing Susan Huntington, *Emerging Professional Liability Exposures for Physicians On the Web,* presentation at the ABA e-Health Law 2000 Seminar, Chicago, Illinois (October 6-7, 2000).

62. American Medical Association, *Online Medical Consultations, Connecting Physicians with Patients,* AMA PRACTICE MANAGEMENT CENTER 1 (April 29, 2010), *available at* www.ama-assn.org/ama1/x-ama/upload/mm/368/consultations.pdf, at 4.

63. Jurisdictions that have no telemedicine laws include Alaska, Delaware, Washington D.C, Massachusetts, Michigan, Missouri, North Dakota, and Oklahoma. American College of Radiology, *Telemedicine Licensing Provisions By State.* www.acr.org/SecondaryMainMenuCategories /GR_Econ/FeaturedCategories/state/state_issues /TelemedicineLicensingProvisionsbyStateDoc8.aspx.

64. U.S. CONST. art. I, § 8, cl. 3; *see also,* Carmen Lewis, *My Computer, My Doctor: A Constitutional Call for Federal Regulation of Cybermedicine,* 32 AMERICAN JOURNAL OF LAW AND MEDICINE 585-609 (2006). *See also,* 25 H.R.S. § 453-1.3 (b)(2010).

65. Thompson, *supra.*

66. " 'Telemedicine' means the use of telecommunications services, including real-time video or web conferencing communication or secure web-based communication to establish a physician-patient relationship, to evaluate a patient, or to treat a patient." 25 H.R.S § 453-1.3 (b)(2010).

67. "Telemedicine services shall include a documented patient evaluation, including history and a discussion of physical symptoms adequate to establish a diagnosis and to identify underlying conditions or contra-indications to the treatment recommended or provided." 25 H.R.S. § 453-1.3 (c)(2010).

68. "Treatment recommendations made via telemedicine, including issuing a prescription via electronic means, shall be held to the same standards of appropriate practice as those in traditional physician-patient settings that do not include a face to face visit but in which prescribing is appropriate, including on-call telephone encounters and encounters for which a follow-up visit is arranged." 25 H.R.S. § 453-1.3 (d)(2010).

69. "Issuing a prescription based solely on an online questionnaire is not treatment for the purposes of this section and does not constitute an acceptable standard of care." 25 HRS § 453-1.3 (d)(2010).

70. "A physician shall not use telemedicine to establish a physician-patient relationship with a patient in this State without a license to practice medicine in Hawaii. Once a provider-patient relationship is established, a patient or physician licensed in this State may use telemedicine for any purpose, including consultation with a medical provider licensed in another state, authorized by this section, or as otherwise provided by law." 25 HRS § 453-1.3 (f)(2010).

71. 22 TEX. ADMIN. CODE §174.4 (2010).

72. "Evaluation of the Patient. Physicians who utilize the Internet must ensure a proper physician-patient relationship is established that at a minimum includes:

(1) establishing that the person requesting the treatment is in fact who the person claims to be;

(2) establishing a diagnosis through the use of acceptable medical practices such as patient history, mental status examination, physical examination, and appropriate diagnostic and laboratory testing to establish diagnoses and identify underlying conditions and/or contraindications to treatment recommended/provided;

(3) discussing with the patient the diagnosis and the evidence for it, the risks and benefits of various treatment options; and

(4) ensuring the availability of the physician or coverage of the patient for appropriate follow-up care." 22 TEX. ADMIN. CODE § 174.4 (a)(2010).

73. Miller, *supra,* quoting Mari Robinson, Executive Director of the Texas Medical Board; *see also* Conde, *supra,* at 19.

74. "Treatment and consultation recommendations made in an online setting, including issuing a prescription via electronic means, will be held to the same standards of appropriate practice as those in traditional (face-to-face) settings. An online or telephonic evaluation by questionnaire does not constitute an acceptable standard of care." 22 TEX. ADMIN. CODE § 174.4 (b) (2010).

75. Conde, *supra,* at 18. Several Texas physicians have been subject to disciplinary action over the past few months for prescribing medications to patients they never actually saw in a face-to-face encounter or for prescribing drugs without establishing a proper physician-patient relationship. For example, a Dr. Rajala prescribed dangerous drugs without maintaining adequate medical records when she wrote 14 prescriptions for hydrocodone and Arthrotec over a 15-month period for a patient with a hip injury without establishing a proper physician-patient relationship. The Board and Dr. Rajala entered into an agreed order requiring Dr. Rajala to complete the physician prescribing course at the University of California San Diego's Physician Assessment and Clinical Education Program or complete 24 hours of continuing medical education in ethics, medical record-keeping and prescribing controlled substances within one year. A Dr. Lengyel failed to maintain adequate medical records, and failed to treat a patient according to the standard of care by **prescribing dangerous drugs without establishing a proper physician-patient relationship.** His medical license was revoked. A Dr. Hinojosa failed to comply with requirements and guidelines for practicing telemedicine; **wrote refill prescriptions for three patients whom he never saw** and whose prior prescriptions he never reviewed; and did not document any therapeutic evaluation that would establish the basic need for such medication. The patients were located in Florida and the prescriptions were written to be filled in Florida, where Dr. Hinojosa has never been licensed to practice medicine. He agreed to voluntarily and permanently surrender his Texas medical license in lieu of further disciplinary proceedings. Texas Medical Board, *Medical Board Disciplines 70 Doctors and Issues 671 Licenses* (February 17, 2010), *available at* www.tmb.state.tx.us/news /press/2010/021710.php.

76. *Id.*

77. *Id.*

78. U.S. CONST. art. I, § 8, cl. 3; *see also,* Carmen Lewis, *My Computer, My Doctor: A Constitutional Call for Federal Regulation of Cybermedicine,* 32 AMERICAN JOURNAL OF LAW AND MEDICINE 585-609 (2006).

79. *Id.,* citing Federal Power Comm'n v. Union Elec. Co., 381 U.S. 90, 94 (1965) and Am. Libraries Ass'n v. Pataki, 969 F. Supp. 160, 161 (S.D.N.Y. 1997), citing Kenneth D. Bassinger, *Dormant Commerce Clause Limits on State Regulation of the Internet: The Transportation Analogy,* 32 GA. L. REV. 889, 904 n. 102 (1998).

80. U.S. Const. art. I, § 8, cl. 3; *see also,* Carmen Lewis, *My Computer, My Doctor: A Constitutional Call for Federal Regulation of Cybermedicine,* 32 American Journal of Law and Medicine 585-609 (2006).

81. Ross D. Silverman, *Regulating Medical Practice In The Cyber Age: Issues And Challenges For State Medical Boards,* 26 American Journal of Law and Medicine 255, 268 (2000).

82. Dobbins, *supra,* at 353.

83. *Id.*

84. Nurse Licensure Compact Administrators, *About, Nurse Licensure Compact,* www.ncsbn.org/156.htm (last accessed May 14, 2010).

85. *Id.*

86. *Id.*

87. Dobbins, *supra* note 47, at 353.

88. Nurse Licensure Compact Administrators, *Map of NLC States,* www.ncsbn.org/158.htm (last accessed May 14, 2010).

Critical Thinking

1. What are the advantages and disadvantages of cybermedicine?

2. What is the downside of the lack of uniform laws governing cybermedicine?

3. Would you consider "visiting" a doctor online? Why or why not?

The *Surprising Reason* Why Heavy Isn't Healthy

It's not just because fat ups your risk of disease. How much you weigh can keep you from getting the same health care everyone else gets. Our *special report* looks at a growing problem in women's health.

GINNY GRAVES

It's shocking, but it's true: Being a woman who's more than 20 pounds overweight may actually hike your risk of getting poor medical treatment. In fact, weighing too much can have surprising—and devastating—health repercussions beyond the usual diabetes and heart-health concerns you've heard about for years. A startling new *Health* magazine investigation reveals that if you're an overweight woman you:

- may have a harder time getting health insurance or have to pay higher premiums;
- are at higher risk of being misdiagnosed or receiving inaccurate dosages of drugs;
- are less likely to find a fertility doctor who will help you get pregnant;
- are less likely to have cancer detected early and get effective treatment for it.

What's going on here? Fat discrimination is part of the problem. A recent Yale study suggested that weight bias can start when a woman is as little as 13 pounds over her highest healthy weight. "Our culture has enormous negativity toward overweight people, and doctors aren't immune," says Harvard Medical School professor Jerome Groopman, MD, author of *How Doctors Think.* "If doctors have negative feelings toward patients, they're more dismissive, they're less patient, and it can cloud their judgment, making them prone to diagnostic errors." With nearly 70 million American women who are considered overweight, the implications of this new information is disturbing, to say the least. Here, what you need to know to get the top-quality health care you deserve—no matter what you weigh.

How Weight Gets in the Way

When Jen Seelaus, from Danbury, Connecticut, went to her doc's office because she was wheezing, she expected to get her asthma medication tweaked. Instead, she was told she'd feel better if she'd just lose some weight. "I didn't go to be lectured about my weight. I was there because I couldn't breathe," says the 5-foot-3, 195-pound woman. "Asthma can be dangerous if it gets out of control, and the nurse practitioner totally ignored that because of my weight."

Seelaus's nurse made a classic diagnostic error, according to Dr. Groopman. "It's called attribution, because your thinking is colored by a stereotype and you attribute the entire clinical picture to that stereotype. Because obesity can cause so many health problems, it's very easy to blame a variety of complaints, from knee pain to breathing troubles, on a patient's weight. That's why doctors—and patients—need to constantly ask, 'What else could this be?'"

There aren't statistics on how many diagnostic errors are due to weight, but the data for the general population is disturbing enough. "Doctors make mistakes in diagnosing 10 to 15 percent of all patients, and in half of those cases it causes real harm," Dr. Groopman says. Based on anecdotal evidence—patients who've told her that their doctors are often too quick to blame symptoms on weight—Rebecca Puhl, PhD, director of Research and Weight Stigma Initiatives at the Rudd Center for Food Policy and Obesity at Yale University, suspects that being heavy could further increase the odds of being misdiagnosed.

Even if doctors are aware of the potential traps they can fall into when diagnosing an overweight patient, extra body fat can literally obscure some illnesses, including heart disease and different types of cancer. "It's more difficult to hear heart and lung sounds in heavy people," says Mary Margaret Huizinga, MD, MPH, director of the Johns Hopkins Digestive Weight Loss Center. "I use an electronic stethoscope, which works well, but I'm very aware of the issues that can crop up in overweight patients. Not all doctors have these stethoscopes—or are aware they need one."

Jeffrey C. King, MD, professor and director of maternal-and-fetal medicine at the University of Louisville School of Medicine, says that "the more tissue between the palpating hand and what you're trying to feel, the harder it is to detect a mass." That may be what happened to Karen Tang [not her real name], a 5-foot-8, 280-pound woman who went to the doctor for pelvic pain. Her doc palpated her uterus but didn't feel anything. "By the time I was referred to a gynecologist, I had a fibroid the size of a melon—so large it was putting pressure on my bladder," she recalls.

Even a routine pelvic exam can be tricky, especially if you've had children. "The vaginal walls become lax and collapse into the middle, obscuring the cervix," Dr. King says. Larger or modified speculums can help, but not all docs have them and they can make the exam more uncomfortable, says Lynda Wolf, MD, a reproductive endocrinologist at Reproductive Medicine Associates of Michigan.

That may explain the disturbing finding that obese women are less likely to get Pap smears than normal-weight women. But doctors may be partly to blame for the screening lapse, too. A University of Connecticut study of more than 1,300 physicians found that 17 percent were reluctant to do pelvic exams on obese women and that 83 percent were hesitant if the patient herself seemed reluctant.

Physical exams aren't the only things hampered by obesity. Large patients may not fit into diagnostic scanning machines—computed tomography (CT) and magnetic resonance imaging (MRI), for instance—and X-rays and ultrasounds may not be as effective, says Raul N. Uppot, MD, a radiologist in the Division of Abdominal Imaging and Intervention at Massachusetts General Hospital in Boston. "Ultrasound is the approach that's the most limited by body fat, because the beams can't penetrate the tissue if you have more than 8 centimeters of subcutaneous fat," he says.

This affects women, in particular, because ultrasound is used to diagnose uterine tumors and ovarian cysts and to evaluate the mother's and baby's health during pregnancy. Just last May, researchers at the University of Texas Southwestern Medical Center at Dallas reported a 20 percent decrease in the ability to detect problems in fetuses of obese women with ultrasound. In another study, obese women were 20 percent more likely to have false-positive results from mammograms—readings that can lead to unnecessary biopsies and anxiety.

Too much body fat can *obscure organs on scans,* giving doctors fuzzy results.

While CT scans are less affected by body fat, getting clear images in heavy patients typically requires a lot more radiation than with normal-weight patients, making it riskier, especially if numerous CT scans are required. But trying to diagnose a health problem without proper imaging is like driving blindfolded. Doctors are sometimes left with little to go on except symptoms and intuition, especially in the emergency room, where physicians make life-and-death decisions in minutes. "If we can't get the imaging because of a patient's weight, and we are concerned about a pulmonary embolism or appendicitis, for example, we have to go ahead and treat based on our clinical impression," says Archana Reddy, MD, a Chicago-area ER physician.

A Big, Fat Health Insurance Problem

Need to lose weight? That's not going to make your insurance company happy. If you're overweight or obese it probably costs them more. Even if you're in an employer's health insurance plan, you may all have to pay higher premiums if there are overweight people in the office filing more health claims.

But the real challenge is for those women who are trying to get private insurance—finding affordable health coverage can be difficult, if not impossible, if you're overweight. Rules vary by insurance company. But, in general, heavier women are likely to take a financial hit. For instance, a woman who is 5 feet 4 inches tall and has no other health problems will likely need a medical exam and pay higher premiums if she weighs more than around 180 or 190 pounds, says John Barrett of Health Insurance Brokers in Pasadena, California. Rates may range from 20 to 100 percent higher, depending on the carrier. And if that 5 foot 4 woman weighs more than around 220? She could be automatically declined coverage.

Women who try to lose weight don't get much help, either. "Weight counseling and early preventive treatment of obesity aren't covered by many plans," says John Wilder Baker, MD, president of the American Society for Metabolic and Bariatric Surgery. And insurance plans often won't cover bariatric surgery or other obesity treatments.

Being overweight can get in the way of effective cancer treatment, too, experts say. The problem: underdosing. "Oncologists usually base chemo on patients' ideal weight rather than their true weight, partly because chemo is so toxic and partly because drug trials typically include only average women, so we don't know the correct dose for bigger women," says Kellie Schneider, MD, a gynecologic oncologist at the University of Alabama at Birmingham. "But underdosing can mean the difference between life and death."

Doctors have long known that obese women are more likely to die of ovarian and breast cancers, but when Dr. Schneider and her colleagues recently gave a group of overweight ovarian cancer patients chemotherapy based on their *actual* weights, they found that the women were as likely to survive the illness as thinner patients. "Doctors aren't intentionally under-treating overweight women," Dr. Schneider says. "We're just working with limited information."

Why Heavy Patients Can't Find Help

There are no studies on how often doctors refuse to treat patients because of their weight. But Sondra Solovay, an Oakland, California, attorney and author of *Tipping the Scales of*

Justice: Fighting Weight-Based Discrimination, says she hears enough anecdotes to believe it's commonplace.

Because of recent studies about various complications, A.J. Yates Jr., MD, associate professor in the Department of Orthopaedic Surgery at the University of Pittsburgh Medical Center, says there are legitimate concerns about operating on patients with a very high body mass index (BMI). But Dr. Yates also notes that some surgeons are reluctant to offer surgery to very overweight patients because the operations are more difficult and time-consuming.

And because data on surgical-complication rates is often calculated without accounting for the higher risk of an obese patient, even a few patients with complications can make the surgeon or hospital look bad to insurance companies. "If hospitals feel they're not looking good they could put subtle pressure on surgeons to avoid risky patients," Dr. Yates says. His concern is that overweight people could be increasingly discriminated against because of this.

Suzy Smith, a 5-foot-3, 400-pound woman from Colonial Beach, Virginia, believes she was one of those people. When her doctor found a large tumor on her kidney, she struggled to find a surgeon who would treat her. Her urologist said that the hospital where he practiced didn't have a table sturdy enough to hold her, and he referred her to a surgeon several hours away. "As soon as that doctor walked in the room, I could tell something was wrong by the look on his face," she says. "He told me he wouldn't operate. He wouldn't risk it," she says. Instead, he offered her cryoablation—a technique that freezes and removes tissue but is less effective than surgery for large tumors.

"I was so shocked," Smith says. "He was basically telling me he wouldn't do the thing that was the most likely to save my life." Finally, in early-December 2008, a doctor removed the tumor. The surgery, after all the preceding drama, was anticlimactic. "It went fantastically well," Smith says. "My doctors were really pleased." But the overall experience, she says, was degrading and disheartening. "Here I was trying to deal with a diagnosis of cancer, worrying that the cancer might spread with every day that went by, and the medical field was closing doors on me left and right."

Infertile couples who are told they can't have in vitro fertilization (IVF) because of the woman's weight also feel doors shutting. Most fertility clinics have stringent rules. "I'd say 95 percent won't do IVF on a woman with a BMI higher than 39 [5-foot-4, weighing 228 pounds, for example], and they usually require an electrocardiogram (EKG) and blood tests if it's higher than 34, because being overweight reduces your chance of getting pregnant and having a healthy pregnancy," says Laurence Jacobs, MD, of Fertility Centers of Illinois. In most cases, he can't accept a patient with a BMI of 40, even if she has no other health issues, because IVF typically takes place in an outpatient setting that's not set up for the higher anesthesia risks associated with obese patients. "No anesthesiologist is going to take that risk for someone who's not willing to make the effort to lose weight," Dr. Jacobs says.

Even more worrisome, a study from Duke University found that obese patients were less likely to receive procedures like cardiac catheterization that can help diagnose and treat heart

How to Get the Care You Deserve

Here, ways women can speak out for better care and more respectful treatment—and get the help they need to reach a healthier weight:

- **Find a physician who isn't fatphobic.** Ask for referrals from heavier friends. Doctors who have struggled with their own weight may be more understanding.
- **Take a friend with you.** "A clinician is much less likely to treat someone badly when there's a witness," says Pat Lyons, RN, co-developer of *A Big Woman's Passport to Best Health,* a guide to overcoming barriers to health care.
- **Be your own advocate.** Have your doc run your numbers so you have all of your measures of health, from body mass index (BMI) to cholesterol and blood sugar. Ask for an assessment of your health based on the big picture.
- **Ask for tools.** Tell your doctor you're interested in sustainable health habits, like walking and eating right. Request a reasonable healthy weight and BMI range so you have goal.
- **Dig deeper.** If you've tried and tried and still can't lose weight, insist that your doc give you more help. For some people there's a medical reason for weight gain that goes beyond lifestyle choices, including medications or conditions that might cause weight gain. "We're trying to educate doctors so they provide obese women with more sensitive and in-depth care," says Keith Bachman, MD, a weight-management expert with Kaiser Permanente's Care Management Institute. The goal: to help doctors see the whole patient and look for all the possible causes of weight gain.
- **Stick to your symptoms.** During your visit say, "Here are the symptoms I'm concerned about. I know some health problems can be caused by weight, but I'd like you to focus on the symptoms I'm here to see you about."
- **Get the doctor you deserve.** If you feel your doctor isn't giving you the kind of care you deserve, find a new one. "When I asked physicians what they would do if they perceived a negative attitude from their doctor, each one said he or she would find another doctor," says Harvard's Jerome Groopman, MD. It's your right to do the same.

disease, perhaps because doctors are concerned about potential complications, says lead author William Yancy Jr., MD, an associate professor at Duke and a staff physician at the VA Medical Center in Durham, North Carolina. Because of the high risk of heart disease in obese patients, the benefits of catheterization may outweigh the risks, he says. "But if the tests aren't performed, heavy patients may not receive appropriate therapy."

Even organ transplants may be withheld because of weight. Patients with BMIs higher than 35—if you're, say, 5 feet

4 inches tall and weigh 205 pounds—are typically less likely to be given a kidney or liver transplant because of the increased risk of postsurgery complications, including infections, blood clots, and pneumonia.

"It's a very difficult issue," says Shawn Pelletier, MD, surgical director of liver transplants at the University of Michigan Health System in Ann Arbor. "We have an obligation to use donor organs in a responsible way. But this is lifesaving surgery, and we don't want to turn people away. Obese kidney-transplant patients may not survive as long as thinner patients, but they live an average of three times longer than if they didn't get the transplant. That's a big benefit, even if there are risks."

Many experts believe the issue goes beyond the strictly medical and into the arena of ethics. "Doctors need to ask themselves, 'Is this obese person less deserving of medical care than the same person would be after weight-loss surgery?'" says Barbara Thompson, vice-chair of the Obesity Action Coalition, a nonprofit advocacy group. "How do we determine whether a person's weight somehow justifies withholding needed medical care or whether bias by providers is the reason treatment is denied?" Yale's Rebecca Puhl asks. "It's an extremely important question with significant implications."

Fat People Get No Respect

When Celina Reeder, a 5-foot-5, 185-pound woman with a torn ligament in her right knee, was told by her surgeon she needed to stop eating so much fast food before he would schedule surgery, the Woodacre, California, woman was astounded. "I left his office feeling ashamed," she recalls. "And I don't even eat fast food! The more I thought about it, the madder I got. So I switched surgeons. Anybody who thinks doctors treat heavy women the same as thin women has obviously never had a weight problem. I really felt like my doctor didn't respect me."

She may have been right. University of Pennsylvania researchers found that more than 50 percent of primary care physicians viewed obese patients as awkward, unattractive, and noncompliant; one third said they were weak-willed, sloppy, and lazy. In addition, researchers at Rice University and the University of Texas School of Public Health in Houston found that as patient BMI increased doctors reported liking their jobs less and having less patience and desire to help the patient.

Whether they know it or not, doctors' attitudes may actually encourage unhealthy behavior. Feeling dissed about their weight can make some women turn to food for comfort. "Stigma is a form of stress, and many obese women cope by eating or refusing to diet," Puhl says. "So weight bias could actually fuel obesity."

Studies have also found that overweight women are more likely to delay doctors' appointments and preventive care, including screenings for cancer, because they don't want to face criticism. "It can be frustrating to treat obese patients,"

admits Lee Green, MD, MPH, a professor of family medicine at the University of Michigan in Ann Arbor. "I spend most of my time treating the consequences of unhealthy lifestyles instead of actual illnesses. People come in complaining of foot or knee pain, and I'm thinking, *Do you not see that you're in pain because you're 60 pounds overweight?* I don't say that, of course. I try to encourage them to lose weight."

Seeing heavy patients was *a waste of time*, doctors admitted in one survey.

Dr. Green seems to be in the minority when it comes to focusing on weight-loss solutions. One study found that just 11 percent of overweight patients received weight-loss counseling when they visited a family-practice doctor.

A Healthy-Weight Wakeup Call

Without a doubt, the medical community needs to take a hard look at the secret biases that may be coloring how they care for overweight women. But some progress is being made. The National Institutes of Health has been encouraging researchers to start identifying and fixing the barriers heavy people face when trying to get health care, says Susan Yanovski, MD, co-director of the Office of Obesity Research at the National Institute of Diabetes and Digestive and Kidney Diseases. And some hospitals are adding larger surgical instruments, wheelchairs, and other equipment.

There's an even bigger problem, though: when heavy women are ignored, the obesity epidemic is ignored, too—and that has to stop, experts say. "Being mistreated or dismissed by your doctor because of your weight is unacceptable. But what's just as important is that doctors are missing an opportunity to help their patients lose weight and improve their health," says Dr. Huizinga of Johns Hopkins. "Doctors and patients need to be able to speak openly about weight-related issues, whether it's the diseases caused by excess weight or the reasons why a patient overeats. That level of conversation requires a certain degree of comfort, and the basis for that is mutual respect, plain and simple," she says. "That's how we can help *all* women get healthier."

Critical Thinking

1. Why are overweight women less likely to receive quality health care?
2. How can being overweight affect your health insurance?
3. How can a doctor's attitude encourage unhealthy behavior?
4. What health benefits are difficult for overweight people to get?

From *Health*, January/February 2010, pp. 142,144–145,198,201. Copyright © 2010 by Ginny Graves. Reprinted by permission of the author.

UNIT 10

Contemporary Health Hazards

Unit Selections

Learning Outcomes

After reading this Unit, you will be able to:

- Describe traumatic brain injury (TBI) and posttraumatic stress disorder (PTSD) and explain why these conditions can be difficult to diagnose.

- Explain the risks associated with the "choking game."

- Understand the relationship between the human papillomavirus and oral cancer.

- Understand the health and environmental risks associated with fracking.

- Explain the risks associated with contracting MRSA.

- Discuss who is most likely to contract MRSA.

- Discuss the risks related to radiation exposure.

Student Website

www.mhhe.com/cls

Internet References

Centers for Disease Control
www.cdc.gov
Environmental Protection Agency
www.epa.gov
Food and Drug Administration
www.fda.gov
World Health Organization
www.who.org

This unit examines a variety of contemporary health hazards that Americans face on a daily basis. What are the most pressing contemporary health hazards today? We've conquered or controlled many of the killers of the 18th and 19th centuries including smallpox, tuberculosis, polio, leprosy, diphtheria, and tetanus. And with the discovery of the germ theory, antibiotics, and the advent of vaccinations and immunizations, most of the diseases that plagued humans are now ancient history. Because of these and other advancements in modern medical science we're living longer and healthier than ever. But new killers have developed in the last century including new and newly emerged infectious diseases and the growing problem of antibiotic resistance. We face newly recognized diseases such as Methicillin-Resistant *Staphlococcus aureus,* (MRSA), Avian Flu, Severe Acute Respiratory Syndrome (SARS), AIDS, mad cow disease, West Nile virus, and drug-resistant tuberculosis have emerged while the primary killers of Americans continues to be heart disease and cancer.

© Tomi/PhotoLink/Getty Images

In addition, some diseases may have their causes rooted in environmental factors. During the 1970s and 1980s, Americans became deeply concerned about environmental changes that affect the air, water, and food we take in. While some improvements have been observed in these areas, much remains to be done, as new areas of concern continue to emerge. Global warming is responsible for climatic changes, including an increase in the number of earthquakes, hurricanes, and other natural disasters such as flooding and rising global temperatures. Rising global temperatures may increase the number of vector-borne diseases as insects who spread disease are increasing and moving north as temperatures rise. Other environmental hazards include the hole in the ozone layer which may be responsible for increasing cases of skin cancer.

While this unit focuses on exogenous factors that influence our state of health, it is important to remember that health is a dynamic state representing the degree of harmony or balance that exists between endogenous and exogenous factors. This concept of balance applies to the environment as well. Due to the intimate relationship that exists between people, animals, and their environment, it is impossible to promote the concept of wellness without also safeguarding the quality of our environment, both the physical and the social.

Six articles were chosen for this unit representing a variety of contemporary health-related hazards. Author Denise Grady addresses radiation concerns following another natural disaster, the earthquake and tsunami that occurred in Japan in the spring of 2011. Radiation from nuclear power plants is a potentially serious problem following earthquakes and tsunamis. While long-term consequences are not known, scientists continue to assess the risk to public health in that country which may also impact the future of nuclear energy. While the disaster in Japan was

natural, a human-created process called liquid fracturing (fracking) may contribute to drinking and ground water pollution. The process, described in "Drilling into the Unknown," is a means of natural gas extraction. Some states, including New York, has put a moratorium on fracking until more is known about the potential hazards associated with the process.

In the article "MRSA: Hospitals Step up Fight. Will It Be Enough?," author Julius A. Karash addresses the growing health problem related to this drug-resistant bacterial infection. It is a particular concern among the institutionalized elderly and in any place where many people are in close contact with each other. MRSA is also a serious risk in the community, spreading among people of all ages and health status who are in close contact such as gyms. This section also addresses a new and growing threat discussed in "The New Sex Cancer." Author Alyssa Giacobbe offers information on oral cancer, which can be caused by the sexually transmitted disease human papillomavirus via oral sex. Men are at risk of oropharyngeal cancer which is also caused by smoking and alcohol consumption. Other issues addressed in this section include the relationship between post-traumatic stress disorder and traumatic brain injuries such as concussions among American soldiers returning from fighting in the Middle East. Finally, the choking game is presented in "Discovering Teenagers' Risky 'Game' Too Late." Author Pauline W. Chen discusses a very dangerous game played by teens in an attempt to get high. They strangle themselves until just before they lose consciousness, typically using a noose. The Centers for Disease Control and Prevention reported 82 deaths related to the choking game and related activities. Many of those who participate try strangulation in the hope of attaining a legal high.

The Warrior's Brain

One family's terrifying medical mystery could represent the military's next big crisis.

ANDREW BAST

B rooke Brown, the wife of Marine Lance Cpl. David Brown, explains how her life changed after her young husband returned home from Iraq with mild Traumatic Brain Injury and PTSD.

The worst was the day Brooke Brown came home to find her husband with a shotgun in his mouth. But there had been plenty of bad days before that: after he returned from a deployment in Iraq, Lance Cpl. David Brown would start shaking in crowded places. Sitting down for a family meal had become nearly impossible: in restaurants he'd frantically search for the quickest exit route. He couldn't concentrate; he couldn't do his job. The Marine Corps placed him on leave prior to discharging him. Brooke quit her job to care for him and the children. The bills piled up.

It sounds like another troubling story of a war vet struggling with PTSD. But Brown's case is more complicated. In addition to the anxiety, he suffered a succession of mild seizures until a devastating grand mal episode sent him to the hospital covered in his own blood, vomit, and excrement. There were also vision problems and excruciating headaches that had plagued him since he'd been knocked to the ground by a series of mortar blasts in Fallujah four years earlier.

Brown, now 23, didn't have any visible injuries, but clearly the man who left for Iraq was not the same man who returned. "Our middle son clings to David; he knows something is wrong," Brooke, 22, explained late this summer. "Our 4-year-old doesn't know what caused it, but he knows Daddy's sick and he needs help."

But what kind of help does Corporal Brown need? His case perplexed civilian doctors and the Department of Veterans Affairs. The headaches and seizures suggest that he is suffering from the aftereffects of an undiagnosed concussion—or, in the current jargon, mild traumatic brain injury (TBI). But some of his symptoms seem consistent with a psychological condition, posttraumatic stress disorder (PTSD). Or could it be both—and if so, are they reinforcing one another in some kind of vicious cycle? The person who knows David better than anyone, his wife, thinks it was hardly a coincidence that one of his worst seizures came on the day last year that his best friend was deployed with the Second Battalion, Eighth Marines, as part of President Obama's surge into Afghanistan.

David Brown's symptoms have placed him at the vanguard of military medicine, where doctors, officials, and politicians are puzzling out the connection between head injuries and PTSD, and the role each plays in both physical and psychological post-combat illness.

Invisible Wounds

The military reports that 144,453 service members have suffered battlefield concussions in the last decade; a study out of Fort Carson argues that that number misses at least 40 percent of cases. By definition, a concussion is a shaking of the brain that results from a blow to the head. Typical symptoms include headache, memory loss, and general confusion. For decades, head injuries were a challenge mainly for civilian doctors, who studied the results of auto accidents and football injuries. The best treatment, it was generally thought, was rest and time. And in the great majority of these civilian cases, the brain heals by itself in as little as a week.

Concussions sustained on the battlefield are another matter, and a vexing one. According to the Department of Veterans Affairs, symptoms such as vision, memory, and speech problems, dizziness, depression, and anxiety last far longer in men and women returning from combat. Why? Doctors suspect that the high-stress combat environment stifles the kind of recovery that would normally occur. More often than not, those unlucky enough to suffer a concussion in Afghanistan, or especially in Iraq, do so in stifling heat, "which can make the effects of a concussion worse," says David Hovda, director of the UCLA Brain Injury Research Center. Then there's the question of reinjury before full recovery. If an injured fighter reports symptoms that match the concussion watch list, he or she is pulled from action for 24 hours. (There's currently no test for a concussion besides self-diagnosis, though the military is actively pursuing biomarker tests that could be done on site.) But in a macho military culture, admitting unseen symptoms that can take you out of the action doesn't happen as often as it should. "If you ain't bleeding, you ain't hurt," says Brooke of the military culture around head injuries.

Blood or not, evidence is mounting that battlefield concussions from these two long-running wars could result in decades of serious and expensive health-care issues for a significant number of veterans. After all, TBI is a relatively new problem of modern warfare. Thanks to technological advances, warriors are surviving what once would have been fatal blasts—but the long-term consequences of the impact are still unknown. Two years ago, the RAND Corporation published a comprehensive study, "The Invisible Wounds of War," which highlighted brain injuries as a massive, and little-understood, mental-health issue for returning combat veterans. This summer the nonprofit journalism site ProPublica chronicled challenges in diagnosis of head trauma and breakdowns in care within the military medical system. Around the same time, the Senate Armed Services Committee called the brass from each of the military branches and the Department of Veterans Affairs to testify on the topic, and at the hearing senators expressed concern that head trauma may be a factor in service-member suicide.

The military's concerns have arisen during something of a boom in concussion research in civilian institutions, and new research in sustained head trauma in athletes shows that repeated concussions can lead to a condition called chronic traumatic encephalopathy. This disorder, which can present 10 to 15 years after the initial trauma, is linked to depression and suicidal thoughts, as well as Parkinson's, dementia, and even a devastating neurological condition resembling Lou Gehrig's disease. Another study found that those who abused drugs and alcohol after a TBI had drastically increased rates of suicide attempts.

Suicide is a serious threat to the military: an August 2010 report by the Department of Defense showed that the military suicide rate comes to one death every 36 hours. In the past, suicide has been associated with PTSD—an issue armed forces across the world have been struggling with for years. "Nostalgia" afflicted Napoleon's troops fighting his endless campaigns far from home. "Traumatic neurosis" and "shell shock" overcame British troops in the trenches of World War I. Col. John Bradley, head of psychiatry at Walter Reed Army Medical Center, describes today's PTSD as the inability to dial back on the instincts necessary for survival in combat even long after one is out of danger. "If you go back to your family and you still feel like you're in mortal danger, that creates a problem," says Bradley. A common estimate inside the military is that 20 percent of veterans in combat experience symptoms of posttraumatic stress. Some 2.1 million service members have been deployed to Iraq and Afghanistan—implying more than 400,000 potential cases.

Connecting the Dots

But in Iraq and Afghanistan, the symptoms of PTSD are often complicated by TBI—a condition seen as a consequence of the fact that, thanks to better battlefield technology and medical care, more soldiers are surviving blasts that proved deadly in previous wars. Figuring out what's caused by PTSD and what's the result of a head injury isn't easy, especially since the symptoms of TBI overlap with those of PTSD. "You may have been injured, may have lost a buddy during an attack," says Bradley. "Traumatic brain injury has both a physical and psychological component, and so does PTSD." After a concussion, one is almost certain to have headaches, but headaches are also common among people with a mental-health disorder. Concussions cause trouble sleeping—and so can PTSD. Difficulty concentrating is common to both. "It's very difficult to determine if it's a psychological problem or the results of an organic brain injury," says Terry Schell, a behavioral scientist at RAND.

The Road Home

Scientists are just starting to understand if and how the two are connected. It's been shown in animal models that a head trauma can make one more susceptible to PTSD. "Minor traumatic brain injury does not necessarily cause PTSD, but it puts the brain in a biochemical and metabolic state that enhances the chances of acquiring posttraumatic stress disorder," says UCLA's Hovda, who is part of a civilian task force of doctors and scientists commissioned by the military to assess how PTSD and TBI affect troops. They'll meet in December to discuss whether troops suffering from both should receive special medical treatment. Hovda also played a key role in the development of the National Intrepid Center of Excellence, a military medical facility in Bethesda, Md., devoted to the care of returning vets who suffer from PTSD and/or head trauma. "When they get to Bethesda, or get home, a lot of times individuals will be suffering from symptoms related to these multiple concussions," he says. "They don't understand that it's related to a brain injury, and they become very depressed and confused."

Murray Stein, a neurologist at the University of California, San Diego, is leading a consortium of doctors and specialists through several clinical trials investigating the long-term effects of concussions mixed with high-stress situations. Stein suspects there's more to the long-term effects of battlefield brain injuries than we now understand. "Right now it's extremely controversial," he says. "It's simply too simplistic to suggest [TBI] and emotional symptoms can't be linked."

There's not a lot research as of yet. Early on in the Iraq War, Col. Charles Hoge, then the director of mental-health research at Walter Reed Army Medical Center, surveyed some 2,700 soldiers about battlefield concussions and PTSD, as well as the extent of their injuries and the state of their current mental and physical health (relying on self-reported measures like days of work missed). In 2008, *The New England Journal of Medicine* published Hoge's findings: battlefield concussions existed, perhaps in significant numbers, but "cognitive problems, rage, sleep disturbance, fatigue, headaches, and other symptoms" that had become commonplace among service members back home resulted almost entirely from PTSD. Hoge argued that attributing postcombat symptoms to the effect of concussions, which "usually resolve rapidly," could lead to a large number of military personnel receiving treatment for the wrong problem—treatment that could actually make things worse for the patient and put undue strain on the health-care system.

In an interview with NEWSWEEK, Hoge agreed that there was a connection between the two conditions. "PTSD and battlefield concussions are interrelated, and they have to be treated as such," he said. But he's also standing by his findings that one should not be confused for the other. In his new book, Once a Warrior, Always a Warrior, published earlier this year as a mental-health handbook for veterans and their families, Hoge reiterates that "concussions/TBIs have also become entangled and confused with PTSD." Battlefield concussions, he writes, are best diagnosed at the time of injury, and the more time that elapses, the more difficult it becomes to link symptoms to the incident.

That much is true: with shoddy records of brain injuries from the early parts of the wars in Iraq and Afghanistan, many veterans who could be afflicted by the long-term effects of battlefield concussions will have little—if any—documentation to rely on in their claims for disability benefits. And as evidenced by Lance Cpl. David Brown, in some cases those men and women could require a significant amount of ongoing care.

The Path Ahead

There's another, unsettling reality, of course: that PTSD and TBI are far from the only culprits for Brown's mystery symptoms. "Headaches are almost useless as a diagnostic," says Barry Willer, professor of psychology at the University of Buffalo and an expert on concussions. He notes that headaches present for a large number of illnesses. And depression, anxiety, and trouble sleeping? Those are often the result of living with an unexplainable illness. In reality, the troops are coming home with myriad medical issues, some new, like TBI; some, like PTSD, as old as war itself; and some a hybrid of the two.

The question is whether we have the tools and treatments to figure out which is which.

Brown finally found some respite thanks to Tim Maxwell, a fellow Marine, who was pierced in the skull with shrapnel in Iraq and later lost his leg to mortar fire. Maxwell has established a quiet network of wounded warriors and maintains a Web site on the topic, SemperMax. Earlier this year, he got wind of Brown's struggle and helped get him back into the Marines and into the TBI ward at the National Naval Medical Center in Bethesda. Today, Brown's back at Camp Lejeune, readmitted to the Marines and working to get medically retired. "I spend most of my time over at the wounded-warrior tent doing rehab," he says. He's taking Topamax, a drug usually prescribed to epileptics to stave off seizures, and it seems to be effective, despite the side effects. "He's lost his speech for 30 minutes a couple of times," Brooke says, but he hasn't had any more grand mal seizures. His wife is fighting for him at every turn. "I'm going to stand by my man," she said in August, and then stiffened her spine. "He stood for me over in Iraq. The least I can do is stand by him now."

Critical Thinking

1. Discuss the relationship between post-traumatic stress disorder (PTSD) and traumatic brain injuries.

2. Address the psychological aspects of traumatic brain injuries.

3. Do veterans suffering from PTSD receive adequate medical treatment?

Discovering Teenagers' Risky "Game" Too Late

Pauline W. Chen, MD

The patient was tall, with legs that extended to the very end of the operating table, a chest barely wider than his 16-year-old hips and a chin covered with pimples and peach fuzz.

He looked like any number of boys I knew in high school, I reflected. And then the other transplant surgeons and I began the operation to remove the dead boy's liver, kidneys, pancreas, lungs and heart.

We knew the organs would be perfect. He had been a healthy teenager, and the cause of death was not a terrible, mutilating car or motorcycle crash.

The boy had hanged himself. He had been discovered early, though not early enough to have survived.

While I had operated on more than a few suicide victims, I had never come across someone so young who had chosen to die in this way. I asked one of the nurses who had spent time with the family about the circumstances. Was he depressed? Had anyone ever suspected? Who found him?

"He was playing the choking game," she said quietly.

I stopped what I was doing and, not believing I had heard correctly, turned to look straight at her.

"You know that game where kids try to get high," she explained. "They strangle themselves until just before they lose consciousness." She put her hand on the boy's arm and continued: "Problem was that this poor kid couldn't wiggle out of the noose he had made for himself. His parents found him hanging by his belt on his bedroom doorknob."

That image comes rushing back whenever I meet another victim or read about the grim mortality statistics associated with this "game." But one thing has haunted me even more in the years since that night. As a doctor who counts adolescents among her patients, I knew nothing about the choking game before I cared for a child who had died playing it.

Some try strangulation in the hopes of attaining a legal high.

Until recently, there has been little attention among health care professionals to this particular form of youthful thrill-seeking. What has been known, however, is that those ages 7 to 21 participate in such activities alone or in groups, holding their breath, strangling one another or dangling in a noose in the hopes of attaining a legal high.

Two years ago the Centers for Disease Control and Prevention reported 82 deaths attributable to the choking game and related activities. This year the C.D.C. released the results of the first statewide survey and found that 1 in 3 eighth graders in Oregon had heard of the game, while more than 1 in 20 had participated.

The popularity of the choking game may be due in part to the misguided belief that it is safe. In one recent study, almost half of the youths surveyed believed there was no risk associated with the game. And unlike other risk-taking behaviors like alcohol or drug abuse, where doctors and parents can counsel teenagers on the dangers involved, no one is countering this gross misperception regarding the safety of near strangulation.

Why? Because like me that night in the operating room, many of my colleagues have no clue that such a game even exists.

This month in the journal *Pediatrics,* researchers from the Rainbow Babies and Children's Hospital in Cleveland reported that almost a third of physicians surveyed were unaware of the choking game. These physicians could not describe any of the 11 warning signs, which include bloodshot eyes and frequent and often severe headaches. And they failed to identify any of the 10 alternative names for the choking game, startlingly benign monikers like "Rush," "Space Monkey," "Purple Dragon" and "Funky Chicken."

"Doctors have a unique opportunity to see and prevent this," the senior author of the study, Dr. Nancy E. Bass, an associate professor of pediatrics and neurology at Case Western Reserve University, said in an interview. "But how are they going to educate parents and patients if they don't know about it?"

In situations where a patient may be contemplating or already participating in choking activities, frank discussions about the warning signs can be particularly powerful. "The sad thing about these cases," Dr. Bass observed, "is that every parent says, 'If we had known what to look for, we probably could have prevented this.'" One set of parents told Dr. Bass that they had noticed knotted scarves and ties on a closet rod in their son's room weeks before his death.

"They had the telltale signs," Dr. Bass said, "but they never knew what to look for."

Broaching the topic can be difficult for parents and doctors alike. Some parents worry that talking about such activities will paradoxically encourage adolescents to participate. "But that's kind of a naïve thought," Dr. Bass countered. "Children can go to the Internet and YouTube to learn about the choking game." In another study published last year, for example, Canadian researchers found 65 videos of the choking game on YouTube over an 11-day period. The videos showed various techniques of strangulation and were viewed almost 175,000 times. But, added Dr. Bass, "these videos don't say that kids can die from doing this."

Few doctors discuss these types of activities with their adolescent patients. Only two doctors in Dr. Bass's study reported ever having tackled the topic because of a lack of time. "Talking about difficult topics is really hard to do," Dr. Bass noted, "when you just have 15 minutes to follow up."

But it is even harder when neither doctor nor patient has any idea of what the activity is or of its lethal consequences.

Based on the results of their study, Dr. Bass and her co-investigators have started programs that educate doctors, particularly those in training, about the warning signs and dangers of strangulation activities. "The choking game may not be as prominent as some of the other topics we cover when we talk with patients," Dr. Bass said, "but it results in death.

"If we don't talk to doctors about this issue, they won't know about the choking game until one of their patients dies."

Critical Thinking

1. Why do some teenagers play the choking game?
2. What are the risks associated with the choking game?
3. What can be done to prevent teens from playing the choking game?

The New Sex Cancer

Doctors used to think this STD threatened only women. Then the men stalled dying.

ALYSSA GIACOBBE

Eric Statler's wisdom teeth were impacted. Inconvenient, sure, but certainly not life threatening. As general manager of a hotel in Idaho's picturesque Clearwater County, Statler spent his 12-hour days charming and chatting up guests, which meant he couldn't afford a week of bloated cheeks and Percocet. Nor, given his myriad responsibilities at the hotel, did Statler feel he could justify time off for at-home recovery. So he procrastinated until the pain was almost unbearable and eating a turkey sandwich felt like chewing tacks.

Two months after he finally underwent the operation. Statler was still waiting for relief—his molars were gone but the pain remained. Not only did he find it excruciating to chew, but now he was losing weight and beginning to feel emotionally beat down. He decided to return to his dentist, who sent him to a local ear, nose, and throat specialist the same day. The ENT needed just minutes to solve the mystery: He took one look at Statler and said, "Son, I think you have cancer."

Statler couldn't believe it. A former college athlete, he still ran nearly every day, never smoked, and drank only a few beers a week. "My wife used to say I was the healthiest man she'd ever known," he says. The average oral cancer patient, by contrast, is a lifelong smoker or heavy drinker in his mid-60s.

But the definition of "average" has slowly been changing, as more and more oral cancer diagnoses are being handed down across the country to otherwise healthy young men. Statler soon learned that he was part of this emerging subset of oral cancer patients, a group of guys who all share one unlikely risk factor: HPV. an undetectable and untreatable STD that may act like tinder for tumors.

An Invisible Enemy

You've probably heard of human papillomavirus, or HPV, the rampant sexually transmitted disease most often associated with cervical cancer in women. How rampant? Odds are good that you once had the virus, you have it now, or you will contract it soon. In fact, the CDC estimates that half of all sexually active people become HPV positive at some time in their lives. With 6 million new infections each year. HPV is the most widely spread and overexposed STD we've ever known—the Kim Kardashian of communicable diseases, if you will.

The reason HPV moves around the way it does has to do with its stealth: In 99 percent of cases, the disease is symptom-free. (The remaining 1 percent present as bumpy, cauliflowery warts on the penis or groin area in men and in and around the vagina in women.) Most people infected with HPV have no idea they have it, who they contracted it from, or that they could be infecting others.

Cancer researchers have known about HPV's connection with cervical cancer since the 1970s, but they've only recently discovered a similar link between the virus and oral cancer. For years, the rate of new head and neck cancers had been declining in tandem with falling smoking rates. But then, after noticing a major upswing in the number of young nonsmokers being diagnosed with oropharyngeal cancer—a form of oral cancer found in the tonsils and in the base of the tongue—doctors at Johns Hopkins acted on a hunch and began testing cancerous tissue for HPV. The resulting study, published in the *New England Journal of Medicine,* revealed that exposure to HPV-16, a high-risk strain known to cause cervical cancer, made patients 32 times as likely to develop oropharyngeal cancer. By comparison, the previous top risk factors—a history of heavy smoking and a history of heavy drinking—were found to increase that risk by just 3 and 2.5 times, respectively.

"HPV is replacing alcohol and smoking as the leading cause of oropharyngeal cancer," says Ted Teknos, M.D., a professor of medicine in the head and neck oncology program at Ohio State University's comprehensive cancer center. HPV fuels cancerous growth in a man's mouth much as it does in a woman's cervix: by integrating into his DNA and hindering the function of proteins that are supposed to reduce cellular stress and suppress tumors.

Figures from the National Cancer Institute reveal that between 1998 and 2008, oropharyngeal cancer rates rose 36 percent in men—or 3.6 percent each year on average. And sometimes its victims are shockingly young, even men in their late 30s, says Robert. Haddad, M.D., chief of the center for head and neck oncology at the Dana-Farber Cancer Institute.

"Many of these cases are missed or diagnosed late because there are no symptoms until it's moved into the lymph nodes; plus, the patient is young and otherwise healthy." he says.

Many doctors view the increase in HPV-related oral cancer as a direct result of a change in sexual practices in the past decade—that is, our orally promiscuous ways. Because HPV is a locally invasive virus, it can spread to your mouth only through direct contact. (In other words, HPV in or around your penis won't "travel" on its own through your body to your mouth.) The most likely way to contract oral HPV is to perform oral sex on an infected partner. However, simply kissing someone who has oral HPV can also lead to infection, according to many researchers who believe that it's possible for HPV to be transmitted through saliva.

It should seem obvious, then, that oral sex is not safer sex—and that your chances of developing oral cancer increase with every type of sexual encounter. According to the same *New England Journal of Medicine* study, people who have had six or more oral sex partners over the course of their lifetime are nearly nine times as likely to develop oropharyngeal cancer.

"Many people don't think oral sex counts as sex," says Gregory Masters, M.D., an oncologist at the Helen F. Graham Cancer Center in Newark, Delaware, and a spokesman for the American Society of Clinical Oncology. "But oral sex comes with risks. And cancer may be one of them."

"Oral sex comes with risks. And cancer may be one of them."

Is Abstinence the Answer?

The day before Brian Hill was diagnosed with stage four oral cancer, he was skiing at Lake Tahoe. "I felt perfectly normal," recalls Hill, a nonsmoker then in his 40s. "I had no sores on my mouth as far as I was aware of, and no pain." He'd grown a beard for the winter, which unfortunately had camouflaged an enlarged, though painless, lymph node. "By the time I felt it, it was the size of an almond," he says.

After a course of antibiotics proved ineffective, an ear, nose, and throat doctor near Hill's home in Santa Fe performed a fine-needle biopsy and delivered the diagnosis: The lymph node contained cancerous tissue.

Hill, the owner of a medical-device company who'd sold his dental implant business a few years earlier, says he considered himself better educated in matters of oral health than the average person. And yet the tumor, which had originated in his right tonsil, had probably gone undetected for as long as 2 years.

At Houston's MD Anderson Cancer Center. Hill's doctors told him they'd been seeing a great number of nonsmokers with oral cancer, but didn't know why. Hill was treated, he recalls, with "everything but the kitchen sink." including chemo, radiation, and surgery to remove the right side of his neck. It was a brutal process during which he suffered from radiation sickness, relied on heavy-duty painkillers, ate through a tube for a year, and lost more than 50 pounds.

Hill eventually learned that his tumor tested positive for HPV-16, the subtype linked to oral cancer, although he had no idea that he had been carrying the virus. Nor would he have: Although gynecologists screen sexually active women for cervical HPV as part of routine annual exams, there is no commercially available HPV test for men and no reliable oral-HPV test for either sex.

Part of the reason no good screening options have been developed is because researchers and doctors share a "why bother?" mentality: In 90 percent of cases, a person's immune system will clear the virus naturally within 2 years, with no lasting implications. Furthermore, unlike cervical HPV—which can be managed by removing infected cells—there's no way to treat oral HPV.

But screening is also challenging because HPV is so very squirrelly: The virus can lie dormant and undetectable, yet transmissible, for years. This is why most doctors say it's pointless for people in monogamous relationships to change their sexual habits in the aftermath of an HPV-positive determination. Chances are, both partners have already been exposed.

For everyone else, however, most doctors do advise a change in sexual practice to reduce risk, including using protection when giving or receiving oral sex, and limiting your number of partners.

That said, there is one other promising preventive measure, at least for the next generation of men: vaccination. Two vaccines currently on the market—Gardasil and Cervarix—target HPV-16: they're 95 percent effective in girls and young women and 90 percent effective in boys and young men when administered before exposure to the strain. But despite the impressive percentages, vaccination is a controversial issue for many parents, in part because the possible side effects include fever, fainting, and (rarely) severe allergic reaction and blood clots. Some parents also have trouble with the idea of protecting their prepubescent kids from a virus related to sex, while other parents, mistakenly believing that HPV affects only girls (in the form of cervical cancer), assume that vaccinating boys is irrelevant. The result: Roughly 4 percent of boys have received the shot. Last year, in a move that may sway hesitant parents, the American Academy of Pediatrics included HPV in its schedule of vaccines for boys.

Got that, dads?

The Dentist Defense

Before you tick off your girlfriend and tell her you've decided to abstain from oral sex, keep in mind that several things have to go wrong for HPV to leave you DOA. First, you need to contract the dangerous HPV-16 strain of the disease (an estimated 1.5 percent of women have it). Next, your immune system has to come up short in trying to clear the virus. And then, even if these two conditions are met, you still may not develop cancer. But if you do? Doctors point out that compared with tobacco-related oral cancer, those cancers associated with HPV are much more beatable.

"The cure rates are in the 80 to 90 percent range, assuming patients are nonsmokers," says Dr. Haddad. "Part of the reason is that these patients are younger and in good shape and can tolerate aggressive treatment."

Consider Bryan Hill. He's been cancer-free for more than a decade, during which he founded the nonprofit Oral Cancer Foundation, a charity that sponsors research, patient support, and public awareness. Statler is also in remission; however, like Hill, he needed radiation, chemotherapy, and extensive surgery—doctors removed 44 cancerous lymph nodes and half his jaw.

Even though Statler's and Hill's cases are success stories, earlier diagnosis would have made their treatment and recovery less invasive and less physically taxing. In most cases, this means spotting a premalignant lesion or change in mouth tissue. While researchers are looking into the possibility of using DNA samples to detect precancerous changes in oral tissue cells, that technology is still years away. Until then, your dentist may be your best hope.

The American Dental Association recommends that dentists perform regular visual and physical exams to look for changes in and around the mouth and throat. No one else knows their way around this part of your body like they do. Ideally, the dentist will catch a tissue change before it becomes dangerous, or spot an abnormal growth in its early stages.

John C. Comisi, D.D.S., a dentist in private practice in Ithaca, New York, says he's caught dozens of precancerous lesions in the mouths of men as young as their 30s. "Anything that looks abnormal or persists over a period of a few weeks should be tested." says Dr. Comisi. "Any abnormality should be treated aggressively and removed. You can't be too sure."

Of course, no dentist will catch everything—just ask Statler, who was told his tumor pain was a toothache. That's why every man should be aware of the possible warning signs of oral cancer: persistent sore throat, hoarseness or unexplained cough, painful sores, any swelling in your lymph nodes or neck, or a change in your voice or trouble swallowing. Your dentist or an ENT specialist should vet any suspicious condition present for longer than 2 weeks.

There's one more thing: Keep enjoying your sex life. You may never contract HPV, let alone develop cancer. But if you live in fear of either possibility, you'll be giving in to an affliction that no surgery or chemotherapy can beat. Statler certainly hasn't backed down: "For now, my wife and I haven't changed what we do in the bedroom." he says. "I just try to have as much sex with her as I can."

"The tumor in his right tonsil had probably gone undetected for 2 years."

Critical Thinking

1. What are the risks associated with infection with human papillomavirus?
2. Why are men at increased risk for oropharyngeal cancer?
3. Why is this called a sex cancer?

Drilling into the Unknown

Fracking is causing a furore in the US and Europe over possible health effects, but are the concerns justified? Peter Aldhous finds the evidence is scarce.

PETER ALDHOUS

You could call it a fracking mess. Fracturing deep shale deposits by injecting them with water, sand and chemicals at high pressure—with the aim of releasing the gas they hold—is causing concern worldwide. In New York State, officials seeking to lift a 2010 moratorium on fracking are sifting through 40,000 public comments on a proposal to regulate the process. Even by the famously opinionated standards of the Empire State, it's an unprecedented response.

Fracking has taken off in a big way in the north-east US in the past few years, particularly in the huge Marcellus Shale formation, which sits beneath New York, Pennsylvania and other Appalachian states. By 2035, US shale gas production is likely to more than double, according to government projections. While that should be good for the climate, providing a cleaner alternative to coal, the dash for gas has triggered its own environmental controversies. Concerns about tainted drinking water lead the way.

So far, evidence that fracking poses serious risks to human health or the environment—beyond the pollution associated with fossil fuel extraction—is scant. But studies are few and hard to interpret, and feelings are running high: neighbours of new fracking operations complain of problems like breathing difficulties, nausea and headaches. "When the public is confused, the public is angry," says Bernard Goldstein, an environmental toxicologist at the University of Pittsburgh, Pennsylvania.

"Neighbours of new fracking operations complain of breathing difficulties and nausea ..."

These concerns could even bring the shale gas bandwagon to a halt. "If action is not taken to reduce the environmental impact ... there is a real risk of serious environmental consequences causing a loss of public confidence that could delay or stop this activity," advisers to US energy secretary Steven Chu concluded late last year.

Officials in New York State are expected to decide on how to proceed by the end of the year. Their deliberations will be watched across the globe. Many nations have shale deposits that could hugely increase natural gas production, but opposition to their exploitation is growing. Lawmakers in France and Bulgaria have voted to ban fracking, and in the UK, small earthquakes triggered by fracking have caused alarm.

In fact, fracking has been around for decades. Traditionally, water was pumped into vertical wells to liberate shallower reserves of "tight gas" trapped in rocks like sandstone. What has changed is the introduction of technology that allows multiple wells to be drilled from the same pad, then run horizontally over thousands of metres through deep shale beds. The amount of water pumped into these wells is far greater than in tight-gas fracking.

The technology was first deployed in Texas in the early 2000s, to little public complaint. It was a different story when production started to take off in Appalachia, where people are not used to oil and gas exploration.

The water used in fracking contains sand, to hold new cracks open, plus small quantities of chemical additives. Their identity is often kept secret by drilling companies, but they may include lubricants like mineral oil, ethylene glycol to prevent scale build-up, and glutaraldehyde to inhibit bacterial growth. Between 10 and 40 per cent of the water flows straight back up the well pipe within a couple of weeks. Once the flowback slows, gas can be collected, along with a small amount of "produced water".

Fracking fluid may be harmful. In addition to the additives, it can pick up toxic salts and volatile organic compounds such as benzene, xylene and phenols from the rock. Geologists say this mixture is unlikely to percolate up through a couple of thousand metres of impermeable rock to reach the shallow groundwater used for drinking. Indeed, the clearest evidence of groundwater pollution comes from a much shallower tight-gas frack. In December, the US Environmental Protection Agency (EPA) reported that groundwater near Pavillion, Wyoming, was contaminated with chemicals including fracking additives. In this case, some fracking had occurred just

372 metres down, within the aquifer from which local people draw their water.

The EPA is now working on a national study of the potential effects on groundwater. It should have initial results by the year's end.

One way fracking water—and methane—could enter groundwater is if the vertical well casing is breached. Methane is not toxic, but it can explode.

Last year, researchers led by Rob Jackson of Duke University in Durham, North Carolina, analysed water from drinking wells above the Marcellus Shale. They found that wells within 1 kilometre of a shale-gas drilling site contained 17 times as much methane as those further away (*Proceedings of the National Academy of Sciences,* DOI: 10.1073/pnas.1100682108). However, the team found no fracking chemicals or salts from the shale, and whether the methane came from the fracked zone or from shallower deposits is in dispute.

Even if groundwater is untainted, the contaminated fracking water must be safely disposed of. In Texas, it has been injected even further below ground, into wells left over from previous drilling. This has caused most of the earthquakes linked to fracking—which still tend to be too small to cause harm. In Appalachia few such deep wells are available. Instead, large companies are recycling their water for future fracks, while smaller operators are faced with expensive water treatment.

Environmental scientists remain worried about illegal discharges and accidents. "You just know there's going to be spillage and contamination," says William Schlesinger, president of the Cary Institute of Ecosystem Studies in Millbrook, New York.

Although the water has caused most concern, many of the ailments blamed on fracking seem more consistent with air pollution. In unpublished work, John Adgate of the Colorado School of Public Health in Denver found that airborne volatile organic compounds spike during the initial flowback period. Could this harm human health? "That's the $64,000 question, and there's not good data," says Adgate.

This lack of data could come to haunt the industry, says Goldstein. In the absence of any studies linking health to actual human exposures to pollution, he argues, fracking will get blamed for clusters of disease—whether or not it is justified. "There will be media attention, lawsuits, and there will be declines in property values," he says. "Industry is piling up problems for the long run, and so is government."

Critical Thinking

1. Discuss the environmental concerns surrounding the fracking process of natural gas selection.

2. What health issues may result from fracking?

3. Overall, are the benefits of fracking worth the risks?

MRSA: Hospitals Step Up Fight. Will It Be Enough?

Julius A. Karash

The drug-resistant bacterial infection MRSA has become so commonplace among the American populace in the last several years that most clinicians now diagnose and treat it as routinely as they do the flu. Still, tens of thousands of Americans with MRSA die each year, putting intense pressure on providers to do more.

Hospitals have instituted a multipronged approach. Certain strategies, like mandating and monitoring frequent hand washing by doctors and staff, are universally accepted, if not universally implemented. Others, such as testing all incoming patients, are much more controversial.

MRSA full name methicillin-resistant *Staphylococcus aureus*—was first identified 50 years ago, but newly compiled data paints an alarming picture. For instance, a June study in the journal Pediatrics found that the number of children hospitalized with MRSA was 10 times higher in 2008 than in 1999, surging from two cases per 1,000 admissions to 21 cases per 1,000 admissions. All told, 30,000 children were hospitalized with MRSA during that 10-year period and 374 died.

Most of the infections were acquired in a community setting, not hospitals, according to the study, led by Jason Newland, M.D., an infectious-disease physician at Children's Mercy Hospitals and Clinics in Kansas City, Mo. The emergence of CA-MRSA—acquired in public places such as playgrounds and health clubs as opposed to health care settings—-complicates experts' efforts to get their arms around the problem.

"What's new of late is we're seeing a blending of these strains," says Russ Olmsted, an epidemiologist at Saint Joseph Mercy Health System in Ann Arbor and president-elect of the Association for Professionals in Infection Control and Epidemiology. "As patients with community-acquired MRSA get admitted to hospitals, those strains are getting transmitted or are adapting to the environment and becoming more like health care-associated MRSA."

The Conundrum

At the same time, hospitals are making progress on certain fronts. For example, researchers led by Deron C. Burton, M.D., reported in the Feb. 18, 2009, issue of *The Journal of the American Medical Association* that central-line catheter-associated bloodstream infections of MRSA declined significantly from 2001 through 2007 in all types of intensive care units except pediatric units, where rates remained static.

"There is some encouraging news," says John Jernigan, M.D., deputy chief of the Prevention and Response Branch of the Division of Healthcare Quality Promotion at the Centers for Disease Control and Prevention. "We have begun to see, using various parameters, some movement in the right direction."

No one disputes that more needs to be done, but infection specialists worry that too much emphasis on MRSA may deflect attention from other drug-resistant infections, such as *Clostridium difficile* and *Acinetobacter.*

Jernigan says MRSA cases represent about 8 percent of the health care-acquired infections reported to the CDC's National Healthcare Safety Network surveillance system. "That means 92 percent are caused by other pathogens, and we don't want to forget about those other problems," he says.

"It is important to remember that MRSA is only one of the important challenges that we face," Jernigan says. "It's a poster child of a large group of problems that we have to deal with in hospitals every day in the United States."

Also complicating matters is a lack of consensus on two key issues: the value of universal MRSA testing of hospital patients, and whether it's fair for Medicare and private insurers to classify health care-acquired infections as "never events" and refuse to pay to treat them.

Amid all the controversy, hospitals have instituted stringent hand-washing campaigns and taken many other measures to keep MRSA and other infections at bay. Far from being complacent, hospital officials know that much work lies ahead of them in this ongoing struggle to protect the health of their patients.

Epidemic or Not?

Health care-acquired infections such as MRSA killed 48,000 Americans in 2006 and cost more than $8 billion to treat, according to a study released in February by Ramanan Laxminarayan, a visiting scholar at Princeton University, and Anup Malani, a professor at the University of Chicago.

MRSA most commonly attacks hospital patients via central-line-related bloodstream infections, urinary catheter-induced infections, ventilator-related pneumonia and surgical-site infections. The billions of dollars in added costs are mostly the result of longer lengths of stay, especially for patients in intensive care units.

A new report by the Centers for Disease Control and Prevention "demonstrates that the steps we're taking to reduce these often-preventable infections are working."

—Kathleen Sebelius, HHS Senretary

Most MRSA cases are not life-threatening, consisting mainly of skin lesions that can be treated with a regimen of antibiotics that are carefully considered so as not to increase resistance. But the bacteria is never fully expunged from the body and infections are likely to recur.

But is MRSA a growing epidemic?

"The qualified answer is, it depends," Olmsted says. "In the U.S. in general, I wouldn't say we have an epidemic, but we have a high endemic rate, which means the background frequency is high compared to other countries."

Olmsted says the prevalence of MRSA among American hospital patients may be three to four times higher than among Canadian hospital patients. "In addition, trends over time that look at frequency of MRSA infections in the entire U.S. population, and not just those in hospitals, indicate significant increases of MRSA over the past 10 years," he says.

"The good news is we still have reasonable susceptibility of MRSA strains to vancomycin, the antibiotic of choice, especially for very serious infection," Olmsted says. "The real concern on the horizon is called vancomycin-resistant *Staph Aureus,* or VRSA. Those are more difficult to treat."

Hospitals Take Up the Challenge

Hospitals have been escalating the fight against MRSA. For example, the person who passes you in a corridor at Truman Medical Centers could very well be a designated observer watching to see if staff members wash their hands when entering and leaving a patient's room.

"Our infection control practitioners are out and about," says Mark Steele, M.D., chief medical officer at Truman Medical Centers in Kansas City, Mo. "We monitor the compliance of all segments of the hospital, with immediate feedback. We also educate the patients. One of the strategies is to have the patients participate in observation and speak up."

Other infection prevention practices at Truman include:

- Cleaning patient rooms and operating rooms with germ-killing bleach.
- Cleaning patients' skin before central-line catheters are inserted.

Enlisting IT in MRSA War

As in any war, the battle against MRSA requires reliable information about the enemy's position. And the faster you can obtain that information and act on it, the better.

That's why more and more hospitals are adding information technology to their arsenal of anti-MRSA weapons.

"Clearly, we think this is a big need for hospitals," says Nicole Latimer, executive director of business intelligence at the Advisory Board Co. "When you have a 30-year history of performing infection prevention through a paper and pencil process or through an Excel spreadsheet process, this is a big change."

The Advisory Board, a for-profit company and think tank based in Washington, D.C., is one of a number of organizations that advocate a major role for IT in the war on MRSA. Another is Advisory Board's technology partner, Vecna Technologies Inc. of Cambridge, Mass. Funded by a National Institutes of Health grant, Vecna developed QC PathFinder software, which went on the market in 2007.

The software is designed to quickly alert hospital staffers when it is determined that a patient is infected, thus enabling a quick response.

"We wanted it to go from a search-and-find exercise, where someone is thumbing through hundreds of pages of microbiology results, to an alert system," Latimer says. "Operational response of the hospital is now within 10 to 15 minutes, rather than within 24 to 48 hours."

Other players in this market include ICNet software. On its website, England-based ICNet says its system is "designed to automate the collection of data as required by the infection control team, thus-providing real-time alerts, reports and analytical tools, which saves considerable ICT [information and communications technology] time and helps to target action more effectively."

—JULIUS KARASH

- Elevating the heads of ventilator patients by at least 30 degrees.
- Isolating patients known to be colonized with MRSA.

Truman also has made adjustments in the antibiotics it uses to treat infections. Keflex and oxacillin have been replaced by Bactrim or clindamycin for outpatients, and sicker patients requiring hospitalization are likely to be given vancomycin.

"I don't think it's becoming significantly more difficult to treat," Steele says, while acknowledging, "It's obviously less easy for hospitals to deal with what's being caught in the community."

In a 2006 report published in the *New England Journal of Medicine,* a team led by Gregory J. Moran, M.D., wrote that "the high prevalence of MRSA among patients with community-associated skin and soft-tissue infections has implications for hospital policies regarding infection control. Our results suggest that strategies used for patients with confirmed MRSA infections should be considered for all patients with purulent skin and soft-tissue infections in areas with a high prevalence of MRSA."

Which strategies work best?

"We see many patients in the emergency department with cutaneous abscesses," Steele says. "Roughly three-quarters of those will be infected with MRSA. Fortunately, most of those are self-limited and amenable to treatment, the primary treatment being incision and drainage. We don't know if antibiotics help these to heal faster or not. That's the subject of an ongoing study I'm involved with now."

Olmsted says hospitals are employing infection prevention "bundles," such as a series of steps to follow when inserting a central-Me catheter. He rites one study that says standardized use of CDC recommendations for centralline insertion has been shown to reduce bloodstream infections by 66 to 70 percent.

But knowing what best practices are and malting sure they are implemented are two different things. "Many hospitals have the right polities in place," Jernigan says. "But we have learned that just having the right policy in place doesn't necessarily translate into effective implementation. Many of the gains we've been seeing have been achieved through better implementation of existing recommendations."

But Is It Enough?

Despite all the efforts being put forth, not everyone thinks hospitals are doing enough to stop MRSA. Several states have passed laws requiring hospitals to screen high-risk patients.

"If hospitals won't take meaningful steps to stop drug-resistant infections, then we'll pass legislation to make sure they do," Washington State Rep. Tom Campbell told the Seattle Times last year.

APIC and the Society for Healthcare Epidemiology of America in 2007 issued a joint statement opposing MRSA screening mandates, saying they are too costly and limit the flexibility of hospital infection-control efforts.

Olmsted says universal MRSA screening legislation represents "a very cement approach to a problem that is fairly fluid and changing all the time. Detection of MRSA on admission is not a one-size-fits-all. You need to use your facility-specific data and decide what measures make sense. It varies considerably by facility."

Steele says "the jury is still out" on the effectiveness of universal MRSA screening. "Our infectious disease experts and infection control people have not felt that, based on the level of evidence we currently have, that's something we should do at this particular time."

Overall, Olmsted cautions that overly stringent measures could result in overtreatment with antibiotics, which would create yet more resistant strains.

Twenty-seven states now require public reporting of hospital-acquired infection rates. Olmsted says he originally was skeptical of public reporting requirements. "However, I will say that it has raised awareness significantly throughout the United States of the problem of health care-acquired infections. In that regard it's been a positive initiative."

In response to concerns about imposing a "severe burden" on hospitals, the CDC on May 7 notified hospitals that it had reversed course and would no longer require them to submit MRSA data to the Buccaneer Data Systems Clinical Data Abstraction Center that they previously reported to the CDC.

Never Ever?

In 2008, the battle against MRSA took on a new dimension when Medicare implemented its "never events" policy. The policy states that Medicare will no longer pay hospitals for treatment of complications such as vascular catheter-associated infections, catheter-associated urinary tract infections and certain surgical-site infections.

"This is really about making hospitals and the health system just a safer place to be," former CMS Acting Administrator Kerry Weems said at the time.

Private insurers are following Medicare's example, but the policy continues to stir debate.

"Somebody who gets the wrong blood type, there's really no gray to that, that should be 100 percent preventable," Steele says. "But infections are a different deal, because there are different susceptibilities to infection. It's not dear that one can prevent 100 percent of infections."

Nonpayment should be decided on a case-by-case basis, Olmstead says, noting that while infections can be prevented in most usages of central-line and urinary-tract catheters, he says it is much more difficult to prevent ventilator-associated pneumonia.

The Road Ahead

Experts agree that a hard road lies ahead in the drive against MRSA and other drug-resistant infections. In its April report, AHRQ stated, "It is unfortunate that HAI rates are not declining. It is evident that more attention devoted to patient safety is needed to ensure that health care does not result in avoidable patient harm."

On the other hand, AHRQ earlier reported that the quality of care delivered in hospitals is improving faster than in any other care setting, and patients are more likely to receive quality of care in a hospital than in any other setting.

Olmsted says hospitals and epidemiologists will "continue to be challenged by new organisms. We can't culture every patient every day while they're in the hospital. If we put our resources into interrupting transmission, with good hand hygiene and cleaning the environment and the patient, that's going to give us a leg up and we'll be ready for whatever organism comes up next."

"There's a lot of work to be done," Jernigan says. "But I think we have come a long way."

Federal policymakers concur. In May, the CDC released *The First State-Specific Healthcare-Associated Infections Summary Data Report.* The report "demonstrates that the steps we're taking to reduce these often-preventable infections are working," Health & Human Services Secretary Kathleen Sebelius said. Citing the 18 percent reduction in the national CLABSI incidence rate, she said HHS, AHRQ and the CDC will work with hospital associations and others "to further reduce blood-stream infection rates through initiatives such as 'On the CUSP: Stop BSI.'"

The American Hospital Association is "committed to improving quality and sharing relevant information with the field," says spokesman Matthew Fenwick, adding, "infection control is a top priority." Though there are "no silver bullets here, we recognize that hospitals need to do more and we are focused upon areas where we can make the most difference," he says.

Critical Thinking

1. Why is MRSA such a concern in hospitals?
2. Who is most at risk for contracting MRSA?
3. Why has MRSA recently emerged? What conditions led to its increase?

Countering Radiation Fears with Just the Facts

DENISE GRADY

As soon as David J. Brenner heard about the undersea earthquake and subsequent tsunami that devastated northern Japan on March 11, he checked a map of the region's nuclear power plants. One, because of its coastal location and reactor design, looked particularly vulnerable: Fukushima Daiichi. He hoped he was wrong.

Less than a day later, ominous reports of failed cooling systems and radiation leaks at that plant began to emerge. Dr. Brenner, director of the Center for Radiological Research at Columbia University—the oldest and largest such center in the world—found himself called on repeatedly to explain what was happening with the failed reactors and to assess the radiation risk to public health, both in Japan and around the world.

Dr. Brenner, 57, a native of Liverpool, England, is a physicist who has spent his career studying the effects of radiation on human health. He has published research showing that CT scans increase the cancer risk in children, and he recently testified before Congress, saying that the widespread use of whole-body X-ray scanners at airports would produce 100 extra cases of cancer each year in the United States.

He thinks CT scanners and the people who use them need more regulation to make sure the scans are medically needed and the doses of radiation as low as possible. He believes that even low doses increase the risk of cancer, and that there is no "safe" level or threshold below which the risk does not rise—even if that risk cannot be measured statistically.

But for all his concern about potential harm from radiation, he does not foresee a public health disaster resulting from the crisis at Fukushima Daiichi.

From the start, he has spoken with a scientist's caution, respect for facts and numbers, and keen appreciation of how much is simply not known or, at this point, even knowable. The situation changes constantly, and the path to the truth can be dicey, twisting through parties with passionate agendas for or against nuclear power, information meted out by government and industry, and public fears of radiation that many scientists consider wildly exaggerated.

How to explain the facts without scaring people needlessly? How to reassure without seeming to sugar-coat or patronize?

The last thing people want, Dr. Brenner said, is a guy like him in a white coat on TV smugly telling them everything is fine.

"People are very worried, which is not surprising," he said. "We want people to be able to make some kind of realistic assessment."

In the week or so after the earthquake, he did about 30 interviews with reporters, he said, "some good, some dreadful."

Some interviewers tried to push him to say the danger was much greater than he believed it to be. He resisted, and canceled one appearance when he realized that the host group had a strong anti-nuclear agenda.

"I try to keep my political views separate from my academic life," he said.

Asked whether he was for or against nuclear power, he paused, then said, "I think there is a role for safe nuclear power."

From the beginning of the troubles at Fukushima Daiichi, he has said that the Japanese plant is not, and will not become, Chernobyl. The Soviet reactor, which had no real containment structure, blew up in 1986 and spewed its contents far and wide. The Japanese reactors, though damaged, do have containment vessels, and the government acted quickly to evacuate people from the areas around the plant.

But he thinks the events in Japan should be a call to action for the United States. "This country and Japan have a fleet of aging nuclear reactors," he said.

Early on, Dr. Brenner said that Fukushima Daiichi would probably turn out to be similar to the 1979 Three Mile Island accident in the United States, which has never been found to have effects on public health. As conditions deteriorated at the Japanese plant, he said he thought the outcome would be somewhat worse than that at Three Mile Island, but not much worse.

But he expects cases of radiation sickness among the workers at the contaminated plant, and, he added, "I fear there will be fatalities."

He said it was possible that there would be some cases of thyroid cancer—probably too few to prove a connection statistically—years from now among people exposed as children to milk, water or produce contaminated with radioactive iodine.

So far, it seems unlikely that the accident will create a vast uninhabitable zone in Japan like the one that Chernobyl left in what is now Ukraine, Dr. Brenner said. Extensive fallout of radioactive cesium occurred at Chernobyl, and it takes many years to decay to safe levels. That kind of fallout has not occurred in Japan.

Over all, he said he thought the Japanese government was doing a good job of providing reliable information to the public—but that it has not always done so. At first, there was a delay in releasing radiation readings around the plant. And when officials announced that radioactive iodine had been found in milk and vegetables, and yet initially declared them safe, Dr. Brenner said, he "screamed loud" and spoke out to reporters about it. There was simply no reason to risk consuming them, he said.

Radioactive iodine is taken up by the thyroid gland, particularly in children, and a vast majority of the 6,000 cases of thyroid cancer caused by the Chernobyl accident occurred because people were not told to stop giving their children local milk. The milk was contaminated because it was produced by cows grazing on grass coated with fallout.

Potassium iodide pills are widely recommended to protect the thyroid gland from radioactive iodine, but Dr. Brenner said it was better just to stop drinking milk until the threat had passed.

His message changed, however, when radioactive iodine turned up in tap water in Tokyo. Though the public was advised that babies, children and pregnant women should not drink the water, Dr. Brenner conceded that some exposure might still be hard to avoid, and that using potassium iodide was a reasonable precaution.

"I've been maybe a little overstrong in saying that potassium iodide doesn't have a role to play," he said. "But usually the problem is milk. To me, the levels in water came as a surprise."

In recent years Dr. Brenner's research has focused on responses to terrorism. He finds himself in the odd position of having directed the development of a machine that he hopes will never be used, the Rapid Automated Biodosimetry Tool, or Rabit. Its purpose is to test blood samples—up to 30,000 a day—for signs that people have been exposed to a significant dose of radiation.

The Rabit was meant to be used in the event of a terrorist attack—a dirty bomb, for instance—in which large numbers of people fearing they had been exposed to radiation might overwhelm clinics and emergency rooms. Small blood samples could be drawn at many locations and sent to the Rabit; people with signs of exposure could be monitored and treated if necessary.

The radiation releases in Japan so far have been much lower than what the Rabit was designed for.

He may have inherited his knack for industrial design from his maternal grandfather, a mechanical engineer who was one of the inventors of the Kit Kat candy bar and the machinery to mass-produce it.

His office holds two prized possessions: a 1961 photograph of John Lennon and George Harrison with Stuart Sutcliffe, the Beatles' original bass player; and the desk used by the first director of the Columbia radiological center, in 1915. It came with a drawerful of tobacco pipes.

On a recent afternoon, the venerable desk was strewn with maps and graphs of radiation levels around the Fukushima plant. Unable to find the one he wanted, Dr. Brenner accused a colleague of having made off with it, and was cheerfully rebuffed. Television interviews were scheduled and a photographer was on the way; he winced and said that lately he had had no time for a haircut.

Critical Thinking

1. What is the risk to public health from the nuclear meltdown?
2. What are the long term consequences?
3. Should Japan and other nations continue to use nuclear energy to supply power? Discuss.

Test-Your-Knowledge Form

We encourage you to photocopy and use this page as a tool to assess how the articles in *Annual Editions* expand on the information in your textbook. By reflecting on the articles you will gain enhanced text information. You can also access this useful form on a product's book support website at www.mhhe.com/cls.

NAME: DATE:

_____

TITLE AND NUMBER OF ARTICLE:

_____

BRIEFLY STATE THE MAIN IDEA OF THIS ARTICLE:

_____

LIST THREE IMPORTANT FACTS THAT THE AUTHOR USES TO SUPPORT THE MAIN IDEA:

_____

WHAT INFORMATION OR IDEAS DISCUSSED IN THIS ARTICLE ARE ALSO DISCUSSED IN YOUR TEXTBOOK OR OTHER READINGS THAT YOU HAVE DONE? LIST THE TEXTBOOK CHAPTERS AND PAGE NUMBERS:

_____

LIST ANY EXAMPLES OF BIAS OR FAULTY REASONING THAT YOU FOUND IN THE ARTICLE:

_____

LIST ANY NEW TERMS/CONCEPTS THAT WERE DISCUSSED IN THE ARTICLE, AND WRITE A SHORT DEFINITION:

NOTES

NOTES